Writings from Japan

Lafcadio Hearn was born in 1850 on the Ionian Island of Santa Maura
(Levkas), the son of a surgeon-major in the British Army and a Greek woman
whom his father seduced before marrying her. Separated from his mother at
an early age, Hearn was brought up by Dublin relatives. Shipped by them to
the United States at the age of nineteen, he lived in a state of near-starvation
until he was first befriended by a printer and then began to make a name for
himself as a crime reporter.

An interest in Creole life and literature lured him in turn to the Vieux
Carré of New Orleans and then to the French West Indies, where he produced the best of his books on a non-Japanese theme, *Two Years in the French
West Indies* (1890). In his forty-first year a commission from *Harper's Weekly*
took him to Japan, where he was to stay for the remaining fourteen years of
his life. He married a Japanese woman, daughter of a samurai family, lived as
a Japanese and eventually assumed Japanese nationality and a Japanese name,
Koizumi Yakumo. While supporting himself as a teacher – his final post was
as Professor of English Literature at the Imperial University of Tokyo – he
poured out book after book about the country of his adoption, the principal
of them being *Glimpses of Unfamiliar Japan* (1894), *Out of the East* (1895),
Kokoro (1896), *Gleanings in Buddha-Fields* (1897), *Exotics and Retrospectives*
(1898), *In Ghostly Japan* (1899), *Shadowings* (1900), *A Japanese Miscellany*
(1901), *Kotto* (1902), *Kwaidan* (1904), *Japan: An Attempt at Interpretation*
(1904) and *The Romance of the Milky Way* (1905). Ailing for many years,
Hearn died of a heart attack in Tokyo in September 1904.

Francis King, novelist and critic, lived for four and a half years in Japan,
where he was Regional Director of the British Council in Kyoto. He is the
author of three works of fiction about the country, *The Custom House*, *The
Waves Behind the Boat* and *The Japanese Umbrella*, and of the non-fiction *Japan*.
His most recent novels are *Act of Darkness* and *Voices in an Empty Room*, both
published in Penguin.

LAFCADIO HEARN

Writings
from Japan

An Anthology Edited
with an Introduction
by Francis King

日本随想

PENGUIN BOOKS

Penguin Books Ltd, Harmondsworth, Middlesex, England
Viking Penguin Inc., 40 West 23rd Street, New York, New York 10010, U.S.A.
Penguin Books Australia Ltd, Ringwood, Victoria, Australia
Penguin Books Canada Ltd, 2801 John Street, Markham, Ontario, Canada L3R 1B4
Penguin Books (N.Z.) Ltd, 182–190 Wairau Road, Auckland 10, New Zealand

This edition first published 1984
Reprinted 1985

Made and printed in Great Britain by
Richard Clay (The Chaucer Press) Ltd, Bungay, Suffolk
Filmset in 10/12 pt Monophoto Palatino by
Northumberland Press Ltd, Gateshead

Contents

Contents

Introduction

Of all the writers and scholars – Pierre Loti, Rudyard Kipling, Arthur Waley, Maurice Dekobra, William Plomer, John Morris, Fosco Maraini, Ruth Benedict, Edwin O. Reischauer, James Kirkup – who have attempted to mediate between Japan and the outside world, Lafcadio Hearn has always been regarded as pre-eminent by the Japanese themselves. Some have been more erudite, intelligent and balanced; others have even written better. But no one else's name is better known to Japanese of every class. How this came about is due in small part to the state of the country when he lived there and in great part to the attitude with which he viewed it.

In 1853, some forty years before Hearn's arrival, a detachment of the United States navy, under Commodore Perry, had forced the Japanese to give American ships access to their ports and so had initiated the inexorable process by which the country, previously sealed off from the rest of the world, had been obliged, hurried step by step, to forfeit its cherished privacy. Feudalism abruptly gave place to a centralization of power, with the creation of ministries – of finance, education, army, navy and so forth – similar to those in the West. Railways, telegraphs, a modern banking system, the introduction of machines into industries previously dependent on hand-labour: it was with a leap of extraordinary daring that all these were achieved in less than half a century.

To acquire the necessary knowledge, successive governments sent their emissaries abroad: to the United States, to Great Britain, to France, to Germany. These emissaries, many of whom were to play a vital role in the creation of the major power now known to us, tended to return with the conviction, also often held by those who had dispatched them, that whatever they had discovered abroad was superior to what they had left behind in Japan. The Westerners who flocked into Japan as diplomats, advisers, teachers, businessmen and journalists shared this conviction: the Japanese must learn to live and behave like the rest of the civilized world.

Such a belief was never Lafcadio Hearn's. He began with the assumption that he had come to this strange, remote country not as an arrogant teacher but as a humble student; and he ended with the symbolic acts of himself becoming a Japanese citizen, of assuming a Japanese name, Koizumi Yakumo, and of instructing his half-Japanese son on his deathbed: 'Put my bones in a jar worth about three sen and bury me in some temple on a hill.'

In his lifetime, the Japanese gratefully recognized in him someone who loved and respected them, who cherished their traditions, who embraced their way of life, and who had none of the Westerner's usual eager, clumsy proposals for their improvement. Now, so many years after his death, this is how they still regard him.

Hearn has come to be identified so much with Japan that few people now care to know anything about the unhappy, turbulent forty years preceding his arrival in the country in which, cantankerous and quarrelsome man that he was, he came nearest to finding happiness and peace.

Lafcadio Hearn had always been known as Patrick Hearn until he emigrated, at the age of nineteen, to America in 1869. His adoption of his bizarre second name, derived from his Ionian island birth-place, Levkas (Santa Maura), and his rejection of his first may perhaps be regarded as symbolic on the one hand of his surrender to his maternal Greek ancestry and on the other hand of his repudiation of whatever was Anglo-Irish in him.

Hearn's father, Charles, had met his mother, Rosa Cassimati, while he was serving as an army doctor on the then remote island of Cythera (Cerigo). It was only when Rosa's family discovered that she was pregnant that they agreed to a marriage. Within a year of each other, in 1849 and 1850, Hearn's older brother, George, and he himself were born on Levkas, to which their father had been transferred. Hearn's memories of the father whom he never saw after his seventh year – he was brought up by a great-aunt in Ireland – were always hostile. 'What if there is "a skeleton in our closet"?' he wrote to his younger brother, Daniel James, who also emigrated to America and there became a farmer. 'Did he not make it?' The 'skeleton in the closet' was their mother's insanity. Speaking hardly a word of English, the bewildered Greek girl had been dispatched with her children to the rigidly Protestant Hearn family home in Dublin in 1851, while Charles Hearn served first in the West Indies and then in the Crimean War. Later, while she was visiting her family in the Ionian Islands, Charles Hearn had their marriage annulled; and after that she never saw any of her three sons. Once she came back to the British Isles in search of them, but she could not discover their whereabouts – each had been farmed out to relatives – and she returned home to her second husband, a Greek lawyer, Cavallini. This atrocious life no doubt accounted for her recurring bouts of mania, culminating in complete insanity for ten years before her death.

In that same letter to his brother Daniel, Hearn wrote:

Whatever there is good in me – and, I believe, whatever there is deeper good in yourself – came from that dark race-soul of which we knew so little. My love of right, my hate of wrong; my admiration for what is beautiful and true; my capacity for faith in man or woman; my sensitiveness to artistic things which gives me what little *success I have*; even that language power whose physical sign is the large eyes of both of us, came from her ... I think only of her, and of you, as imaging her possibly, all my life – rarely of him. It is the mother who makes us, makes at least all that makes the nobler man, not his strength or powers of calculation, but his heart and power to love.

From the mother, too – he might have added, but did not – came that growing paranoia which drove him to quarrel with almost everyone who had ever befriended him, much like that other literary wanderer, D. H. Lawrence.

It was as, in effect, a remittance man that Hearn's relatives, despairing of his iconoclasm, his rebelliousness and his inability to settle to any occupation, dispatched him to the United States. After a bitter period, during which he kept starvation at bay only by such menial jobs as running messages and peddling mirrors from door to door, he first got a job in Cincinnati with a kindly printer, in whose shop he used to sleep, and then was taken on by the Cincinnati *Enquirer* as a cub reporter. It was on the *Enquirer* that, exhibiting a love of the macabre that was to remain with him all his life, he made his name with the reporting of a number of lurid murder cases, the chief of which was 'The Tan Yard Case' of 1874.

Constantly falling out with editors, usually because, following his own capricious bent, he tended to write more frequently about what interested him than about what was likely to interest his readers, he also failed in his attempts to start a satirical weekly magazine entitled *Ye Giglampz* and to open a restaurant called, aptly, The Hard Times. Increasingly fascinated by Creole life and literature, he lived for a time in the Vieux Carré of New Orleans, where he produced *La Cuisine Créole* (1885) and a collection of Louisiana Negro proverbs, *Ghombo Zhêbes* (1885). A sojourn in the French West Indies resulted in the best of his books on a non-Japanese subject, his *Two Years in the French West Indies* (1890).

It was a commission from *Harper's Weekly* that took him to Japan; but, even before he arrived there, he started one of those acrimonious disputes so typical of his life, with the long-suffering firm. But for that dispute, he might never have taken a job in the country and so made his home there for the rest of his days. His *Glimpses of Unfamiliar Japan*, first and freshest of his collections of essays on Japanese themes, derived from the *Harper's* commission.

The extent of Hearn's continuing fame in Japan is at once indicated by a visit to Matsue. It was to this remote provincial town on the Japanese Sea that he travelled for four days by rickshaw in order to take up the first of his appointments as a teacher of English language and literature at a secondary school; it was there that he met his wife, Setsuko Koizumi, only daughter of an impoverished samurai family; and though, while he lived there, he would often grumble in his letters to his Western correspondents – he had no one congenial to whom to talk, the Siberian cold would put him underground, he could not survive exclusively on Japanese fare – yet Matsue was to remain for him, through the ensuing years of growing discouragement and dis-illusion, an earthly paradise. At Matsue there is no one who has not heard of Hearn. Even a child can lead one to the site of the school, now demolished, where he taught; to the house where he lived after his marriage; and to the Lafcadio Hearn Museum, next to the house.

The Museum, or Yakumo-Kinen-Kan, was built in 1936 out of money contributed by his Japanese admirers. The size of a modest public lavatory, it is, says a notice, modelled on the Goethe Museum in Weimar 'with Greek additions'. These additions were presumably made as a complimentary reference to Hearn's maternal ancestry. It is easy to smile at this architectural tribute, and many foreigners, including myself, have done so. But we might ask ourselves: Is there a Joseph Conrad Museum in England? Or a Thomas Mann Museum in the United States? The building contains Hearn's manuscripts and books; articles of clothing, among them some yellowing woollen underwear; and other of his personal possessions. There are a number of photographs of Hearn with his pupils. Everyone in them is staring at the camera, except for Hearn, whose head is always turned aside. This is because at the age of sixteen he lost the sight of an eye during a scuffle with some schoolfellows, and the strain to which the other eye was subsequently put (he would use a magnifying glass and a telescope but seldom spectacles) caused it to become increasingly protuberant – 'my Cyclops eye', he called it.

Hearn had always been humiliatingly conscious of the inadequacy of his size no less than of the unattractiveness of his looks; and I should guess that this sense of physical inferiority had much to do with his decision, after many years of homelessness, to make Japan his home. In Japan, his diminutive size did not matter, since it was not below the average; and the Japanese did not regard him as either handsome or ugly, merely as a *gaijin* (foreigner). In any case, Japanese women of that period cared far less than Western ones about a man's appearance, setting more store on social position, ability to support a family and intellectual or artistic eminence. Even on his first arrival in Matsue, Hearn was regarded as a man of importance, with a salary the equal of that of the Governor. Within a few years he was supporting no less than ten of his in-laws.

There must, of course, have been other psychological factors involved in Hearn's decision to adopt an alien way of life, even to the extent of obliging his Tokyo colleagues and pupils, many of them used to the comfort of Western chairs, to squat on the floor beside him, of marrying a Japanese, of bringing up his children in the Japanese style, of adopting Japanese nationality and of taking his wife's family name as his own. All his life, until he came to Japan, Hearn had been oppressed by the feeling that he belonged nowhere. In Ireland, as a swarthy child with gold ear-rings in his ears, and later in England, he was always an exotic, a wop, a dago; but unable to speak his mother's language and having lost all touch with her, he could not feel that he was truly Greek. In France, where he was sent to school for a brief period, he was taunted with being an Englishman. In America he was one of innumerable impoverished Irish immigrants. But worse than his consciousness that he had no true nationality (in fact he was a British subject until he became a Japanese one) was his consciousness, aggravated by his physical abnormality, that he was in some ineradicable way unlike others and set apart from them. Like so many other voluntary exiles – there are a host of them resident in Japan today – he found that this disturbing sense of alienation from his fellow men was appeased by a wholly alien environment. Now he could console himself: of course he was not like others – he was a Westerner, they were Japanese! The difference was merely one of pigmentation, of tradition, of upbringing; it was not that terrible other difference within the psyche itself.

Lastly, there was the fascination which, all his life, darker skins exerted on him. It is not generally known that in 1875, at the age of twenty-five, Hearn went through a marriage ceremony with a mulatto, a former slave, called Althea or Mattie Foley (there is some doubt as to her baptismal first name). But the laws of the time against miscegenation made the union void and she and Hearn separated after a few months (O. W. Forst in his *Young Hearn* tells the story in interesting detail). Of this match Henry Watkin, the middle-aged printer from England who befriended Hearn in his early years and whom Hearn used to call 'Dear Old Dad', wrote as follows:

His unfortunate marriage was the result not of contempt for existing notions ... but of a desire that is native to all humanity, that of being loved. His sensitiveness of his personal defects was so deep, and the feeling that owing to them all doors were closed to him was so great, that it seemed to him that love of even one of earth's social outcasts was too great a boon to be cast aside.

But this, one surmises, is not the whole diagnosis. Throughout his whole adult life, in Cincinatti, in New Orleans, in Martinique and then in Japan, he was to feel the pull of that attraction, like some dangerously hidden current. What was its power over him? May it not have been that whenever he embarked on another such liaison, he was unconsciously taking on himself the role of his father seducing a girl from an alien and 'lesser' race, but taking it on himself each time with the intention that he would succeed where his father had so brutally and shamefully failed? Hearn, too, failed at first;

but apart from the success of his literary work, the only other unqualified success in his life was his marriage to Setsuko Koizumi. He had managed to carry through what his father could not carry through, and so at last had been able simultaneously to prove his superiority over his father and to expiate vicariously the wrong done to his mother.

Hearn had never been happier than at Matsue; and he was never to be so happy again. Driven to abandon his earthly paradise because of his fear of the winters beside the Japan Sea – 'I fear a few more winters of this kind will put me underground,' he wrote to the English Japanologist Basil Hall Chamberlain – he took up a teaching post in Kyushu, the southern island of Japan, at a government college in Kumamoto. He found the town 'devilishly ugly and commonplace'; and he hated the curriculum, the evidence all around him of the New Japan and, above all, the earthquakes – he had, he confessed, 'a really disgusting fear of them'. So the wanderer moved on: at first to Kobe, most Western of all cities in Japan except for the capital, where he worked for the English-language *Chronicle*, and then to the Imperial University in Tokyo, where he occupied the Chair of English Literature. Year by year his complaints multiplied and his persecution mania, always latent, became more acute. One by one he repelled those who had been generous and helpful to him, often using as his pretext some imagined slight or injury of which the astonished former friend was wholly unaware. To his half-sister in England, with whom he had started an affectionate correspondence, he suddenly sent only the empty envelope which contained the last letter she had written to him; Basil Hall Chamberlain, who had done so much to help him, he also disinherited; to Fenellosa, the great Spanish-American scholar, he wrote a letter beginning:

My dear Professor – I have been meditating, and after the meditation I came to the conclusion not to visit your charming new home again – not at least before 1900. I suppose that I am a beast and an ape; but nevertheless I hope to make you understand . . .

Chamberlain, most sympathetic of men, bore him no resentment and even went to pains after Hearn's death to make excuses for his behaviour:

Lafcadio's dropping of his friends seemed to me to have its roots in that very quality which made the chief charm of his works. I mean his idealism.

13

Friends, when he first made them, were for him more than mere mortal men, they stood endowed with every perfection ... But he was not emotional merely; another side of his mind had the keen insight of a man of science. Thus he soon came to see that his idols had clay feet, and – being so purely subjective in his judgements – he was indignant with them for having, as he thought, deceived him. Add to this that the rigid character of his philosophical opinions made him perforce despise, as intellectual weaklings, all those who did not share them, or shared them only in a lukewarm manner – and his disillusionment with a series of friends with whom he had once thought to find intellectual sympathy is seen to have been inevitable ... Thus it was hardly possible for him to retain old ties of friendship except with a few men whom he met on the plane of everyday life apart from the higher intellectual interests. Lafcadio himself was a greater sufferer from all this than anyone else; for he possessed the affectionate disposition of a child, and suffered poignantly when sympathy was withdrawn or – what amounted to the same – when he himself withdrew it. He was much to be pitied – always wishing to love, and discovering each time that his love had been misplaced.

Hearn was less indulgent to himself and more perceptive. He saw that the sense of opposition from others, the feeling that he had a grievance, the rankling of some imagined injustice or betrayal, were goads essential to the full functioning of his creative talent.

... *Unless somebody does or says something horribly mean to me, I can't do certain kinds of work* – the tiresome kinds, that compel a great deal of thinking ... Pain is therefore to me of exceeding value betimes; and everybody who does me a wrong indirectly does me a right ... Whenever I begin to forget one new burn, new caustic from some unexpected quarter is poured into my brain; then the new pain forces other work. It strikes me as being possibly a peculiar morbid condition.

'Possibly a peculiar morbid condition'; as one reads the dismal story of Hearn's last years, his slow physical disintegration seems to be accompanied by a mental and spiritual disintegration equally distressing.

Typical of his worsening mania was the incident which brought to a close his work as lecturer at the Imperial University. An Englishman arrived in Hearn's lecture-room, introduced himself and announced that he would like to stay to hear him conduct his class. The intrusion was perhaps ill-mannered; but Hearn's frenzy was out of all proportion to the mildness of this offence. Going home, he at once dashed off a letter of resignation in terms so violent that the President had no course but to accept it. Shortly after, in 1904, he died, to be buried in the land of his adoption, at the Zoshigaya Public Cemetery in Tokyo.

Unfortunately, we have no verb 'to Japanese', as the equivalent of 'to Americanize', 'to Anglicize', 'to gallicize'. Perhaps in the case of Hearn 'to japan' would be the most suitable, for just as, after japanning, the natural grain of a piece of wood is lost forever under a hard coat of lacquer, so, after Hearn had been thoroughly 'japanned', it became increasingly difficult to trace his original European and American characteristics under the carapace he had built about himself.

His assumption of the personality of Koizumi Yakumo (Yakumo means 'eight clouds'), the Japanese head of a family burdened by the manifold responsibilities imposed on him and sustained by the manifold services which he in turn can impose, was so successful that one Japanese authority has written of him that 'he is almost as Japanese as the haiku', and another, a Buddhist, told me that the only explanation of Hearn's uncanny knowledge and understanding of Japan and the Japanese was that, in some previous existence, he must have been a native of the country.

It is certainly remarkable that it was only after his arrival in Japan, at the age of forty, that he began to produce the books for which he is now remembered. A book like his *Two Years in the French West Indies* (1890) still has its interest, but it suffers from a style as exuberant and lush as the vegetation of the area with which it deals. Japan taught him the value of understatement, hint and allusion, and a far more chastened, more poetic style was at once the result.

When I first went to Japan, I prepared myself by reading a number of books on its history, its customs and its culture. Most were of a more recent date than Hearn's; but on my arrival, I realized that it was his that had given me the most accurate idea of what, superficialities apart, I should find there.

In making this selection from the books that, even when in chronic pain from the heart condition that eventually killed him, he poured out to make up a corpus of work on Japan unrivalled even today by any other Western writer, I have adopted three categories: Recollections, Reflections and Relations. The first consists of accounts of his own experiences; the second of meditations on aspects of

Japanese life; and the third of tales, many of them concerned with the supernatural and adapted from Japanese sources.

In transliterating from the Japanese, Hearn followed what has come to be known as the Hepburn system. Consonants are pronounced approximately as in English, the vowels as in Spanish or Italian, with an accent to differentiate long *o* and *u* from short *o* and *u*.

PART ONE

Recollections

追憶

My First Day in the Orient

追憶

'Do not fail to write down your first impressions as soon as possible,' said a kind English professor whom I had the pleasure of meeting soon after my arrival in Japan: 'they are evanescent, you know; they will never come to you again, once they have faded out; and yet of all the strange sensations you may receive in this country you will feel none so charming as these.' I am trying now to reproduce them from the hasty notes of the time, and find that they were even more fugitive than charming; something has evaporated from all my recollections of them — something impossible to recall. I neglected the friendly advice, in spite of all resolves to obey it: I could not, in those first weeks, resign myself to remain indoors and write, while there was yet so much to see and hear and feel in the sun-steeped ways of the wonderful Japanese city. Still, even could I revive all the lost sensations of those first experiences, I doubt if I could express and fix them in words. The first charm of Japan is intangible and volatile as a perfume.

It began for me with my first kuruma-ride out of the European quarter of Yokohama into the Japanese town; and so much as I can recall of it is hereafter set down.

I

It is with the delicious surprise of the first journey through Japanese streets — unable to make one's kuruma-runner understand anything but gestures, frantic gestures to roll on anywhere, everywhere, since all is unspeakably pleasurable and new — that one first receives the real sensation of being in the Orient, in this Far East so much read of, so long dreamed of, yet, as the eyes bear witness, heretofore all unknown. There is a romance even in the first full consciousness of this rather commonplace fact; but for me this consciousness is transfigured inexpressibly by the divine beauty of the day. There is some charm unutterable in the morning air, cool with the coolness of Japanese spring and wind-waves from the snowy cone of Fuji; a charm perhaps due rather to softest lucidity than to any positive tone – an atmospheric limpidity, extraordinary, with only a suggestion of blue in it, through which the most distant objects appear focused with amazing sharpness. The sun is only pleasantly warm; the jinrikisha, or kuruma, is the most cosy little vehicle imaginable; and the street-vistas, as seen above the dancing white mushroom-shaped hat of my sandaled runner, have an allurement of which I fancy that I could never weary.

Elfish everything seems; for everything as well as everybody is small, and queer, and mysterious: the little houses under their blue roofs, the little shop-fronts hung with blue, and the smiling little people in their blue costumes. The illusion is only broken by the occasional passing of a tall foreigner, and by divers shop-signs bearing announcements in absurd attempts at English. Nevertheless, such discords only serve to emphasize reality; they never materially lessen the fascination of the funny little streets.

'Tis at first a delightfully odd confusion only, as you look down one of them, through an interminable flutter of flags and swaying of dark blue drapery, all made beautiful and mysterious with Japanese or Chinese lettering. For there are no immediately discernible laws of construction or decoration: each building seems to have a fantastic prettiness of its own; nothing is exactly like anything else, and all is bewilderingly novel. But gradually, after an hour passed in the quarter, the eye begins to recognize in a vague way some general plan in the construction of these low, light, queerly gabled wooden houses, mostly unpainted, with their first stories all open to the street, and thin strips of roofing sloping above each shop-front, like awnings, back to the miniature balconies of paper-screened second stories. You begin to understand the common plan of the tiny shops, with their matted floors well raised above the street level, and the general perpendicular arrangement of sign-lettering, whether undulating on drapery or glimmering on gilded and lacquered sign-boards. You observe that the same rich dark blue which dominates in popular costume rules also in shop draperies, though there is a sprinkling of other tints — bright blue and white and red (no greens or yellows). And then you note also that the dresses of the laborers are lettered with the same wonderful lettering as the shop draperies. No arabesques could produce such an effect. As modified for decorative purposes, these ideographs have a speaking symmetry which no design without a meaning could possess. As they appear on the back of a workman's frock — pure white on dark blue — and large enough to be easily read at a great distance (indicating some guild or company of which the wearer is a member or employee), they give to the poor cheap garment a factitious appearance of splendor.

And finally, while you are still puzzling over the mystery of things, there will come to you like a revelation the knowledge that most of the amazing picturesqueness of these streets is simply due to the profusion of Chinese and Japanese characters in white, black, blue or gold, decorating everything — even surfaces of doorposts and paper screens. Perhaps, then, for one moment, you will imagine the effect of English lettering substituted for those magical characters; and the mere idea will give to whatever aesthetic sentiment you may possess a brutal shock, and you will become, as I have become, an enemy of the Romaji-Kwai — that society founded for the ugly utilitarian purpose of introducing the use of English letters in writing Japanese

I'

An ideograph does not make upon the Japanese brain any impression similar to that created in the Occidental brain by a letter or combination of letters — dull, inanimate symbols of vocal sounds. To the Japanese brain an ideograph is a vivid picture: it lives; it speaks; it gesticulates. And the whole space of a Japanese street is full of such living characters — figures that cry out to the eyes, words that smile or grimace like faces.

What such lettering is, compared with our own lifeless types, can be understood only by those who have lived in the farthest East. For even the printed characters of Japanese or Chinese imported texts give no suggestion of the possible beauty of the same characters as modified for decorative inscriptions, for sculptural use, or for the commonest advertising purposes. No rigid convention fetters the fancy of the calligrapher or designer: each strives to make his characters more beautiful than any others; and generations upon generations of artists have been toiling from time immemorial with like emulation, so that through centuries and centuries of tireless effort and study, the primitive hieroglyph or ideograph has been evolved into a thing of beauty indescribable. It consists only of a certain number of brush-strokes; but in each stroke there is an undiscoverable secret art of grace, proportion, imperceptible curve, which actually makes it seem alive, and bears witness that even during the lightning-moment of its creation the artist felt with his brush for the ideal shape of the stroke *equally along its entire length*, from head to tail. But the art of the strokes is not all; the art of their combination is that which produces the enchantment, often so as to astonish the Japanese themselves. It is not surprising, indeed, considering the strangely personal, animate, esoteric aspect of Japanese lettering, that there should be wonderful legends of calligraphy, relating how words written by holy experts became incarnate, and descended from their tablets to hold converse with mankind.

III

My kurumaya calls himself 'Cha.' He has a white hat which looks like the top of an enormous mushroom; a short blue wide-sleeved jacket; blue drawers, close-fitting as 'tights,' and reaching to his ankles; and light straw sandals bound upon his bare feet with cords of palmetto-fibre. Doubtless he typifies all the patience, endurance, and insidious coaxing powers of his class. He has already manifested his power to make me give him more than the law allows; and I have been warned against him in vain. For the first sensation of having a human being for a horse, trotting between shafts, unwearyingly bobbing up and down before you for hours, is alone enough to evoke a feeling of compassion. And when this human being, thus trotting between shafts, with all his hopes, memories, sentiments, and com-prehensions, happens to have the gentlest smile, and the power to return the least favor by an apparent display of infinite gratitude, this compassion becomes sympathy, and provokes unreasoning impulses to self-sacrifice. I think the sight of the profuse perspiration has also something to do with the feeling, for it makes one think of the cost of heart-beats and muscle-contractions, likewise of chills, congestions, and pleurisy. Cha's clothing is drenched; and he mops his face with a small sky-blue towel, with figures of bamboo-sprays and sparrows in white upon it, which towel he carries wrapped about his wrist as he runs.

That, however, which attracts me in Cha — Cha considered not as a motive power at all, but as a personality — I am rapidly learning to discern in the multitudes of faces turned toward us as we roll through these miniature streets. And perhaps the supremely pleasurable impression of this morning is that produced by the singular gentleness of popular scrutiny. Everybody looks at you curiously; but there is never anything disagreeable, much less hostile in the gaze: most commonly it is accompanied by a smile or half-smile. And the ultimate consequence of all these kindly curious looks and smiles is that the stranger finds himself thinking of fairy-land. Hackneyed to the degree of provocation this statement no doubt is: everybody describing the sensations of his first Japanese day talks of the land as fairy-land, and of its people as fairy-folk. Yet there is a natural reason for this unanimity in choice of terms to describe what is almost impossible to describe more accurately at the first essay. To find one's self suddenly in a world where everything is upon a smaller and daintier scale than with us — a world of lesser and seemingly kindlier beings, all smiling at you as if to wish you well — a world where all movement is slow and soft, and voices are hushed — a world where land, life, and sky are unlike all that one has known elsewhere — this is surely the realization, for imaginations nourished with English folklore, of the old dream of a World of Elves.

IV

The traveler who enters suddenly into a period of social change — especially change from a feudal past to a democratic present — is likely to regret the decay of things beautiful and the ugliness of things new. What of both I may yet discover in Japan I know not; but today, in these exotic streets, the old and the new mingle so well that one seems to set off the other. The line of tiny white telegraph poles carrying the world's news to papers printed in a mixture of Chinese and Japanese characters; an electric bell in some tea-house with an

Oriental riddle of text pasted beside the ivory button; a shop of American sewing-machines next to the shop of a maker of Buddhist images; the establishment of a photographer beside the establishment of a manufacturer of straw sandals: all these present no striking incongruities, for each sample of Occidental innovation is set into an Oriental frame that seems adaptable to any picture. But on the first day, at least, the Old alone is new for the stranger, and suffices to absorb his attention. It then appears to him that everything Japanese is delicate, exquisite, admirable — even a pair of common wooden chopsticks in a paper bag with a little drawing upon it; even a package of toothpicks of cherry-wood, bound with a paper wrapper wonderfully lettered in three different colors; even the little sky-blue towel, with designs of flying sparrows upon it, which the jinrikisha man uses to wipe his face. The bank bills, the commonest copper coins, are things of beauty. Even the piece of plaited colored string used by the shopkeeper in tying up your last purchase is a pretty curiosity. Curiosities and dainty objects bewilder you by their very multitude: on either side of you, wherever you turn your eyes, are countless wonderful things as yet incomprehensible.

But it is perilous to look at them. Every time you dare to look, something obliges you to buy it — unless, as may often happen, the smiling vender invites your inspection of so many varieties of one article, each specially and all unspeakably desirable, that you flee away out of mere terror at your own impulses. The shopkeeper never asks you to buy; but his wares are enchanted, and if you once begin buying you are lost. Cheapness means only a temptation to commit bankruptcy; for the resources of irresistible artistic cheapness are inexhaustible. The largest steamer that crosses the Pacific could not contain what you wish to purchase. For, although you may not, perhaps, confess the fact to yourself, what you really want to buy is not the contents of a shop; you want the shop and the shopkeeper, and streets of shops with their draperies and their habitants, the whole city and the bay and the mountains begirdling it, and Fujiyama's white witchery overhanging it in the speckless sky, all Japan, in very truth, with its magical trees and luminous atmosphere, with all its cities and towns and temples, and forty millions of the most lovable people in the universe.

Now there comes to my mind something I once heard said by

a practical American on hearing of a great fire in Japan: 'Oh! those people can afford fires; their houses are so cheaply built.' It is true that the frail wooden houses of the common people can be cheaply and quickly replaced; but that which was within them to make them beautiful cannot — and every fire is an art tragedy. For this is the land of infinite hand-made variety; machinery has not yet been able to introduce sameness and utilitarian ugliness in cheap production (except in response to foreign demand for bad taste to suit vulgar markets), and each object made by the artist or artisan differs still from all others, even of his own making. And each time something beautiful perishes by fire, it is a something representing an individual idea.

Happily the art impulse itself, in this country of conflagrations, has a vitality which survives each generation of artists, and defies the flame that changes their labor to ashes or melts it to shapelessness. The idea whose symbol has perished will reappear again in other creations — perhaps after the passing of a century — modified, indeed, yet recognizably of kin to the thought of the past. And every artist is a ghostly worker. Not by years of groping and sacrifice does he find his highest expression; the sacrificial past is within him; his art is an inheritance; his fingers are guided by the dead in the delineation of a flying bird, of the vapors of mountains, of the colors of the morning and evening, of the shape of branches and the spring burst of flowers: generations of skilled workmen have given him their cunning, and revive in the wonder of his drawing. What was conscious effort in the beginning became unconscious in later centuries — becomes almost automatic in the living man — becomes the art instinctive. Wherefore, one colored print by a Hokusai or Hiroshige, originally sold for less than a cent, may have more real art in it than many a Western painting valued at more than the worth of a whole Japanese street.

v

Here are Hokusai's own figures walking about in straw rain-coats, and immense mushroom-shaped hats of straw, and straw sandals — bare-limbed peasants, deeply tanned by wind and sun; and patient-faced mothers with smiling bald babies on their backs, toddling by upon their geta (high, noisy, wooden clogs), and robed merchants squatting and smoking their little brass pipes among the countless riddles of the shops.

Then I notice how small and shapely the feet of the people are – whether bare brown feet of peasants, or beautiful feet of children wearing tiny, tiny geta, or feet of young girls in snowy tabi. The tabi, the white digitated stocking, gives to a small light foot a mythological aspect – the white cleft grace of the foot of a fauness. Clad or bare the Japanese foot has the antique symmetry: it has not yet been distorted by the infamous foot-gear which has deformed the feet of Occidentals.

... Of every pair of Japanese wooden clogs, one makes in walking a slightly different sound from the other, as *kring* to *krang*; so that the echo of the walker's steps has an alternate rhythm of tones. On a pavement, such as that of a railway station, the sound obtains immense sonority; and a crowd will sometimes intentionally fall into step. with the drollest conceivable result of drawling wooden noise.

VI

'Tera e yuke!'

I have been obliged to return to the European hotel – not because of the noon-meal, as I really begrudge myself the time necessary to eat it, but because I cannot make Cha understand that I want to visit a Buddhist temple. Now Cha understands; my landlord has uttered the mystical words:

'Tera e yuke!'

A few minutes of running along broad thoroughfares lined with gardens and costly ugly European buildings; then passing the bridge of a canal stocked with unpainted sharp-prowed craft of extraordinary construction, we again plunge into narrow, low, bright, pretty streets – into another part of the Japanese city. And Cha runs at the top of his speed between more rows of little ark-shaped houses, narrower above than below; between other unfamiliar lines of little open shops. And always over the shops little strips of blue-tiled roof slope back to the paper-screened chamber of upper floors; and from all the façades hang draperies dark blue, or white, or crimson – foot-breadths of texture covered with beautiful Japanese lettering, white on blue, red on black, black on white. But all this flies by swiftly as a dream. Once more we cross a canal; we rush up a narrow street rising to meet a hill; and Cha, halting suddenly before an immense flight of broad stone steps, sets the shafts of his vehicle on the ground that I may dismount, and pointing to the steps, exclaims:

'Tera!'

I dismount, and ascend them, and, reaching a broad terrace, find myself face to face with a wonderful gate, topped by a tilted, peaked, many-cornered Chinese roof. It is all strangely carven, this gate. Dragons are intertwined in a frieze above its open doors; and the panels of the doors themselves are similarly sculptured; and there are gargoyles — grotesque lion heads — protruding from the caves. And the whole is gray, stone-colored; to me, nevertheless, the carvings do not seem to have the fixity of sculpture; all the snakeries and dragonries appear to undulate with a swarming motion, elusively, in eddyings as of water.

I turn a moment to look back through the glorious light. Sea and sky mingle in the same beautiful pale clear blue. Below me the billowing of bluish roofs reaches to the verge of the unruffled bay on the right, and to the feet of the green wooded hills flanking the city on two sides. Beyond that semicircle of green hills rises a lofty range of serrated mountains, indigo silhouettes. And enormously high above the line of them towers an apparition indescribably lovely — one solitary snowy cone, so filmily exquisite, so spiritually white, that but for its immemorially familiar outline one would surely deem it a shape of cloud. Invisible its base remains, being the same delicious tint as the sky: only above the eternal snow-line its dreamy cone appears, seeming to hang, the ghost of a peak, between the luminous land and the luminous heaven — the sacred and matchless mountain, Fujiyama.

And suddenly, a singular sensation comes upon me as I stand before this weirdly sculptured portal — a sensation of dream and doubt. It seems to me that the steps, and the dragon-swarming gate, and the blue sky arching over the roofs of the town, and the ghostly beauty of Fuji, and the shadow of myself there stretching upon the gray masonry, must all vanish presently. Why such a feeling? Doubtless because the forms before me — the curved roofs, the coiling dragons, the Chinese grotesqueries of carving — do not really appear to me as things new, but as things dreamed: the sight of them must have stirred to life forgotten memories of picture-books. A moment, and the delusion vanishes; the romance of reality returns, with freshened consciousness of all that which is truly and deliciously new; the magical transparencies of distance, the wondrous delicacy of the tones of the living picture, the enormous height of the summer blue, and the white soft witchery of the Japanese sun.

V₁I

I pass on and climb more steps to a second gate with similar gargoyles and swarming of dragons, and enter a court where graceful votive lanterns of stone stand like monuments. On my right and left two great grotesque stone lions are sitting — the lions of Buddha, male and female. Beyond is a long low light building, with curved and gabled roof of blue tiles, and three wooden steps before its entrance. Its sides are simple wooden screens covered with thin white paper. This is the temple.

On the steps I take off my shoes; a young man slides aside the screens closing the entrance, and bows me a gracious welcome. And I go in, feeling under my feet a softness of matting thick as bedding. An immense square apartment is before me, full of an unfamiliar sweet smell — the scent of Japanese incense; but after the full blaze of the sun, the paper-filtered light here is dim as moonshine; for a minute or two I can see nothing but gleams of gilding in a soft gloom. Then, my eyes becoming accustomed to the obscurity, I perceive against the paper-paned screens surrounding the sanctuary on three sides shapes of enormous flowers cutting like silhouettes against the vague white light. I approach and find them to be paper flowers — symbolic lotus-blossoms beautifully colored, with curling leaves gilded on the upper surface and bright green beneath. At the dark end of the apartment, facing the entrance, is the altar of Buddha, a rich and lofty altar, covered with bronzes and gilded utensils clustered to right and left of a shrine like a tiny gold temple. But I see no statue; only a mystery of unfamiliar shapes of burnished metal, relieved against darkness, a darkness behind the shrine and altar — whether recess or inner sanctuary I cannot distinguish.

*

The young attendant who ushered me into the temple now approaches, and, to my great surprise, exclaims in excellent English, pointing to a richly decorated gilded object between groups of candelabra on the altar·

'That is the shrine of Buddha.'

'And I would like to make an offering to Buddha,' I respond.

'It is not necessary,' he says, with a polite smile.

But I insist; and he places the little offering for me upon the altar. Then he invites me to his own room, in a wing of the building — a large luminous room, without furniture, beautifully matted. And we sit down upon the floor and chat. He tells me he is a student in the temple. He learned English in Tōkyō, and speaks it with a curious accent, but with fine choice of words. Finally he asks me:

'Are you a Christian?'

And I answer truthfully:

'No.'

'Are you a Buddhist?'

'Not exactly.'

'Why do you make offerings if you do not believe in Buddha?'

'I revere the beauty of his teaching, and the faith of those who follow it.'

'Are there Buddhists in England and America?'

'There are, at least, a great many interested in Buddhist philosophy.'

And he takes from an alcove a little book, and gives it to me to examine. It is an English copy of Olcott's *Buddhist Catechism*.

'Why is there no image of Buddha in your temple?' I ask.

'There is a small one in the shrine upon the altar,' the student answers; 'but the shrine is closed. And we have several large ones. But the image of Buddha is not exposed here every day — only upon festal days. And some images are exposed only once or twice a year.'

From my place, I can see, between the open paper screens, men and women ascending the steps, to kneel and pray before the entrance of the temple. They kneel with such naïve reverence, so gracefully and so naturally, that the kneeling of our Occidental devotees seems a clumsy stumbling by comparison. Some only join their hands; others clap them three times loudly and slowly; then they bow their heads, pray silently for a moment, and rise and depart. The shortness of the prayers impresses me as something novel and interesting. From time to time I hear the clink and rattle of brazen coin into the great wooden money-box at the entrance.

I turn to the young student, and ask him:

'Why do they clap their hands three times before they pray?'

He answers:

'Three times for the Sansai, the Three Powers: Heaven, Earth, Man.'

'But do they clap their hands to call the Gods, as Japanese clap their hands to summon their attendants?'

'Oh, no!' he replies. 'The clapping of hands represents only the awakening from the Dream of the Long Night.'[1]

'What night? What dream?'

He hesitates some moments before making answer:

'The Buddha said: All beings are only dreaming in this fleeting world of unhappiness.'

'Then the clapping of hands signifies that in prayer the soul awakens from such dreaming?'

'Yes.'

'You understand what I mean by the word "soul"?'

'Oh, yes! Buddhists believe the soul always was — always will be.

'Even in Nirvana?'

'Yes.'

While we are thus chatting the Chief Priest of the temple enters — a very aged man — accompanied by two young priests, and I am presented to them; and the three bow very low, showing me the glossy crowns of their smoothly shaven heads, before seating themselves in the fashion of gods upon the floor. I observe they do not smile; these are the first Japanese I have seen who do not smile; their faces are impassive as the faces of images. But their long eyes observe me very closely, while the student interprets their questions, and while I attempt to tell them something about the translations of the Sutras in our *Sacred Books of the East*, and about the labors

1. I do not think this explanation is correct; but it is interesting, as the first which ꞏ obtained upon the subject. Properly speaking, Buddhist worshipers should not clap the hands, but only rub them softly together. Shintō worshipers always clap their hands four times.

of Beal and Burnouf and Feer and Davids and Kern, and others. They listen without change of countenance, and utter no word in response to the young student's translation of my remarks. Tea, however, is brought in and set before me in a tiny cup, placed in a little brazen saucer, shaped like a lotus-leaf; and I am invited to partake of some little sugar-cakes (kwashi), stamped with a figure which I recognize as the Swastika, the ancient Indian symbol of the Wheel of the Law.

As I rise to go, all rise with me; and at the steps the student asks for my name and address.

'For,' he adds, 'you will not see me here again, as I am going to leave the temple. But I will visit you.'

'And your name?' I ask.

'Call me Akira,' he answers.

At the threshold I bow my goodbye; and they all bow very, very low — one blue-black head, three glossy heads like balls of ivory. And as I go, only Akira smiles.

VIII

'Tera?' queries Cha, with his immense white hat in his hand, as I resume my seat in the jinrikisha at the foot of the steps. Which no doubt means, do I want to see any more temples? Most certainly I do: I have not yet seen Buddha.

'Yes, tera, Cha.'

And again begins the long panorama of mysterious shops and tilted eaves, and fantastic riddles written over everything. I have no idea in what direction Cha is running. I only know that the streets seem to become always narrower as we go, and that some of the houses look like great wickerwork pigeon-cages only, and that we pass over several bridges before we halt again at the foot of another hill. There is a lofty flight of steps here also, and before them a structure which I know is both a gate and a symbol, imposing, yet in no manner resembling the great Buddhist gateway seen before. Astonishingly simple all the lines of it are: it has no carving, no coloring, no lettering upon it; yet it has a weird solemnity, an enigmatic beauty. It is a torii.

'Miya,' observes Cha. Not a tera this time, but a shrine of the gods of the more ancient faith of the land — a miya.

I am standing before a Shintō symbol; I see for the first time, out of a picture at least, a torii. How to describe a torii to those who have never looked at one even in a photograph or engraving? Two lofty columns, like gate-pillars, supporting horizontally two cross-beams, the lower and lighter beam having its ends fitted into the columns a little distance below their summits; the uppermost and larger beam supported upon the tops of the columns, and projecting well beyond them to right and left. That is a torii: the construction varying little in design, whether made of stone, wood, or metal. But this description can give no correct idea of the appearance of a torii, of its majestic aspect, of its mystical suggestiveness as a gateway. The first time you see a noble one, you will imagine, perhaps, that you see the colossal model of some beautiful Chinese letter towering against the sky; for all the lines of the thing have the grace of an animated ideograph — have the bold angles and curves of characters made with four sweeps of a master-brush.[2]

Passing the torii I ascend a flight of perhaps one hundred stone steps, and find at their summit a second torii, from whose lower cross-beam hangs festooned the mystic shimenawa. It is in this case a hempen rope of perhaps two inches in diameter through its greater length, but tapering off at either end like a snake. Sometimes the shimenawa is made of bronze, when the torii itself is of bronze; but according to tradition it should be made of straw, and most commonly is. For it represents the straw rope which the deity Futo-tama-no-mikoto stretched behind the Sun-goddess, Ama-terasu-oho-mi-Kami, after Ame-no-ta-jikara-wo-no-Kami, the Heavenly-handstrength-god, had pulled her out, as is told in that ancient myth of Shintō which Professor Chamberlain has translated.[3] And the shimenawa, in its

2. Various writers, following the opinion of the Japanologue Satow, have stated that the torii was originally a bird-perch for fowls offered up to the gods at Shintō shrines — 'not as food, but to give warning of daybreak.' The etymology of the word is said to be 'bird-rest' by some authorities; but Aston, not less of an authority, derives it from words which would give simply the meaning of a gateway. See Chamberlain's *Things Japanese*, pp. 429, 430.

3. Professor Basil Hall Chamberlain has held the extraordinary position of Professor of *Japanese* in the Imperial University of Japan — no small honor to English philology!

commoner and simpler form, has pendent tufts of straw along its entire length, at regular intervals, because originally made, tradition declares, of grass pulled up by the roots which protruded from the twist of it.

Advancing beyond this torii, I find myself in a sort of park or pleasure-ground on the summit of the hill. There is a small temple on the right; it is closed up; and I have read so much about the disappointing vacuity of Shintō temples that I do not regret the absence of its guardian. And I see before me what is infinitely more interesting – a grove of cherry-trees covered with something unutterably beautiful – a dazzling mist of snowy blossoms clinging like summer cloud-fleece about every branch and twig; and the ground beneath them and the path before me, is white with the soft, thick, odorous snow of fallen petals.

Beyond this loveliness are flower-plots surrounding tiny shrines; and marvelous grotto-work, full of monsters – dragons and mythologic beings chiseled in the rock; and miniature landscape work with tiny groves of dwarf trees, and lilliputian lakes, and microscopic brooks and bridges and cascades. Here, also, are swings for children. And here are belvederes, perched on the verge of the hill, wherefrom the whole fair city, and the whole smooth bay speckled with fishing-sails no bigger than pin-heads, and the far, faint, high promontories reaching into the sea, are all visible in one delicious view – blue-penciled in a beauty of ghostly haze indescribable.

Why should the trees be so lovely in Japan? With us, a plum or cherry tree in flower is not an astonishing sight; but here it is a miracle of beauty so bewildering that, however much you may have previously read about it, the real spectacle strikes you dumb. You see no leaves – only one great filmy mist of petals. Is it that the trees have been so long domesticated and caressed by man in this land of the Gods, that they have acquired souls, and strive to show their gratitude, like women loved, by making themselves more beautiful for man's sake? Assuredly they have mastered men's hearts by their loveliness, like beautiful slaves. That is to say, Japanese hearts. Apparently there have been some foreign tourists of the brutal class in this place, since it has been deemed necessary to set up inscriptions in English announcing that 'IT IS FORBIDDEN TO INJURE THE TREES.'

33

IX

'Tera?'

'Yes, Cha, tera.'

But only for a brief while do I traverse Japanese streets. The houses separate, become scattered along the feet of the hills: the city thins away through little valleys, and vanishes at last behind. And we follow a curving road overlooking the sea. Green hills slope steeply down to the edge of the way on the right; on the left, far below, spreads a vast stretch of dun sand and salty pools to a line of surf so distant that it is discernible only as a moving white thread. The tide is out; and thousands of cockle-gatherers are scattered over the sands, at such distances that their stooping figures, dotting the glimmering sea-bed, appear no larger than gnats. And some are coming along the road before us, returning from their search with well-filled baskets – girls with faces almost as rosy as the faces of English girls.

As the jinrikisha rattles on, the hills dominating the road grow higher. All at once Cha halts again before the steepest and loftiest flight of temple steps I have yet seen.

I climb and climb and climb, halting perforce betimes, to ease the violent aching of my quadriceps muscles; reach the top completely out of breath; and find myself between two lions of stone; one showing his fangs, the other with jaws closed. Before me stands the temple, at the farther end of a small bare plateau surrounded on three sides by low cliffs – a small temple, looking very old and gray. From a rocky height to the left of the building, a little cataract tumbles down into a pool, ringed in by a palisade. The voice of the water drowns all other sounds. A sharp wind is blowing from the ocean: the place is chill even in the sun, and bleak, and desolate, as if no prayer had been uttered in it for a hundred years.

Cha taps and calls, while I take off my shoes upon the worn wooden steps of the temple; and after a minute of waiting, we hear a muffled step approaching and a hollow cough behind the paper screens. They slide open; and an old white-robed priest appears, and motions me, with a low bow, to enter. He has a kindly face; and his smile of welcome seems to me one of the most exquisite I have ever been greeted with. Then he coughs again, so badly that I think if I ever come here another time, I shall ask for him in vain.

I go in, feeling that soft, spotless, cushioned matting beneath my feet with which the floors of all Japanese buildings are covered. I pass the indispensable bell and lacquered reading-desk; and before me I see other screens only, stretching from floor to ceiling. The old man, still coughing, slides back one of these upon the right, and waves me into the dimness of an inner sanctuary, haunted by faint odors of incense. A colossal bronze lamp, with snarling gilded dragons coiled about its columnar stem, is the first object I discern; and, in passing, it, my shoulder sets ringing a festoon of little bells suspended from the lotus-shaped summit of it. Then I reach the altar, gropingly, unable yet to distinguish forms clearly. But the priest, sliding back screen after screen, pours in light upon the gilded brasses and the inscriptions; and I look for the image of the Deity or presiding Spirit between the altar-groups of convoluted candelabra. And I see – only a mirror, a round, pale disk of polished metal, and my own face therein, and behind this mockery of me a phantom of the far sea.

Only a mirror! Symbolizing what? Illusion? Or that the Universe exists for us solely as the reflection of our own souls? Or the old Chinese teaching that we must seek the Buddha only in our own hearts? Perhaps some day I shall be able to find out all these things.

As I sit on the temple steps, putting on my shoes preparatory to going, the kind old priest approaches me again, and, bowing, presents a bowl. I hastily drop some coins in it, imagining it to be a Buddhist almsbowl, before discovering it to be full of hot water. But the old man's beautiful courtesy saves me from feeling all the grossness of my mistake. Without a word, and still preserving his kindly smile, he takes the bowl away, and, returning presently with another bowl, empty, fills it with hot water from a little kettle, and makes a sign to me to drink.

Tea is most usually offered to visitors at temples; but this little shrine is very, very poor; and I have a suspicion that the old priest suffers betimes for want of what no fellow-creature should be permitted to need. As I descend the windy steps to the roadway I see him still looking after me, and I hear once more his hollow cough.

Then the mockery of the mirror recurs to me. I am beginning to wonder whether I shall ever be able to discover that which I seek – outside of myself! That is, outside of my own imagination.

x

'Tera?' once more queries Cha.

'Tera, no — it is getting late. Hotel, Cha.'

But Cha, turning the corner of a narrow street, on our homeward route, halts the jinrikisha before a shrine or tiny temple scarcely larger than the smallest of Japanese shops, yet more of a surprise to me than any of the larger sacred edifices already visited. For, on either side of the entrance, stand two monster-figures, nude, blood-red, demoniac, fearfully muscled, with feet like lions, and hands brandishing gilded thunderbolts, and eyes of delirious fury; the guardians of holy things, the Ni-Ō, or 'Two Kings.'[4] And right between these crimson monsters a young girl stands looking at us; her slight figure, in robe of silver-gray and girdle of iris-violet, relieved deliciously against the twilight darkness of the interior. Her face, impassive and curiously delicate, would charm wherever seen; but here, by strange contrast with the frightful grotesqueries on either side of her, it produces an effect unimaginable. Then I find myself wondering whether my feeling of repulsion toward those twin monstrosities be altogether just, seeing that so charming a maiden deems them worthy of veneration. And they even cease to seem ugly as I watch her standing there between them, dainty and slender as some splendid moth, and always naïvely gazing at the foreigner, utterly unconscious that they might have seemed to him both unholy and uncomely.

What are they? Artistically they are Buddhist transformations of Brahma and of Indra. Enveloped by the absorbing, all-transforming magical atmosphere of Buddhism, Indra can now wield his thunderbolts only in defense of the faith which has dethroned him: he has become

4. These Ni-Ō, however, the first I saw in Japan, were very clumsy figures. There are magnificent Ni-Ō to be seen in some of the great temple gateways in Tōkyō, Kyōto, and elsewhere. The grandest of all are those in the Ni-Ō Mon, or 'Two Kings' Gate,' of the huge Tōdaiji temple at Nara. They are eight hundred years old. It is impossible not to admire the conception of stormy dignity and hurricane-force embodied in those colossal figures.

Prayers are addressed to the Ni-Ō, especially by pilgrims. Most of their statues are disfigured by little pellets of white paper, which people chew into a pulp and then spit at them. There is a curious superstition that if the pellet sticks to the statue the prayer is heard: if, on the other hand, it falls to the ground, the prayer will not be answered.

a keeper of the temple gates; nay, has even become a servant of Bosatsu (Bodhisattvas), for this is only a shrine of Kwannon, Goddess of Mercy, not yet a Buddha.

'Hotel, Cha, hotel!' I cry out again, for the way is long, and the sun sinking – sinking in the softest imaginable glow of topazine light. I have not seen Shaka (so the Japanese have transformed the name Sakya-Muni); I have not looked upon the face of the Buddha. Perhaps I may be able to find his image tomorrow, somewhere in this wilderness of wooden streets, or upon the summit of some yet unvisited hill.

The sun is gone; the topaz-light is gone; and Cha stops to light his lantern of paper; and we hurry on again, between two long lines of painted paper lanterns suspended before the shops: so closely set, so level those lines are, that they seem two interminable strings of pearls of fire. And suddenly a sound – solemn, profound, mighty – peals to my ears over the roofs of the town, the voice of the tsurigane, the great temple-bell of Nogiyama.

All too short the day seemed. Yet my eyes have been so long dazzled by the great white light, and so confused by the sorcery of that interminable maze of mysterious signs which made each street vista seem a glimpse into some enormous *grimoire*, that they are now weary even of the soft glowing of all these paper lanterns, likewise covered with characters that look like texts from a Book of Magic. And I feel at last the coming of that drowsiness which always follows enchantment.

XI

'Amma-kamishimo-go-hyakmon!'

A woman's voice ringing through the night, chanting in a tone of singular sweetness words of which each syllable comes through my open window like a wavelet of flute-sound. My Japanese servant, who speaks a little English, has told me what they mean, those words:

'Amma-kamishimo-go-hyakmon!'

And always between these long, sweet calls I hear a plaintive whistle, one long note first, then two short ones in another key. It is the whistle of the amma, the poor blind woman who earns her living by shampooing the sick or the weary, and whose whistle warns pedestrians and drivers of vehicles to take heed for her sake, as she cannot see. And she sings also that the weary and the sick may call her in.

'Amma-kamishimo-go-hyakmon!'

The saddest melody, but the sweetest voice. Her cry signifies that for the sum of 'five hundred mon' she will come and rub your weary body 'above and below,' and make the weariness or the pain go away. Five hundred mon are the equivalent of five sen (Japanese cents); there are ten rin to a sen, and ten mon to one rin. The strange sweetness of the voice is haunting – makes me even wish to have some pains, that I might pay five hundred mon to have them driven away.

I lie down to sleep, and I dream. I see Chinese texts – multitudinous, weird, mysterious – fleeing by me, all in one direction; ideographs white and dark, upon sign-boards, upon paper screens, upon the backs of sandaled men. They seem to live, these ideographs, with conscious life; they are moving their parts, moving with a movement as of insects, monstrously, like *phasmidae*. I am rolling always through low, narrow, luminous streets in a phantom jinrikisha, whose wheels make no sound. And always, always, I see the huge white mushroom-shaped hat of Cha dancing up and down before me as he runs.

The Chief City of the Province of the Gods

追憶

I

The first of the noises of a Matsue day comes to the sleeper like the throbbing of a slow, enormous pulse exactly under his ear. It is a great, soft, dull buffet of sound — like a heartbeat in its regularity, in its muffled depth, in the way it quakes up through one's pillow so as to be felt rather than heard. It is simply the pounding of the ponderous pestle of the kometsuki, the cleaner of rice — a sort of colossal wooden mallet with a handle about fifteen feet long horizontally balanced on a pivot. By treading with all his force on the end of the handle, the naked kometsuki elevates the pestle, which is then allowed to fall back by its own weight into the rice-tub. The measured muffled echoing of its fall seems to me the most pathetic of all sounds of Japanese life; it is the beating, indeed, of the Pulse of the Land.

Then the boom of the great bell of Tōkōji, the Zen-shū temple, shakes over the town; then come melancholy echoes of drumming from the tiny little temple of Jizō in the street Zaimokuchō, near my house, signaling the Buddhist hour of morning prayer. And finally the cries of the earliest itinerant venders begin — 'Daikoyai! kabuya-kabu!' — the sellers of daikon and other strange vegetables. 'Moyaya-moya!' — the plaintive call of the women who sell little thin slips of kindling-wood for the lighting of charcoal fires.

II

Roused thus by these earliest sounds of the city's wakening life, I slide open my little Japanese paper window to look out upon the morning over a soft green cloud of spring foliage rising from the

39

river-bounded garden below. Before me, tremulously mirroring everything upon its farther side, glimmers the broad glassy mouth of the
Ōhashigawa, opening into the grand Shinji Lake, which spreads out
broadly to the right in a dim gray frame of peaks. Just opposite to
me, across the stream, the blue-pointed Japanese dwellings have their
to[1] all closed; they are still shut up like boxes, for it is not yet sunrise, although it is day.

But oh, the charm of the vision — those first ghostly love-colors
of a morning steeped in mist soft as sleep itself resolved into a visible
exhalation! Long reaches of faintly tinted vapor cloud the far lake
verge — long nebulous bands, such as you may have seen in old
Japanese picture-books, and must have deemed only artistic whim-
sicalities unless you had previously looked upon the real phenomena.
All the bases of the mountains are veiled by them, and they
stretch athwart the loftier peaks at different heights like immeasurable
lengths of gauze (this singular appearance the Japanese term
'shelving'),[2] so that the lake appears incomparably larger than it really
is, and not an actual lake, but a beautiful spectral sea of the same
tint as the dawn-sky and mixing with it, while peak-tips rise like islands
from the brume, and visionary strips of hill ranges figure as league-
long causeways stretching out of sight — an exquisite chaos, ever
changing aspect as the delicate fogs rise, slowly, very slowly. As the
sun's yellow rim comes into sight, fine thin lines of warmer tone —
spectral violets and opalines — shoot across the flood, tree-tops take
tender fire, and the unpainted façades of high edifices across the water
change their wood-color to vapory gold through the delicious haze.

Looking sunward, up the long Ōhashigawa, beyond the many-
pillared wooden bridge, one high-pooped junk, just hoisting sail, seems
to me the most fantastically beautiful craft I ever saw — a dream of
Orient seas, so idealized by the vapor is it; the ghost of a junk, but
a ghost that catches the light as clouds do; a shape of gold mist,
seemingly semi-diaphanous, and suspended in pale blue light.

---

1. Thick solid sliding shutters of unpainted wood, which in Japanese houses serve
both as shutters and as doors.
2. Tanabiku.

III

And now from the river-front touching my garden there rises to me a sound of clapping of hands — one, two, three, four claps — but the owner of the hands is screened from view by the shrubbery. At the same time, however, I see men and women descending the stone steps of the wharves on the opposite side of the Ōhashigawa, all with little blue towels tucked into their girdles. They wash their faces and hands and rinse their mouths — the customary ablution preliminary to Shintō prayer. Then they turn their faces to the sunrise and clap their hands four times and pray. From the long high white bridge come other clappings, like echoes, and others again from far light graceful craft, curved like new moons — extraordinary boats, in which I see bare-limbed fishermen standing with foreheads bowed to the golden East. Now the clappings multiply — multiply at last into an almost continuous volleying of sharp sounds. For all the population are saluting the rising sun — O-Hi-San, the Lady of Fire — Ama-terasu-oho-mi-Kami, the Lady of the Great Light.[3] 'Konnichi-Sama! Hail this day to thee, divinest Day-Maker! Thanks unutterable unto thee, for this thy sweet light, making beautiful the world!' So, doubtless, the thought, if not the utterance, of countless hearts. Some turn to the sun only, clapping their hands; yet many turn also to the West, to holy Kitzuki, the immemorial shrine; and not a few turn their faces successively to all the points of heaven, murmuring the names of a hundred gods; and others, again, after having saluted the Lady of Fire, look toward high Ichibata, toward the place of the great temple of Yakushi-Nyorai, who giveth sight to the blind — not clapping their hands as in Shintō worship, but only rubbing the palms softly together after the Buddhist manner. But all — for in this most antique province of Japan all Buddhists are Shintōists likewise — utter the archaic words of Shintō prayer: 'Harai tamai kiyome tamai to Kami imi tami.'

Prayer to the most ancient gods who reigned before the coming of the Buddha, and who still reign here in their own Izumo-land — in the Land of Reed Plains, in the Place of the Issuing of Clouds; prayer to the deities of primal chaos and primeval sea and of the beginnings of the world — strange gods with long weird names, kindred

3. Ama-terasu-oho-mi-Kami literally signifies 'the Heaven-Shining-Great-August-Divinity.' (See Professor Chamberlain's translation of the Kojiki.)

of U-hiji-ni-no-Kami, the First Mud-Lord, kindred of Su-hiji-ni-no-Kami, the First Sand-Lady; prayer to those who came after them – the gods of strength and beauty, the world-fashioners, makers of mountains and the isles, ancestors of those sovereigns whose lineage still is named 'The Sun's Succession;' prayer to the Three Thousand Gods 'residing within the provinces,' and to the Eight Hundred Myriads who dwell in the azure Takama-no-hara – in the blue Plain of High Heaven. 'Nippon-koku-chū-yaoyorozu-no-Kami-gami-sama!'

IV

'Ho–ke-kyō!'

My uguisu is awake at last, and utters his morning prayer. You do not know what an uguisu is? An uguisu is a holy little bird that professes Buddhism. All uguisu have professed Buddhism from time immemorial; all uguisu preach alike to men the excellence of the divine Sutra.

'Ho–ke-kyō!'

In the Japanese tongue, Ho-ke-kyō; in Sanskrit, Saddharma-Pundarika: *The Sutra of the Lotus of the Good Law*, the divine book of the Nichiren sect. Very brief, indeed, is my little feathered Buddhist's confession of faith – only the sacred name reiterated over and over again like a litany, with liquid bursts of twittering between.

'Ho–ke-kyō!'

Only this one phrase, but how deliciously he utters it! With what slow amorous ecstasy he dwells upon its golden syllables!

It hath been written: 'He who shall keep, read, teach, or write this Sutra shall obtain eight hundred good qualities of the Eye. He shall see the whole Triple Universe down to the great hell Aviki, and up to the extremity of existence. He shall obtain twelve hundred good qualities of the Ear. He shall hear all sounds in the Triple Universe – sounds of gods, goblins, demons, and beings not human.'

'Ho–ke-kyō!'

A single word only. But it is also written: 'He who shall joyfully accept but a single word from this Sutra, incalculably greater shall be his merit than the merit of one who should supply all beings in the four hundred thousand Asankhyeyas of worlds with all the necessaries for happiness.'

'Ho—ke-kyō!'

Always he makes a reverent little pause after uttering it and before shrilling out his ecstatic warble — his bird-hymn of praise. First the warble; then a pause of about five seconds, then a slow, sweet, solemn utterance of the holy name in a tone as of meditative wonder; then another pause; then another wild, rich, passionate warble. Could you see him, you would marvel how so powerful and penetrating a soprano could ripple from so minute a throat; for he is one of the very tiniest of all feathered singers, yet his chant can be heard far across the broad river, and children going to school pause daily on the bridge, a whole cho away, to listen to his song. And uncomely withal: a neutral-tinted mite, almost lost in his immense box-cage of hinoki wood, darkened with paper screens over its little wire-grated windows, for he loves the gloom.

Delicate he is and exacting even to tyranny. All his diet must be laboriously triturated and weighed in scales, and measured out to him at precisely the same hour each day. It demands all possible care and attention merely to keep him alive. He is precious, nevertheless. 'Far and from the uttermost coasts is the price of him,' so rare he is. Indeed, I could not have afforded to buy him. He was sent to me by one of the sweetest ladies in Japan, daughter of the governor of Izumo, who, thinking the foreign teacher might feel lonesome during a brief illness, made him the exquisite gift of this dainty creature.

V

The clapping of hands has ceased; the toil of the day begins; continually louder and louder the pattering of geta over the bridge. It is a sound never to be forgotten, this pattering of geta over the Ōhashi — rapid, merry, musical, like the sound of an enormous dance; and a dance it veritably is. The whole population is moving on tiptoe, and the multitudinous twinkling of feet over the verge of the sunlit roadway is an astonishment. All those feet are small, symmetrical — light as the feet of figures painted on Greek vases — and the step is always taken toes first; indeed, with geta it could be taken no other way, for the heel touches neither the geta nor the ground, and the foot is tilted forward by the wedge-shaped wooden sole. Merely to stand upon a pair of geta is difficult for one unaccustomed to their use, yet you see Japanese children running at full speed in geta with soles at least three inches high, held to the foot only by a forestrap fastened between the great toe and the other toes, and they never trip and the geta never falls off. Still more curious is the spectacle of men walking in bokkuri or takageta, a wooden sole with wooden supports at least five inches high fitted underneath it so as to make the whole structure seem the lacquered model of a wooden bench. But the wearers stride as freely as if they had nothing upon their feet.

Now children begin to appear, hurrying to school. The undulation of the wide sleeves of their pretty speckled robes, as they run, looks precisely like a fluttering of extraordinary butterflies. The junks spread their great white or yellow wings, and the funnels of the little steamers which have been slumbering all night by the wharves begin to smoke.

One of the tiny lake steamers lying at the opposite wharf has just opened its steam-throat to utter the most unimaginable, piercing, desperate, furious howl. When that cry is heard everybody laughs. The other little steamboats utter only plaintive mooings, but unto this particular vessel – newly built and launched by a rival company – there has been given a voice expressive to the most amazing degree of reckless hostility and savage defiance. The good people of Matsue, upon hearing its voice for the first time, gave it forth with a new and just name – Ōkami-Maru. 'Maru' signifies a steamship. 'Ōkami' signifies a wolf.

VI

A very curious little object now comes slowly floating down the river, and I do not think that you could possibly guess what it is.

The Hotoke, or Buddhas, and the beneficent Kami are not the only divinities worshiped by the Japanese of the poorer classes. The deities of evil, or at least some of them, are duly propitiated upon certain occasions, and requited by offerings whenever they graciously vouchsafe to inflict a temporary ill instead of an irremediable misfortune.[4] (After all, this is no more irrational than the thanksgiving

4. 'The gods who do harm are to be appeased, so that they may not punish those who have offended them.' Such are the words of the great Shintō teacher, Hirata, as translated by Mr Satow in his article *The Revival of Pure Shintau*.

prayer at the close of the hurricane season in the West Indies, after the destruction by storm of twenty-two thousand lives.) So men sometimes pray to Ekibiogami, the God of Pestilence, and to Kaze-no-Kami, the God of Wind and of Bad Colds, and to Hoso-no-Kami, the God of Smallpox, and to divers evil genii.

Now when a person is certainly going to get well of smallpox a feast is given to the Hoso-no-Kami, much as a feast is given to the Fox-God when a possessing fox has promised to allow himself to be cast out. Upon a sando-wara, or small straw mat, such as is used to close the end of a rice-bale, one or more kawarake, or small earthenware vessels, are placed. These are filled with a preparation of rice and red beans, called adzukimeshi, whereof both Inari-Sama and Hoso-no-Kami are supposed to be very fond. Little bamboo wands with gohei (paper cuttings) fastened to them are then planted either in the mat or in the adzukimeshi, and the color of these gohei must be red. (Be it observed that the gohei of other Kami are always white.) This offering is then either suspended to a tree, or set afloat in some running stream at a considerable distance from the home of the convalescent. This is called 'seeing the God off.'

VII

The long white bridge with its pillars of iron is recognizably modern. It was, in fact, opened to the public only last spring with great ceremony. According to some most ancient custom, when a new bridge has been built the first persons to pass over it must be the happiest of the community. So the authorities of Matsue sought for the happiest folk, and selected two aged men who had both been married for more than half a century, and who had had not less than twelve children, and had never lost any of them. These good patriarchs first crossed the bridge accompanied by their venerable wives, and followed by their grown-up children, grandchildren, and great-grandchildren, amidst a great clamor of rejoicing, the showering of fireworks, and the firing of cannon.

But the ancient bridge so recently replaced by this structure was much more picturesque, curving across the flood and supported upon multitudinous feet, like a long-legged centipede of the innocuous kind. For three hundred years it had stood over the stream firmly and well, and it had its particular tradition.

When Horiō Yoshiharu, the great general who became daimyō of Izumo in the Keichō era, first undertook to put a bridge over the mouth of this river, the builders labored in vain; for there appeared to be no solid bottom for the pillars of the bridge to rest upon. Millions of great stones were cast into the river to no purpose, for the work constructed by day was swept away or swallowed up by night. Nevertheless, at last the bridge was built, but the pillars began to sink soon after it was finished; then a flood carried half of it away, and as often as it was repaired so often it was wrecked. Then a human sacrifice was made to appease the vexed spirits of the flood. A man was buried alive in the river-bed below the place of the middle pillar, where the current is most treacherous, and thereafter the bridge remained immovable for three hundred years.

This victim was one Gensuke, who had lived in the street Saikamachi; for it had been determined that the first man who should cross the bridge wearing hakama without a machi[5] should be put under the bridge; and Gensuke sought to pass over not having a machi in his hakama, so they sacrificed him. Wherefore the midmost pillar of the bridge was for three hundred years called by his name — Gensuke-bashira. It is averred that upon moonless nights a ghostly fire flitted about that pillar — always in the dead watch hour between two and three; and the color of the light was red, though I am assured that in Japan, as in other lands, the fires of the dead are most often blue.

VIII

Now some say that Gensuke was not the name of a man, but the name of an era, corrupted by local dialect into the semblance of a personal appellation. Yet so profoundly is the legend believed that when the new bridge was being built thousands of country-folk were afraid to come to town; for a rumor arose that a new victim was needed, who was to be chosen from among them, and that it had been determined to make the choice from those who still wore their hair in queues after the ancient manner. Wherefore hundreds of aged

5. Machi, a stiff piece of pasteboard or other material sewn into the waist of the hakama at the back, so as to keep the folds of the garment perpendicular and neat-looking.

men cut off their queues. Then another rumor was circulated to the effect that the police had been secretly instructed to seize the one thousandth person of those who crossed the new bridge the first day, and to treat him after the manner of Gensuke. And at the time of the great festival of the Rice-God, when the city is usually thronged by farmers coming to worship at the many shrines of Inari, this year there came but few; and the loss to local commerce was estimated at several thousand yen.

IX

The vapors have vanished, sharply revealing a beautiful little islet in the lake, lying scarcely half a mile away — a low, narrow strip of land with a Shintō shrine upon it, shadowed by giant pines; not pines like ours, but huge, gnarled, shaggy, tortuous shapes, vast-reaching like ancient oaks. Through a glass one can easily discern a torii, and before it two symbolic lions of stone (Kara-shishi), one with its head broken off, doubtless by its having been overturned and dashed about by heavy waves during some great storm. This islet is sacred to Benten, the Goddess of Eloquence and Beauty, wherefore it is called Benten-no-shima. But it is more commonly called Yome-ga-shima, or 'The Island of the Young Wife,' by reason of a legend. It is said that it arose in one night, noiselessly as a dream, bearing up from the depths of the lake the body of a drowned woman who had been very lovely, very pious, and very unhappy. The people, deeming this a sign from heaven, consecrated the islet to Benten, and thereon built a shrine unto her, planted trees about it, set a torii before it, and made a rampart about it with great curiously-shaped stones; and there they buried the drowned woman.

Now the sky is blue down to the horizon, the air is a caress of spring. I go forth to wander through the queer old city.

X

I perceive that upon the sliding doors, or immediately above the principal entrance of nearly every house, are pasted oblong white papers bearing ideographic inscriptions; and overhanging every threshold I see the sacred emblem of Shintō, the little rice-straw rope with its long fringe of pendent stalks. The white papers at once interest me; for they are ofuda, or holy texts and charms, of which I am a devout collector. Nearly all are from temples in Matsue or its vicinity; and the Buddhist ones indicate by the sacred words upon them to what particular shū, or sect, the family belongs — for nearly every soul in this community professes some form of Buddhism as well as the all-dominant and more ancient faith of Shintō. And even one quite ignorant of Japanese ideographs can nearly always distinguish at a glance the formula of the great Nichiren sect from the peculiar appearance of the column of characters composing it, all bristling with long sharp points and banneret zigzags, like an army; the famous text *Namu-myō-hō-ren-ge-kyō*, inscribed of old upon the flag of the great captain Kato Kiyomasa, the extirpator of Spanish Christianity, the glorious *vir ter execrandus* of the Jesuits. Any pilgrim belonging to this sect has the right to call at whatever door bears the above formula and ask for alms or food.

But by far the greater number of the ofuda are Shintō. Upon almost every door there is one ofuda especially likely to attract the attention of a stranger, because at the foot of the column of ideographs composing its text there are two small figures of foxes, a black and a white fox, facing each other in a sitting posture, each with a little bunch of rice-straw in its mouth, instead of the more usual emblematic key. These ofuda are from the great Inari temple of Oshiroyama,[6] within the castle grounds, and are charms against fire. They represent, indeed, the only form of assurance against fire yet known in Matsue — so far, at least, as wooden dwellings are concerned. And although a single spark and a high wind are sufficient in combination to obliterate a larger city in one day, great fires are unknown in Matsue, and small ones are of rare occurrence.

The charm is peculiar to the city; and of the Inari in question this tradition exists:

When Naomasu, the grandson of Iyeyasu, first came to Matsue to rule the province, there entered into his presence a beautiful boy, who said: 'I came hither from the home of your august father in Echizen, to protect you from all harm. But I have no dwelling-place, and am staying therefore at the Buddhist temple of Fu-mon-in. Now

6. Kushi-no-ki-Matsuhira-Inari-Daimyōjin.

if you will make for me a dwelling within the castle grounds, I will protect from fire the buildings there and the houses of the city, and your other residence likewise which is in the capital. For I am Inari Shinyemon.' With these words he vanished from sight. Therefore Naomasu dedicated to him the great temple which still stands in the castle grounds, surrounded by one thousand foxes of stone.

XI

I now turn into a narrow little street, which, although so ancient that its dwarfed two-story houses have the look of things grown up from the ground, is called the Street of the New Timber. New the timber may have been one hundred and fifty years ago; but the tints of the structures would ravish an artist — the sombre ashen tones of the wood-work, the furry browns of old thatch, ribbed and patched and edged with the warm soft green of those velvety herbs and mosses which flourish upon Japanese roofs.

However, the perspective of the street frames in a vision more surprising than any details of its mouldering homes. Between very lofty bamboo poles, higher than any of the dwellings, and planted on both sides of the street in lines, extraordinary black nets are stretched, like prodigious cobwebs against the sky, evoking sudden memories of those monster spiders which figure in Japanese mythology and in the picture-books of the old artists. But these are only fishing-nets of silken thread; and this is the street of the fishermen. I take my way to the great bridge.

XII

A stupendous ghost!

Looking eastward from the great bridge over those sharply beautiful mountains, green and blue, which tooth the horizon, I see a glorious spectre towering to the sky. Its base is effaced by far mists: out of the air the thing would seem to have shaped itself — a phantom cone, diaphanously gray below, vaporously white above, with a dream of perpetual snow — the mighty mountain of Daisen.

At the first approach of winter it will in one night become all blanched from foot to crest; and then its snowy pyramid so much resembles that Sacred Mountain, often compared by poets to a white inverted fan, half opened, hanging in the sky, that it is called Izumo-Fuji, 'the Fuji of Izumo.' But it is really in Hōki, not in Izumo, though it cannot be seen from any part of Hōki to such advantage as from here. It is the one sublime spectacle of this charming land; but it is visible only when the air is very pure. Many are the marvelous legends related concerning it, and somewhere upon its mysterious summit the Tengu are believed to dwell.

XIII

At the farther end of the bridge, close to the wharf where the little steamboats are, is a very small Jizō temple (Jizō-dō). Here are kept many bronze drags; and whenever any one has been drowned and the body not recovered, these are borrowed from the little temple and the river is dragged. If the body be thus found, a new drag must be presented to the temple.

From here, half a mile southward to the great Shintō temple of Tenjin, deity of scholarship and calligraphy, broadly stretches Tenjinmachi, the Street of the Rich Merchants, all draped on either side with dark blue hangings, over which undulate with every windy palpitation from the lake white wondrous ideographs, which are names and signs, while down the wide way, in white perspective, diminishes a long line of telegraph poles.

Beyond the temple of Tenjin the city is again divided by a river, the Shindotegawa, over which arches the bridge Tenjin-bashi. Again beyond this other large quarters extend to the hills and curve along the lake shore. But in the space between the two rivers is the richest and busiest life of the city, and also the vast and curious quarter of the temples. In this islanded district are likewise the theatres, and the place where wrestling-matches are held, and most of the resorts of pleasure.

Parallel with Tenjinmachi runs the great street of the Buddhist temples, or Teramachi, of which the eastern side is one unbroken succession of temples – a solid front of court walls tile-capped, with imposing gateways at regular intervals. Above this long stretch of tile-capped wall rise the beautiful tilted massive lines of gray-blue temple roofs against the sky. Here all the sects dwell side by side in harmony — Nichiren-shū, Shingon-shū, Zen-shū, Tendai-shū, even that Shin-shū, unpopular in Izumo because those who follow its teaching strictly must not worship the Kami. Behind each temple court there is a cemetery, or hakaba; and eastward beyond these are other temples, and beyond them yet others — masses of Buddhist architecture mixed with shreds of gardens and miniature homesteads, a huge labyrinth of mouldering courts and fragments of streets.

Today, as usual, I find I can pass a few hours very profitably in visiting the temples; in looking at the ancient images seated within the cups of golden lotus-flowers under their aureoles of gold; in buying curious mamori; in examining the sculptures of the cemeteries, where I can nearly always find some dreaming Kwannon or smiling Jizō well worth the visit.

The great courts of Buddhist temples are places of rare interest for one who loves to watch the life of the people; for these have been for unremembered centuries the playing-places of the children. Generations of happy infants have been amused in them. All the nurses, and little girls who carry tiny brothers or sisters upon their backs, go thither every morning that the sun shines; hundreds of children join them; and they play at strange, funny games — 'Oni-gokko,' or the game of Devil, 'Kage-Oni,' which signifies the Shadow and the Demon, and 'Mekusan-gokko,' which is a sort of 'blindman's buff.'

Also, during the long summer evenings, these temples are wrestling-grounds, free to all who love wrestling; and in many of them there is a dohyō-ba, or wrestling-ring. Robust young laborers and sinewy artisans come to these courts to test their strength after the day's tasks are done, and here the fame of more than one now noted wrestler was first made. When a youth has shown himself able to overmatch at wrestling all others in his own district, he is challenged by champions of other districts; and if he can overcome these also, he may hope eventually to become a skilled and popular professional wrestler.

It is also in the temple courts that the sacred dances are performed and that public speeches are made. It is in the temple courts, too, that the most curious toys are sold, on the occasion of the great holidays — toys most of which have a religious signification. There are grand old trees, and ponds full of tame fish, which put up their heads to beg for food when your shadow falls upon the water. The holy lotus is cultivated therein.

'Though growing in the foulest slime, the flower remains pure and undefiled.

'And the soul of him who remains ever pure in the midst of temptation is likened unto the lotus.

'Therefore is the lotus carven or painted upon the furniture of temples; therefore also does it appear in all the representations of our Lord Buddha.

'In Paradise the blessed shall sit at ease enthroned upon the cups of golden lotus-flowers.'[7]

A bugle-call rings through the quaint street; and round the corner of the last temple come marching a troop of handsome young riflemen, uniformed somewhat like French light infantry, marching by fours so perfectly that all the gaitered legs move as if belonging to a single body, and every sword-bayonet catches the sun at exactly the same angle, as the column wheels into view. These are the students of the Shihan-Gakkō, the College of Teachers, performing their daily military exercises. Their professors give them lectures upon the microscopic study of cellular tissues, upon the segregation of developing nerve structure, upon spectrum analysis, upon the evolution of the color sense, and upon the cultivation of bacteria in glycerine infusions. And they are none the less modest and knightly in manner for all their modern knowledge, nor the less reverentially devoted to their dear old fathers and mothers whose ideas were shaped in the era of feudalism.

XIV

Here come a band of pilgrims, with yellow straw overcoats, 'rain-coats' (mino), and enormous yellow straw hats, mushroom-shaped, of which the down-curving rim partly hides the face. All carry staffs, and wear their robes well girded up so as to leave free the lower limbs, which are inclosed in white cotton leggings of a peculiar and indescribable kind. Precisely the same sort of costume was worn by the same class of travelers many centuries ago; and just as you now see them trooping by — whole families wandering together, the pilgrim child clinging

7. From an English composition by one of my Japanese pupils.

to the father's hand – so may you see them pass in quaint procession across the faded pages of Japanese picture-books a hundred years old.

At intervals they halt before some shop-front to look at the many curious things which they greatly enjoy seeing, but which they have no money to buy.

I myself have become so accustomed to surprises, to interesting or extraordinary sights, that when a day happens to pass during which nothing remarkable has been heard or seen I feel vaguely discontented. But such blank days are rare: they occur in my own case only when the weather is too detestable to permit of going out-of-doors. For with ever so little money one can always obtain the pleasure of looking at curious things. And this has been one of the chief pleasures of the people in Japan for centuries and centuries, for the nation has passed its generations of lives in making or seeking such things. To divert one's self seems, indeed, the main purpose of Japanese existence, beginning with the opening of the baby's wondering eyes. The faces of the people have an indescribable look of patient expectancy – the air of waiting for something interesting to make its appearance. If it fail to appear, they will travel to find it: they are astonishing pedestrians and tireless pilgrims, and I think they make pilgrimages not more for the sake of pleasing the gods than of pleasing themselves by the sight of rare and pretty things. For every temple is a museum, and every hill and valley throughout the land has its temple and its wonders.

Even the poorest farmer, one so poor that he cannot afford to eat a grain of his own rice, can afford to make a pilgrimage of a month's duration; and during that season when the growing rice needs least attention hundreds of thousands of the poorest go on pilgrimages. This is possible, because from ancient times it has been the custom for everybody to help pilgrims a little; and they can always find rest and shelter at particular inns (kichinyado) which receive pilgrims only, and where they are charged merely the cost of the wood used to cook their food.

But multitudes of the poor undertake pilgrimages requiring much more than a month to perform, such as the pilgrimage to the thirty-three great temples of Kwannon, or that to the eighty-eight temples of Kōbōdaishi; and these, though years be needed to accomplish them, are as nothing compared to the enormous Sengaji, the pilgrimage to the thousand temples of the Nichiren sect. The time of a generation may pass ere this can be made. One may begin it in early youth, and complete it only when youth is long past. Yet there are several in Matsue, men and women, who have made this tremendous pilgrimage, seeing all Japan, and supporting themselves not merely by begging, but by some kinds of itinerant peddling.

The pilgrim who desires to perform this pilgrimage carries on his shoulders a small box, shaped like a Buddhist shrine, in which he keeps his spare clothes and food. He also carries a little brazen gong, which he constantly sounds while passing through a city or village, at the same time chanting the *Namu-myō-hō-ren-ge-kyō*; and he always bears with him a little blank book, in which the priest of every temple visited stamps the temple seal in red ink. The pilgrimage over, this book with its one thousand seal impressions becomes an heirloom in the family of the pilgrim.

XV

I too must make divers pilgrimages, for all about the city, beyond the waters or beyond the hills, lie holy places immemorially old.

Kitzuki, founded by the ancient gods, who 'made stout the pillars upon the nethermost rock bottom, and made high the cross-beams to the Plain of High Heaven' — Kitzuki, the Holy of Holies, whose high-priest claims descent from the Goddess of the Sun; and Ichibata, famed shrine of Yakushi-Nyorai, who giveth sight to the blind — Ichibata-no-Yakushi, whose lofty temple is approached by six hundred and forty steps of stone; and Kiomidzu, shrine of Kwannon of the Eleven Faces, before whose altar the sacred fire has burned without ceasing for a thousand years; and Sada, where the Sacred Snake lies coiled forever on the sambo of the gods; and Oba, with its temples of Izanami and Izanagi, parents of gods and men, the makers of the world; and Yaegaki, whither lovers go to pray for unions with the beloved; and Kaka, Kaka-ura, Kaka-no-Kukedo San — all these I hope to see.

But of all places, Kaka-ura! Assuredly I must go to Kaka.

Few pilgrims go thither by sea, and boatmen are forbidden to go there if there be even wind enough 'to move three hairs.' So that whoever wishes to visit Kaka must either wait for a period of dead calm – very rare upon the coast of the Japanese Sea – or journey thereunto by land; and by land the way is difficult and wearisome. But I must see Kaka. For at Kaka, in a great cavern by the sea, there is a famous Jizō of stone; and each night, it is said, the ghosts of little children climb to the high cavern and pile up before the statue small heaps of pebbles; and every morning, in the soft sand, there may be seen the fresh prints of tiny naked feet, the feet of the infant ghosts. It is also said that in the cavern there is a rock out of which comes a stream of milk, as from a woman's breast; and the white stream flows forever, and the phantom children drink of it. Pilgrims bring with them gifts of small straw sandals – the zori that children wear – and leave them before the cavern, that the feet of the little ghosts may not be wounded by the sharp rocks. And the pilgrim treads with caution, lest he should overturn any of the many heaps of stones; for if this be done the children cry.

XVI

The city proper is as level as a table, but is bounded on two sides by low demilunes of charming hills shadowed with evergreen foliage and crowned with temples or shrines. There are thirty-five thousand souls dwelling in ten thousand houses forming thirty-three principal and many smaller streets; and from each end of almost every street, beyond the hills, the lake, or the eastern rice-fields, a mountain summit is always visible – green, blue, or gray according to distance. One may ride, walk, or go by boat to any quarter of the town; for it is not only divided by two rivers, but is also intersected by numbers of canals crossed by queer little bridges curved like a well-bent bow. Architecturally (despite such constructions in European style as the College of Teachers, the great public school, the Kenchō, the new post-office), it is much like other quaint Japanese towns; the structure of its temples, taverns, shops, and private dwellings is the same as in other cities of the western coast. But doubtless owing to the fact that Matsue remained a feudal stronghold until a time within the memory of thousands still living, those feudal distinctions of caste so sharply drawn in ancient times are yet indicated with singular exactness by the varying architecture of different districts. The city can be definitely divided into three architectural quarters: the district of the merchants and shop-keepers, forming the heart of the settlement, where all the houses are two stories high; the district of the temples, including nearly the whole southeastern part of the town; and the district or districts of the shizoku (formerly called samurai), comprising a vast number of large, roomy, garden-girt, one-story dwellings. From these elegant homes, in feudal days, could be summoned at a moment's notice five thousand 'two-sworded men' with their armed retainers, making a fighting total for the city alone of probably not less than thirteen thousand warriors. More than one third of all the city buildings were then samurai homes; for Matsue was the military centre of the most ancient province of Japan. At both ends of the town, which curves in a crescent along the lake shore, were the two main settlements of samurai; but just as some of the most important temples are situated outside of the temple district, so were many of the finest homesteads of this knightly caste situated in other quarters. They mustered most thickly, however, about the castle, which stands today on the summit of its citadel hill — the Oshiroyama — solid as when first built long centuries ago, a vast and sinister shape, all iron-gray, rising against the sky from a cyclopean foundation of stone. Fantastically grim the thing is, and grotesquely complex in detail; looking somewhat like a huge pagoda, of which the second, third, and fourth stories have been squeezed down and telescoped into one another by their own weight. Crested at its summit, like a feudal helmet, with two colossal fishes of bronze lifting their curved bodies skyward from either angle of the roof, and bristling with horned gables and gargoyled eaves and tilted puzzles of tiled roofing at every story, the creation is a veritable architectural dragon, made up of magnificent monstrosities — a dragon, moreover, full of eyes set at all conceivable angles, above, below, and on every side. From under the black scowl of the loftiest eaves, looking east and south, the whole city can be seen at a single glance, as in the vision of a soaring hawk; and from the northern angle the view plunges down three hundred feet to the castle road, where walking figures of men appear no larger than flies.

XVII

The grim castle has its legend.

It is related that, in accordance with some primitive and barbarous custom, precisely like that of which so terrible a souvenir has been preserved for us in the most pathetic of Servian ballads, 'The Foundation of Skadra,' a maiden of Matsue was interred alive under the walls of the castle at the time of its erection, as a sacrifice to some forgotten gods. Her name has never been recorded; nothing concerning her is remembered except that she was beautiful and very fond of dancing.

Now after the castle had been built, it is said that a law had to be passed forbidding that any girl should dance in the streets of Matsue. For whenever any maiden danced the hill Oshiroyama would shudder, and the great castle quiver from basement to summit.

XVIII

One may still sometimes hear in the streets a very humorous song, which everyone in town formerly knew by heart, celebrating the Seven Wonders of Matsue. For Matsue was formerly divided into seven quarters, in each of which some extraordinary object or person was to be seen. It is now divided into five religious districts, each containing a temple of the state religion. People living within those districts are called ujiko, and the temple the ujigami, or dwelling-place of the tutelary god. The ujiko must support the ujigami. (Every village and town has at least one ujigami.)

There is probably not one of the multitudinous temples of Matsue which has not some marvelous tradition attached to it; each of the districts has many legends; and I think that each of the thirty-three streets has its own special ghost story. Of these ghost stories I cite two specimens: they are quite representative of one variety of Japanese folklore.

Near to the Fu-mon-in temple, which is in the northeastern quarter, there is a bridge called Adzuki-togi-bashi, or The Bridge of the Washing of Peas. For it was said in other years that nightly a phantom woman sat beneath that bridge washing phantom peas. There is an exquisite Japanese iris-flower, of rainbow-violet color, which flower is named kaki-tsubata; and there is a song about that flower called kaki-tsubata-no-uta. Now this song must never be sung near the Adzuki-togi-bashi, because, for some strange reason which seems to have been forgotten, the ghosts haunting that place become so angry upon hearing it that to sing it there is to expose one's self to the most frightful calamities. There was once a samurai who feared nothing, who one night went to the bridge and loudly sang the song. No ghost appearing, he laughed and went home. At the gate of his house he met a beautiful tall woman whom he had never seen before, and who, bowing, presented him with a lacquered box (fumi-bako) such as women keep their letters in. He bowed to her in his knightly way; but she said, 'I am only the servant — this is my mistress's gift,' and vanished out of his sight. Opening the box, he saw the bleeding head of a young child. Entering his house, he found upon the floor of the guest-room the dead body of his own infant son with the head torn off.

Of the cemetery Dai-Oji, which is in the street called Naka-baramachi, this story is told:

In Nakabaramachi there is an ameya, or little shop in which midzu-ame is sold — the amber-tinted syrup, made of malt, which is given to children when milk cannot be obtained for them. Every night at a late hour there came to that shop a very pale woman, all in white, to buy one rin[8] worth of midzu-ame. The ame-seller wondered that she was so thin and pale, and often questioned her kindly; but she answered nothing. At last one night he followed her, out of curiosity. She went to the cemetery; and he became afraid and returned.

The next night the woman came again, but bought no midzu-ame, and only beckoned to the man to go with her. He followed her, with friends, into the cemetery. She walked to a certain tomb, and there disappeared; and they heard, under the ground, the crying of a child. Opening the tomb, they saw within it the corpse of the woman who nightly visited the ameya, with a living infant, laughing to see the lantern light, and beside the infant a little cup of midzu-ame. For the mother had been prematurely buried; the child was born in the tomb, and the ghost of the mother had thus provided for it — love being stronger than death.

XIX

Over the Tenjin-bashi, or Bridge of Tenjin, and through small streets and narrow of densely populated districts, and past many a tenantless

8. *Rin*, one tenth of one cent. A small round copper coin with a square hole in the middle.

and mouldering feudal homestead, I make my way to the extreme southwestern end of the city, to watch the sunset from a little sobaya[9] facing the lake. For to see the sun sink from this sobaya is one of the delights of Matsue.

There are no such sunsets in Japan as in the tropics: the light is gentle as a light of dreams; there are no furies of color; there are no chromatic violences in nature in this Orient. All in sea or sky is tint rather than color, and tint vapor-toned. I think that the exquisite taste of the race in the matter of colors and of tints, as exemplified in the dyes of their wonderful textures, is largely attributable to the sober and delicate beauty of nature's tones in this all-temperate world where nothing is garish.

Before me the fair vast lake sleeps, softly luminous, far-ringed with chains of blue volcanic hills shaped like a sierra. On my right, at its eastern end, the most ancient quarter of the city spreads its roofs of blue-gray tile; the houses crowd thickly down to the shore, to dip their wooden feet into the flood. With a glass I can see my own windows and the far-spreading of the roofs beyond, and above all else the green citadel with its grim castle, grotesquely peaked. The sun begins to set, and exquisite astonishments of tinting appear in water and sky.

Dead rich purples cloud broadly behind and above the indigo blackness of the serrated hills — mist purples, fading upwards, smokily into faint vermilions and dim gold, which again melt up through ghostliest greens into the blue. The deeper waters of the lake, far away, take a tender violet indescribable, and the silhouette of the pine-shadowed island seems to float in that sea of soft sweet color. But the shallower and nearer is cut from the deeper water by the current as sharply as by a line drawn, and all the surface on this side of that line is a shimmering bronze — old rich ruddy gold-bronze.

All the fainter colors change every five minutes — wondrously change and shift like tones and shades of fine shot-silks.

XX

Often in the streets at night, especially on the nights of sacred festivals (matsuri), one's attention will be attracted to some small booth by

9. An inn where soba is sold.

the spectacle of an admiring and perfectly silent crowd pressing before it. As soon as one can get a chance to look one finds there is nothing to look at but a few vases containing sprays of flowers, or perhaps some light gracious branches freshly cut from a blossoming tree. It is simply a little flower-show, or, more correctly, a free exhibition of master skill in the arrangement of flowers. For the Japanese do not brutally chop off flower-heads to work them up into meaningless masses of color, as we barbarians do: they love nature too well for that; they know how much the natural charm of the flower depends upon its setting and mounting, its relation to leaf and stem, and they select a single graceful branch or spray just as nature made it. At first you will not, as a Western stranger, comprehend such an exhibition at all: you are yet a savage in such matters compared with the commonest coolies about you. But even while you are still wondering at popular interest in this simple little show, the charm of it will begin to grow upon you, will become a revelation to you; and, despite your Occidental idea of self-superiority, you will feel humbled by the discovery that all flower displays you have ever seen abroad were only monstrosities in comparison with the natural beauty of those few simple sprays. You will also observe how much the white or pale blue screen behind the flowers enhances the effect by lamp or lantern light. For the screen has been arranged with the special purpose of showing the exquisiteness of plant shadows; and the sharp silhouettes of sprays and blossoms cast thereon are beautiful beyond the imagining of any Western decorative artist.

XXI

It is still the season of mists in this land whose most ancient name signifies the Place of the Issuing of Clouds. With the passing of twilight a faint ghostly brume rises over lake and landscape, spectrally veiling surfaces, slowly obliterating distances. As I lean over the parapet of the Tenjin-bashi, on my homeward way, to take one last look eastward, I find that the mountains have already been effaced. Before me there is only a shadowy flood far vanishing into vagueness without a horizon — the phantom of a sea. And I become suddenly aware that little white things are fluttering slowly down into it from the fingers of a woman standing upon the bridge beside me, and murmuring something in a low sweet voice. She is praying for her dead child. Each of those little papers she is dropping into the current bears a tiny picture of Jizō, and perhaps a little inscription. For when a child dies the mother buys a small woodcut (hanko) of Jizō, and with it prints the image of the divinity upon one hundred little papers. And she sometimes also writes upon the papers words signifying 'For the sake of . . .' – inscribing never the living, but the kaimyō or soul-name only, which the Buddhist priest has given to the dead, and which is written also upon the little commemorative tablet kept within the Buddhist household shrine, or butsuma. Then, upon a fixed day (most commonly the forty-ninth day after the burial), she goes to some place of running water and drops the little papers therein one by one; repeating, as each slips through her fingers, the holy invocation, '*Namu Jizō, Dai Bosatsu!*'

Doubtless this pious little woman, praying beside me in the dusk, is very poor. Were she not, she would hire a boat and scatter her tiny papers far away upon the bosom of the lake. (It is now only after dark that this may be done; for the police – I know not why – have been instructed to prevent the pretty rite just as in the open ports they have been instructed to prohibit the launching of the little straw boats of the dead, the shōryōbune.)

But why should the papers be cast into running water? A good old Tendai priest tells me that originally the rite was only for the souls of the drowned. But now these gentle hearts believe that all waters flow downward to the Shadow-world and through the Sai-no-Kawara, where Jizō is.

XXII

At home again, I slide open once more my little paper window, and look out upon the night. I see the paper lanterns flitting over the bridge, like a long shimmering of fireflies. I see the spectres of a hundred lights trembling upon the black flood. I see the broad shōji of dwellings beyond the river suffused with the soft yellow radiance of invisible lamps; and upon those lighted spaces I can discern slender moving shadows, silhouettes of graceful women. Devoutly do I pray that glass may never become universally adopted in Japan – there would be no more delicious shadows.

I listen to the voices of the city awhile. I hear the great bell of Tōkōji rolling its soft Buddhist thunder across the dark, and the songs of the night-walkers whose hearts have been made merry with wine, and the long sonorous chanting of the night-peddlers.

'U-mu-don-yai-soba-yai!' It is the seller of hot soba, Japanese buckwheat making his last round.

'Umai handan, machibito endan, usemono ninsō kasō kichikyō no urainai!' The cry of the itinerant fortune-teller.

'Ame-yu!' The musical cry of the seller of midzu-ame, the sweet amber syrup which children love.

'Amai!' The shrilling call of the seller of amazaké, sweet rice wine.

'Kawachi-no-kuni-hiotan-yama-koi-no-tsuji-ura!' The peddler of love-papers, of divining-papers, pretty tinted things with little shadowy pictures upon them. When held near a fire or a lamp, words written upon them with invisible ink begin to appear. These are always about sweethearts, and sometimes tell one what he does not wish to know. The fortunate ones who read them believe themselves still more fortunate; the unlucky abandon all hope; the jealous become even more jealous than they were before.

From all over the city there rises into the night a sound like the bubbling and booming of great frogs in a marsh — the echoing of the tiny drums of the dancing-girls, of the charming geisha. Like the rolling of a waterfall continually reverberates the multitudinous pattering of geta upon the bridge. A new light rises in the east; the moon is wheeling up from behind the peaks, very large and weird and wan through the white vapors. Again I hear the sounds of the clapping of many hands. For the wayfarers are paying obeisance to O-Tsuki-San: from the long bridge they are saluting the coming of the White Moon-Lady.[10]

I sleep, to dream of little children, in some mouldering mossy temple court, playing at the game of Shadows and of Demons.

---

10. According to the mythology of the *Kojiki* the Moon-Deity is a male divinity. But the common people know nothing of the *Kojiki*, written in an archaic Japanese which only the learned can read; and they address the moon as O-Tsuki-San, or 'Lady Moon,' just as the old Greek idyllists did.

In the Cave of the Children's Ghosts

追憶

I

It is forbidden to go to Kaka if there be wind enough 'to move three hairs.'

Now an absolutely windless day is rare on this wild western coast. Over the Japanese Sea, from Korea, or China, or boreal Sibera, some west or northwest breeze is nearly always blowing. So that I have had to wait many long months for a good chance to visit Kaka.

Taking the shortest route, one goes first to Mitsu-ura from Matsue, either by kuruma or on foot. By kuruma this little journey occupies nearly two hours and a half, though the distance is scarcely seven miles, the road being one of the worst in all Izumo. You leave Matsue to enter at once into a broad plain, level as a lake, all occupied by rice-fields and walled in by wooded hills. The path, barely wide enough for a single vehicle, traverses this green desolation, climbs the heights beyond it, and descends again into another and larger level of rice-fields surrounded also by hills. The path over the second line of hills is much steeper; then a third rice-plain must be crossed and a third chain of green altitudes, lofty enough to merit the name of mountains. Of course one must make the ascent on foot: it is no small labor for a kurumaya to pull even an empty kuruma up to the top; and how he manages to do so without breaking the little vehicle is a mystery, for the path is stony and rough as the bed of torrent. A tiresome climb I find it; but the landscape view from the summit is more than compensation.

Then descending, there remains a fourth and last wide level of rice-fields to traverse. The absolute flatness of the great plains between the ranges, and the singular way in which these latter 'fence off' the country into sections, are matters for surprise even in a land of surprises like Japan. Beyond the fourth rice-valley there is a fourth hill-chain, lower and richly wooded, on reaching the base of which the traveler must finally abandon his kuruma, and proceed over the hills on foot. Behind them lies the sea. But the very worst bit of the journey now begins. The path makes an easy winding ascent between bamboo growths and young pine and other vegetation for a shaded quarter of a mile, passing before various little shrines and pretty homesteads surrounded by high-hedged gardens. Then it suddenly breaks into steps, or rather ruins of steps — partly hewn in the rock, partly built, everywhere breached and worn — which descend, all edgeless, in a manner amazingly precipitous, to the village of Mitsu-ura. With straw sandals, which never slip, the country folk can nimbly hurry up or down such a path; but with foreign footgear one slips at nearly every step; and when you reach the bottom at last, the wonder of how you managed to get there, even with the assistance of your faithful kurumaya, keeps you for a moment quite unconscious of the fact that you are already in Mitsu-ura.

II

Mitsu-ura stands with its back to the mountains, at the end of a small deep bay hemmed in by very high cliffs. There is only one narrow strip of beach at the foot of the heights; and the village owes its existence to the fact, for beaches are rare on this part of the coast. Crowded between the cliffs and the sea, the houses have a painfully compressed aspect; and somehow the greater number gives one the impression of things created out of wrecks of junks. The little streets, or rather alleys, are full of boats and skeletons of boats and boat timbers; and everywhere, suspended from bamboo poles much taller than the houses, immense bright brown fishing-nets are drying in the sun. The whole curve of the beach is also lined with boats, lying side by side, so that I wonder how it will be possible to get to the water's edge without climbing over them. There is no hotel; but I find hospitality in a fisherman's dwelling, while my kurumaya goes somewhere to hire a boat for Kaka-ura.

In less than ten minutes there is a crowd of several hundred people about the house, half-clad adults and perfectly naked boys. They blockade the building; they obscure the light by filling up the doorways and climbing into the windows to look at the foreigner. The aged proprietor of the cottage protests in vain, says harsh things; the crowd only thickens. Then all the sliding screens are closed. But in the paper panes there are holes; and at all the lower holes the curious take regular turns at peeping. At a higher hole I do some peeping myself. The crowd is not prepossessing: it is squalid, dull-featured, remarkably ugly. But it is gentle and silent; and there are one or two pretty faces in it which seem extraordinary by reason of the general homeliness of the rest.

At last my kurumaya has succeeded in making arrangements for a boat; and I effect a sortie to the beach, followed by the kurumaya, and by all my besiegers. Boats have been moved to make a passage for us, and we embark without trouble of any sort. Our crew consists of two scullers — an old man at the stern, wearing only a rokushaku about his loins, and an old woman at the bow, fully robed and wearing an immense straw hat shaped like a mushroom. Both of course stand to their work and it would be hard to say which is the stronger or more skillful sculler. We passengers squat Oriental fashion upon a mat in the centre of the boat, where a hibachi, well stocked with glowing charcoal, invites us to smoke.

III

The day is clear blue to the end of the world, with a faint wind from the east, barely enough to wrinkle the sea, certainly more than enough to 'move three hairs.' Nevertheless the boatwoman and the boatman do not seem anxious; and I begin to wonder whether the famous prohibition is not a myth. So delightful the transparent water looks, that before we have left the bay I have to yield to its temptation by plunging in and swimming after the boat. When I climb back on board we are rounding the promontory on the right; and the little vessel begins to rock. Even under this thin wind the sea is moving in long swells. And as we pass into the open, following the westward trend of the land, we find ourselves gliding over an ink-black depth, in front of one of the very grimmest coasts I ever saw.

A tremendous line of dark iron-colored cliffs, towering sheer from the sea without a beach, and with never a speck of green below their summits, and here and there along this terrible front, monstrous beetlings, breaches, fissures, earthquake rendings, and topplings-down. Enormous fractures show lines of strata pitched up skyward, or plunging down into the ocean with the long fall of cubic miles of cliff. Before fantastic gaps, prodigious masses of rock, of all nightmarish shapes, rise from profundities unfathomed. And though the wind today seems trying to hold its breath, white breakers are reaching far up the cliffs, and dashing their foam into the faces of the splintered crags. We are too far to hear the thunder of them; but their ominous sheet-lightning fully explains to me the story of the three hairs. Along this goblin coast on a wild day there would be no possible chance for the strongest swimmer or the stoutest boat; there is no place for the foot, no hold for the hand, nothing, but the sea raving against a precipice of iron. Even today, under the feeblest breath imaginable, great swells deluge us with spray as they splash past. And for two long hours this jagged frowning coast towers by: and, as we toil on, rocks rise around us like black teeth; and always, far away, the foam-bursts gleam at the feet of the implacable cliffs. But there are no sounds save the lapping and plashing of passing swells, and the monotonous creaking of the sculls upon their pegs of wood.

At last, at last, a bay – a beautiful large bay, with a demilune of soft green hills about it, overtopped by far blue mountains – and in the very farthest point of the bay a miniature village, in front of which many junks are riding at anchor: Kaka-ura.

But we do not go to Kaka-ura yet; the Kukedo are not there. We cross the broad opening of the bay. journey along another half mile of ghastly sea-precipice, and finally make for a lofty promontory of naked Plutonic rock. We pass by its menacing foot, slip along its side, and lo! at an angle opens the arched mouth of a wonderful cavern, broad, lofty, and full of light, with no floor but the sea. Beneath us, as we slip into it, I can see rocks fully twenty feet down. The water is clear as air. This is the Shin-Kukedo, called the *New* Cavern, though assuredly older than human record by a hundred thousand years.

IV

A more beautiful sea-cave could scarcely be imagined. The sea, tunneling the tall promontory through and through, has also, like a great architect, ribbed and groined and polished its mighty work. The arch of the entrance is certainly twenty feet above the deep water, and fifteen wide; and trillions of wave tongues have licked the vault and walls into wondrous smoothness. As we proceed, the rock-roof steadily heightens and the way widens. Then we unexpectedly glide under a heavy shower of fresh water, dripping from overhead. This spring is called the ō-chōzubachi or mitarashi[1] of Shin-Kukedo-San. From the high vault at this point it is believed that a great stone will detach itself and fall upon any evil-hearted person who should attempt to enter the cave. I safely pass through the ordeal!

Suddenly, as we advance, the boatwoman takes a stone from the bottom of the boat, and with it begins to rap heavily on the bow· and the hollow echoing is reiterated with thundering repercussions through all the cave. And in another instant we pass into a great burst of light, coming from the mouth of a magnificent and lofty archway on the left, opening into the cavern at right angles. This explains the singular illumination of the long vault, which at first seemed to come from beneath; for while the opening was still invisible all the water appeared to be suffused with light. Through this grand arch, between outlying rocks, a strip of beautiful green undulating coast appears, over miles of azure water. We glide on toward the third entrance to the Kukedo, opposite to that by which we came in; and enter the dwelling-place of the Kami and the Hotoke, for this grotto is sacred both to Shintō and to Buddhist faith. Here the Kukedo reaches its greatest altitude and breadth. Its vault is fully forty feet above the water, and its walls thirty feet apart. Far up on the right, near the roof, is a projecting white rock, and above the rock an orifice wherefrom a slow stream drips, seeming white as the rock itself.

This is the legendary Fountain of Jizō, the fountain of milk at which the souls of dead children drink. Sometimes it flows more swiftly, sometimes more slowly; but it never ceases by night or day. And mothers suffering from want of milk come hither to pray that milk

1. Such are the names given to the water-vessels or cisterns at which Shintō worshipers must wash their hands and rinse their mouths ere praying to the Kami. A mitarashi or ō-chozubachi is placed before every Shintō temple. The pilgrim to Shin-Kukedo-San should perform this ceremonial ablution at the little rock-spring above described, before entering the sacred cave. Here even the gods of the cave are said to wash after having passed through the sea-water.

may be given unto them; and their prayer is heard. And mothers having more milk than their infants need come hither also, and pray to Jizō that so much as they can give may be taken for the dead children; and their prayer is heard, and their milk diminishes.

At least thus the peasants of Izumo say.

And the echoing of the swells leaping against the rocks without, the rushing and rippling of the tide against the walls, the heavy rain of percolating water, sounds of lapping and gurgling and plashing, and sounds of mysterious origin coming from no visible where, make it difficult for us to hear each other speak. The cavern seems full of voices, as if a host of invisible beings were holding tumultuous converse.

Below us all the deeply lying rocks are naked to view as if seen through glass. It seems to me that nothing could be more delightful than to swim through this cave and let one's self drift with the sea-currents through all its cool shadows. But as I am on the point of jumping in, all the other occupants of the boat utter wild cries of protest. It is certain death! men who jumped in here only six months ago were never heard of again! this is sacred water, Kami-no-umi! And as if to conjure away my temptation, the boatwoman again seizes her little stone and raps fearfully upon the bow. On finding, however, that I am not sufficiently deterred by these stories of sudden death and disappearance, she suddenly screams into my ear the magical word:

'SAMÉ!'

Sharks! I have no longer any desire whatever to swim through the many-sounding halls of Shin-Kukedo-San. I have lived in the tropics!

And we start forthwith for Kyū-Kukedo-San, the Ancient Cavern.

v

For the ghastly fancies about the Kami-no-umi, the word 'samé' afforded a satisfactory explanation. But why that long, loud, weird rapping on the bow with a stone evidently kept on board for no other purpose? There was an exaggerated earnestness about the action which gave me an uncanny sensation — something like that which moves a man while walking at night upon a lonesome road, full of queer shadows, to sing at the top of his voice. The boatwoman at first declares that the rapping was made only for the sake of the singular echo. But after some cautious further questioning, I discover a much more sinister reason for the performance. Moreover, I learn that all the seamen and seawomen of this coast do the same thing when passing through perilous places, or places believed to be haunted by the Ma. What are the Ma?

Goblins!

VI

From the caves of the Kami we retrace our course for about a quarter of a mile; then make directly for an immense perpendicular wrinkle in the long line of black cliffs. Immediately before it a huge dark rock towers from the sea, whipped by the foam of breaking swells. Rounding it, we glide behind it into still water and shadow, the shadow of a monstrous cleft in the precipice of the coast. And suddenly, at an unsuspected angle, the mouth of another cavern yawns before us; and in another moment our boat touches its threshold of stone with a little shock that sends a long sonorous echo, like the sound of a temple drum, booming through all the abysmal place. A single glance tells me whither we have come. Far within the dusk I see the face of a Jizō, smiling in pale stone, and before him, and all about him, a weird congregation of gray shapes without shape — a host of fantasticalities that strangely suggest the wreck of a cemetery. From the sea the ribbed floor of the cavern slopes high through deepening shadows back to the black mouths of a farther grotto; and all that slope is covered with hundreds and thousands of forms like shattered haka. But as the eyes grow accustomed to the gloaming it becomes manifest that these were never haka; they are only little towers of stone and pebbles deftly piled up by long and patient labor.

'Shinda kodomo no shigoto,' my kurumaya murmurs with a compassionate smile; 'all this is the work of the dead children.'

And we disembark. By counsel, I take off my shoes and put on a pair of zori, or straw sandals, provided for me, as the rock is extremely slippery. The others land barefoot. But how to proceed soon becomes a puzzle: the countless stone-piles stand so close together that no space for the foot seems to be left between them.

'Mada michi ga arimasŭ!' the boatwoman announces, leading the way. There is a path.

Following after her, we squeeze ourselves between the wall of the cavern on the right and some large rocks, and discover a very, very narrow passage left open between the stone-towers. But we are warned to be careful for the sake of the little ghosts: if any of their work be overturned, they will cry. So we move very cautiously and slowly across the cave to a space bare of stone-heaps, where the rocky floor is covered with a thin layer of sand, detritus of a crumbling ledge above it. And in that sand I see light prints of little feet, children's feet, tiny naked feet, only three or four inches long — *the footprints of the infant ghosts.*

Had we come earlier, the boatwoman says, we should have seen many more. For 'tis at night, when the soil of the cavern is moist with dews and drippings from the roof, that They leave Their footprints upon it; but when the heat of the day comes, and the sand and the rocks dry up, the prints of the little feet vanish away.

There are only three footprints visible, but these are singularly distinct. One points toward the wall of the cavern; the others toward the sea. Here and there, upon ledges of projections of the rock, all about the cavern, tiny straw sandals — children's zori — are lying: offerings of pilgrims to the little ones, that their feet may not be wounded by the stones. But all the ghostly footprints are prints of naked feet.

Then we advance, picking our way very, very carefully between the stone-towers, toward the mouth of the inner grotto, and reach the statue of Jizō before it. A seated Jizō, carven in granite, holding in one hand the mystic jewel by virtue of which all wishes may be fulfilled; in the other his shakujō, or pilgrim's staff. Before him (strange condescension of Shintō faith!) a little torii has been erected, and a pair of gohei! Evidently this gentle divinity has no enemies; at the feet of the lover of children's ghosts, both creeds unite in tender homage.

I said feet. But this subterranean Jizō has only one foot. The carven lotus on which he reposes has been fractured and broken: two great petals are missing; and the right foot, which must have rested upon one of them, has been knocked off at the ankle. This, I learn upon inquiry, has been done by the waves. In times of great storm the billows rush into the cavern like raging Oni, and sweep all the little stone-towers into shingle as they come, and dash the statues against the rocks. But always during the first still night after the tempest the work is reconstructed as before!

'Hotoke ga shimpai shite: naki-naki tsumi naoshi-masŭ.' They make mourning, the hotoke; weeping, they pile up the stones again, they rebuild their towers of prayer.

All about the black mouth of the inner grotto the bone-colored rock bears some resemblance to a vast pair of yawning jaws. Downward from this sinister portal the cavern-floor slopes into a deeper and darker aperture. And within it, as one's eyes become accustomed to the gloom, a still larger vision of stone-towers is disclosed; and beyond them, in a nook of the grotto, three other statues of Jizō smile, each one with a torii before it. Here I have the misfortune to upset first one stone-pile and then another, while trying to proceed. My kurumaya, almost simultaneously, ruins a third. To atone, therefore, we must build six new towers, or double the number of those which we have cast down. And while we are thus busied, the boatwoman tells of two fishermen who remained in the cavern through all one night, and heard the humming of the viewless gathering, and sounds of speech, like the speech of children murmuring in multitude

VII

Only at night do the shadowy children come to build their little stone-heaps at the feet of the Jizō; and it is said that every night the stones are changed. When I ask why they do not work by day, when there is none to see them, I am answered: 'O-Hi-San[2] might see them; *the dead exceedingly fear the Lady-Sun.*'

To the question, 'Why do they come from the sea?' I can get no satisfactory answer. But doubtless in the quaint imagination of this people, as also in that of many another, there lingers still the primitive idea of some communication, mysterious and awful, between the world of waters and the world of the dead. It is always over the sea, after the Feast of Souls, that the spirits pass murmuring back to their dim realm, in those elfish little ships of straw which are launched for them upon the sixteenth day of the seventh moon. Even when these are

2. 'The August Fire-Lady;' or, 'the August Sun-Lady,' Ama-terasu-oho-mi-Kami.

launched upon rivers, or when floating lanterns are set adrift upon lakes or canals to light the ghosts upon their way, or when a mother bereaved drops into some running stream one hundred little prints of Jizō for the sake of her lost darling, the vague idea behind the pious act is that all waters flow to the sea and the sea itself unto the 'Nether-distant Land.'

Some time, somewhere, this day will come back to me at night, with its visions and sounds: the dusky cavern, and its gray hosts of stone climbing back into darkness, and the faint prints of little naked feet, and the weirdly smiling images. and the broken syllables of the waters, inward-borne, multiplied by husky echoings, blending into one vast ghostly whispering, like the humming of the Sai-no-Kawara.

And over the black-blue bay we glide to the rocky beach of Kaka-ura.

VIII

As at Mitsu-ura, the water's edge is occupied by a serried line of fishing-boats, each with its nose to the sea; and behind these are ranks of others; and it is only just barely possible to squeeze one's way between them over the beach to the drowsy, pretty, quaint little streets behind them. Everybody seems to be asleep when we first land: the only living creature visible is a cat, sitting on the stern of a boat; and even that cat, according to Japanese beliefs, might not be a real cat, but an o-baké or a nekomata – in short, a goblin-cat, *for it has a long tail*. It is hard work to discover the solitary hotel: there are no signs; and every house seems a private house, either a fisherman's or a farmer's. But the little place is worth wandering about in. A kind of yellow stucco is here employed to cover the exterior of walls; and this light warm tint under the bright blue day gives to the miniature streets a more than cheerful aspect.

When we do finally discover the hotel, we have to wait quite a good while before going in; for nothing is ready; everybody is asleep or away, though all the screens and sliding-doors are open. Evidently there are no thieves in Kaka-ura. The hotel is on a little hillock, and is approached from the main street (the rest are only miniature alleys) by two little flights of stone steps. Immediately across the way I see a Zen temple and a Shintō temple, almost side by side.

At last a pretty young woman, naked to the waist, with a bosom like a Naiad, comes running down the street to the hotel at a surprising speed, bowing low with a smile as she hurries by us into the house. This little person is the waiting-maid of the inn, O-Kayo-San – a name signifying 'Years of Bliss.' Presently she reappears at the threshold, fully robed in a nice kimono, and gracefully invites us to enter, which we are only too glad to do. The room is neat and spacious; Shintō kakemono from Kitzuki are suspended in the toko and upon the walls; and in one corner I see a very handsome Zen-butsudan, or household shrine. (The form of the shrine, as well as the objects of worship therein, vary according to the sect of the worshipers.) Suddenly I become aware that it is growing strangely dark; and, looking about me, perceive that all the doors and windows and other apertures of the inn are densely blocked up by a silent, smiling crowd which has gathered to look at me. I could not have believed there were so many people in Kaka-ura.

In a Japanese house, during the hot season, everything is thrown open to the breeze. All the shōji or sliding paper-screens, which serve for windows; and all the opaque paper-screens (fusuma) used in other seasons to separate apartments, are removed. There is nothing left between floor and roof save the frame or skeleton of the building; the dwelling is literally *unwalled,* and may be seen through in any direction. The landlord, finding the crowd embarrassing, closes up the building in front. The silent, smiling crowd goes to the rear. The rear is also closed. Then the crowd masses to right and left of the house; and both sides have to be closed, which makes it unsufferably hot. And the crowd make gentle protest.

Wherefore our host, being displeased, rebukes the multitude with argument and reason, yet without lifting his voice. (Never do these people lift up their voices in anger.) And what he says I strive to translate, with emphases, as follows:

'You-as-for! outrageousness doing – *what* marvelous is?

'*Theatre* is not!

'*Juggler* is not!

'*Wrestler* is not!

'*What* amusing is?

'Honorable *Guest* this is!

'Now august-to-eat-time-is; to-look-at *evil* matter is. *Honorable-returning-time-in-*to-look-at-as-for-is-good.'

But outside, soft laughing voices continue to plead; pleading, shrewdly enough, only with the feminine portion of the family: the landlord's heart is less easily touched. And these, too, have their arguments:

'Oba-San!

'O-Kayo-San!

'Shōji-to-open-condescend! — want to see!

'*Though-we-look-at, Thing-that-by-looking-at-is-worn-out-it-is-not!*

'So that not-to-hinder looking-at is good.

'Hasten therefore to open!'

As for myself, I would gladly protest against this sealing-up, for there is nothing offensive nor even embarrassing in the gaze of these innocent, gentle people; but as the landlord seems to be personally annoyed, I do not like to interfere. The crowd, however, does not go away: it continues to increase, waiting for my exit. And there is one high window in the rear, of which the paper-panes contain some holes; and I see shadows of little people climbing up to get to the holes. Presently there is an eye at every hole.

When I approach the window, the peepers drop noiselessly to the ground, with little timid bursts of laughter, and run away. But they soon come back again. A more charming crowd could hardly be imagined: nearly all boys and girls, half-naked because of the heat, but fresh and clean as flower-buds. Many of the faces are surprisingly pretty: there are but very few which are not extremely pleasing. But where are the men, and the old women? Truly, this population seems not of Kaka-ura, but rather of the Sai-no-Kawara. The boys look like little Jizō.

During dinner, I amuse myself by poking pears and little pieces of radish through the holes in the shōji. At first there is much hesitation and silvery laughter; but in a little while the silhouette of a tiny hand reaches up cautiously, and a pear vanishes away. Then a second pear is taken, without snatching, as softly as if a ghost had appropriated it. Thereafter hesitation ceases, despite the effort of one elderly woman to create a panic by crying out the word 'Mahōtsukai,' 'wizard.' By the time the dinner is over and the shōji removed, we have all become good friends. Then the crowd resumes its silent observation from the four cardinal points.

I never saw a more striking difference in the appearance of two village populations than that between the youth of Mitsu-ura and of Kaka. Yet the villages are but two hours' sailing distance apart. In remoter Japan, as in certain islands of the West Indies, particular physical types are developed apparently among communities but slightly isolated; on one side of a mountain a population may be remarkably attractive, while upon the other you may find a hamlet whose inhabitants are decidedly unprepossessing. But nowhere in this country have I seen a prettier *jeunesse* than that of Kaka-ura.

'Returning-time-in-to-look-at-as-for-is-good.' As we descend to the bay, the whole of Kaka-ura, including even the long-invisible ancients of the village, accompanies us; making no sound except the pattering of geta. Thus we are escorted to our boat. Into all the other craft drawn up on the beach the younger folk clamber lightly and seat themselves on the prows and the gunwales to gaze at the marvelous *Thing-that-by-looking-at-worn-out-is-not*. And all smile, but say nothing, even to each other: somehow the experience gives me the sensation of being asleep; it is so soft, so gentle, and so queer withal, just like things seen in dreams. And as we glide away over the blue lucent water I look back to see the people all waiting and gazing still from the great semicircle of boats; all the slender brown child-limbs dangling from the prows; all the velvety-black heads motionless in the sun; all the boy-faces smiling Jizō-smiles; all the black soft eyes still watching, tirelessly watching, the *Thing-that-by-looking-at-worn-out-is-not*. And as the scene, too swiftly receding, diminishes to the width of a kakemono, I vainly wish that I could buy this last vision of it, to place it in my toko, and delight my soul betimes with gazing thereon. Yet another moment, and we round a rocky point; and Kaka-ura vanishes from my sight forever. So all things pass away.

Assuredly those impressions which longest haunt recollection are the most transitory: we remember many more instants than minutes, more minutes than hours; and who remembers an entire day? The sum of the remembered happiness of a lifetime is the creation of seconds. What is more fugitive than a smile? Yet when does the memory of a vanished smile expire? Or the soft regret which that memory may evoke?

Regret for a single individual smile is something common to normal human nature; but regret for the smile of a population, for a smile considered as an abstract quality, is certainly a rare sensation, and one to be obtained, I fancy, only in this Orient land whose people smile forever like their own gods of stone. And this precious experience is already mine; I am regretting the smile of Kaka.

Simultaneously there comes the recollection of a strangely grim Buddhist legend. Once the Buddha smiled; and by the wondrous radiance of that smile were countless worlds illuminated. But there came a Voice, saying: *It is not real! It cannot last!* And the light passed.

At the Market
of the Dead

追
憶

I

It is just past five o'clock in the afternoon. Through the open door of my little study the rising breeze of evening is beginning to disturb the papers on my desk, and the white fire of the Japanese sun is taking that pale amber tone which tells that the heat of the day is over. There is not a cloud in the blue — not even one of those beautiful white filamentary things, like ghosts of silken floss, which usually swim in this most ethereal of earthly skies even in the driest weather.

A sudden shadow at the door. Akira, the young Buddhist student, stands at the threshold slipping his white feet out of the sandal-thongs preparatory to entering, and smiling like the god Jizō.

'Ah! komban, Akira.'

'Tonight,' says Akira, seating himself upon the floor in the posture of Buddha upon the Lotus, 'the Bon-ichi will be held. Perhaps you would like to see it?'

'Oh, Akira, all things in this country I should like to see. But tell me, I pray you, unto what may the Bon-ichi be likened?'

'The Bon-ichi,' answers Akira, 'is a market at which will be sold all things required for the Festival of the Dead; and the Festival of the Dead will begin tomorrow, when all the altars of the temples and all the shrines in the homes of good Buddhists will be made beautiful.'

'Then I want to see the Bon-ichi, Akira, and I should also like to see a Buddhist shrine — a household shrine.'

'Yes, will you come to my room?' asks Akira. 'It is not far — in the Street of the Aged Men, beyond the Street of the Stony River, and near to the Street Everlasting. There is a butsuma there — a household shrine — and on the way I will tell you about the Bonku.'

So, for the first time I learn those things — which I am now about to write.

From the thirteenth to the fifteenth day of July is held the Festival of the Dead — the Bommatsuri or Bonku — by some Europeans called the Feast of Lanterns. But in many places there are two such festivals annually; for those who still follow the ancient reckoning of time by moons hold that the Bommatsuri should fall on the thirteenth, fourteenth, and fifteenth days of the seventh month of the antique calendar, which corresponds to a later period of the year.

Early on the morning of the thirteenth, new mats of purest rice straw, woven expressly for the festival, are spread upon all Buddhist altars and within each butsuma or butsudan — the little shrine before which the morning and evening prayers are offered up in every believing home. Shrines and altars are likewise decorated with beautiful embellishments of colored paper, and with flowers and sprigs of certain hallowed plants — always real lotus-flowers when obtainable, otherwise lotus-flowers of paper, and fresh branches of shikimi (anise) and of misohagi (lespedeza). Then a tiny lacquered table — a zen — such as Japanese meals are usually served upon, is placed upon the altar, and the food offerings are laid on it. But in the smaller shrines of Japanese homes the offerings are more often simply laid upon the rice matting, wrapped in fresh lotus-leaves.

These offerings consist of the foods called somen, resembling our vermicelli, gozen, which is boiled rice, dango, a sort of tiny dumpling, eggplant, and fruits according to season — frequently uri and saikwa, slices of melon and watermelon, and plums and peaches. Often sweet cakes and dainties are added. Sometimes the offering is only O-sho-jin-gu (honorable uncooked food); more usually it is O-rio-gu (honorable boiled food); but it never includes, of course, fish, meats, or wine. Clear water is given to the shadowy guest, and is sprinkled from time to time upon the altar or within the shrine with a branch of misohagi; tea is poured out every hour for the viewless visitors, and everything is daintily served up in little plates and cups and bowls, as for living guests, with hashi (chopsticks) laid beside the offering. So for three days the dead are feasted.

At sunset, pine torches, fixed in the ground before each home, are kindled to guide the spirit-visitors. Sometimes, also, on the first evening of the Bommatsuri, welcome fires (mukaebi) are lighted along the shore of the sea or lake or river by which the village or city is situated – neither more nor less than one hundred and eight fires; this number having some mystic signification in the philosophy of Buddhism. And charming lanterns are suspended each night at the entrances of homes – the Lanterns of the Festival of the Dead – lanterns of special forms and colors, beautifully painted with suggestions of landscape and shapes of flowers, and always decorated with a peculiar fringe of paper streamers.

Also, on the same night, those who have dead friends go to the cemeteries and make offerings there, and pray, and burn incense, and pour out water for the ghosts. Flowers are placed there in the bamboo vases set beside each haka, and lanterns are lighted and hung up before the tombs, but these lanterns have no designs upon them.

At sunset on the evening of the fifteenth only the offerings called Segaki are made in the temples. Then are fed the ghosts of the circle of Penance, called Gakidō, the place of hungry spirits; and then also are fed by the priests those ghosts having no other friends among the living to care for them. Very, very small these offerings are – like the offerings to the gods.

III

Now this, Akira tells me, is the origin of the Segaki, as the same is related in the holy book Busetsuuran-bongyo:

Dai-Mokenren, the great disciple of Buddha, obtained by merit the Six Supernatural Powers. And by virtue of them it was given him to see the soul of his mother in the Gakidō – the world of spirits doomed to suffer hunger in expiation of faults committed in a previous life. Mokenren saw that his mother suffered much, he grieved exceedingly because of her pain, and he filled a bowl with choicest food and sent it to her. He saw her try to eat; but each time that she tried to lift the food to her lips it would change into fire and burning embers, so that she could not eat. Then Mokenren asked the Teacher what he could do to relieve his mother from pain. And the Teacher made answer: 'On the fifteenth day of the seventh month, feed the ghosts of the great priests of all countries.' And Mokenren, having done so, saw that his mother was freed from the state of gaki, and that she was dancing for joy.[1] This is the origin also of the dances called Bon-odori, which are danced on the third night of the Festival of the Dead throughout Japan.

Upon the third and last night there is a weirdly beautiful ceremony, more touching than that of the Segaki, stranger than the Bon-odori – the ceremony of farewell. All that the living may do to please the dead has been done; the time allotted by the powers of the unseen worlds unto the ghostly visitants is well-nigh past, and their friends must send them all back again.

Everything has been prepared for them. In each home small boats made of barley straw closely woven have been freighted with supplies of choice food, with tiny lanterns, and written messages of faith and love. Seldom more than two feet in length are these boats; but the dead require little room. And the frail craft are launched on canal, lake, sea, or river – each with a miniature lantern glowing at the prow, and incense burning at the stern. And if the night be fair, they voyage long. Down all the creeks and rivers and canals the phantom fleets go glimmering to the sea; and all the sea sparkles to the horizon with the lights of the dead, and the sea wind is fragrant with incense.

But alas! it is now forbidden in the great seaports to launch the shōryōbune, 'the boats of the blessed ghosts.'

IV

It is so narrow, the Street of the Aged Men, that by stretching out one's arms one can touch the figured sign-draperies before its tiny shops on both sides at once. And these little ark-shaped houses really seem toy-houses; that in which Akira lives is even smaller than the rest, having no shop in it, and no miniature second story. It is all closed up. Akira slides back the wooden amado which forms the door, and then the paper-paned screens behind it; and the tiny structure, thus opened, with its light unpainted woodwork and painted paper partitions, looks

1. It is related in the same book that Ananda having asked the Buddha how came Mokenren's mother to suffer in the Gakidō, the Teacher replied that in a previous incarnation she had refused, through cupidity, to feed certain visiting priests.

something like a great bird-cage. But the rush matting of the elevated floor is fresh, sweet-smelling, spotless; and as we take off our footgear to mount upon it, I see that all within is neat, curious, and pretty.

'The woman has gone out,' says Akira, setting the smoking-box (hibachi) in the middle of the floor, and spreading beside it a little mat for me to squat upon.

'But what is this, Akira?' I ask, pointing to a thin board suspended by a ribbon on the wall — a board so cut from the middle of a branch as to leave the bark along its edges There are two columns of mysterious signs exquisitely painted upon it.

'Oh, that is a calendar,' answers Akira. 'On the right side are the names of the months having thirty-one days; on the left, the names of those having less. Now here is a household shrine.'

Occupying the alcove, which is an indispensable part of the structure of Japanese guest-rooms, is a native cabinet painted with figures of flying birds; and on this cabinet stands the butsuma. It is a small lacquered and gilded shrine, with little doors modeled after those of a temple gate — a shrine very quaint, very much dilapidated (one door has lost its hinges), but still a dainty thing despite its crackled lacquer and faded gilding. Akira opens it with a sort of compassionate smile; and I look inside for the image. There is none; only a wooden tablet with a band of white paper attached to it, bearing Japanese characters — the name of a dead baby girl — and a vase of expiring flowers, a tiny print of Kwannon, the Goddess of Mercy, and a cup filled with ashes of incense.

'Tomorrow,' Akira says, 'she will decorate this, and make the offerings of food to the little one.'

Hanging from the ceiling, on the opposite side of the room, and in front of the shrine, is a wonderful, charming, funny, white-and-rosy mask — the face of a laughing, chubby girl with two mysterious spots upon her forehead, the face of Otafuku.[2] It twirls round and round in the soft air-current coming through the open shōji; and every time those funny black eyes, half-shut with laughter, look at me, I cannot help smiling. And hanging still higher, I see little Shintō emblems of paper (gohei), a miniature mitre-shaped cap in likeness of those worn in the sacred dances, a pasteboard emblem of the magic gem

2. A deity of good fortune.

(Niō-i hōjiu) which the gods bear in their hands, a small Japanese doll, and a little wind-wheel which will spin around with the least puff of air, and other indescribable toys, mostly symbolic, such as are sold on festal days in the courts of the temples – the playthings of the dead child.

'Komban!' exclaims a very gentle voice behind us. The mother is standing there, smiling as if pleased at the stranger's interest in her butsuma – a middle-aged woman of the poorest class, not comely, but with a most kindly face. We return her evening greeting; and while I sit down upon the little mat laid before the hibachi, Akira whispers something to her, with the result that a small kettle is at once set to boil over a very small charcoal furnace. We are probably going to have some tea.

As Akira takes his seat before me, on the other side of the hibachi, I ask him:

'What was the name I saw on the tablet?'

'The name which you saw,' he answers, 'was not the real name. The real name is written upon the other side. After death another name is given by the priest. A dead boy is called Ryochi Dōji; a dead girl, Mioyo Dōnyo.'

While we are speaking, the woman approaches the little shrine, opens it, arranges the objects in it, lights the tiny lamp, and with joined hands and bowed head begins to pray. Totally unembarrassed by our presence and our chatter she seems, as one accustomed to do what is right and beautiful heedless of human opinion; praying with that brave, true frankness which belongs to the poor only of this world – those simple souls who never have any secret to hide, either from each other or from heaven, and of whom Ruskin nobly said, *'These are our holiest.'* I do not know what words her heart is murmuring: I hear only at moments that soft sibilant sound, made by gently drawing the breath through the lips, which among this kind of people is a token of humblest desire to please.

As I watch the tender little rite, I become aware of something dimly astir in the mystery of my own life – vaguely, indefinably familiar, like a memory ancestral, like the revival of a sensation forgotten two thousand years. Blended in some strange way it seems to be with my faint knowledge of an elder world, whose household gods were also the beloved dead; and there is a weird sweetness in this place, like a shadowing of Lares.

Then, her brief prayer over, she turns to her miniature furnace again. She talks and laughs with Akira; she prepares the tea, pours it out in tiny cups and serves it to us, kneeling in that graceful attitude — picturesque, traditional — which for six hundred years has been the attitude of the Japanese woman serving tea. Verily, no small part of the life of the women of Japan is spent thus in serving little cups of tea. Even as a ghost, she appears in popular prints offering to somebody spectral tea-cups of spectral tea. Of all Japanese ghost-pictures, I know of none more pathetic than that in which the phantom of a woman kneeling humbly offers to her haunted and remorseful murderer a little cup of tea!

'Now let us go to the Bon-ichi,' says Akira, rising; 'she must go there herself soon, and it is already getting dark Sayōnara!'

It is indeed almost dark as we leave the little house: stars are pointing in the strip of sky above the street; but it is a beautiful night for a walk, with a tepid breeze blowing at intervals, and sending long flutterings through the miles of shop draperies. The market is in the narrow street at the verge of the city, just below the hill where the great Buddhist temple of Zoto-Kuin stands — in the Motomachi, only ten squares away.

v

The curious narrow street is one long blaze of lights — lights of lantern signs, lights of torches and lamps illuminating unfamiliar rows of little stands and booths set out in the thoroughfare before all the shopfronts on each side; making two far-converging lines of multi-colored fire. Between these moves a dense throng, filling the night with a clatter of geta that drowns even the tide-like murmuring of voices and the cries of the merchant. But how gentle the movement! — there is no jostling, no rudeness; everybody, even the weakest and smallest, has a chance to see everything; and there are many things to see.

'Hasu-no-hana! — hasu-no-ha!' Here are the venders of lotus-flowers for the tombs and the altars, of lotus-leaves in which to wrap the food of the beloved ghosts. The leaves, folded into bundles, are heaped upon tiny tables; the lotus-flowers, buds and blossoms intermingled, are fixed upright in immense bunches, supported by light frames of bamboo.

'Ogara! – ogara-ya!' White sheaves of long peeled rods. These are hemp-sticks. The thinner ends can be broken up into hashi for the use of the ghosts; the rest must be consumed in the mukaebi. Rightly all these sticks should be made of pine; but pine is too scarce and dear for the poor folk of this district, so the ogara are substituted.

'Kawarake! – kawarake-ya!' The dishes of the ghosts: small red shallow platters of unglazed earthenware; primeval pottery wrought after a fashion which now exists only for the dead – pottery shaped after a tradition older than the religion of Buddha.

'Ya-bondoro-wa-irimasenka?' The lanterns – the 'bon' lanterns – which will light the returning feet of the ghosts. All are beautiful. Some are hexagonal, like the lanterns of the great shrines; and some have the form of stars; and some are like great luminous eggs. They are decorated with exquisite paintings of lotus-flowers, and with fringes of paper streamers choicely colored, or perhaps broad white paper ribbons in which charming suggestions of lotus-blossoms have been scissored out. And here are dead-white lanterns, round like moons; these are for the cemeteries.

'O-kazari! O-kazari-ya!' The venders of all articles of decoration for the Festival of the Dead. 'Komo-demo! – nandemo!' Here are the fresh, white mats of rice straw for the butsumas and the altars; and here are the warauma, little horses made out of wisps of straw, for the dead to ride; and the waraushi, little oxen of straw which will do shadowy labor for them. All honorably cheap – O-yasui! Here also are the branches of shikimi for the altars, and sprays of misohagi wherewith to sprinkle water upon the Segaki.

'O-kazari-mono-wa-irimasenka!' Exquisite scarlet and white tassels of strings of rice grains, like finest bead-work; and wonderful paper decorations for the butsuma; and incense-sticks (senko) of all varieties, from the commonest, at a couple of cents a bundle, to the extremely dear, at one yen – long, light, chocolate-colored, brittle rods, slender as a pencil-lead, each bundle secured by straps of gilded and colored paper. You take one, light an end, and set the other end upright in a vessel containing soft ashes; it will continue to smoulder, filling the air with fragrance, until wholly consumed.

'Hotaru-ni-kirigisu! — o-kodomo-shu-no-onagusa-mi — oyasuku-makemasu!' Eh! what is all this? A little booth shaped like a sentry-box, all made of laths, covered with a red-and-white chess pattern of paper; and out of this frail structure issues a shrilling keen as the sound of leaking steam. 'Oh, that is only insects,' says Akira, laughing; 'nothing to do with the Bonku.' Insects, yes! — in cages! The shrilling is made by scores of huge green crickets, each prisoned in a tiny bamboo cage by itself. 'They are fed with eggplant and melon rind,' continues Akira, 'and sold to children to play with.' And there are also beautiful little cages full of fireflies — cages covered with brown mosquito-netting, upon each of which some simple but very pretty design in bright colors has been dashed by a Japanese brush. One cricket and cage, two cents. Fifteen fireflies and cage, five cents.

Here on a street corner squats a blue-robed boy behind a low wooden table, selling wooden boxes about as big as match-boxes, with red paper hinges. Beside the piles of these little boxes on the table are shallow dishes filled with clear water, in which extraordinary thin flat shapes are floating — shapes of flowers, trees, birds, boats, men, and women. Open a box; it costs only two cents. Inside, wrapped in tissue paper, are bundles of little pale sticks, like round match-sticks, with pink ends. Drop one into the water, it instantly unrolls and expands into the likeness of a lotus-flower. Another transforms itself into a fish. A third becomes a boat. A fourth changes to an owl. A fifth becomes a tea-plant, covered with leaves and blossoms ... So delicate are these things that, once immersed, you cannot handle them without breaking them. They are made of seaweed.

'Tsukuri hana! — tsukuri-hana-wa-irimasenka?' The sellers of artificial flowers, marvelous chrysanthemums and lotus-plants of paper, imitations of bud and leaf and flower so cunningly wrought that the eye alone cannot detect the beautiful trickery. It is only right that these should cost much more than their living counterparts.

VI

High above the thronging and the clamor and the myriad fires of the merchants, the great Shingon temple at the end of the radiant street towers upon its hill against the starry night, weirdly, like a dream — strangely illuminated by rows of paper lanterns hung all along

85

its curving eaves; and the flowing of the crowd bears me thither. Out of the broad entrance, over a dark gliding mass which I know to be heads and shoulders of crowding worshipers, beams a broad band of yellow light; and before reaching the lion-guarded steps I hear the continuous clanging of the temple gong, each clang the signal of an offering and a prayer. Doubtless a cataract of cash is pouring into the great alms-chest; for tonight is the Festival of Yakushi-Nyorai, the Physician of Souls. Borne to the steps at last, I find myself able to halt a moment, despite the pressure of the throng, before the stand of a lantern-seller selling the most beautiful lanterns that I have ever seen. Each is a gigantic lotus-flower of paper, so perfectly made in every detail as to seem a great living blossom freshly plucked; the petals are crimson at their bases, paling to white at their tips; the calyx is a faultless mimicry of nature, and beneath it hangs a beautiful fringe of paper cuttings, colored with the colors of the flower, green below the calyx, white in the middle, crimson at the ends. In the heart of the blossom is set a microscopic oil-lamp of baked clay; and this being lighted, all the flower becomes luminous, diaphanous — a lotus of white crimson fire. There is a slender gilded wooden hoop by which to hang it up, and the price is four cents! How can people afford to make such things for four cents, even in this country of astounding cheapness?

Akira is trying to tell me something about the hyaku-hachi-no-mukaebi, the Hundred and Eight Fires, to be lighted tomorrow evening, which bear some figurative relation unto the Hundred and Eight Foolish Desires; but I cannot hear him for the clatter of the geta and the komageta, the wooden clogs and wooden sandals of the worshipers ascending to the shrine of Yakushi-Nyorai. The light straw sandals of the poorer men, the zōri and the waraji, are silent; the great clatter is really made by the delicate feet of women and girls, balancing themselves carefully upon their noisy geta. And most of these little feet are clad with spotless tabi, white as a white lotus. White feet of little blue-robed mothers they mostly are — mothers climbing patiently and smilingly, with pretty placid babies at their backs, up the hill to Buddha.

And while through the tinted lantern light I wander on with the gentle noisy people, up the great steps of stone, between other displays of lotus-blossoms, between other high hedge-rows of paper flowers, my thought suddenly goes back to the little broken shrine in the poor woman's room, with the humble playthings hanging before it, and the laughing, twirling mask of Otafuku. I see the happy, funny little eyes, oblique and silky-shadowed like Otafuku's own, which used to look at those toys — toys in which the fresh child-senses found a charm that I can but faintly divine, a delight hereditary, ancestral. I see the tender little creature being borne, as it was doubtless borne many times, through just such a peaceful throng as this, in just such a lukewarm, luminous night, peeping over the mother's shoulder, softly clinging at her neck with tiny hands.

Somewhere among this multitude she is — the mother. She will feel again tonight the faint touch of little hands, yet will not turn her head to look and laugh, as in other days.

By the Japanese Sea

I

It is the fifteenth day of the seventh month — and I am in Hōki.

The blanched road winds along a coast of low cliffs — the coast of the Japanese Sea. Always on the left, over a narrow strip of stony land, or a heaping of dunes, its vast expanse appears, blue-wrinkling to that pale horizon beyond which Korea lies, under the same white sun. Sometimes, through sudden gaps in the cliff's verge, there flashes to us the running of the surf. Always upon the right another sea — a silent sea of green, reaching to far misty ranges of wooded hills, with huge pale peaks behind them — a vast level of rice-fields, over whose surface soundless waves keep chasing each other under the same great breath that moves the blue today from Chōsen to Japan.

Though during the week the sky has remained unclouded, the sea has for several days been growing angrier; and now the muttering of its surf sounds far into the land. They say that it always roughens thus during the period of the Festival of the Dead — the three days of the Bon, which are the thirteenth, fourteenth, and fifteenth of the seventh month by the ancient calendar. And on the sixteenth day, after the shōryōbune, which are the Ships of Souls, have been launched, no one dares to enter it: no boats can then be hired; all the fishermen remain at home. For on that day the sea is the highway of the dead, who must pass back over its waters to their mysterious home; and therefore upon that day is it called Hotoke-umi — the Buddha-Flood — the Tide of the Returning Ghosts. And ever upon the night of that sixteenth day — whether the sea be calm or tumultuous — all its surface shimmers with faint lights gliding out to the open — the dim fires of the dead; and there is heard a murmuring of voices, like the murmur of a city far off — the indistinguishable speech of souls.

II

But it may happen that some vessel, belated in spite of desperate effort to reach port, may find herself far out at sea upon the night of the sixteenth day. Then will the dead rise tall about the ship, and reach long hands and murmur: 'Tago, tago o-kure! — tago o-kure!'[1] Never may they be refused; but, before the bucket is given, the bottom of it must be knocked out. Woe to all on board should an entire tago be suffered to fall even by accident into the sea! — for the dead would at once use it to fill and sink the ship.

Nor are the dead the only powers invisible dreaded in the time of the Hotoke-umi. Then are the Ma most powerful, and the Kappa.[2]

But in all times the swimmer fears the Kappa, the Ape of Waters, hideous and obscene, who reaches up from the deeps to draw men down, and to devour their entrails.

Only their entrails.

The corpse of him who has been seized by the Kappa may be cast on shore after many days. Unless long battered against the rocks by

1. 'A bucket honorably condescend [to give].'

2. The Kappa is not properly a sea goblin, but a river goblin, and haunts the sea only in the neighbourhood of river mouths.

About a mile and a half from Matsue, at the little village of Kawachi-mura, on the river called Kawachi, stands a little temple called Kawako-no-miya, or the Miya of the Kappa. (In Izumo, among the common people, the word 'Kappa' is not used, but the term 'Kawako,' or 'The Child of the River.') In this little shrine is preserved a document said to have been signed by a Kappa. The story goes that in ancient times the Kappa dwelling in the Kawachi used to seize and destroy many of the inhabitants of the village and many domestic animals. One day, however, while trying to seize a horse that had entered the river to drink the Kappa got its head twisted in some way under the belly-band of the horse, and the terrified animal, rushing out of the water, dragged the Kappa into a field. There the owner of the horse and a number of peasants seized and bound the Kappa. All the villagers gathered to see the monster which bowed its head to the ground, and audibly begged for mercy. The peasants desired to kill the goblin at once; but the owner of the horse, who happened to be the head man of the mura, said: 'It is better to make it swear never again to touch any person or animal belonging to Kawachi-mura.' A written form of oath was prepared and read to the Kappa. It said that It could not write, but that It would sign the paper by dipping Its hand in ink, and pressing the imprint thereof at the bottom of the document. This having been agreed to and done, the Kappa was set free. From that time forward no inhabitant or animal of Kawachi-mura was ever assaulted by the goblin.

heavy surf, or nibbled by fishes, it will show no outward wound. But it will be light and hollow – empty like a long-dried gourd.

III

Betimes, as we journey on, the monotony of undulating blue on the left, or the monotony of billowing green upon the right, is broken by the gray apparition of a cemetery – a cemetery so long that our jinrikisha men, at full run, take a full quarter of an hour to pass the huge congregation of its perpendicular stones. Such visions always indicate the approach of villages; but the villages prove to be as surprisingly small as the cemeteries are surprisingly large. By hundreds of thousands do the silent populations of the hakaba outnumber the folk of the hamlets to which they belong – tiny thatched settlements sprinkled along the leagues of coast, and sheltered from the wind only by ranks of sombre pines. Legions on legions of stones – a host of sinister witnesses of the cost of the present to the past – and old, old, old! – hundreds so long in place that they have been worn into shapelessness merely by the blowing of sand from the dunes, and their inscriptions utterly effaced. It is as if one were passing through the burial-ground of all who ever lived on this wind-blown shore since the being of the land.

And in all these hakaba – for it is the Bon – there are new lanterns before the newer tombs – the white lanterns which are the lanterns of graves. Tonight the cemeteries will be all aglow with lights like the fires of a city for multitude. But there are also unnumbered tombs before which no lanterns are – elder myriads, each the token of a family extinct, or of which the absent descendants have forgotten even the name. Dim generations whose ghosts have none to call them back, no local memories to love – so long ago obliterated were all things related to their lives.

IV

Now many of these villages are only fishing settlements, and in them stand old thatched homes of men who sailed away on some eve of tempest, and never came back. Yet each drowned sailor has his tomb in the neighbouring hakaba, and beneath it something of him has been buried.

What?

Among these people of the west something is always preserved which in other lands is cast away without a thought — the hozo-no-o, the flower-stalk of a life, the navel-string of the newly-born. It is enwrapped carefully in many wrappings; and upon its outermost covering are written the names of the father, the mother, and the infant, together with the date and hour of birth — and it is kept in the family o-mamori-bukuro. The daughter, becoming a bride, bears it with her to her new home; for the son it is preserved by his parents. It is buried with the dead; and should one die in a foreign land, or perish at sea, it is entombed in lieu of the body.

v

Concerning them that go down into the sea in ships, and stay there, strange beliefs prevail on this far coast — beliefs more primitive, assuredly, than the gentle faith which hangs white lanterns before the tombs. Some hold that the drowned never journey to the Meido. They quiver forever in the currents; they billow in the swaying of tides; they toil in the wake of the junks; they shout in the plunging of breakers. 'Tis their white hands that toss in the leap of the surf; their clutch that clatters the shingle, or seizes the swimmer's feet in the pull of the undertow. And the seamen speak euphemistically of the O-baké, the honorable ghosts, and fear them with a great fear.

Wherefore cats are kept on board!

A cat, they aver, has power to keep the O-baké away. How or why, I have not yet found any to tell me. I know only that cats are deemed to have power over the dead. If a cat be left alone with a corpse, will not the corpse rise and dance? And of all cats a mike-neko, or cat of three colors, is most prized on this account by sailors. But if they cannot obtain one — and cats of three colors are rare — they will take another kind of cat; and nearly every trading junk has a cat; and when the junk comes into port, its cat may generally be seen — peeping through some little window in the vessel's side, or squatting in the opening where the great rudder works — that is, if the weather be fair and the sea still.

VI

But these primitive and ghastly beliefs do not affect the beautiful practices of Buddhist faith in the time of the Bon; and from all these little villages the shōryōbune are launched upon the sixteenth day. They are much more elaborately and expensively constructed on this coast than in some other parts of Japan; for though made of straw only woven over a skeleton framework, they are charming models of junks, complete in every detail. Some are between three and four feet long. On the white paper sail is written the kaimyō or soul-name of the dead. There is a small water-vessel on board, filled with fresh water, and an incense-cup; and along the gunwales flutter little paper banners bearing the mystic manji which is the Sanskrit swastika.[3]

The form of the shōryōbune and the customs in regard to the time and manner of launching them differ much in different provinces. In most places they are launched for the family dead in general, wherever buried; and they are in some places launched only at night, with small lanterns on board. And I am told also that it is the custom at certain sea-villages to launch the lanterns all by themselves, in lieu of the shōryōbune proper — lanterns of a particular kind being manufactured for that purpose only.

But on the Izumo coast, and elsewhere along this western shore, the soul-boats are launched only for those who have been drowned at sea, and the launching takes place in the morning instead of at night. Once every year, for ten years after death, a shōryōbune is launched; in the eleventh year the ceremony ceases. Several shōryōbune which I saw at Inasa were really beautiful, and must have cost a rather large sum for poor fisher-folk to pay. But the ship-carpenter who made them said that all the relatives of a drowned man contribute to purchase the little vessel, year after year.

VII

Near a sleepy little village called Kami-ichi I make a brief halt in order to visit a famous sacred tree. It is in a grove close to the public highway, but upon a low hill. Entering the grove, I find myself in a sort of miniature glen surrounded on three sides by very low cliffs, above

3. The Buddhist symbol 卍 .

which enormous pines are growing, incalculably old. Their vast coiling roots have forced their way through the face of the cliffs, splitting rocks; and their mingling crests make a green twilight in the hollow. One pushes out three huge roots of a very singular shape; and the ends of these have been wrapped about with long white papers bearing written prayers, and with offerings of seaweed. The shape of these roots, rather than any tradition, would seem to have made the tree sacred in popular belief: it is the object of a special cult; and a little torii has been erected before it, bearing a votive annunciation of the most artless and curious kind. I cannot venture to offer a translation of it — though for the anthropologist and folk-lorist it certainly possesses peculiar interest. The worship of the tree, or at least of the Kami supposed to dwell therein, is one rare survival of a phallic cult probably common to most primitive races, and formerly widespread in Japan. Indeed it was suppressed by the government scarcely more than a generation ago. On the opposite side of the little hollow, carefully posed upon a great loose rock, I see something equally artless and almost equally curious — a kitōja-no-mono, or ex-voto. Two straw figures joined together and reclining side by side: a straw man and a straw woman. The workmanship is childishly clumsy; but still the woman can be distinguished from the man by the ingenious attempt to imitate the female coiffure with a straw wisp. And as the man is represented with a queue — now worn only by aged survivors of the feudal era — I suspect that this kitōja-no-mono was made after some ancient and strictly conventional model.

Now this queer ex-voto tells its own story. Two who loved each other were separated by the fault of the man, the charm of some jorō, perhaps, having been the temptation to faithlessness. Then the wronged one came here and prayed the Kami to dispel the delusion of passion and touch the erring heart. The prayer has been heard: the pair have been reunited; and *she* has therefore made these two quaint effigies with her own hands, and brought them to the Kami of the pine — tokens of her innocent faith and her grateful heart.

VIII

Night falls as we reach the pretty hamlet of Hamamura, our last resting-place by the sea, for tomorrow our way lies inland. The inn at which we lodge is very small, but very clean and cosy; and there is a delightful bath of natural hot water; for the yadoya is situated close to a natural spring. This spring, so strangely close to the sea beach, also furnishes, I am told, the baths of all the houses in the village.

The best room is placed at our disposal; but I linger awhile to examine a very fine shōryōbune, waiting, upon a bench near the street entrance, to be launched tomorrow. It seems to have been finished but a short time ago; for fresh clippings of straw lie scattered around it, and the kaimyō has not yet been written upon its sail. I am surprised to hear that it belongs to a poor widow and her son, both of whom are employed by the hotel.

I was hoping to see the Bon-odori at Hamamaura, but I am disappointed. At all the villages the police have prohibited the dance. Fear of cholera has resulted in stringent sanitary regulations. In Hamamura the people have been ordered to use no water for drinking, cooking, or washing except the hot water of their own volcanic springs.

A little middle-aged woman, with a remarkably sweet voice, comes to wait upon us at supper-time. Her teeth are blackened and her eyebrows shaved after the fashion of married women twenty years ago; nevertheless her face is still a pleasant one, and in her youth she must have been uncommonly pretty. Though acting as a servant, it appears that she is related to the family owning the inn, and that she is treated with the consideration due to kindred. She tells us that the shōryōbune is to be launched for her husband and brother — both fishermen of the village, who perished in sight of their own home eight years ago. The priest of the neighbouring Zen temple is to come in the morning to write the kaimyō upon the sail, as none of the household are skilled in writing the Chinese characters.

I make her the customary little gift, and, through my attendant, ask her various questions about her history. She was married to a man much older than herself, with whom she lived very happily; and her brother, a youth of eighteen, dwelt with them. They had a good boat and a little piece of ground, and she was skillful at the loom; so they managed to live well. In summer the fishermen fish at night: when all the fleet is out, it is pretty to see the line of torch-fires in the offing, two or three miles away, like a string of stars. They do not go out when the weather is threatening; but in certain months the great storms (taifu) come so quickly that the boats are overtaken almost before they have time to hoist sail. Still as a temple pond the sea was on the night when her husband and brother last sailed away; the taifu rose before daybreak. What followed, she relates with a simple pathos that I cannot reproduce in our less artless tongue.

'All the boats had come back except my husband's; for my husband and my brother had gone out farther than the others, so they were not able to return as quickly. And all the people were looking and waiting. And every minute the waves seemed to be growing higher and the wind more terrible; and the other boats had to be dragged far up on the shore to save them. Then suddenly we saw my husband's boat coming, very, very quickly. We were so glad! It came quite near, so that I could see the face of my husband and the face of my brother. But suddenly a great wave struck it upon one side, and it turned down into the water, and it did not come up again. And then we saw my husband and my brother swimming; but we could see them only when the waves lifted them up. Tall like hills the waves were, and the head of my husband, and the head of my brother would go up, up, up, and then down, and each time they rose to the top of a wave so that we could see them they would cry out, "Tasukete! tasukete!"⁴ But the strong men were afraid; the sea was too terrible; I was only a woman! Then my brother could not be seen any more. My husband was old, but very strong; and he swam a long time – so near that I could see his face was like the face of one in fear – and he called "Tasukete!" But none could help him; and he also went down at last. And yet I could see his face before he went down.

'And for a long time after, every night, I used to see his face as I saw it then, so that I could not rest, but only weep. And I prayed and prayed to the Buddhas and to the Kami-Sama that I might not dream that dream. Now it never comes; but I can still see his face, even while I speak ... In that time my son was only a little child.'

Not without sobs can she conclude her simple recital. Then, suddenly bowing her head to the matting, and wiping away her tears with her sleeve, she humbly prays our pardon for this little exhibition of emotion, and laughs – the soft low laugh *de rigueur* of Japanese

4. 'Help! help!'

politeness. This, I must confess, touches me still more than the story itself. At a fitting moment my Japanese attendant delicately changes the theme, and begins a light chat about our journey, and the danna-sama's interest in the old customs and legends of the coast. And he succeeds in amusing her by some relation of our wanderings in Izumo.

She asks whither we are going. My attendant answers probably as far as Tottori.

'Aa! Tottori! Sō degozarimasu ka? . . . Now, there is an old story – the Story of the Futon of Tottori. But the danna-sama knows that story?'

Indeed, the danna-sama does not, and begs earnestly to hear it. And the story is set down, somewhat as I learn it through the lips of my interpreter.

IX

Many years ago, a very small yadoya in Tottori town received its first guest, an itinerant merchant. He was received with more than common kindness, for the landlord desired to make a good name for his little inn. It was a new inn, but as its owner was poor, most of its dōgu – furniture and utensils – had been purchased from the furuteya.[5] Nevertheless, everything was clean, comforting, and pretty. The guest ate heartily and drank plenty of good warm saké; after which his bed was prepared on the soft floor, and he laid himself down to sleep.

[But here I must interrupt the story for a few moments, to say a word about Japanese beds. Never, unless some inmate happen to be sick, do you see a bed in any Japanese house by day, though you visit all the rooms and peep into all the corners. In fact, no bed exists, in the Occidental meaning of the word. That which the Japanese call bed has no bedstead, no spring, no mattress, no sheets, no blankets. It consists of thick quilts only, stuffed, or, rather, padded with cotton, which are called futon. A certain number of futon are laid down upon the tatami (the floor mats), and a certain number of others are used for coverings. The wealthy can lie upon five or six quilts, and cover themselves with as many as they please, while poor folk must content themselves with two or three. And of course there are many kinds,

5. Furuteya, the establishment of a dealer in second-hand wares – furute.

from the servant's cotton futon which is no larger than a Western hearth rug, and not much thicker, to the heavy and superb futon silk, eight feet long by seven broad, which only the kanemochi can afford. Besides these there is the yogi, a massive quilt made with wide sleeves like a kimono, in which you can find much comfort when the weather is extremely cold. All such things are neatly folded up and stowed out of sight by day in alcoves contrived in the wall and closed with fusuma — pretty sliding screen doors covered with opaque paper usually decorated with dainty designs. There also are kept those curious wooden pillows, invented to preserve the Japanese coiffure from becoming disarranged during sleep.

The pillow has a certain sacredness; but the origin and the precise nature of the beliefs concerning it I have not been able to learn. Only this I know, that to touch it with the foot is considered very wrong; and that if it be kicked or moved thus, even by accident, the clumsiness must be atoned for by lifting the pillow to the forehead with the hands, and replacing it in its original position respectfully, with the word 'go-men,' signifying, I pray to be excused.]

Now, as a rule, one sleeps soundly after having drunk plenty of warm saké, especially if the night be cool and the bed very snug. But the guest, having slept but a very little while, was aroused by the sound of voices in his room — voices of children, always asking each other the same questions:

'Ani-San samukarō?'

'Omae samukarō?'

The presence of children in his room might annoy the guest, but could not surprise him, for in these Japanese hotels there are no doors, but only papered sliding screens between room and room. So it seemed to him that some children must have wandered into his apartment, by mistake, in the dark. He uttered some gentle rebuke. For a moment only there was silence; then a sweet, thin, plaintive voice queried, close to his ear, 'Ani-San samukarō?' ('Elder Brother probably is cold?'), and another sweet voice made answer caressingly, 'Omae samukarō?' ('Nay, thou probably art cold?')

He arose and rekindled the candle in the andon,[6] and looked about

6. Andon, a paper lantern of peculiar construction, used as a night light. Some forms of the andon are remarkably beautiful.

the room. There was no one. The shōji were all closed. He examined the cupboards; they were empty. Wondering, he lay down again, leaving the light still burning; and immediately the voices spoke again, complainingly, close to his pillow:

'Ani-San samukarō?'

'Omae samukarō?'

Then, for the first time, he felt a chill creep over him, which was not the chill of the night. Again and again he heard, and each time he became more afraid. For he knew that the voices were *in the futon!* It was the covering of the bed that cried out thus.

He gathered hurriedly together the few articles belonging to him, and, descending the stairs, aroused the landlord and told what had passed. Then the host, much angered, made reply: 'That to make pleased the honorable guest everything has been done, the truth is; but the honorable guest too much august saké having drank, bad dreams has seen.' Nevertheless the guest insisted upon paying at once that which he owed, and seeking lodging elsewhere.

Next evening there came another guest who asked for a room for the night. At a late hour the landlord was aroused by his lodger with the same story. And this lodger, strange to say, had not taken any saké. Suspecting some envious plot to ruin his business, the landlord answered passionately: 'Thee to please all things honorably have been done: nevertheless, ill-omened and vexatious words thou utterest. And that my inn my means-of-livelihood is — that also thou knowest. Wherefore that such things be spoken, right-there-is-none!' Then the guest, getting into a passion, loudly said things much more evil; and the two parted in hot anger.

But after the guest was gone, the landlord, thinking all this very strange, ascended to the empty room to examine the futon. And while there, he heard the voices, and he discovered that the guests had said only the truth. It was one covering — only one — which cried out. The rest were silent. He took the covering into his own room, and for the remainder of the night lay down beneath it. And the voices continued until the hour of dawn: 'Ani-San samukarō?' 'Omae samukarō?' So that he could not sleep.

But at break of day he rose up and went out to find the owner of the furuteya at which the futon had been purchased. The dealer knew nothing. He had bought the futon from a smaller shop, and the keeper of that shop had purchased it from a still poorer dealer dwelling in the farthest suburb of the city. And the innkeeper went from one to the other, asking questions.

Then at last it was found that the futon had belonged to a poor family, and had been bought from the landlord of a little house in which the family had lived, in the neighborhood of the town. And the story of the futon was this:

The rent of the little house was only sixty sen a month, but even this was a great deal for the poor folks to pay. The father could earn only two or three yen a month, and the mother was ill and could not work; and there were two children — a boy of six years and a boy of eight. And they were strangers in Tottori.

One winter's day the father sickened; and after a week of suffering he died, and was buried. Then the long-sick mother followed him, and the children were left alone. They knew no one whom they could ask for aid; and in order to live they began to sell what there was to sell.

That was not much: the clothes of the dead father and mother, and most of their own; some quilts of cotton, and a few poor household utensils — hibachi, bowls, cups, and other trifles. Every day they sold something, until there was nothing left but one futon. And a day came when they had nothing to eat; and the rent was not paid.

The terrible Dai-kan had arrived, the season of greatest cold; and the snow had drifted too high that day for them to wander far from the little house. So they could only lie down under their one futon, and shiver together, and compassionate each other in their own childish way:

'Ani-San, samukarō?'

'Omae samukarō?'

They had no fire, nor anything with which to make fire; and the darkness came; and the icy wind screamed into the little house.

They were afraid of the wind, but they were more afraid of the house-owner, who roused them roughly to demand his rent. He was a hard man, with an evil face. And finding there was none to pay him, he turned the children into the snow, and took their one futon away from them, and locked up the house.

They had but one thin blue kimono each, for all their other clothes had been sold to buy food; and they had nowhere to go. There was a temple of Kwannon not far away, but the snow was too high for them to reach it. So when the landlord was gone, they crept back behind the house. There the drowsiness of cold fell upon them, and they slept, embracing each other to keep warm. And while they slept, the gods covered them with a new futon – ghostly-white and very beautiful. And they did not feel cold any more. For many days they slept there; then somebody found them, and a bed was made for them in the hakaba of the Temple of Kwannon-of-the-Thousand-Arms.

And the innkeeper, having heard these things, gave the futon to the priests of the temple, and caused the kyō to be recited for the little souls. And the futon ceased thereafter to speak.

x

One legend recalls another; and I hear tonight many strange ones. The most remarkable is a tale which my attendant suddenly remembers, – a legend of Izumo.

Once there lived in the Izumo village called Mochida-no-ura a peasant who was so poor that he was afraid to have children. And each time that his wife bore him a child he cast it into the river, and pretended that it had been born dead. Sometimes it was a son, sometimes a daughter; but always the infant was thrown into the river at night. Six were murdered thus.

But, as the years passed, the peasant found himself more prosperous. He had been able to purchase land and to lay by money. And at last his wife bore him a seventh child – a boy.

Then the man said: 'Now we can support a child, and we shall need a son to aid us when we are old. And this boy is beautiful. So we will bring him up.'

And the infant thrived; and each day the hard peasant wondered more at his own heart – for each day he knew that he loved his son more.

One summer's night he walked out into his garden, carrying his child in his arms. The little one was five months old.

And the night was so beautiful, with its great moon that the peasant cried out:

'Aa! kon ya medzurashii e yo da!' ('Ah! tonight truly a wondrously beautiful night is!')

Then the infant, looking up into his face and speaking the speech of a man, said:

'Why, father! *the* LAST *time you threw me away* the night was just like this, and the moon looked just the same, did it not?'[7]

And thereafter the child remained as other children of the same age, and spoke no word

The peasant became a monk.

XI

After the supper and the bath, feeling too warm to sleep, I wander out alone to visit the village hakaba, a long cemetery upon a sandhill, or rather a prodigious dune, thinly covered at its summit with soil, but revealing through its crumbling flanks the story of its creation by ancient tides, mightier than tides of today.

I wade to my knees in sand to reach the cemetery. It is a warm moonlight night, with a great breeze. There are many bon-lanterns (bondōrō), but the sea-wind has blown out most of them; only a few here and there still shed a soft white glow – pretty shrine-shaped cases of wood, with apertures of symbolic outline, covered with white paper. Visitors beside myself there are none, for it is late. But much gentle work has been done here today, for all the bamboo vases have been furnished with fresh flowers or sprays, and the water basins filled with fresh water, and the monuments cleansed and beautified. And in the farthest nook of the cemetery I find, before one very humble tomb, a pretty zen or lacquered dining tray, covered with dishes and bowls containing a perfect dainty little Japanese repast. There is also a pair of new chopsticks, and a little cup of tea, and some of the dishes are still warm. A loving woman's work; the prints of her little sandals are fresh upon the path.

7. 'Ototsun! washi wo shimai ni shitesashita toki mo, chōdo kon ya no yona tsuki yo data-ne?' – Izumo dialect.

XII

There is an Irish folk-saying that any dream may be remembered if the dreamer, after awakening, forbear to scratch his head in the effort to recall it. But should he forget this precaution, never can the dream be brought back to memory: as well try to re-form the curlings of a smoke-wreath blown away.

Nine hundred and ninety-nine of a thousand dreams are indeed hopelessly evaporative. But certain rare dreams, which come when fancy has been strangely impressed by unfamiliar experiences – dreams particularly apt to occur in time of travel – remain in recollection, imaged with all the vividness of real events.

Of such was the dream I dreamed at Hamamura, after having seen and heard those things previously written down.

Some pale broad paved place – perhaps the thought of a temple court – tinted by a faint sun; and before me a woman, neither young nor old, seated at the base of a great gray pedestal that supported I know not what, for I could look only at the woman's face. Awhile I thought that I remembered her – a woman of Izumo; then she seemed a weirdness. Her lips were moving, but her eyes remained closed, and I could not choose but look at her.

And in a voice that seemed to come thin through distance of years she began a soft wailing chant; and, as I listened, vague memories came to me of a Celtic lullaby. And as she sang, she loosed with one hand her long black hair, till it fell coiling upon the stones. And, having fallen, it was no longer black, but blue – pale day-blue – and was moving sinuously, crawling with swift blue ripplings to and fro. And then, suddenly, I became aware that the ripplings were far, very far away, and that the woman was gone. There was only the sea, blue-billowing to the verge of heaven, with long slow flashings of soundless surf.

And wakening, I heard in the night the muttering of the real sea – the vast husky speech of the Hotoke-Umi – *the Tide of the Returning Ghosts.*

Beside the Sea

追
憶

I

The Buddhist priests had announced that a ségaki-service, in behalf of all the drowned folk of Yaidzu, would be held on the shore at two o'clock in the afternoon. Yaidzu is an ancient place – it is mentioned, under the name of 'Yakidzu,' in the oldest chronicles of Japan – and for thousands of years the fishers of Yaidzu have been regularly paying their toll of life to the great deep. And the announcement of the priests reminded me of something very much older than Buddhism – the fancy that the spirits of the drowned move with the waters forever. According to this belief, the sea off Yaidzu must be thick with souls ...

Early in the afternoon I went to the shore to observe preparations; and I found a multitude of people already there assembled. It was a burning July day, not a speck of cloud visible; and the coarse shingle of the slope, under the blaze of sun, was radiating heat like slag just raked from a furnace. But those fisher-folk, tanned to all tints of bronze, did not mind the sun: they sat on the scorching stones, and waited. The sea was at ebb, and gentle – moving in slow, long, lazy ripples.

Upon the beach there had been erected a kind of rude altar, about four feet high; and on this had been placed an immense ihai, or mortuary tablet, of unpainted wood – the back of the tablet being turned to the sea. The ihai bore, in large Chinese characters, the inscription *Sangai-Ban-Rei-I* – signifying 'Resting-place [or seat] of the myriad [innumerable] spirits of the Three States of Existence.' Various food-offerings had been set before this tablet – including a bowl of cooked rice; rice-cakes; eggplants; pears; and, piled upon a fresh lotus-leaf, a quantity of what is called hyaku-mi-no-onjiki. It is really a mixture of rice and sliced eggplant, though the name implies one hundred different kinds of nourishment. In the bowl of boiled rice tiny sticks were fixed, with cuttings of colored paper attached to them. I also observed candles, a censer, some bundles of incense-rods, a vessel of water, and a pair of bamboo cups containing sprays of the sacred plant shikimi.[1] Beside the water-vessel there had been laid a bunch of misohagi,[2] with which to sprinkle water upon the food-offerings, according to the prescriptions of the rite.

To each of the four posts supporting the altar a freshly cut bamboo had been attached; and other bamboos had been planted in the beach, to right and left of the structure; and to every bamboo was fastened a little banner inscribed with Chinese characters. The banners of the bamboos at the four corners of the altar bore the names and attributes of the Four Deva Kings — Zōchō Tennō, guardian of the West; Jikoku Tennō, guardian of the East; Tamon Tennō, guardian of the North; and Kōmoku Tennō, guardian of the South.

In front of the altar straw-mattings had been laid, so as to cover a space of beach about thirty feet long by fifteen wide; and above this matted space awnings of blue cotton had been rigged up, to shelter the priests from the sun. I squatted down awhile under the awnings to make a rough drawing (afterwards corrected and elaborated by a Japanese friend) of the altar and the offerings.

The service was not held at the appointed time: it must have been nearly three o'clock when the priests made their appearance. There were seven of them, in vestments of great ceremony; and they were accompanied by acolytes carrying bells, books, stools, reading-stands, and other necessary furniture. Priests and acolytes took their places under the blue awning; the spectators standing outside, in the sun. Only one of the priests — the chief officiant — sat facing the altar; the others, with their acolytes, seated themselves to right and left of him, so as to form two ranks, facing each other.

1. *Illicium religiosum.*
2. A kind of bush-clover.

II

After some preliminary rearrangement of the offerings upon the altar, and the kindling of some incense-rods, the ceremony proper began with a Buddhist hymn, or gâthâ, which was chanted to the accompaniment of hyōshigi[3] and of bells. There were two bells – a large deep-sounding bell; and a small bell of very sweet tone – in charge of a little boy. The big bell was tapped slowly; the little bell was sounded rapidly; and the hyōshigi rattled almost like a pair of castanets. And the effect of the gâthâ as chanted by all the officiants in unison, with this extraordinary instrumentation, was not less impressive than strange:

> *Biku Bikuni*
> *Hosshin hoji*
> *Ikki jō-jiki,*
> *Fusé jippō,*
> *Kyū-jin kokū,*
> *Shūhen hōkai,*
> *Mijin setchū*
> *Sho-u kokudo,*
> *Issai gaki;*
> *Senbō kyūmétsu,*
> *Sansen chishu,*
> *Naishi koya,*
> *Shō-kijin to,*
> *Shōrai shushi ...*

This brief sonorous metre seemed to me particularly well adapted for invocatory or incantatory chanting; and the gâthâ of the ségaki-service was indeed a veritable incantation – as the following free translation will make manifest:

'We, Bhikshus and Bhikunis, devoutly presenting this vessel of pure food, do offer the same to all, without exception, of the Pretas dwelling in the Ten Directions of Space, in the surrounding Dharma-worlds, and in every part of the Earth – not excepting the smallest atom of dust within a temple. And also to the spirits of those long

---

3. Hyōshigi are small blocks of hard wood, which are used, either for signaling or for musical purposes, by striking them quickly together so as to produce a succession of sharp dry sounds.

dead and passed away, and likewise unto the Lord-Spirits of mountain and river and soil, and of waste places. Hither deign therefore to approach and to gather, all ye goblins! We now, out of our pity and compassion, desire to give you food. We wish that each and all of you may enjoy this our food-gift. And moreover we shall pray, doing homage to all the Buddhas and to all the Heavenly Ones who dwell within the Zones of Formlessness, that you, and that all beings having desire, may be enabled to obtain contentment. We shall pray that all of you, by virtue of the utterance of the dhâranîs, and by the enjoyment of this food-offering, may find the higher knowledge, and be freed from every pain, and soon obtain rebirth in the Zone Celestial – there to know every bliss, moving freely in all the Ten Directions, and finding everywhere delight. Awaken within yourselves the Bodhi-Mind! Follow the Way of Enlightenment! Rise to Buddhahood! Turn ye no more backward! – neither linger on the path! Let such among you as first obtain the Way vow each to lead up the rest, and so become free! Also we beseech you now to watch over us and to guard us, by night and by day. And help us even now to obtain our desire in bestowing this food upon you, that the merit produced by this action may be extended to all beings dwelling within the Dharma-worlds, and that the power of this merit may help to spread the Truth through all those Dharma-worlds, and help all beings therein to find the Supreme Enlightenment, and to obtain all wisdom. And we now pray that all your acts hereafter may serve to gain for you the merit that will help you to Buddhahood. And thus we desire that you quickly become Buddhas.'

Then began the most curious part of the service – namely, the sprinkling and the presentation of the food-offerings, with recitation of certain dhâranîs, or magical verses, composed of talismanic Sanskrit words. This portion of the rite was brief; but to recount all its details would require much space, every utterance or gesture of the officiant being made according to rule. For example, the hands and fingers of the priest, during the recital of any dhâranî, must be held in a position prescribed for that particular dhâranî. But the principal incidents of this complicated ritual are about as follows:

First of all is recited, seven times, the Dhârani of Invitation, to summon the spirits from the Ten Directions of Space. During its recitation the officiant must hold out his right hand, with the tip of the middle finger touching the tip of the thumb, and the rest of the fingers extended. Then is recited, with a different, but equally weird gesture, the Dhârânî of the Breaking of the Gates of Hell. Next is repeated the *Se-Kanrō* verse, or Dhârânî of the Bestowal of the Amrita, by virtue of which it is supposed that the food-offerings are transformed, for the sake of the ghosts, into heavenly nectar and ambrosia. And thereafter is chanted, three times, an invocation to the Five Tathâgatas:

'Salutation to Hōshō Nyōrai — hereby besought to relieve [the Pretas] from the karma of all desire, and to fill them with bliss!

'Salutation to Myō-Shikishin-Nyōrai — besought to take away from them every imperfection of form!

'Salutation to Kanrō-Ō-Nyōrai — besought to purify their bodies and their minds, and to give them peace of heart!

'Salutation to Kobaku-Shin-Nyōrai — besought to favor them with the delight of excellent taste!

'Salutation to Rifui-Nyōrai — besought to free them from all their fears, and to deliver them out of the World of Hungry Spirits!'

The book *Bongyō Ségaki-Monben* says:

'When the officiants have thus recited the names of the Five Tathâgatas, then, by the grace of the power of those Buddhas, all the Pretas shall be liberated from the karma of their former errors, shall experience immeasurable bliss, shall receive excellent features and complete bodies, shall be rid of all their terrors, and, after having partaken of the food-offerings which have been changed for them into amrita of delightful taste, shall soon be reborn into the Pure Land [Jodo].'

After the invocation of the Five Tathâgatas, other verses are recited; and during this recitation the food-offerings are removed, one by one. (There is a mysterious regulation that, after having been taken from the altar, they must not be placed under a willow-tree, a peach-tree, or a pomegranate-tree.) Last of all is recited the Dhârânî of Dismissal, seven times — the priest each time snapping his fingers as a signal to the ghosts that they are free to return. This is called the *Hakken*, or Sending-Away.

III

The sea never ebbs far on this steep coast, though it often rises tremendously, breaking into the town; and its gentler moods are not to be trusted. By way of precaution the posts of the ihai-stand had been driven deeply into the beach. The event proved that this precaution had not been taken in vain; for the rite began, owing to the delay of the priests, only with the turn of the tide. Even while the gâthâ was being chanted, the sea roughened and darkened; and then – as if the outer deep responded – the thunder-roll of a great breaker suddenly smothered the voices of the singers and the clanging of the bells. Soon another heavy surge boomed along the shore, then another; and during the reciting of the dhâranîs the service could be heard only in the intervals of wave-bursts, while the foam sheeted up the slope, whirling and hissing even to within a few paces of the altar ...

And again I found myself thinking of the old belief in some dim relation between the dead and the sea. In that moment the primitive fancy appeared to me much more reasonable and more humane than the ghastly doctrine of a Preta-world, with its thirty-six orders of hideous misery – its swarms of goblins hungering and burning! ... Nay, the poor dead! – why should they be thus deformed and doomed by human judgement? Wiser and kindlier to dream of them as mingling with flood and wind and cloud – or quickening the heart of the flower – or flushing the cheek of the fruit – or shrilling with the cicadæ in forest-solitudes – or thinly humming in summer-dusk with the gathering of the gnats ... I do not believe – I do not wish to believe in hungry ghosts ... Ghosts break up, I suppose, into soul-dust at the touch of death – though their atoms, doubtless, thereafter recombine with other dust for the making of other ghosts ... Still, I cannot convince myself that even the grosser substance of vanished being ever completely dies, however dissolved or scattered – fleeting in the gale – floating in the mists – shuddering in the leaf – flickering in the light of waters – or tossed on some desolate coast in a thunder of surf, to whiten and writhe in the clatter of shingle ...

*

As the ceremony ended, a fisherman mounted lightly to the top of one of the awning-posts; and there, gymnastically poised, he began to shower down upon the crowd a quantity of very small rice-cakes, which the young folks scrambled for, with shouts of laughter. After the uncanny solemnity of that rite, the outburst of merriment was almost startling; but I found it also very natural, and pleasant, and human. Meanwhile the seven priests departed in many-colored procession — their acolytes trudging wearily behind them, under much weight of stands and stools and bells. Soon the assembly scattered, all the rice-cakes having been distributed and appropriated; then the altar, the awnings, the mattings were removed; and in a surprisingly short time every trace of the strange ceremony had disappeared ... I looked about me; I was alone upon the beach ... There was no sound but the sound of the returning tide: a muttering enormous, appalling — as of some Life innominable, that had been at peace, awakened to immeasurable pain ...

Drifting

A typhoon was coming; and I sat on the sea-wall in a great wind to look at the breakers; and old Amano Jinsuké sat beside me. Southeast all was black-blue gloom, except the sea, which had a strange and tawny color. Enormous surges were already towering in. A hundred yards away they crumbled over with thunder and earthquake, and sent their foam leaping and sheeting up the slope, to spring at our faces. After each long crash, the sound of the shingle retreating was exactly like the roar of a railway train at full speed. I told Amano Jinsuké that it made me afraid; and he smiled.

'I swam for two nights and two days,' he said, 'in a sea worse than this. I was nineteen years old at the time. Out of a crew of eight, I was the only man saved.

'Our ship was called the *Fukuju Maru*;[1] she was owned by Mayéda Jingorō, of this town! All of the crew but one were Yaidzu men. The captain was Saito Kichiyēmon, a man more than sixty years of age; he lived in Jō-no-Koshi – the street just behind us. There was another old man on board, called Nito Shōshichi, who lived in the Araya quarter. Then there was Terao Kankichi, forty-two years old; his brother Minosuké, a lad of sixteen, was also with us. The Terao folk lived in Araya. Then there was Saito Heikichi, thirty years old; and there was a man called Matsushirō; he came from Suō, but had settled in Yaidzu. Washino Otokichi was another of the crew; he lived in Jō-no-Koshi, and was only twenty-one. I was the youngest on board – excepting Terao Minosuké.

'We sailed from Yaidzu on the morning of the tenth day of the seventh month of Manyen Gwannen[2] – the Year of the Ape – bound for Sanuki. On the night of the eleventh, in the Kishū offing, we

1. The word Fukuju signifies 'Fortunate Longevity.'
2. That is to say, the first, or coronation-year, of the Period Manyen – 1860–61.

were caught by a typhoon from the southeast. A little before midnight, the ship capsized. As I felt her going over, I caught a plank, and threw it out, and jumped. It was blowing fearfully at the time; and the night was so dark that I could see only a few feet away; but I was lucky enough to find that plank, and put it under me. In another moment the ship was gone. Near me in the water were Washino Otokichi and the Terao brothers and the man Matsushirō – all swimming. There was no sign of the rest: they probably went down with the ship. We five kept calling to each other as we went up and down with the great seas; and I found that everyone except Terao Kankichi had a plank or a timber of some sort. I cried to Kankichi: "Elder brother, you have children, and I am very young – let me give you this plank!" He shouted back: "In this sea a plank is dangerous! Keep away from timber, Jinyō! – you may get hurt!" Before I could answer him, a wave like a black mountain burst over us. I was a long time under; and when I came up again, there was no sign of Kankichi. The younger men were still swimming; but they had been swept away to the left of me; I could not see them. We shouted to each other. I tried to keep with the waves – the others called to me: "Jinyō! Jinyō! come this way – this way!" But I knew that to go in their direction would be very dangerous; for every time that a wave struck me sideways, I was taken under. So I called back to them: "Keep with the tide! – keep with the current!" But they did not seem to understand; and they still called to me: "Kocchi é koi! – kocchi é koi!"[3] – and their voices each time sounded more and more far away. I became afraid to answer ... The drowned call to you like that when they want company: Kocchi é koi! – kocchi é koi! ...

'After a little time the calling ceased; and I heard only the sea and the wind and the rain. It was so dark that one could see the waves only at the moment they went by – high black shadows, each with a great pull. By the pull of them I guessed how to direct myself. The rain kept them from breaking much; had it not been for the rain, no man could have lived long in such a sea. And hour after hour the wind became worse, and the swells grew higher; and I prayed for help to Jizō-Sama of Ogawa all that night ... Lights?

3. 'Come this way!'

— yes, there were lights in the water, but not many: the large kind, that shine like candles ...

At dawn the sea looked ugly — a muddy green; and the waves were like hills; and the wind was terrible. Rain and spray made a fog over the water; and there was no horizon. But even if there had been land in sight I could have done nothing except try to keep afloat. I felt hungry — very hungry; and the pain of the hunger soon became hard to bear. All that day I went up and down with the great waves — drifting under the wind and the rain; and there was no sign of land. I did not know where I was going: under that sky one could not tell east from west.

'After dark the wind lulled; but the rain still poured, and all was black. The pain of the hunger passed; but I felt weak — so weak that I thought I must go under. Then I heard the voices calling me, just as they had called me the night before: "Kocchi é koi! — kocchi é koi!" ... And, all at once, I saw the four men of the *Fukuju Maru* — not swimming, but standing by me — Terao Kankichi, and Terao Minosuké, and Washino Otokichi, and the man Matsushirō. All looked at me with angry faces; and the boy Minosuké cried out, as in reproach: "Here I have to fix the helm; and you, Jinsuké, do nothing but sleep!" Then Terao Kankichi — the one to whom I had offered the plank — bent over me with a kakemono in his hands, and half-unrolled it, and said: "Jinyō! here I have a picture of Amida Buddha — see! Now indeed you must repeat the *Nembutsu!*" He spoke strangely, in a way that made me afraid: I looked at the figure of the Buddha; and I repeated the prayer in great fear — "Namu Amida Butsu! — namu Amida Butsu!"[4] In the same moment a pain, like the pain of fire, stung through my thighs and hips; and I found that I had rolled off the plank into the sea. The pain had been caused by a great katsuo-no-éboshi ... You never saw a katsuo-no-éboshi? It is a jelly-fish shaped like the éboshi, or cap, of a Shintō priest; and we call it the katsuo-no-éboshi because the katsuo-fish [bonito] feed upon it. When that thing appears anywhere, the fishermen expect to catch many katsuo. The body is clear like glass; but underneath there is a kind of purple fringe, and long purple strings; and when those strings touch you, the pain is very great, and lasts for a long

4. This invocation, signifying 'Salutation to the Buddha Amitâbha,' is commonly repeated as a prayer for the dead.

time ... That pain revived me; if I had not been stung I might never have awakened. I got on the plank again, and prayed to Jizō-Sama of Ogawa, and to Kompira-Sama; and I was able to keep awake until morning.

'Before daylight the rain stopped, and the sky began to clear; for I could see some stars. At dawn I got drowsy again; and I was awakened by a blow on the head. A large sea-bird had struck me. The sun was rising behind clouds; and the waves had become gentle. Presently a small brown bird flew by my face, a coast-bird (I do not know its real name); and I thought that there must be land in sight. I looked behind me, and I saw mountains. I did not recognize the shapes of them: they were blue — seemed to be nine or ten *ri* distant. I made up my mind to paddle towards them, though I had little hope of getting to shore. I was feeling hungry again — terribly hungry!

'I paddled toward the mountains, hour after hour. Once more I fell asleep; and once again a sea-bird struck me. All day I paddled. Toward evening I could tell, from the look of the mountains, that I was approaching them; but I knew that it would take me two days to reach the shore. I had almost ceased to hope when I caught sight of a ship, a big junk. She was sailing toward me; but I saw that, unless I could swim faster, she would pass me at a great distance. It was my last chance: so I dropped the plank, and swam as fast as I could. I did get within about two chō of her: then I shouted. But I could see nobody on deck; and I got no answer. In another minute she had passed beyond me. The sun was setting; and I despaired. All of a sudden a man came on deck, and shouted to me: "Don't try to swim! don't tire yourself — we are going to send a boat!" I saw the sail lowered at the same time; and I felt so glad that new strength seemed to come to me; I swam on fast. Then the junk dropped a little boat; and as the boat came toward me, a man called out: "Is there anybody else? — have you dropped anything?" I answered: "I had nothing but a plank" ... In the same instant all my strength was gone: I felt the men in the boat pulling me up; but I could neither speak nor move, and everything became dark.

'After a time I heard the voices again — the voices of the men of the *Fukuju Maru*: "Jinyō! Jinyō!" — and I was frightened. Then somebody shook me, and said: "*Oi! oi!*[5] it is only a dream!" — and

5. As we should say, 'Hey! hey!' — to call attention.

I saw that I was lying in the junk, under a hanging lantern (for it was night); and beside me an old man, a stranger, was kneeling, with a cup of boiled rice in his hand. "Try to eat a little," he said, very kindly. I wanted to sit up, but could not; then he fed me himself, out of the cup. When it was empty I asked for more; but the old man answered: "Not now; you must sleep first." I heard him say to someone else: "Give him nothing more until I tell you: if you let him eat much, he will die." I slept again; and twice more that night I was given rice – soft-boiled rice – one small cupful at a time.

'In the morning I felt much better; and the old man, who had brought me the rice, came and questioned me. When he heard about the loss of our ship, and the time that I had been in the water, he expressed great pity for me. He told me that I had drifted, in those two nights and days, more than twenty-five *ri*.[6] "We went after your plank," he said, "and picked it up. Perhaps you would like to present it some day to the temple of Kompira-Sama." I thanked him, but answered that I wanted to offer it to the temple of Jizō-Sama of Ogawa, at Yaidzu; for it was to Jizō-Sama of Ogawa that I had most often prayed for help.

'The kind old man was the captain, and also the owner, of the junk. She was a Banshū ship, and was bound for the port of Kuki, in Kishū ... You write the name, Ku-ki, with the character for "demon" – so that it means the Nine Demons ... All the men of the ship were very good to me. I was naked, except for a loincloth, when I came on board; and they found clothes for me. One gave me an under-robe, and another an upper-robe, and another a girdle; several gave me towels and sandals; and all of them together made up a gift of money for me, amounting to between six and seven ryō.

'When we reached Kuki – a nice little place, though it has a queer name – the captain took me to a good inn; and after a few days' rest I got strong again. Then the governor of the district, the Jitō, as we called him in those days, sent for me, and heard my story, and had it written down. He told me that he would have to send a report of the matter to the Jitō of the Yaidzu district, after which he would find means to send me home. But the Banshū captain

6. That is to say, about sixty-three English miles.

who had saved me offered to take me home in his own ship, and also to act as messenger for the Jitō; and there was much argument between the two. At that time we had no telegraph and no post; and to send a special messenger (hikyaku), from Kuki to Yaidzu,[7] would have cost at least fifty ryō. But, on the other hand, there were particular laws and customs about such matters – laws very different from those of today. Meanwhile a Yaidzu ship came to the neighboring port of Arasha; and a woman of Kuki, who happened to be at Arasha, told the Yaidzu captain that I was at Kuki. The Yaidzu ship then came to Kuki; and the Jitō decided to send me home in charge of the Yaidzu captain, giving him a written order.

'Altogether, it was about a month from the time of the loss of the *Fukuju Maru* when I returned to Yaidzu. We reached the harbor at night; and I did not go home at once: it would have frightened my people. Although no certain news of the loss of our ship had then been received at Yaidzu, several things belonging to her had been picked up by fishing-craft; and as the typhoon had come very suddenly, with a terrible sea, it was generally believed that the *Fukuju Maru* had gone down, and that all of us had been drowned ... None of the other men were ever heard of again ... I went that night to the house of a friend; and in the morning I sent word to my parents and brother; and they came for me ...

'Once every year I go to the temple of Kompira in Sanuki: all who have been saved from shipwreck go there to give thanks. And I often go to the temple of Jizō-Sama of Ogawa. If you will come with me there tomorrow, I will show you that plank.'

---

7. The distance is more than one hundred and fifty miles.

In Yokohama

A good sight indeed has met us today — a good daybreak — a beautiful rising; for we have seen the Perfectly Enlightened, who has crossed the stream — *Hemavatasutta*

I

The Jizō-Dō was not easy to find, being hidden away in a court behind a street of small shops; and the entrance to the court itself — a very narrow opening between two houses — being veiled at every puff of wind by the fluttering sign-drapery of a dealer in second-hand clothing.

Because of the heat, the shōji of the little temple had been removed, leaving the sanctuary open to view on three sides. I saw the usual Buddhist furniture — service-bell, reading-desk, and scarlet lacquered mokugyo — disposed upon the yellow matting. The altar supported a stone Jizō, wearing a bib for the sake of child ghosts; and above the statue, upon a long shelf, were smaller images gilded and painted — another Jizō, aureoled from head to feet, a radiant Amida, a sweet-faced Kwannon, and a gruesome figure of the Judge of Souls. Still higher were suspended a confused multitude of votive offerings, including two framed prints taken from American illustrated papers: a view of the Philadelphia Exhibition, and a portrait of Adelaide Neilson in the character of Juliet. In lieu of the usual flower vases before the houzon there were jars of glass bearing the inscription: '*Reine Claude au jus; conservation garantie. Toussaint Cosnard: Bordeaux.*' And the box filled with incense-rods bore the legend: '*Rich in flavor — Pinhead Cigarettes.*' To the innocent folk who gave them, and who could never hope in this world to make costlier gifts, these ex-votos seemed beautiful because strange; and in spite of incongruities it seemed to me that the little temple did really look pretty.

A screen, with weird figures of Arhats creating dragons, masked the further chamber; and the song of an unseen uguisu sweetened the hush of the place. A red cat came from behind the screen to look at us, and retired again, as if to convey a message. Presently appeared an aged nun, who welcomed us and bade us enter, her smoothly shaven head shining like a moon at every reverence. We doffed our footgear, and followed her behind the screen into a little room that opened upon a garden; and we saw the old priest seated upon a cushion, and writing at a very low table. He laid aside his brush to greet us; and we also took our places on cushions before him. Very pleasant his face was to look upon: all wrinkles written there by the ebb of life spake of that which was good.

The nun brought us tea, and sweetmeats stamped with the Wheel of the Law; the red cat curled itself up beside me; and the priest talked to us. His voice was deep and gentle; there were bronze tones in it, like the rich murmurings which follow each peal of a temple bell. We coaxed him to tell us about himself. He was eighty-eight years of age, and his eyes and ears were still as those of a young man; but he could not walk because of chronic rheumatism. For twenty years he had been occupied in writing a religious history of Japan, to be completed in three hundred volumes; and he had already completed two hundred and thirty. The rest he hoped to write during the coming year. I saw on a small book-shelf behind him the imposing array of neatly bound MSS.

'But the plan upon which he works,' said my student interpreter, 'is quite wrong. His history will never be published; it is full of impossible stories – miracles and fairy-tales.'

(I thought I should like to read the stories.)

'For one who has reached such an age,' I said, 'you seem very strong.'

'The signs are that I shall live some years longer,' replied the old man, 'though I wish to live only long enough to finish my history. Then, as I am helpless and cannot move about, I want to die so as to get a new body. I suppose I must have committed some fault in a former life, to be crippled as I am. But I am glad to feel that I am nearing the Shore.'

'He means the shore of the Sea of Death and Birth,' says my interpreter. 'The ship whereby we cross, you know, is the Ship of the Good Law; and the farthest shore is Nehan – Nirvana.'

Are all our bodily weaknesses and misfortunes,' I asked, 'the results of errors committed in other births?'

'That which we are,' the old man answered, 'is the consequence of that which we have been. We say in Japan the consequence of mangō and ingō – the two classes of actions.'

'Evil and good?' I queried.

'Greater and lesser. There are no perfect actions. Every act contains both merit and demerit, just as even the best painting has defects and excellences. But when the sum of good in any action exceeds the sum of evil, just as in a good painting the merits outweigh the faults, then the result is progress. And gradually by such progress will all evil be eliminated.'

'But how,' I asked, 'can the result of actions affect the physical conditions? The child follows the way of his fathers, inherits their strength or their weakness; yet not from them does he receive his soul.'

'The chain of causes and effects is not easy to explain in a few words. To understand all you should study the Dai-jō or Greater Vehicle; also the Shō-jō, or Lesser Vehicle. There you will learn that the world itself exists only because of acts. Even as one learning to write, at first writes only with great difficulty, but afterward, becoming skillful, writes without knowledge of any effort, so the tendency of acts continually repeated is to form habit. And such tendencies persist far beyond this life.'

'Can any man obtain the power to remember his former births?'

'That is very rare,' the old man answered, shaking his head. 'To have such memory one should first become a Bosatsu [Bodhissattva].'

'Is it not possible to become a Bosatsu?'

'Not in this age. This is the Period of Corruption. First there was the Period of True Doctrine, when life was long; and after it came the Period of Images, during which men departed from the highest truth; and now the world is degenerate. It is not now possible by good deeds to become a Buddha, because the world is too corrupt and life is too short. But devout persons may attain the Gokuraku [Paradise] by virtue of merit, and by constantly repeating the Nembutsu; and in the Gokuraku, they may be able to practice the true doctrine. For the days are longer there, and life also is very long.'

'I have read in our translations of the Sutras,' I said, 'that by virtue of good deeds men may be reborn in happier and yet happier conditions successively, each time obtaining more perfect faculties, each time surrounded by higher joys. Riches are spoken of, and strength and beauty, and graceful women, and all that people desire in this temporary world. Wherefore I cannot help thinking that the way of progress must continually grow more difficult the further one proceeds. For if these texts be true, the more one succeeds in detaching one's self from the things of the senses, the more powerful become the temptations to return to them. So that the reward of virtue would seem itself to be made an obstacle in the path.'

'Not so!' replied the old man. 'They, who by self-mastery reach such conditions of temporary happiness, have gained spiritual force also, and some knowledge of truth. Their strength to conquer themselves increases more and more with every triumph, until they reach at last that world of Apparitional Birth, in which the lower forms of temptation have no existence.'

The red cat stirred uneasily at a sound of geta, then went to the entrance, followed by the nun. There were some visitors waiting; and the priest begged us to excuse him a little while, that he might attend to their spiritual wants. We made place quickly for them, and they came in — poor pleasant folk, who saluted us kindly: a mother bereaved, desiring to have prayers said for the happiness of her little dead boy; a young wife to obtain the pity of the Buddha for her ailing husband; a father and daughter to seek divine help for somebody that had gone very far away. The priest spoke caressingly to all, giving to the mother some little prints of Jizō, giving a paper of blest rice to the wife, and on behalf of the father and daughter, preparing some holy texts. Involuntarily there came to me the idea of all the countless innocent prayers thus being daily made in countless temples; the idea of all the fears and hopes and heartaches of simple love; the idea of all the humble sorrows unheard by any save the gods. The student began to examine the old man's books, and I began to think of the unthinkable.

Life — life as unity, uncreated, without beginning, of which we know the luminous shadows only; life forever striving against death, and always conquered yet always surviving — what is it? — why is it? A myriad times the universe is dissipated – a myriad times again evolved; and the same life vanishes with every vanishing, only to reappear in another cycling. The Cosmos becomes a nebula, the nebula a Cosmos: eternally the swarms of suns and worlds are born; eternally they die. But after each tremendous integration the flaming spheres cool down and ripen into life; and the life ripens into Thought. The ghost in each one of us must have passed through the burning of a million suns – must survive the awful vanishing of countless future universes. May not Memory somehow and somewhere also survive? Are we sure that in ways and forms unknowable it does not, as infinite vision – remembrance of the Future in the Past? Perhaps in the Night-without-end, as in deeps of Nirvana, dreams of all that has ever been, of all that can ever be, are being perpetually dreamed.

The parishioners uttered their thanks, made their little offerings to Jizō, and retired, saluting us as they went. We resumed our former places beside the little writing-table, and the old man said:

'It is the priest, perhaps, who among all men best knows what sorrow is in the world. I have heard that in the countries of the West there is also much suffering, although the Western nations are so rich.'

'Yes,' I made answer; 'and I think that in Western countries there is more unhappiness than in Japan. For the rich there are larger pleasures, but for the poor greater pains. Our life is much more difficult to live; and, perhaps for that reason, our thoughts are more troubled by the mystery of the world.'

The priest seemed interested, but said nothing. With the interpreter's help, I continued:

'There are three great questions by which the minds of many men in the Western countries are perpetually tormented. These questions we call "the Whence, the Whither, and the Why," meaning, Whence Life? Whither does it go? Why does it exist and suffer? Our highest Western Science declares them riddles impossible to solve, yet confesses at the same time that the heart of man can find no peace till they are solved. All religions have attempted explanations; and all their explanations are different. I have searched Buddhist books for answers to these questions, and I found answers which seemed to me better than any others. Still, they did not satisfy me, being incomplete. From your own lips I hope to obtain some answers to the first and the third questions at least. I do not ask for proof or for arguments of any kind: I ask only to know doctrine. Was the beginning of all things in universal Mind?'

To this question I really expected no definite answer, having, in the Sutra called Sabbâsava, read about 'those things which ought not to be considered,' and about the Six Absurd Notions, and the words of the rebuke to such as debate within themselves: '*This is a being: whence did it come? Whither will it go?*' But the answer came, measured and musical, like a chant:

'All things considered as individual have come into being, through forms innumerable of development and reproduction, out of the universal Mind. Potentially within that mind they had existed from eternity. But between that we call Mind and that we call Substance there is no difference of essence. What we name Substance is only the sum of our own sensations and perceptions; and these themselves are but phenomena of Mind. Of Substance-in-itself we have not any knowledge. We know nothing beyond the phases of our mind, and these phases are wrought in it by outer influence or power, to which we give the name Substance. But Substance and Mind in themselves are only two phases of one infinite Entity.'

'There are Western teachers also,' I said, 'who teach a like doctrine; and the most profound researches of our modern science seem to demonstrate that what we term Matter has no absolute existence. But concerning that infinite Entity of which you speak, is there any Buddhist teaching as to when and how It first produced those two forms which in name we still distinguish as Mind and Substance?'

'Buddhism,' the old priest answered, 'does not teach, as other religions do, that things have been produced by creation. The one and only Reality is the universal Mind, called in Japanese Shinnyo[1] – the Reality-in-its-very-self, infinite and eternal. Now this infinite Mind within Itself beheld Its own sentiency. And, even as one who in hallucination assumes apparitions to be actualities, so the universal Entity took for external existences that which It beheld only within Itself. We call this illusion Mu-myo,[2] signifying "without radiance," or "void of illumination."'

1. Sanskrit: *Bhûta-Tathatâ.*   2. Sanskrit: *Avidya.*

'The word has been translated by some Western scholars,' I observed, 'as "Ignorance."'

'So I have been told. But the idea conveyed by the word we use is not the idea expressed by the term "ignorance." It is rather the idea of enlightenment misdirected, or of illusion.'

'And what has been taught,' I asked, 'concerning the time of that illusion?'

'The time of the primal illusion is said to be Mu-shi, "beyond beginning," in the incalculable past. From Shinnyo emanated the first distinction of the Self and the Not-Self, whence have arisen all individual existences, whether of Spirit or of Substance, and all those passions and desires, likewise, which influence the conditions of being through countless births. Thus the universe is the emanation of the infinite Entity; yet it cannot be said that we are the creations of that Entity. The original Self of each of us is the universal Mind; and within each of us the universal Self exists, together with the effects of the primal illusion. And this state of the original Self enwrapped in the results of illusion, we call Nyōrai-zō,[3] or the Womb of the Buddha. The end for which we should all strive is simply our return to the infinite Original Self, which is the essence of Buddha.'

'There is another subject of doubt,' I said, 'about which I much desire to know the teaching of Buddhism. Our Western science declares that the visible universe has been evolved and dissolved successively innumerable times during the infinite past, and must also vanish and reappear through countless cycles in the infinite future. In our translations of the ancient Indian philosophy, and of the sacred texts of the Buddhists, the same thing is declared. But is it not also taught that there shall come at last for all things a time of ultimate vanishing and of perpetual rest?'

He answered: 'The Shō-jō indeed teaches that the universe has appeared and disappeared over and over again, times beyond reckoning in the past, and that it must continue to be alternately dissolved and reformed through unimaginable eternities to come. But we are

---

3. Sanskrit: *Tathâgata-gharba.* The term 'Tathâgata' (Japanese *Nyōrai*) is the highest title of a Buddha. It signifies 'One whose coming is like the coming of his predecessors.'

also taught that all things shall enter finally and forever, into the state of Nehan.'[4]

An irreverent yet irrepressible fancy suddenly arose within me. I could not help thinking of Absolute Rest as expressed by the scientific formula of 274° centigrade below zero, or 525°·2 Fahrenheit. But I only said:

'For the Western mind it is difficult to think of absolute rest as a condition of bliss. Does the Buddhist idea of Nehan include the idea of infinite stillness, of universal immobility?'

'No,' replied the priest. 'Nehan is the condition of Absolute Self-sufficiency, the state of all-knowing, all-perceiving. We do not suppose it a state of total inaction, but the supreme condition of freedom from all restraint. It is true that we cannot imagine a bodiless condition of perception or knowledge; because all our ideas and sensations belong to the condition of the body. But we believe that Nehan is the state of infinite vision and infinite wisdom and infinite spiritual peace.'

The red cat leaped upon the priest's knees, and there curled itself into a posture of lazy comfort. The old man caressed it; and my companion observed, with a little laugh:

'See how fat it is! Perhaps it may have performed some good deeds in a previous life.'

'Do the conditions of animals,' I asked, 'also depend upon merit and demerit in previous existences?'

The priest answered me seriously:

'All conditions of being depend upon conditions pre-existing, and Life is One. To be born into the world of men is fortunate; there we have some enlightenment, and chances of gaining merit. But the state of an animal is a state of obscurity of mind, deserving our pity and benevolence. No animal can be considered truly fortunate; yet even in the life of animals there are countless differences of condition.'

A little silence followed, softly broken by the purring of the cat. I looked at the picture of Adelaide Neilson, just visible above the top of the screen; and I thought of Juliet, and wondered what the

4. Nirvana.

priest would say about Shakespeare's wondrous story of passion and sorrow, were I able to relate it worthily in Japanese. Then suddenly, like an answer to that wonder, came a memory of the two hundred and fifteenth verse of the *Dhammapada*: *'From love comes grief; from grief comes fear: one who is free from love knows neither grief nor fear.'*

'Does Buddhism,' I asked, 'teach that all sexual love ought to be suppressed? Is such love of necessity a hindrance to enlightenment? I know that Buddhist priests, excepting those of the Shin-shū, are forbidden to marry; but I do not know what is the teaching concerning celibacy and marriage among the laity.'

'Marriage may be either a hindrance or a help on the Path,' the old man said, 'according to conditions. All depends upon conditions. If the love of wife and child should cause a man to become too much attached to the temporary advantages of this unhappy world, then such love would be a hindrance. But, on the contrary, if the love of wife and child should enable a man to live more purely and more unselfishly than he could do in a state of celibacy, then marriage would be a very great help to him in the Perfect Way. Many are the dangers of marriage for the wise; but for those of little understanding the dangers of celibacy are greater. And even the illusion of passion may sometimes lead noble natures to the higher knowledge. There is a story of this. Dai-Mokukenren,[5] whom the people call Mokuren, was a disciple of Shaka.[6] He was a very comely man; and a girl became enamored of him. As he belonged already to the Order, she despaired of being ever able to have him for her husband; and she grieved in secret. But at last she found courage to go to the Lord Buddha, and to speak all her heart to him. Even while she was speaking, he cast a deep sleep upon her; and she dreamed she was the happy wife of Mokuren. Years of contentment seemed to pass in her dream; and after them years of joy and sorrow mingled; and suddenly her husband was taken away from her by death. Then she knew such sorrow that she wondered how she could live; and she awoke in that pain, and saw the Buddha smile. And he said to her: "Little Sister, thou hast seen. Choose now as thou wilt — either to be the bride of Mokuren, or to seek the higher Way upon which he has entered." Then she cut off her

5. Sanskrit: *Mahâmaudgalyâyana.*   6. The Japanese rendering of Sakyamuni.

hair, and became a nun, and in aftertime attained to the condition of one never to be reborn.'

For a moment it seemed to me that the story did not show how love's illusion could lead to self-conquest; that the girl's conversion was only the direct result of painful knowledge forced upon her, not a consequence of her love. But presently I reflected that the vision accorded her could have produced no high result in a selfish or unworthy soul. I thought of disadvantages unspeakable which the possession of foreknowledge might involve in the present order of life; and felt it was a blessed thing for most of us that the future shaped itself behind a veil. Then I dreamed that the power to lift that veil might be evolved or won, just so soon as such a faculty should be of real benefit to men, but not before; and I asked:

'Can the power to see the Future be obtained through enlightenment?'

The priest answered:

'Yes. When we reach that state of enlightenment in which we obtain the Roku-Jindzū, or Six Mysterious Faculties, then we can see the Future as well as the Past. Such power comes at the same time as the power of remembering former births. But to attain to that condition of knowledge, in the present age of the world, is very difficult.'

My companion made me a stealthy sign that it was time to say goodbye. We had stayed rather long — even by the measure of Japanese etiquette, which is generous to a fault in these matters. I thanked the master of the temple for his kindness in replying to my fantastic questions, and ventured to add:

'There are a hundred other things about which I should like to ask you, but today I have taken too much of your time. May I come again?'

'It will make me very happy,' he said. 'Be pleased to come again as soon as you desire. I hope you will not fail to ask about all things which are still obscure to you. It is by earnest inquiry that truth may be known and illusions dispelled. Nay, come often — that I may speak to you of the Shō-jō. And these I pray you to accept.'

He gave me two little packages. One contained white sand — sand from the holy temple of Zenkōji, whither all good souls make pilgrimage after death. The other contained a very small white stone, said to be a shari, or relic of the body of a Buddha.

I hoped to visit the kind old man many times again. But a school contract took me out of the city and over the mountains; and I saw him no more.

II

Five years, all spent far away from treaty ports, slowly flitted by before I saw the Jizō-Dō again. Many changes had taken place both without and within me during that time. The beautiful illusion of Japan, the almost weird charm that comes with one's first entrance into her magical atmosphere, had, indeed, stayed with me very long, but had totally faded out at last. I had learned to see the Far East without its glamor. And I had mourned not a little for the sensations of the past.

But one day they all came back to me — just for a moment. I was in Yokohama, gazing once more from the Bluff at the divine spectre of Fuji haunting the April morning. In that enormous spring blaze of blue light, the feeling of my first Japanese day returned, the feeling of my first delighted wonder in the radiance of an un-known fairy-world full of beautiful riddles — an Elf-land having a special sun and a tinted atmosphere of its own. Again I knew myself steeped in a dream of luminous peace; again all visible things assumed for me a delicious immateriality. Again the Orient heaven — flecked only with thinnest white ghosts of cloud, all shadowless as Souls entering into Nirvana — became for me the very sky of Buddha; and the colors of the morning seemed deepening into those of the traditional hour of His birth, when trees long dead burst into blossom, and winds were perfumed, and all creatures living found themselves possessed of loving hearts. The air seemed pregnant with even such a vague sweetness, as if the Teacher were about to come again; and all faces passing seemed to smile with premonition of the celestial advent.

Then the ghostliness went away, and things looked earthly; and I thought of all the illusions I had known, and of the illusions of the world as Life, and of the universe itself as illusion. Whereupon the name Mu-myō returned to memory; and I was moved immediately to seek the ancient thinker of the Jizō-Dō.

The quarter had been much changed: old houses had vanished, and new ones dovetailed wondrously together. I discovered the court at last nevertheless, and saw the little temple just as I had remembered it. Before the entrance women were standing; and a young priest I had never seen before was playing with a baby; and the small brown hands of the infant were stroking his shaven face. It was a kindly face, and intelligent, with very long eyes.

'Five years ago,' I said to him, in clumsy Japanese, 'I visited this temple. In that time there was an aged bonsan here.'

The young bonsan gave the baby into the arms of one who seemed to be its mother, and responded:

'Yes. He died — that old priest; and I am now in his place. Honorably please to enter.'

I entered. The little sanctuary no longer looked interesting: all its innocent prettiness was gone. Jizō still smiled over his bib; but the other divinities had disappeared, and likewise many votive offerings — including the picture of Adelaide Neilson. The priest tried to make me comfortable in the chamber where the old man used to write, and set a smoking-box before me. I looked for the books in the corner; they also had vanished. Everything seemed to have been changed.

I asked:

'When did he die?'

'Only last winter,' replied the incumbent, 'in the Period of Greatest Cold. As he could not move his feet, he suffered much from the cold. This is his ihai.'

He went to an alcove containing shelves incumbered with a bewilderment of objects indescribable — old wrecks, perhaps, of sacred things — and opened the doors of a very small butsudan, placed between glass jars full of flowers. Inside I saw the mortuary tablet — fresh black lacquer and gold. He lighted a lamplet before it, set a rod of incense smouldering, and said:

'Pardon my rude absence a little while; for there are parishioners waiting.'

So left alone, I looked at the ihai and watched the steady flame of the tiny lamp and the blue, slow, upcurlings of incense — wondering if the spirit of the old priest was there. After a moment I felt as if he really were, and spoke to him without words. Then I noticed that the flower vases on either side of the butsudan still bore the name of Toussaint Cosnard of Bordeaux, and that the incense-box maintained its familiar legend of richly flavored cigarettes. Looking about the room I also perceived the red cat, fast asleep in a sunny corner. I went to it, and stroked it; but it knew me not, and scarcely opened its drowsy eyes. It was sleeker than ever, and seemed happy. Near the entrance I heard a plaintive murmuring; then the voice of the priest, reiterating sympathetically some half-comprehended answer to his queries: '*A woman of nineteen, yes. And a man of twenty-seven, is it?*' Then I rose to go.

'Pardon,' said the priest, looking up from his writing, while the poor women saluted me, 'yet one little moment more!'

'Nay,' I answered; 'I would not interrupt you. I came only to see the old man, and I have seen his ihai. This, my little offering, was for him. Please to accept it for yourself.'

'Will you not wait a moment, that I may know your name?'

'Perhaps I shall come again,' I said evasively. 'Is the old nun also dead?'

'Oh no! she is still taking care of the temple. She has gone out, but will presently return. Will you not wait? Do you wish nothing?'

'Only a prayer,' I answered. 'My name makes no difference. A man of forty-four. Pray that he may obtain whatever is best for him.'

The priest wrote something down. Certainly that which I had bidden him pray for was not the wish of my 'heart of hearts.' But I knew the Lord Buddha would never hearken to any foolish prayer for the return of lost illusions.

追
憶

1

25 July. Three extraordinary visits have been made to my house this week.

The first was that of the professional well-cleaners. For once every year all wells must be emptied and cleansed, lest the God of Wells, Suijin-Sama, be wroth. On this occasion I learned some things relating to Japanese wells and the tutelar deity of them, who has two names, being also called Mizuha-nome-no-mikoto.

Suijin-Sama protects all wells, keeping their water sweet and cool, provided that house-owners observe his laws of cleanliness, which are rigid. To those who break them sickness comes, and death. Rarely the god manifests himself, taking the form of a serpent. I have never seen any temple dedicated to him. But once each month a Shintō priest visits the homes of pious families having wells, and he repeats certain ancient prayers to the Well-God, and plants nobori, little paper flags, which are symbols, at the edge of the well. After the well had been cleaned, also, this is done. Then the first bucket of the new water must be drawn up by a man; for if a woman first draw water, the well will always thereafter remain muddy.

The god has little servants to help him in his work. These are the small fishes the Japanese call funa.[1] One or two funa are kept in every well, to clear the water of larvae. When a well is cleaned, great care is taken of the little fish. It was on the occasion of the coming of the well-cleaners that I first learned of the existence of a pair of funa in my own well. They were placed in a tub of cool

1. A sort of small silver carp.

water while the well was refilling, and thereafter were replunged into their solitude.

The water of my well is clear and ice-cold. But now I can never drink of it without a thought of those two small white lives circling always in darkness, and startled through untold years by the descent of plashing buckets.

The second curious visit was that of the district firemen, in full costume, with their hand-engines. According to ancient custom, they make a round of all their district once a year during the dry spell, and throw water over the hot roofs, and receive some small perquisite from each wealthy householder. There is a belief that when it has not rained for a long time roofs may be ignited by the mere heat of the sun. The firemen played with their hose upon my roofs, trees, and garden, producing considerable refreshment; and in return I bestowed on them wherewith to buy saké.

The third visit was that of a deputation of children asking for some help to celebrate fittingly the festival of Jizō, who has a shrine on the other side of the street, exactly opposite my house. I was very glad to contribute to their fund, for I love the gentle god, and I knew the festival would be delightful. Early next morning, I saw that the shrine had already been decked with flowers and votive lanterns. A new bib had been put about Jizō's neck, and a Buddhist repast set before him. Later on, carpenters constructed a dancing-platform in the temple court for the children to dance upon; and before sundown the toy-sellers had erected and stocked a small street of booths inside the precincts. After dark I went out into a great glory of lantern fires to see the children dance; and I found, perched before my gate, an enormous dragonfly more than three feet long. It was a token of the children's gratitude for the little help I had given them — a kazari, a decoration. I was startled for the moment by the realism of the thing; but upon close examination I discovered that the body was a pine branch wrapped with colored paper, the four wings were four fire-shovels, and the gleaming head was a little teapot. The whole was lighted by a candle so placed as to make extraordinary shadows, which formed part of the design. It was a wonderful instance of art sense working without a speck of artistic material, yet it was all the labor of a poor little child only eight years old!

II

30 July. The next house to mine, on the south side — a low, dingy structure — is that of a dyer. You can always tell where a Japanese dyer is by the long pieces of silk or cotton stretched between bamboo poles before his door to dry in the sun — broad bands of rich azure, of purple, of rose, pale blue, pearl gray. Yesterday my neighbor coaxed me to pay the family a visit; and after having been led through the front part of their little dwelling, I was surprised to find myself looking from a rear veranda at a garden worthy of some old Kyōto palace. There was a dainty landscape in miniature, and a pond of clear water peopled by goldfish having wonderfully compound tails.

When I had enjoyed this spectacle awhile, the dyer led me to a small room fitted up as a Buddhist chapel. Though everything had had to be made on a reduced scale, I did not remember to have seen a more artistic display in any temple. He told me it had cost him about fifteen hundred yen. I did not understand how even that sum could have sufficed. There were three elaborately carven altars — a triple blaze of gold lacquer-work; a number of charming Buddhist images; many exquisite vessels; an ebony reading-desk; a mokugyō;[2] two fine bells — in short, all the paraphernalia of a temple in miniature. My host had studied at a Buddhist temple in his youth, and knew the sutras, of which he had all that are used by the Jōdo sect. He told me that he could celebrate any of the ordinary services. Daily, at a fixed hour, the whole family assembled in the chapel for prayers; and he generally read the Kyō for them. But on extraordinary occasions a Buddhist priest from the neighboring temple would come to officiate.

He told me a queer story about robbers. Dyers are peculiarly liable to be visited by robbers; partly by reason of the value of

2. A hollow wooden block shaped like a dolphin's head. It is tapped in accompaniment to the chanting of the Buddhist sutras.

the silks intrusted to them, and also because the business is known to be lucrative. One evening the family were robbed. The master was out of the city; his old mother, his wife, and a female servant were the only persons in the house at the time. Three men, having their faces masked and carrying long swords, entered the door. One asked the servant whether any of the apprentices were still in the building; and she, hoping to frighten the invaders away, answered that the young men were all still at work. But the robbers were not disturbed by this assurance. One posted himself at the entrance, the other two strode into the sleeping-apartment. The women started up in alarm, and the wife asked, 'Why do you wish to kill us?' He who seemed to be the leader answered, 'We do not wish to kill you; we want money only. But if we do not get it, then it will be this' — striking his sword into the matting. The old mother said, 'Be so kind as not to frighten my daughter-in-law, and I will give you whatever money there is in the house. But you ought to know there cannot be much, as my son has gone to Kyōto.' She handed them the money-drawer and her own purse. There were just twenty-seven yen and eighty-four sen. The head robber counted it, and said, quite gently, 'We do not want to frighten you. We know you are a very devout believer in Buddhism, and we think you would not tell a lie. Is this all?' 'Yes, it is all,' she answered. 'I am, as you say, a believer in the teaching of the Buddha, and if you come to rob me now, I believe it is only because I myself, in some former life, once robbed you. This is my punishment for that fault, and so, instead of wishing to deceive you, I feel grateful at this opportunity to atone for the wrong which I did to you in my previous state of existence.' The robber laughed, and said, 'You are a good old woman, and we believe you. If you were poor, we would not rob you at all. Now we only want a couple of kimono and this' — laying his hand on a very fine silk overdress. The old woman replied, 'All my son's kimono I can give you, but I beg you will not take that, for it does not belong to my son, and was confided to us only for dyeing. What is ours I can give, but I cannot give what belongs to another.' 'That is quite right,' approved the robber, 'and we shall not take it.'

After receiving a few robes, the robbers said goodnight, very politely, but ordered the women not to look after them. The old servant was still near the door. As the chief robber passed her, he

said, 'You told us a lie, so take that!' — and struck her senseless
None of the robbers were ever caught.

III

29 August. When a body has been burned, according to the funeral
rites of certain Buddhist sects, search is made among the ashes for
a little bone called the Hotoke-San, or 'Lord Buddha,' popularly
supposed to be a little bone of the throat. What bone it really is
I do not know, never having had a chance to examine such a relic.

According to the shape of this little bone when found after the
burning, the future condition of the dead may be predicted. Should
the next state to which the soul is destined be one of happiness,
the bone will have the form of a small image of Buddha. But if
the next birth is to be unhappy, then the bone will have either
an ugly shape, or no shape at all.

A little boy, the son of a neighboring tobacconist, died the night
before last, and today the corpse was burned. The little bone left
over from the burning was discovered to have the form of three
Buddhas — San-Tai — which may have afforded some spiritual consola-
tion to the bereaved parents.[3]

IV

13 September. A letter from Matsue, Izumo, tells me that the old
man who used to supply me with pipe-stems is dead. (A Japanese
pipe, you must know, consists of three pieces, usually — a metal
bowl large enough to hold a pea, a metal mouthpiece, and a bamboo
stem which is renewed at regular intervals.) He used to stain his
pipestems very prettily: some looked like porcupine quills, and some
like cylinders of snakeskin. He lived in a queer narrow little street
at the verge of the city. I know the street because in it there is
a famous statue of Jizō called Shiroko-Jizō — 'White-Child-Jizō' —

3. At the great temple of Tennōji, at Ōsaka, all such bones are dropped into
a vault; and according *to the sound each makes in falling,* further evidence about the
Gōsho is said to be obtained. After a hundred years from the time of beginning
this curious collection, all these bones are to be ground into a kind of paste, out
of which a colossal statue of Buddha is to be made.

which I once went to see. They whiten its face, like the face of a dancing-girl, for some reason which I have never been able to find out.

The old man had a daughter, O-Masu, about whom a story is told. O-Masu is still alive. She has been a happy wife for many years; but she is dumb. Long ago, an angry mob sacked and destroyed the dwelling and the storehouses of a rice speculator in the city. His money, including a quantity of gold coin (koban), was scattered through the street. The rioters — rude, honest peasants — did not want it: they wished to destroy, not to steal. But O-Masu's father, the same evening, picked up a koban from the mud, and took it home. Later on a neighbor denounced him, and secured his arrest. The judge before whom he was summoned tried to obtain certain evidence by cross-questioning O-Masu, then a shy girl of fifteen. She felt that if she continued to answer she would be made, in spite of herself, to give testimony unfavorable to her father; that she was in the presence of a trained inquisitor, capable, without effort, of forcing her to acknowledge everything she knew. She ceased to speak, and a stream of blood gushed from her mouth. She had silenced herself forever by simply biting off her tongue. Her father was acquitted. A merchant who admired the act demanded her in marriage, and supported her father in his old age.

V

10 October. There is said to be one day — only one — in the life of a child during which it can remember and speak of its former birth.

On the very day that it becomes exactly two years old, the child is taken by its mother into the most quiet part of the house, and is placed in a mi, or rice-winnowing basket. The child sits down in the mi. Then the mother says, calling the child by name, 'Omae no zensé wa, nande attakane? — iute, gōran.'[4] Then the child always answers in one word. For some mysterious reason, no more lengthy reply is ever given. Often the answer is so enigmatic that some priest or fortune-teller must be asked to interpret it. For instance, yesterday, the little son of a copper-smith living near us answered

4. 'Thy previous life as for — what was it? Honorably look [or please look] and tell?'

only 'Umé' to the magical question. Now umé might mean a plum-flower, a plum, or a girl's name — 'Flower-on-the-Plum.' Could it mean that the boy remembered having been a girl? Or that he had been a plum-tree? 'Souls of men do not enter plum-trees,' said a neighbor. A fortune-teller this morning declared, on being questioned about the riddle, that the boy had probably been a scholar, poet, or statesman, because the plum-tree is the symbol of Tenjin, patron of scholars, statesmen, and men of letters.

VI

17 November. An astonishing book might be written about those things in Japanese life which no foreigner can understand. Such a book should include the study of certain rare but terrible results of anger.

As a national rule, the Japanese seldom allow themselves to show anger. Even among the common classes, any serious menace is apt to take the form of a smiling assurance that your favor shall be remembered, and that its recipient is grateful. (Do not suppose, however, that this is ironical, in our sense of the word: it is only euphemistic, ugly things not being called by their real names.) But this smiling assurance may possibly mean death. When vengeance comes, it comes unexpectedly. Neither distance nor time, within the empire, can offer any obstacles to the avenger who can walk fifty miles a day, whose whole baggage can be tied up in a very small towel, and whose patience is almost infinite. He may choose a knife, but is much more likely to use a sword — a Japanese sword. This, in Japanese hands, is the deadliest of weapons; and the killing of ten or twelve persons by one angry man may occupy less than a minute. It does not often happen that the murderer thinks of trying to escape. Ancient custom requires that, having taken another life, he should take his own; wherefore to fall into the hands of the police would be to disgrace his name. He has made his preparations beforehand, written his letters, arranged for his funeral, perhaps — as in one appalling instance last year — even chiseled his own tombstone. Having fully accomplished his revenge, he kills himself.

There has just occurred, not far from the city, at the village called Sugikamimura, one of those tragedies which are difficult to understand. The chief actors were Narumatsu Ichirō, a young shopkeeper; his wife, O-Noto, twenty years of age, to whom he had been married only a year; and O-Noto's maternal uncle, one Sugimoto Kasaku, a man of violent temper, who had once been in prison. The tragedy was in four acts.

ACT I. *Scene: Interior of public bathhouse. Sugimoto Kasaku in the bath. Enter Narumatsu Ichirō, who strips, gets into the smoking water without noticing his relative, and cries out:*

'*Aa!* as if one should be in Jigoku, so hot this water is!'

(The word 'Jigoku' signifies the Buddhist hell; but, in common parlance, it also signifies a prison – this time an unfortunate coincidence.)

Kasaku (*terribly angry*): 'A raw baby, you, to seek a hard quarrel! What do you not like?'

Ichirō (*surprised and alarmed, but rallying against the tone of Kasaku*): 'Nay! What? That I said need not by you be explained. Though I said the water was hot, your help to make it hotter was not asked.'

Kasaku (*now dangerous*): 'Though for my own fault, not once, but twice in the hell of prison I had been, what should there be wonderful in it? Either an idiot child or a low scoundrel you must be!'

(*Each eyes the other for a spring, but each hesitates, although things no Japanese should suffer himself to say have been said. They are too evenly matched, the old and the young.*)

Kasaku (*growing cooler as Ichirō becomes angrier*): 'A child, a raw child, to quarrel with *me!* What should a baby do with a wife? Your wife is my blood, mine – the blood of the man from hell! Give her back to my house.'

Ichirō (*desperately, now fully assured Kasaku is physically the better man*): 'Return my wife? You say to return her? Right quickly shall she be returned, at once!'

So far everything is clear enough. Then Ichirō hurries home, caresses his wife, assures her of his love, tells her all, and sends her, not to Kasaku's house, but to that of her brother. Two days later, a little after dark, O-Noto is called to the door by her husband, and the two disappear in the night.

ACT II. *Night scene. House of Kasaku closed; light appears through chinks of sliding shutters. Shadow of a woman approaches. Sound of knocking. Shutters slide back.*

Wife of Kasaku (recognizing O-Noto): 'Aa! aa! Joyful it is to see you! Deign to enter, and some honorable tea to take.'

O-Noto (speaking very sweetly): 'Thanks indeed. But where is Kasaku San?'

Wife of Kasaku: 'To the other village he has gone, but must soon return. Deign to come in and wait for him.'

O-Noto (still more sweetly). 'Very great thanks. A little, and I come. But first I must tell my brother.'

(Bows, and slips off into the darkness, and becomes a shadow again, which joins another shadow. The two shadows remain motionless.)

ACT III. *Scene: Bank of a river at night, fringed by pines. Silhouette of the house of Kasaku far away. O-Noto and Ichirō under the trees, Ichirō with a lantern. Both have white towels tightly bound round their heads; their robes are girded well up, and their sleeves caught back with tasuki cords, to leave the arms free. Each carries a long sword.*

It is the hour, as the Japanese most expressively say, 'when the sound of the river is loudest.' There is no other sound but a long occasional humming of wind in the needles of the pines; for it is late autumn, and the frogs are silent. The two shadows do not speak, and the sound of the river grows louder.

Suddenly there is the noise of a plash far off – somebody crossing the shallow stream; then an echo of wooden sandals – irregular, staggering – the footsteps of a drunkard, coming nearer and nearer. The drunkard lifts up his voice: it is Kasaku's voice. He sings:

> 'Suita okata ni suirarete;
> Ya-ton-ton!'[5]

– a song of love and wine.

Immediately the two shadows start toward the singer at a run – a noiseless flitting, for their feet are shod with waraji. Kasaku still sings. Suddenly a loose stone turns under him; he wrenches his ankle, and utters a growl of anger. Almost in the same instant a lantern is held close to his face. Perhaps for thirty seconds it remains

---

5. The meaning is, 'Give to the beloved one a little more [wine].' The 'Ya-ton-ton' is only a burden, without exact meaning, like our own 'With a hey! and a ho!' etc.

there. No one speaks. The yellow light shows three strangely in-expressive masks rather than visages. Kasaku sobers at once — recognizing the faces, remembering the incident of the bathhouse, and seeing the swords. But he is not afraid, and presently bursts into a mocking laugh.

'Hé! hé! The Ichirō pair! And so you take me, too, for a baby? What are you doing with such things in your hands? Let me show you how to use them.'

But Ichirō, who has dropped the lantern, suddenly delivers, with the full swing of both hands, a sword-slash that nearly severs Kasaku's right arm from the shoulder; and as the victim staggers, the sword of the woman cleaves through his left shoulder. He falls with one fearful cry, *'Hitogoroshi!'* which means 'murder.' But he does not cry again. For ten whole minutes the swords are busy with him. The lantern, still glowing, lights the ghastliness. Two belated pedestrians approach, hear, see, drop their wooden sandals from their feet, and flee back into the darkness without a word. Ichirō and O-Noto sit down by the lantern to take breath, for the work was hard.

The son of Kasaku, a boy of fourteen, comes running to find his father. He has heard the song, then the cry; but he has not yet learned fear. The two suffer him to approach. As he nears O-Noto, the woman seizes him, flings him down, twists his slender arms under her knees, and clutches the sword. But Ichirō, still panting, cries, 'No! no! Not the boy! He did us no wrong!' O-Noto releases him. He is too stupefied to move. She slaps his face terribly, crying, 'Go!' He runs, not daring to shriek.

Ichirō and O-Noto leave the chopped mass, walk to the house of Kasaku, and call loudly. There is no reply — only the pathetic, crouching silence of women and children waiting death. But they are bidden not to fear. Then Ichirō cries:

'Honorable funeral prepare! Kasaku by my hand is now dead!'

'And by mine!' shrills O-Noto.

Then the footsteps recede.

ACT IV. *Scene: Interior of Ichirō's house. Three persons kneeling in the guest-room: Ichirō, his wife, and an aged woman, who is weeping.*

Ichirō: 'And now, mother, to leave you alone in this world, though you have no other son, is indeed an evil thing. I can only pray your forgiveness. But my uncle will always care for you, and to his house you must go at once, since it is time we two should die. No common, vulgar death shall we have, but an elegant, splendid death – *Rippana!* And you must not see it. Now go.'

She passes away, with a wail. The doors are solidly barred behind her. All is ready.

O-Noto thrusts the point of the sword into her throat. But she still struggles. With a last kind word Ichirō ends her pain by a stroke that severs the head.

And then?

Then he takes his writing-box, prepares the inkstone, grinds some ink, chooses a good brush, and, on carefully selected paper, composes five poems, of which this is the last:

> *Meido yori*
> *Yu dempō ga*
> *Aru naraba,*
> *Hayaku an chaku*
> *Mōshi okuran.*[6]

Then he cuts his own throat perfectly well.

Now, it was clearly shown, during the official investigation of these facts, that Ichirō and his wife had been universally liked, and had been from their childhood noted for amiability.

The scientific problem of the origin of the Japanese has never yet been solved. But sometimes it seems to me that those who argue in favor of a partly Malay origin have some psychological evidence in their favor. Under the submissive sweetness of the gentlest Japanese woman – a sweetness of which the Occidental can scarcely form any idea – there exist possibilities of hardness absolutely inconceivable without ocular evidence. A thousand times she can forgive, can sacrifice herself in a thousand ways, unutterably touching; but let one particular soul-nerve be stung, and fire shall forgive sooner than she. Then there may suddenly appear in that frail-seeming woman an incredible courage, an appalling, measured, tireless purpose of honest vengeance. Under all the amazing self-control and patience of the

---

6. The meaning is about as follows: 'If from the Meido it be possible to send letters or telegrams, I shall write and forward news of our speedy safe arrival there.'

man there exists an adamantine something very dangerous to reach. Touch it wantonly, and there can be no pardon. But resentment is seldom likely to be excited by mere hazard. Motives are keenly judged. An error can be forgiven; deliberate malice never.

In the house of any rich family the guest is likely to be shown some of the heirlooms. Among these are almost sure to be certain articles belonging to those elaborate tea ceremonies peculiar to Japan. A pretty little box, perhaps, will be set before you. Opening it, you see only a beautiful silk bag, closed with a silk running-cord decked with tiny tassels. Very soft and choice the silk is, and elaborately figured. What marvel can be hidden under such a covering? You open the bag, and see within another bag, of a different quality of silk, but very fine. Open that, and lo! a third, which contains a fourth, which contains a fifth, which contains a sixth, which contains a seventh bag, which contains the strangest, roughest, hardest vessel of Chinese clay that you ever beheld. Yet it is not only curious but precious: it may be more than a thousand years old.

Even thus have centuries of the highest social culture wrapped the Japanese character about with many priceless soft coverings of courtesy, of delicacy, of patience, of sweetness, of moral sentiment. But underneath these charming multiple coverings there remains the primitive clay, hard as iron; kneaded perhaps with all the mettle of the Mongol, all the dangerous suppleness of the Malay.

VII

28 December. Beyond the high fence inclosing my garden in the rear rise the thatched roofs of some very small houses occupied by families of the poorest class. From one of these little dwellings there continually issues a sound of groaning – deep groaning of a man in pain. I have heard it for more than a week, both night and day, but latterly the sounds have been growing longer and louder, as if every breath were an agony: 'Somebody there is very sick,' says Manyemon, my old interpreter, with an expression of extreme sympathy.

The sounds have begun to make me nervous. I reply, rather brutally, 'I think it would be better for all concerned if that somebody were dead.'

Manyemon makes three times a quick, sudden gesture with both hands, as if to throw off the influence of my wicked words, mutters a little Buddhist prayer, and leaves me with a look of reproach. Then, conscience-stricken, I send a servant to inquire if the sick person has a doctor, and whether any aid can be given. Presently the servant returns with the information that a doctor is regularly attending the sufferer, and that nothing else can be done.

I notice, however, that, in spite of his cobwebby gestures, Manyemon's patient nerves have also become affected by those sounds. He has even confessed that he wants to stay in the little front room, near the street, so as to be away from them as far as possible. I can neither write nor read. My study being in the extreme rear, the groaning is there almost as audible as if the sick man were in the room itself. There is always in such utterances of suffering a certain ghastly timbre by which the intensity of the suffering can be estimated; and I keep asking myself, How can it be possible for the human being making those sounds by which I am tortured, to endure much longer?

It is a positive relief, later in the morning, to hear the moaning drowned by the beating of a little Buddhist drum in the sick man's room, and the chanting of the *Namu-myō-hō-ren-ge-kyō* by a multitude of voices. Evidently there is a gathering of priests and relatives in the house. 'Somebody is going to die,' Manyemon says. And he also repeats the holy words of praise to the Lotus of the Good Law.

The chanting and the tapping of the drum continue for several hours. As they cease, the groaning is heard again. Every breath a groan! Toward evening it grows worse — horrible. Then it suddenly stops. There is a dead silence of minutes. And then we hear a passionate burst of weeping — the weeping of a woman — and voices calling a name. 'Ah! somebody is dead!' Manyemon says.

We hold council. Manyemon has found out that the people are miserably poor; and I, because my conscience smites me, propose to send them the amount of the funeral expenses, a very small sum. Manyemon thinks I wish to do this out of pure benevolence, and says pretty things. We send the servant with a kind message, and instructions to learn if possible the history of the dead man. I cannot help suspecting some sort of tragedy; and a Japanese tragedy is generally interesting.

*

29 December. As I had surmised, the story of the dead man was worth learning. The family consisted of four – the father and mother, both very old and feeble, and two sons. It was the eldest son, a man of thirty-four, who had died. He had been sick for seven years. The younger brother, a kurumaya, had been the sole support of the whole family. He had no vehicle of his own, but hired one, paying five sen a day for the use of it. Though strong and a swift runner, he could earn little: there is in these days too much competition for the business to be profitable. It taxed all his powers to support his parents and his ailing brother; nor could he have done it without unfailing self-denial. He never indulged himself even to the extent of a cup of saké; he remained unmarried; he lived only for his filial and fraternal duty.

This was the story of the dead brother: When about twenty years of age, and following the occupation of a fish-seller, he had fallen in love with a pretty servant at an inn. The girl returned his affection. They pledged themselves to each other. But difficulties arose in the way of their marriage. The girl was pretty enough to have attracted the attention of a man of some means, who demanded her hand in the customary way. She disliked him; but the conditions he was able to offer decided her parents in his favor. Despairing of union, the two lovers resolved to perform jōshi. Somewhere or other they met at night, renewed their pledge in wine, and bade farewell to the world. The young man then killed his sweetheart with one blow of a sword, and immediately afterward cut his own throat with the same weapon. But people rushed into the room before he had expired, took away the sword, sent for the police, and summoned a military surgeon from the garrison. The would-be suicide was removed to the hospital, skillfully nursed back to health, and after some months of convalescence was put on trial for murder.

What sentence was passed I could not fully learn. In those days, Japanese judges used a good deal of personal discretion when dealing with emotional crime; and their exercise of pity had not yet been restricted by codes framed upon Western models. Perhaps in this case they thought that to have survived a jōshi was in itself a severe punishment. Public opinion is less merciful, in such instances, than law. After a term of imprisonment the miserable man was allowed to return to his family, but was placed under perpetual police surveillance. The people shrank from him. He made the mistake of living on. Only his parents and brother remained to him. And soon he became a victim of unspeakable physical suffering; yet he clung to life.

The old wound in his throat, although treated at the time as skill-fully as circumstances permitted, began to cause terrible pain. After its apparent healing, some slow cancerous growth commenced to spread from it, reaching into the breathing-passages above and below where the sword-blade had passed. The surgeon's knife, the torture of the cautery, could only delay the end. But the man lingered through seven years of continually increasing agony. There are dark beliefs about the results of betraying the dead — of breaking the mutual promise to travel together to the Meido. Men said that the hand of the murdered girl always reopened the wound — undid by night all that the surgeon could accomplish by day. For at night the pain invariably increased, becoming most terrible at the precise hour of the attempted shinjū!

Meanwhile, through abstemiousness and extraordinary self-denial, the family found means to pay for medicines, for attendance, and for more nourishing food than they themselves ever indulged in. They prolonged by all possible means the life that was their shame, their poverty, their burden. And now that death has taken away that burden, they weep!

Perhaps all of us learn to love that which we train ourselves to make sacrifices for, whatever pain it may cause. Indeed, the question might be asked whether we do not love most that which causes us most pain.

At a Railway Station

Seventh day of the sixth Month;
twenty-sixth of Meiji

Yesterday a telegram from Fukuoka announced that a desperate criminal captured there would be brought for trial to Kumamoto today, on the train due at noon. A Kumamoto policeman had gone to Fukuoka to take the prisoner in charge.

Four years ago a strong thief entered some house by night in the Street of the Wrestlers, terrified and bound the inmates, and carried away a number of valuable things. Tracked skillfully by the police, he was captured within twenty-four hours — even before he could dispose of his plunder. But as he was being taken to the police station he burst his bonds, snatched the sword of his captor, killed him, and escaped. Nothing more was heard of him until last week.

Then a Kumamoto detective, happening to visit the Fukuoka prison, saw among the toilers a face that had been four years photographed upon his brain. 'Who is that man?' he asked the guard. 'A thief,' was the reply, 'registered here as Kusabé.' The detective walked up to the prisoner and said:

'Kusabé is not your name. Nomura Teïchi, you are needed in Kumamoto for murder.' The felon confessed all.

I went with a great throng of people to witness the arrival at the station. I expected to hear and see anger; I even feared possibilities of violence. The murdered officer had been much liked; his relatives would certainly be among the spectators; and a Kumamoto crowd is not very gentle. I also thought to find many police on duty. My anticipations were wrong.

The train halted in the usual scene of hurry and noise, scurry and clatter of passengers wearing geta, screaming of boys wanting to sell Japanese newspapers and Kumamoto lemonade. Outside the barrier we waited for nearly five minutes. Then, pushed through the wicket by a police-sergeant, the prisoner appeared – a large wild-looking man, with head bowed down, and arms fastened behind his back. Prisoner and guard both halted in front of the wicket; and the people pressed forward to see – but in silence. Then the officer called out:

'Sugihara San! Sugihara O-Kibi! is she present?'

A slight small woman standing near me, with a child on her back, answered, 'Hai!' and advanced through the press. This was the widow of the murdered man; the child she carried was his son. At a wave of the officer's hand the crowd fell back, so as to leave a clear space about the prisoner and his escort. In that space the woman with the child stood facing the murderer. The hush was of death.

Not to the woman at all, but the child only, did the officer then speak. He spoke low, but so clearly that I could catch every syllable:

'Little one, this is the man who killed your father four years ago. You had not yet been born; you were in your mother's womb. That you have no father to love you now is the doing of this man. Look at him' – here the officer, putting a hand to the prisoner's chin, sternly forced him to lift his eyes – 'look well at him, little boy! Do not be afraid. It is painful; but it is your duty. Look at him!'

Over the mother's shoulder the boy gazed with eyes widely open, as in fear; then he began to sob; then tears came; but steadily and obediently he still looked – looked – looked – straight into the cringing face.

The crowd seemed to have stopped breathing.

I saw the prisoner's features distort; I saw him suddenly dash himself down upon his knees despite his fetters, and beat his face into the dust, crying out the while in a passion of hoarse remorse that made one's heart shake:

'Pardon! pardon! pardon me, little one! That I did – not for hate was it done; but in mad fear only, in my desire to escape. Very, very wicked I have been; great unspeakable wrong have I done you! But now for my sin I go to die. I wish to die; I am glad to die! Therefore, O little one, be pitiful! – forgive me!'

The child still cried silently. The officer raised the shaking criminal: the dumb crowd parted left and right to let them by. Then, quite suddenly, the whole multitude began to sob. And as the bronzed guardian passed, I saw what I had never seen before — what few men ever see — what I shall probably never see again — the tears of a Japanese policeman.

The crowd ebbed, and left me musing on the strange morality of the spectacle. Here was justice unswerving yet compassionate, forcing knowledge of a crime by the pathetic witness of its simplest result. Here was desperate remorse, praying only for pardon before death. And here was a populace — perhaps the most dangerous in the empire when angered — comprehending all, touched by all, satisfied with the contrition and the shame, and filled, not with wrath, but only with the great sorrow of the sin — through simple deep experience of the difficulties of life and the weaknesses of human nature.

But the most significant, because the most Oriental, fact of the episode was that the appeal to remorse had been made through the criminal's sense of fatherhood — that potential love of children which is so large a part of the soul of every Japanese.

There is a story that the most famous of all Japanese robbers, Ishikawa Goëmon, once by night entering a house to kill and steal, was charmed by the smile of a baby which reached out hands to him, and that he remained playing with the little creature until all chance of carrying out his purpose was lost.

It is not hard to believe this story. Every year the police records tell of compassion shown to children by professional criminals. Some months ago a terrible murder case was reported in the local papers, the slaughter of a household by robbers. Seven persons had been literally hewn to pieces while asleep; but the police discovered a little boy quite unharmed, crying alone in a pool of blood; and they found evidence unmistakable that the men who slew must have taken great care not to hurt the child.

In Cholera-Time

China's chief ally in the late war, being deaf and blind, knew nothing, and still knows nothing, of treaties or of peace. It followed the returning armies of Japan, invaded the victorious empire, and killed about thirty thousand people during the hot season. It is still slaying; and the funeral-pyres burn continually. Sometimes the smoke and the odor come wind-blown into my garden down from the hills behind the town, just to remind me that the cost of burning an adult of my own size is eighty sen — about half a dollar in American money at the present rate of exchange.

From the upper balcony of my house, the whole length of a Japanese street, with its rows of little shops, is visible down to the bay. Out of various houses in that street I have seen cholera-patients conveyed to the hospital — the last one (only this morning) my neighbor across the way, who kept a porcelain shop. He was removed by force, in spite of the tears and cries of his family. The sanitary law forbids the treatment of cholera in private houses; yet people try to hide their sick, in spite of fines and other penalties, because the public cholera-hospitals are overcrowded and roughly managed, and the patients are entirely separated from all who love them. But the police are not often deceived: they soon discover unreported cases, and come with litters and coolies. It seems cruel; but sanitary law must be cruel. My neighbor's wife followed the litter, crying, until the police obliged her to return to her desolate little shop. It is now closed up, and will probably never be opened again by the owners.

Such tragedies end as quickly as they begin. The bereaved, so soon as the law allows, remove their pathetic belongings, and disappear; and the ordinary life of the street goes on, by day and by night, exactly as if nothing particular had happened. Itinerant venders, with their bamboo poles and baskets or buckets or boxes, pass the empty houses, and utter their accustomed cries; religious processions go by, chanting fragments of sutras; the blind shampooer blows his melancholy whistle; the private watchman makes his heavy staff boom upon the gutter-flags; the boy who sells confectionery still taps his drum, and sings a love song with a plaintive sweet voice, like a girl's:

'*You and I together* ... I remained long; yet in the moment of going I thought I had only just come.

'*You and I together* ... Still I think of the tea. Old or new tea of Uji it might have seemed to others; but to me it was Gyokorō tea, of the beautiful yellow of the yamabuki flower.

'*You and I together* ... I am the telegraph-operator; you are the one who waits the message. I send my heart, and you receive it. What care we now if the posts should fall, if the wires be broken?'

And the children sport as usual. They chase one another with screams and laughter; they dance in chorus; they catch dragon-flies and tie them to long strings; they sing burdens of the war, about cutting off Chinese heads:

'*Chan-chan bozu no
Kubi wo hané!*'

Sometimes a child vanishes; but the survivors continue their play. And this is wisdom.

It costs only forty-four sen to burn a child. The son of one of my neighbors was burned a few days ago. The little stones with which he used to play lie there in the sun just as he left them ... Curious, this child-love of stones! Stones are the toys not only of the children of the poor, but of all children at one period of existence: no matter how well supplied with other playthings, every Japanese child wants sometimes to play with stones. To the child-mind a stone is a marvelous thing, and ought so to be, since even to the understanding of the mathematician there can be nothing more wonderful than a common stone. The tiny urchin suspects the stone to be much more than it seems, which is an excellent suspicion; and if stupid grown-up folk did not untruthfully tell him that his plaything is not worth thinking about, he would never tire of it, and would always be finding something new and extraordinary in it. Only a very great mind could answer all a child's questions about stones.

According to popular faith, my neighbor's darling is now playing with small ghostly stones in the Dry Bed of the River of Souls — wondering, perhaps, why they cast no shadows. The true poetry in the legend of the Sai-no-Kawara is the absolute naturalness of its principal idea — the phantom-continuation of that play which all little Japanese children play with stones.

II

The pipe-stem seller used to make his round with two large boxes suspended from a bamboo pole balanced upon his shoulder: one box containing stems of various diameters, lengths, and colors, together with tools for fitting them into metal pipes; and the other box containing a baby — his own baby. Sometimes I saw it peeping over the edge of the box, and smiling at the passers-by; sometimes I saw it lying, well wrapped up and fast asleep, in the bottom of the box; sometimes I saw it playing with toys. Many people, I was told, used to give it toys. One of the toys bore a curious resemblance to a mortuary tablet (ihai); and this I always observed in the box, whether the child were asleep or awake.

The other day I discovered that the pipe-stem seller had abandoned his bamboo pole and suspended boxes. He was coming up the street with a little hand-cart just big enough to hold his wares and his baby, and evidently built for that purpose in two compartments. Perhaps the baby had become too heavy for the more primitive method of conveyance. Above the cart fluttered a small white flag, bearing in cursive characters the legend *Kiseru-rao kae* (pipe-stems exchanged), and a brief petition for 'honorable help,' *O-tasuké wo negaimasu.* The child seemed well and happy; and I again saw the tablet-shaped object which had so often attracted my notice before. It was now fastened upright to a high box in the cart facing the infant's bed. As I watched the cart approaching, I suddenly felt convinced that the tablet was really an ihai: the sun shone full upon it, and there was no mistaking the conventional Buddhist text. This aroused my curiosity; and I asked Manyemon to tell the pipe-stem seller that we had a number of pipes needing fresh stems, which was true. Presently the cartlet drew up at our gate, and I went to look at it.

The child was not afraid, even of a foreign face — a pretty boy. He lisped and laughed and held out his arms, being evidently used to petting; and while playing with him I looked closely at the tablet. It was a Shinshū ihai, bearing a woman's kaimyō, or posthumous name; and Manyemon translated the Chinese characters for me: *Revered and of good rank in the Mansion of Excellence, the thirty-first day of the third month of the twenty-eighth year of Meiji.* Meantime a servant had fetched the pipes which needed new stems; and I glanced at the face of the artisan as he worked. It was the face of a man past middle age, with those worn, sympathetic lines about the mouth, dry beds of old smiles, which give to so many Japanese faces an indescribable expression of resigned gentleness. Presently Manyemon began to ask questions; and when Manyemon asks questions, not to reply is possible for the wicked only. Sometimes behind that dear innocent old head I think I see the dawning of an aureole — the aureole of the Bosatsu.

The pipe-stem seller answered by telling his story. Two months after the birth of their little boy, his wife had died. In the last hour of her illness she had said: 'From what time I die till three full years be past I pray you to leave the child always united with the Shadow of me: never let him be separated from my ihai, so that I may continue to care for him and to nurse him — since thou knowest that he should have the breast for three years. This, my last asking, I entreat thee, do not forget.' But the mother being dead, the father could not labor as he had been wont to do, and also take care of so young a child, requiring continual attention both night and day; and he was too poor to hire a nurse. So he took to selling pipe-stems, as he could thus make a little money without leaving the child even for a minute alone. He could not afford to buy milk; but he had fed the boy for more than a year with rice gruel and amé syrup.

I said that the child looked very strong, and none the worse for lack of milk.

'That,' declared Manyemon, in a tone of conviction bordering on reproof, 'is because the dead mother nurses him. How should he want for milk?'

And the boy laughed softly, as if conscious of a ghostly caress.

A Letter from Japan

Here, in this quiet suburb, where the green peace is broken only by the voices of children at play and the shrilling of cicadæ, it is difficult to imagine that, a few hundred miles away, there is being carried on one of the most tremendous wars of modern times, between armies aggregating more than half a million of men, or that, on the intervening sea, a hundred ships of war have been battling. This contest, between the mightiest of Western powers and a people that began to study Western science only within the recollection of many persons still in vigorous life, is, on one side at least, a struggle for national existence. It was inevitable, this struggle − might perhaps have been delayed, but certainly not averted. Japan has boldly challenged an empire capable of threatening simultaneously the civilizations of the East and the West − a medieval power that, unless vigorously checked, seems destined to absorb Scandinavia and to dominate China. For all industrial civilization the contest is one of vast moment; for Japan it is probably the supreme crisis in her national life. As to what her fleets and her armies have been doing, the world is fully informed; but as to what her people are doing at home, little has been written.

To inexperienced observation they would appear to be doing nothing unusual; and this strange calm is worthy of record. At the beginning of hostilities an Imperial mandate was issued, bidding all non-combatants to pursue their avocations as usual, and to trouble themselves as little as possible about exterior events; and this command has been obeyed to the letter. It would be natural to suppose that all the sacrifices, tragedies, and uncertainties of the contest had thrown their gloom over the life of the capital in especial; but there is really nothing whatever to indicate a condition of anxiety or depression.

On the contrary, one is astonished by the joyous tone of public confidence, and the admirably restrained pride of the nation in its victories. Western tides have strewn the coast with Japanese corpses; regiments have been blown out of existence in the storming of positions defended by wire-entanglements; battleships have been lost: yet at no moment has there been the least public excitement. The people are following their daily occupations just as they did before the war; the cheery aspect of things is just the same; the theatres and flower displays are not less well patronized. The life of Tōkyō has been, to outward seeming, hardly more affected by the events of the war than the life of nature beyond it, where the flowers are blooming and the butterflies hovering as in other summers. Except after the news of some great victory — celebrated with fireworks and lantern processions — there are no signs of public emotion; and but for the frequent distribution of newspaper extras, by runners ringing bells, you could almost persuade yourself that the whole story of the war is an evil dream.

Yet there has been, of necessity, a vast amount of suffering — viewless and voiceless suffering — repressed by that sense of social and patriotic duty which is Japanese religion. As a seventeen-syllable poem of the hour tells us, the news of every victory must bring pain as well as joy:

> *Gōgwai no*
> *Tabi teki mikata*
> *Goké ga fuè.*

'Each time that an extra is circulated the widows of foes and friends have increased in multitude.'

The great quiet and the smiling tearlessness testify to the more than Spartan discipline of the race. Anciently the people were trained, not only to conceal their emotions, but to speak in a cheerful voice and to show a pleasant face under any stress of moral suffering; and they are obedient to that teaching today. It would still be thought a shame to betray personal sorrow for the loss of those who die for Emperor and fatherland. The public seem to view the events of the war as they would watch the scenes of a popular play. They are interested without being excited; and their extraordinary self-control is particularly shown in various manifestations of the 'Play-impulse.'

Everywhere the theatres are producing war dramas (based upon actual fact); the newspapers and magazines are publishing war stories and novels; the cinematograph exhibits the monstrous methods of modern warfare, the numberless industries are turning out objects of art or utility designed to commemorate the Japanese triumphs.

But the present psychological condition, the cheerful and even playful tone of public feeling, can be indicated less by any general statement than by the mention of ordinary facts – everyday matters recorded in the writer's diary.

Never before were the photographers so busy; It is said that they have not been able to fulfill half of the demands made upon them. The hundreds of thousands of men sent to the war wished to leave photographs with their families, and also to take with them portraits of parents, children, and other beloved persons. The nation was being photographed during the past six months.

A fact of sociological interest is that photography has added something new to the poetry of the domestic faith. From the time of its first introduction, photography became popular in Japan; and none of those superstitions, which inspire fear of the camera among less civilized races, offered any obstacle to the rapid development of a new industry. It is true that there exists some queer-folk beliefs about photographs – ideas of mysterious relation between the sun-picture and the person imaged. For example: if, in the photograph of a group, one figure appear indistinct or blurred, that is thought to be an omen of sickness or death. But this superstition has its industrial value: It has compelled photographers to be careful about their work – especially in these days of war, when everybody wants to have a good clear portrait, because the portrait might be needed for another purpose than preservation in an album.

During the last twenty years there has gradually come into existence the custom of placing the photograph of a dead parent, brother, husband, or child, beside the mortuary tablet kept in the Buddhist household shrine. For this reason, also, the departing soldier wishes to leave at home a good likeness of himself.

The rites of domestic affection, in old samurai families, are not confined to the cult of the dead. On certain occasions, the picture

153

of the absent parent, husband, brother, or betrothed, is placed in the alcove of the guest-room, and a feast is laid out before it. The photograph, in such cases, is fixed upon a little stand (dai); and the feast is served as if the person were present. This pretty custom of preparing a meal for the absent is probably more ancient than any art of portraiture; but the modern photograph adds to the human poetry of the rite. In feudal time it was the rule to set the repast facing the direction in which the absent person had gone — north, south, east, or west. After a brief interval the covers of the vessels containing the cooked food were lifted and examined. If the lacquered inner surface was thickly beaded with vapor, all was well; but if the surface was dry, that was an omen of death, a sign that the disembodied spirit had returned to absorb the essence of the offerings.

As might have been expected, in a country where the 'play-impulse' is stronger, perhaps, than in any other part of the world, the *Zeitgeist* found manifestation in the flower displays of the year. I visited those in my neighborhood, which is the Quarter of the Gardeners. This quarter is famous for its azaleas (tsutsuji); and every spring the azalea gardens attract thousands of visitors, not only by the wonderful exhibition then made of shrubs which look like solid masses of blossom (ranging up from snowy white, through all shades of pink, to a flamboyant purple), but also by displays of effigies: groups of figures ingeniously formed with living leaves and flowers. These figures, life-size, usually represent famous incidents of history or drama. In many cases — though not in all — the bodies and the costumes are composed of foliage and flowers trained to grow about a framework; while the faces, feet, and hands are represented by some kind of flesh-colored composition.

This year, however, a majority of the displays represented scenes of the war, such as an engagement between Japanese infantry and mounted Cossacks, a night attack by torpedo boats, the sinking of a battleship. In the last-mentioned display, Russian bluejackets appeared, swimming for their lives in a rough sea, the pasteboard waves and the swimming figures being made to rise and fall by the pulling of a string, while the crackling of quick-firing guns was imitated by a mechanism contrived with sheets of zinc.

It is said that Admiral Tōgō sent to Tōkyō for some flowering-trees in pots – inasmuch as his responsibilities allowed him no chance of seeing the cherry-flowers and the plum-blossoms in their season – and that the gardeners responded even too generously.

Almost immediately after the beginning of hostilities, thousands of 'war pictures' – mostly cheap lithographs – were published. The drawing and coloring were better than those of the prints issued at the time of the war with China; but the details were to a great extent imaginary – altogether imaginary as to the appearance of Russian troops. Pictures of the engagements with the Russian fleet were effective, despite some lurid exaggeration. The most startling things were pictures of Russian defeats in Korea, published before a single military engagement had taken place; the artist had 'flushed to anticipate the scene.' In these prints the Russians were depicted as fleeing in utter rout, leaving their officers – very fine-looking officers – dead upon the field, while the Japanese infantry, with dreadfully determined faces, were coming up at a double. The propriety and the wisdom of thus pictorially predicting victory, and easy victory to boot, may be questioned. But I am told that the custom of so doing is an old one; and it is thought that to realize the common hope thus imaginatively is lucky. At all events, there is no attempt at deception in these pictorial undertakings; they help to keep up the public courage, and they ought to be pleasing to the gods.

Some of the earlier pictures have now been realized in grim fact. The victories in China had been similarly foreshadowed: they amply justified the faith of the artist … Today the war pictures continue to multiply; but they have changed character. The inexorable truth of the photograph, and the sketches of the war correspondent, now bring all the vividness and violence of fact to help the artist's imagination. There was something naïve and theatrical in the drawings of anticipation; but the pictures of the hour represent the most tragic reality – always becoming more terrible. At this writing, Japan has yet lost no single battle; but not a few of her victories have been dearly won.

To enumerate even a tenth of the various articles ornamented with designs inspired by the war – articles such as combs, clasps, fans, brooches, card-cases, purses – would require a volume. Even cakes and confectionery are stamped with naval or military designs; and the glass or paper windows of shops — not to mention the sign-boards — have pictures of Japanese victories painted upon them. At night the shop lanterns proclaim the pride of the nation in its fleets and armies; and a whole chapter might easily be written about the new designs in transparencies and toy lanterns. A new revolving lantern — turned by the air-current which its own flame creates — has become very popular. It represents a charge of Japanese infantry upon Russian defenses; and holes pierced in the colored paper, so as to produce a continuous vivid flashing while the transparency revolves, suggest the exploding of shells and the volleying of machine guns.

Some displays of the art-impulse, as inspired by the war, have been made in directions entirely unfamiliar to Western experience — in the manufacture, for example, of women's hair ornaments and dress materials. Dress goods decorated with war pictures have actually become a fashion, especially crêpe silks for underwear, and figured silk linings for cloaks and sleeves. More remarkable than these are the new hairpins; by hairpins I mean those long double-pronged ornaments of flexible metal which are called kanzashi, and are more or less ornamented according to the age of the wearer. (The kanzashi made for young girls are highly decorative; those worn by older folk are plain, or adorned only with a ball of coral or polished stone.) The new hairpins might be called commemorative: one, of which the decoration represents a British and a Japanese flag intercrossed, celebrates the Anglo-Japanese alliance; another represents an officer's cap and sword; and the best of all is surmounted by a tiny metal model of a battleship. The battleship-pin is not merely fantastic: it is actually pretty!

As might have been expected, military and naval subjects occupy a large place among the year's designs for toweling. The towel designs celebrating naval victories have been particularly successful: they are mostly in white, on a blue ground; or in black, on a white ground. One of the best — blue and white — represented only a flock of gulls wheeling about the masthead of a sunken iron-clad, and, far away, the silhouettes of Japanese battleships passing to the horizon ... What especially struck me in this, and in several other designs, was the original manner in which the Japanese artist had seized upon the traits of the modern battleship — the powerful and sinister lines of its shape — just as he would have caught for us the typical character of a beetle or a lobster. The lines have been just enough exaggerated to convey, at one glance, the real impression made by the aspect of these iron monsters — a vague impression of bulk and force and menace, very difficult to express by ordinary methods of drawing.

Besides towels decorated with artistic sketches of this sort, there have been placed upon the market many kinds of towels bearing comic war pictures — caricatures or cartoons which are amusing without being malignant. It will be remembered that at the time of the first attack made upon the Port Arthur squadron, several of the Russian officers were in the Dalny theater, never dreaming that the Japanese would dare to strike the first blow. This incident has been made the subject of a towel design. At one end of the towel is a comic study of the faces of the Russians, delightedly watching the gyrations of a ballet dancer. At the other end is a study of the same commanders when they find, on returning to the port, only the masts of their battleships above water. Another towel shows a procession of fish in front of a surgeon's office — waiting their turns to be relieved of sundry bayonets, swords, revolvers, and rifles, which have stuck in their throats. A third towel picture represents a Russian diver examining, with a prodigious magnifying-glass, the holes made by torpedoes in the hull of a sunken cruiser. Comic verses or legends, in cursive text, are printed beside these pictures.

The great house of Mitsui, which placed the best of these designs on the market, also produced some beautiful souvenirs of the war, in the shape of fukusa. (A fukusa is an ornamental silk covering, or wrapper, put over presents sent to friends on certain occasions, and returned after the present has been received.) These are made of the heaviest and costliest silk, and inclosed within appropriately decorated covers. Upon one fukusa is a colored picture of the cruisers *Nisshin* and *Kasuga*, under full steam; and upon another has been printed, in beautiful Chinese characters, the full text of the Imperial Declaration of War.

But the strangest things that I have seen in this line of production were silk dresses for baby girls — figured stuffs which, when looked at from a little distance, appeared incomparably pretty, owing to the masterly juxtaposition of tints and colors. On closer inspection the charming design proved to be composed entirely of war pictures, or, rather, fragments of pictures, blended into one astonishing combination:

naval battles; burning warships; submarine mines exploding; torpedo boats attacking; charges of Cossacks repulsed by Japanese infantry; artillery rushing into position; storming of forts; long lines of soldiery advancing through mist. Here were colors of blood and fire, tints of morning haze and evening glow, noon-blue and starred night-purple, sea-gray and field-green — most wonderful thing! ... I suppose that the child of a military or naval officer might, without impropriety, be clad in such a robe. But then — the unspeakable pity of things!

The war toys are innumerable: I can attempt to mention only a few of the more remarkable kinds.

Japanese children play many sorts of card games, some of which are old, others quite new. There are poetical card games, for example, played with a pack of which each card bears the text of a poem, or part of a poem; and the player should be able to remember the name of the author of any quotation in the set. Then there are geographical card games, in which each of the cards used bears the name, and perhaps a little picture, of some famous site, town, or temple; and the player should be able to remember the district and province in which the mentioned place is situated. The latest novelty in this line is a pack of cards with pictures upon them of the Russian war vessels; and the player should be able to state what has become of every vessel named, whether sunk, disabled, or confined in Port Arthur.

There is another card game in which the battleships, cruisers, and torpedo craft of both Japan and Russia are represented. The winner in this game destroys his 'captures' by tearing the cards taken. But the shops keep packages of each class of warship cards in stock; and when all the destroyers or cruisers of one country have been put *hors de combat*, the defeated party can purchase new vessels abroad. One torpedo boat costs about one farthing; but five torpedo boats can be bought for a penny.

The toy-shops are crammed with models of battleships — in wood, clay, porcelain, lead, and tin — of many sizes and prices. Some of the larger ones, moved by clockwork, are named after Japanese battleships: *Shikishima, Fuji, Mikasa*. One mechanical toy represents the sinking of a Russian vessel by a Japanese torpedo boat. Among cheaper things of this class is a box of colored sand, for the representation of naval engagements. Children arrange the sand so as to resemble waves; and with each box of sand are sold two fleets of tiny leaden vessels. The Japanese ships are white, and the Russian black; and explosions of torpedoes are to be figured by small cuttings of vermilion paper, planted in the sand.

The children of the poorest classes make their own war toys; and I have been wondering whether those ancient feudal laws (translated by Professor Wigmore) which fixed the cost and quality of toys to be given to children did not help to develop that ingenuity which the little folk display. Recently I saw a group of children in our neighborhood playing at the siege of Port Arthur, with fleets improvised out of scraps of wood and some rusty nails. A tub of water represented Port Arthur. Battleships were figured by bits of plank, into which chop-sticks had been fixed to represent masts, and rolls of paper to represent funnels. Little flags, appropriately colored, were fastened to the masts with rice paste. Torpedo boats were imaged by splinters, into each of which a short thick nail had been planted to indicate a smokestack. Stationary submarine mines were represented by small squares of wood, each having one long nail driven into it; and these little things, when dropped into water with the nail-head downwards, would keep up a curious bobbing motion for a long time. Other squares of wood, having clusters of short nails driven into them, represented floating mines: and the mimic battleships were made to drag for these, with lines of thread. The pictures in the Japanese papers had doubtless helped the children to imagine the events of the war with tolerable accuracy.

Naval caps for children have become, of course, more in vogue than ever before. Some of the caps bear, in Chinese characters of burnished metal, the name of a battleship, or the words *Nippon Teikoku* (Empire of Japan) — disposed like the characters upon the cap of a blue-jacket. On some caps, however, the ship's name appears in English letters — *Yashima*, *Fuji*, etc.

The play-impulse, I had almost forgotten to say, is shared by the soldiers themselves, though most of those called to the front do not expect to return in the body. They ask only to be remembered at the Spirit-Invoking Shrine (Shōkonsha), where the shades of all who die for Emperor and country are believed to gather. The men of the regiments temporarily quartered in our suburb, on their way to the war, found time to play at mimic war with the small folk of the neighborhood. (At all times Japanese soldiers are very kind to children; and the children here march with them, join in their military songs, and correctly salute their officers, feeling sure that the gravest officer will return the salute of a little child.) When the last regiment went away, the men distributed toys among the children assembled at the station to give them a parting cheer — hairpins, with military symbols for ornament, to the girls; wooden infantry and tin cavalry to the boys. The oddest present was a small clay model of a Russian soldier's head, presented with the jocose promise: 'If we come back, we shall bring you some real ones.' In the top of the head there is a small wire loop, to which a rubber string can be attached. At the time of the war with China, little clay models of Chinese heads, with very long queues, were favorite toys.

The war has also suggested a variety of new designs for that charming object, the toko-niwa. Few of my readers know what a toko-niwa, or 'alcove-garden,' is. It is a miniature garden — perhaps less than two feet square — contrived within an ornamental shallow basin of porcelain or other material, and placed in the alcove of a guest-room by way of decoration. You may see there a tiny pond; a streamlet crossed by humped bridges of Chinese pattern; dwarf trees forming a grove, and shading the model of a Shintō temple; imitations in baked clay of stone lanterns — perhaps even the appearance of a hamlet of thatched cottages. If the toko-niwa be not too small, you may see real fish swimming in the pond, or a pet tortoise crawling among the rockwork. Sometimes the miniature garden represents Hōrai, and the palace of the Dragon-King.

Two new varieties have come into fashion. One is a model of Port Arthur, showing the harbor and the forts; and with the materials for the display there is sold a little map, showing how to place certain tiny battleships, representing the imprisoned and the investing fleets. The other toko-niwa represents a Korean or Chinese landscape, with hill ranges and rivers and woods; and the appearance of a battle is created by masses of toy soldiers — cavalry, infantry, and artillery — in all positions of attack and defense. Minute forts of baked clay, bristling with cannon about the size of small pins, occupy elevated positions. When properly arranged the effect is panoramic. The soldiers in the foreground are about an inch long; those a little farther away about half as long; and those upon the hills are no larger than flies.

But the most remarkable novelty of this sort yet produced is a kind of toko-niwa recently on display at a famous shop in Ginza. A label bearing the inscription *Kaï-téï no Ikken* (View of the Ocean-Bed) sufficiently explained the design. The suïbon, or 'water-tray,' containing the display was half filled with rocks and sand so as to resemble a sea-bottom; and little fishes appeared swarming in the foreground. A little farther back, upon an elevation, stood Otohimé, the Dragon-King's daughter, surrounded by her maiden attendants, and gazing, with just the shadow of a smile, at two men in naval uniform who were shaking hands – dead heroes of the war: Admiral Makaroff and Commander Hirosé! ... These had esteemed each other in life; and it was a happy thought thus to represent their friendly meeting in the world of Spirits.

Though his name is perhaps unfamiliar to English readers, Commander Takeo Hirosé has become, deservedly, one of Japan's national heroes. On the 27th of March, during the second attempt made to block the entrance to Port Arthur, he was killed while endeavoring to help a comrade, a comrade who had formerly saved him from death. For five years Hirosé had been a naval attaché at St Petersburg, and had made many friends in Russian naval and military circles. From boyhood his life had been devoted to study and duty; and it was commonly said of him that he had no particle of selfishness in his nature. Unlike most of his brother officers, he remained unmarried, holding that no man who might be called on at any moment to lay down his life for his country had a moral right to marry. The only amusements in which he was ever known to indulge were physical exercises; and he was acknowledged one of the best jūjutsu (wrestlers) in the empire. The heroism of his death, at the age of thirty-six, had much less to do with the honors paid to his memory than the self-denying heroism of his life.

Now his picture is in thousands of homes, and his name is celebrated in every village. It is celebrated also by the manufacture of various souvenirs, which are sold by myriads. For example, there is a new fashion in sleeve-buttons, called Kinen-botan, or 'Commemoration-buttons.' Each button bears a miniature portrait of the commander, with the inscription *Shichi-shō hōkoku*, 'Even in seven successive lives – for love of country.' It is recorded that Hirosé often cited, to friends who criticized his ascetic devotion to duty, the famous utterance of Kusunoki Masashigé, who declared, ere laying down his life for the Emperor Go-Daigo, that he desired to die for his sovereign in seven successive existences.

But the highest honor paid to the memory of Hirosé is of a sort now possible only in the East, though once possible also in the West, when the Greek or Roman patriot-hero might be raised, by the common love of his people, to the place of the Immortals . . . Wine-cups of porcelain have been made, decorated with his portrait; and beneath the portrait appears, in ideographs of gold, the inscription *Gunshin Hirosé Chūsa*. The character 'gun' signifies war; the character 'shin,' a god – either in the sense of *divus* or *deus*, according to circumstances; and the Chinese text, read in the Japanese way, is *Ikusa no Kami*. Whether that stern and valiant spirit is really invoked by the millions who believe that no brave soul is doomed to extinction, no well-spent life laid down in vain, no heroism cast away, I do not know. But, in any event, human affection and gratitude can go no farther than this; and it must be confessed that Old Japan is still able to confer honors worth dying for.

Boys and girls in all the children's schools are now singing the Song of Hirosé Chūsa, which is a marching song. The words and the music are published in a little booklet, with a portrait of the late commander upon the cover. Everywhere, and at all hours of the day, one hears this song being sung:

'He whose every word and deed gave to men an example of what the war-folk of the Empire of Nippon should be – Commander Hirosé: is he really dead?

'Though the body die, the spirit dies not. He who wished to be reborn seven times into this world, for the sake of serving his country, for the sake of requiting the Imperial favor – Commander Hirosé: has he really died?

' "Since I am a son of the Country of the Gods, the fire of the evil-hearted Russians cannot touch me!" The sturdy Takeo who spoke thus: can he really be dead? ...

'Nay! that glorious war-death meant undying fame; beyond a thousand years the valiant heart shall live; as to a god of war shall reverence be paid to him ...'

Observing the playful confidence of this wonderful people in their struggle for existence against the mightiest power of the West — their perfect trust in the wisdom of their leaders and the valor of their armies, the good humor of their irony when mocking the enemy's blunders, their strange capacity to find, in the world-stirring events of the hour, the same amusement that they would find in watching a melodrama — one is tempted to ask: 'What would be the moral consequence of a national defeat?' ... It would depend, I think, upon circumstances. Were Kuropatkin able to fulfill his rash threat of invading Japan, the nation would probably rise as one man. But otherwise the ' nowledge of any great disaster would be bravely borne. From time unknown Japan has been a land of cataclysms — earthquakes that ruin cities in the space of a moment; tidal waves, two hundred miles long, sweeping whole coast populations out of existence; floods submerging hundreds of leagues of well-tilled fields; eruptions burying provinces. Calamities like this have disciplined the race in resignation and in patience; and it has been well trained also to bear with courage all the misfortunes of war. Even by the foreign peoples that have been most closely in contact with her, the capacities of Japan remained unguessed. Perhaps her power to resist aggression is far surpassed by her power to endure.

In a Japanese Hospital

追
憶

I

The last patient of the evening, a boy less than four years old, is received by nurses and surgeons with smiles and gentle flatteries, to which he does not at all respond ... He is both afraid and angry – especially angry – at finding himself in an hospital tonight: some indiscreet person assured him that he was being taken to the theatre; and he sang for joy on the way, forgetting the pain of his arm; and this is not the theatre! There are doctors here – doctors that hurt people ... He lets himself be stripped, and bears the examination without wincing; but when told that he must lie down upon a certain low table, under an electric lamp, he utters a very emphatic Iya![1] ... The experience inherited from his ancestors has assured him that to lie down in the presence of a possible enemy is not good; and by the same ghostly wisdom he has divined that the smile of the surgeon was intended to deceive ... 'But it will be so nice upon the table!' coaxingly observes a young nurse; 'see the pretty red cloth!' 'Iya!' repeats the little man – made only more wary by this appeal to aesthetic sentiment ... So they lay hands upon him – two surgeons and two nurses – lift him deftly, bear him to the table with the red cloth. Then he shouts his small cry of war – for he comes of good fighting stock – and, to the general alarm, battles most valiantly, in spite of that broken arm. But lo! a white wet cloth descends upon his eyes and mouth, and he cannot cry, and there is a strange sweet smell in his nostrils, and the voices and the lights have floated very, very far away, and he is sinking, sinking, sinking into wavy darkness ... The slight limbs relax; for a moment the breast heaves quickly, in the last fight of the lungs against the paralyzing anaesthetic: then

1. 'No!'

all motion stops ... Now the cloth is removed; and the face reappears – all the anger and pain gone out of it. So smile the little gods that watch the sleep of the dead ... Quickly the ends of the fractured bone are brought into place with a clear snap; bandages and cotton and plaster of Paris, and yet more bandages, are rapidly applied by expert hands; the face and little hands are sponged. Then the patient, still insensible, is wrapped in a blanket and taken away ... Interval, between entrance and exit: twelve minutes and a half.

Nothing is commonplace as seen for the first time; and the really painless details of the incident – the stifling of the cry, the sudden numbing of will, the subsequent pallid calm of the little face – so simulated tragedy as to set imagination wandering in darksome ways ... A single wicked blow would have produced exactly the same results of silence and smiling rest. Countless times in the countless ages of the past it must have done so; countless times passion must have discerned, in the sudden passionless beauty of the stricken, the eternal consequence of the act ... *Till the heavens be no more they shall not awake, nor be roused out of their sleep.* 'Till the heavens be no more' – but after? Thereafter – perhaps: yet never again the same ...

But I felt that I had been startled more than touched by that sudden suppression of the personality, the Self – because of the mystery thereby made manifest. In one moment – under the vapor of a chemical – voice, motion, will, thought, all pleasure and pain and memory, had ceased to be; the whole life of the budding senses – the delicate machinery of the little brain, with its possible priceless inheritance from countless generations – had been stilled and stopped as by the very touch of death. And there remained, to all outward seeming, only the form, the simulacrum – a doll of plastic flesh, with the faint unconscious smile of an icon ...

The faces of the little stone Buddhas, who dream by roadsides or above the graves, have the soft charm of Japanese infancy. They resemble the faces of children asleep; and you must have seen Japanese children asleep to know the curious beauty of the immature features – the vague sweetness of the lines of lids and lips. In the art of the Buddhist image-maker, the peace of the divine condition is suggested by the same shadowy smile that makes beautiful the slumber of the child.

II

The memory of icons naturally evoked remembrance of those powers which icons do but symbolize; and presently I found myself thinking that, to the vision of a God, the entire course of a human life would appear much like the incident which I had just witnessed – a coming, a crying and struggling, and a sudden vanishing of personality under the resistless anaesthetic of death. (I am not speaking of a cosmic divinity, to whom the interval between the kindling and the extinction of a sun would seem as brief as seems to us the flash of a firefly in the night: I mean an anthropomorphic God.) According to Herbert Spencer, the tiny consciousness of a gnat can distinguish intervals of time representing something between the ten-thousandth and the fifteen-thousandth part of a second. For a being as mentally superior to man as man to the gnat, would not the time of a generation appear but an instant? Would such a being perceive our human existence at all, except as a budding and a withering, a ceaseless swift succession of apparitions and disparitions, a mere phenomenon of fermentation peculiar to the surface of a cooling planet? Of course, were he to study that phenomenon in detail, somewhat as we study ferments under the lens, he would not see the smile of the babe change instantaneously to the laughter of the skull; but I fancy that whatever might psychologically happen, between the first smile of rosy flesh and the last dull grin of bone, would remain for him as indistinguishable as the gnat's ten or fifteen thousand wing-beats per second remain for us. I doubt whether the God of a system, or even of a single world, could sympathize with our emotions any more than we ourselves can sympathize with the life that thrills in a droplet of putrid water ...

But what is this human creature that, in the sight of a God, might seem to rise from earth merely to weep and laugh one moment in the light, ere crumbling back to clay again? A form evolved, in the course of a hundred million years, from out of some shapeless speck of primordial slime. But this knowledge of the evolution nowise illuminates the secret of the life in itself – the secret of the sentiency struggling against destruction through all those million centuries – ever contriving and building, to baffle death, more and more astounding complexities of substance, more and yet more marvelous complexities of mind — and able at last to prolong the term of its being from the primal duration of an instant to the possible human age of a hundred years. The sentiency is the riddle of riddles. Thought has been proved a compounding of sensation. But the simplest sensation perceptible is itself a compound or the result of a compounding — perhaps the shock of a fusion — the flash of a blending; and the mystery of life remains the most inscrutable, the most tremendous, the most appalling of enigmas.

From the terror of that mystery our fathers sought to save their world by uttering the black decree: *'On pain of sword and fire, on peril of the Everlasting Death,* THOU SHALT NOT THINK!'

But the elder wisdom of the East proclaimed: *Fear not to think, O child of the Abyss, upon the Depth that gave thee birth! Divining that Formless out of which thou hast come, into which thou must dissolve again, thou shalt know thy Being timeless, and infinitely One! . . '*

Fuji-no-Yama

Kité miréba,
Sahodo madé nashi,
Fuji no Yama!

Seen on close approach, the mountain of Fuji does not come up to expectation — *Japanese proverbial philosophy*

The most beautiful sight in Japan, and certainly one of the most beautiful in the world, is the distant apparition of Fuji on cloudless days — more especially days of spring and autumn, when the greater part of the peak is covered with late or with early snows. You can seldom distinguish the snowless base, which remains the same color as the sky: you perceive only the white cone seeming to hang in heaven; and the Japanese comparison of its shape to an inverted half-open fan is made wonderfully exact by the fine streaks that spread downward from the notched top, like shadows of fan-ribs. Even lighter than a fan the vision appears — rather the ghost or dream of a fan; yet the material reality a hundred miles away is grandiose among the mountains of the globe. Rising to a height of nearly 12,500 feet, Fuji is visible from thirteen provinces of the Empire. Nevertheless it is one of the easiest of lofty mountains to climb; and for a thousand years it has been scaled every summer by multitudes of pilgrims. For it is not only a sacred mountain, but the most sacred mountain of Japan, the holiest eminence of the land that is called Divine, the Supreme Altar of the Sun; and to ascend it at least once in a life-time is the duty of all who reverence the ancient gods. So from every district of the Empire pilgrims annually wend their way to Fuji; and in nearly all the provinces there are pilgrim-societies — Fuji-Kō — organized for the purpose of aiding those desiring to visit the sacred peak. If this act of faith cannot be performed by everybody in person, it can at least be performed by proxy. Any hamlet, however remote, can occasionally send one representative to pray before the shrine of the divinity of Fuji, and to salute the rising sun from that sublime eminence. Thus a single company of Fuji pilgrims may be composed of men from a hundred different settlements.

By both of the national religions Fuji is held in reverence. The Shintō deity of Fuji is the beautiful goddess Ko-no-hana-saku-ya-himé – she who brought forth her children in fire without pain, and whose name signifies 'Radiant-blooming-as-the-flowers-of-the-trees,' or, according to some commentators, 'Causing-the-flowers-to-blossom-brightly.' On the summit is her temple; and in ancient books it is recorded that mortal eyes have beheld her hovering, like a luminous cloud, above the verge of the crater. Her viewless servants watch and wait by the precipices to hurl down whomsoever presumes to approach her shrine with unpurified heart ... Buddhism loves the grand peak because its form is like the white bud of the Sacred Flower, and because the eight cusps of its top, like the eight petals of the Lotus, symbolize the Eight Intelligences of Perception, Purpose, Speech, Conduct, Living, Effort, Mindfulness, and Contemplation.

But the legends and traditions about Fuji, the stories of its rising out of the earth in a single night – of the shower of pierced jewels once flung down from it, of the first temple built upon its summit eleven hundred years ago, of the Luminous Maiden that lured to the crater an emperor who was never seen afterward, but is still worshiped at a little shrine erected on the place of his vanishing, of the sand that daily rolled down by pilgrim feet nightly reascends to its former position – have not all these things been written in books? There is really very little left for me to tell about Fuji except my own experience of climbing it.

I made the ascent by way of Gotemba – the least picturesque, but perhaps also the least difficult of the six or seven routes open to choice. Gotemba is a little village chiefly consisting of pilgrim-inns. You reach it from Tōkyō in about three hours by the Tōkaidō railway, which rises for miles as it approaches the neighborhood of the mighty volcano. Gotemba is considerably more than two thousand feet above the sea, and therefore comparatively cool in the hottest season. The open country about it slopes to Fuji; but the slope is so gradual that the table-land seems almost level to the eye. From Gotemba in perfectly clear weather the mountain looks uncomfortably near — formidable by proximity — though actually miles away. During the rainy season it may appear and disappear alternately many times in one day, like an enormous spectre. But on the gray August morning when I entered Gotemba as a pilgrim, the landscape was muffled in vapors; and Fuji was totally invisible. I arrived too late to attempt the ascent on the same day; but I made my preparations at once for the day following, and engaged a couple of gōriki ('strong-pull men'), or experienced guides. I felt quite secure on seeing their broad honest faces and sturdy bearing. They supplied me with a pilgrim-staff, heavy blue tabi (that is to say, cleft-stockings, to be used with sandals), a straw hat shaped like Fuji, and the rest of a pilgrim's outfit, telling me to be ready to start with them at four o'clock in the morning.

What is hereafter set down consists of notes taken on the journey, but afterwards amended and expanded — for notes made while climbing are necessarily hurried and imperfect.

1

24 August 1897

From strings stretched above the balcony upon which my inn-room opens, hundreds of towels are hung like flags, blue towels and white, having printed upon them in Chinese characters the names of pilgrim-companies and of the divinity of Fuji. These are gifts to the house, and serve as advertisements ... Raining from a uniformly grey sky. Fuji always invisible.

25 August

3.30 a.m. — No sleep — tumult all night of parties returning late from the mountain, or arriving for the pilgrimage — constant clapping of hands to summon servants — banqueting and singing in the adjoining chambers, with alarming bursts of laughter every few minutes ... Breakfast of soup, fish, and rice. Gōriki arrive in professional costume, and find me ready. Nevertheless they insist that I shall undress again and put on heavy underclothing, warning me that even when it is Doyō (the period of greatest summer heat) at the foot of the mountain, it is Daikan (the period of greatest winter cold) at the top. Then they start in advance, carrying provisions and bundles of heavy clothing ... A kuruma waits for me, with three runners, two to pull, and one to push, as the work will be hard uphill. By kuruma I can go to the height of five thousand feet.

Morning black and slightly chill, with fine rain; but I shall soon be above the rain-clouds ... The lights of the town vanish behind us; the kuruma is rolling along a country-road. Outside of the swinging penumbra made by the paper-lantern of the foremost runner, nothing is clearly visible; but I can vaguely distinguish silhouettes of trees and, from time to time, of houses — peasants' houses with steep roofs.

Gray wan light slowly suffuses the moist air; day is dawning through drizzle ... Gradually the landscape defines with its colors. The way lies through thin woods. Occasionally we pass houses with high thatched roofs that look like farmhouses; but cultivated land is nowhere visible ...

Open country with scattered clumps of trees — larch and pine. Nothing in the horizon but scraggy tree-tops above what seems to be the rim of a vast down. No sign whatever of Fuji ... For the first time I notice that the road is black — black sand and cinders apparently, volcanic cinders: the wheels of the kuruma and the feet of the runners sink into it with a crunching sound.

The rain has stopped, and the sky becomes a clearer gray ... The trees decrease in size and number as we advance.

What I have been taking for the horizon, in front of us, suddenly breaks open, and begins to roll smokily away to left and right. In the great rift part of a dark-blue mass appears — a portion of Fuji. Almost at the same moment the sun pierces the clouds behind us; but the road now enters a copse covering the base of a low ridge, and the view is cut off ... Halt at a little house among the trees – a pilgrims' resting-place – and there find the gōriki, who have advanced much more rapidly than my runners, waiting for us. Buy eggs, which a gōriki rolls up in a narrow strip of straw matting, tying the matting tightly with straw cord between the eggs, so that the string of eggs has somewhat the appearance of a string of sausages ... Hire a horse.

*

Sky clears as we proceed; white sunlight floods everything. Road reascends; and we emerge again on the moorland. And, right in front, Fuji appears — naked to the summit — stupendous — startling as if newly risen from the earth. Nothing could be more beautiful. A vast blue cone — warm-blue, almost violet through the vapors not yet lifted by the sun — with two white streaklets near the top which are great gullies full of snow, though they look from here scarcely an inch long. But the charm of the apparition is much less the charm of color than of symmetry — a symmetry of beautiful bending lines with a curve like the curve of a cable stretched over a space too wide to allow of pulling taut. (This comparison did not at once suggest itself: the first impression given me by the grace of those lines was an impression of femininity; I found myself thinking of some exquisite sloping of shoulders toward the neck.) I can imagine nothing more difficult to draw at sight. But the Japanese artist, through his marvelous skill with the writing-brush — the skill inherited from generations of calligraphists — easily faces the riddle: he outlines the silhouette with two flowing strokes made in the fraction of a second, and manages to hit the exact truth of the curves — much as a professional archer might hit a mark, without consciously taking aim, through long exact habit of hand and eye.

II

I see the gōriki hurrying forward far away, one of them carrying the eggs round his neck! ... Now there are no more trees worthy of the name, only scattered stunted growths resembling shrubs. The black road curves across a vast grassy down; and here and there I see large black patches in the green surface — bare spaces of ashes and scoriae; showing that this thin green skin covers some enormous volcanic deposit of recent date ... As a matter of history, all this district was buried two yards deep in 1707 by an eruption from the side of Fuji. Even in far-off Tōkyō the rain of ashes covered roofs to a depth of sixteen centimetres. There are no farms in this region, because there is little true soil; and there is no water. But volcanic destruction is not eternal destruction; eruptions at last prove fertilizing; and the divine 'Princess-who-causes-the-flowers-to-blossom-brightly' will make this waste to smile again in future hundreds of years.

*

... The black openings in the green surface become more numerous and larger. A few dwarf-shrubs still mingle with the coarse grass ... The vapors are lifting; and Fuji is changing color. It is no longer a glowing blue, but a dead sombre blue. Irregularities previously hidden by rising ground appear in the lower part of the grand curves. One of these to the left. shaped like a camel's hump, represents the focus of the last great eruption.

The land is not now green with black patches, but black with green patches; and the green patches dwindle visibly in the direction of the peak. The shrubby growths have disappeared. The wheels of the kuruma and the feet of the runners sink deeper into the volcanic sand ... The horse is now attached to the kuruma with ropes, and I am able to advance more rapidly. Still the mountain seems far away; but we are really running up its flank at a height of more than five thousand feet.

Fuji has ceased to be blue of any shade. It is black — charcoal-black — a frightful extinct heap of visible ashes and cinders and slaggy lava ... Most of the green has disappeared. Likewise all of the illusion. The tremendous naked black reality — always becoming more sharply, more grimly, more atrociously defined — is a stupefaction, a nightmare ... Above — miles above — the snow patches glare and gleam against that blackness — hideously. I think of a gleam of white teeth I once saw in a skull — a woman's skull — otherwise burnt to a sooty crisp.

So one of the fairest, if not the fairest, of earthly visions resolves itself into a spectacle of horror and death ... But have not all human ideals of beauty, like the beauty of Fuji seen from afar, been created by forces of death and pain? Are not all, in their kind, but composites of death, beheld in retrospective through the magical haze of inherited memory?

III

The green has utterly vanished; all is black. There is no road, only the broad waste of black sand sloping and narrowing up to those dazzling, grinning patches of snow. But there is a track — a yellowish track made by thousands and thousands of cast-off sandals of straw (waraji), flung aside by pilgrims. Straw sandals quickly wear out upon this black grit; and every pilgrim carries several pairs for the journey. Had I to make the ascent alone, I could find the path by following that wake of broken sandals — a yellow streak zigzagging up out of sight across the blackness.

6.40 a.m. — We reach Tarōbō, first of the ten stations on the ascent: height, 6,000 feet. The station is a large wooden house, of which two rooms have been fitted up as a shop for the sale of staves, hats, raincoats, sandals — everything pilgrims need. I find there a peripatetic photographer offering for sale photographs of the mountain which are really very good as well as very cheap ... Here the gōriki take their first meal; and I rest. The kuruma can go no further; and I dismiss my three runners, but keep the horse, a docile and surefooted creature; for I can venture to ride him up to Ni-gō-goséki, or Station No. 2½.

Start for No. 2½ up the slant of black sand, keeping the horse at a walk. No. 2½ is shut up for the season ... Slope now becomes steep as a stairway, and further riding would be dangerous. Alight and make ready for the climb. Cold wind blowing so strongly that I have to tie on my hat tightly. One of the gōriki unwinds from about his waist a long stout cotton girdle, and, giving me one end to hold, passes the other over his shoulder for the pull. Then he proceeds over the sand at an angle, with a steady short step, and I follow; the other guide keeping closely behind me to provide against any slip.

There is nothing very difficult about this climbing, except the weariness of walking through sand and cinders: it is like walking over dunes ... We mount by zigzags. The sand moves with the wind; and I have a slightly nervous sense — the feeling only, not the perception; for I keep my eyes on the sand — of height growing above depth ... Have to watch my steps carefully, and to use my staff constantly, as the slant is now very steep ... We are in a white fog — passing through clouds! Even if I wished to look back, I could see nothing through this vapor; but I have not the least wish to look back. The wind has suddenly ceased — cut off, perhaps, by a ridge; and there is a silence that I remember from West Indian days: the Peace of High Places. It is broken only by the crunching of the ashes beneath our feet. I can distinctly hear my heart beat ... The guide tells me that I stoop too much, orders me to walk upright, and always in stepping to put down the heel first. I do this, and find it relieving. But climbing through this tiresome mixture of ashes and sand begins to be trying. I am perspiring and panting. The guide bids me keep my honorable mouth closed, and breathe only through my honorable nose.

We are out of the fog again ... All at once I perceive above us, at a little distance, something like a square hole in the face of the mountain – a door! It is the door of the third station – a wooden hut half-buried in black drift ... How delightful to squat again, even in a blue cloud of wood-smoke and under smoke-blackened rafters! Time, 8.30 a.m. Height, 7,085 feet.

In spite of the wood-smoke the station is comfortable enough inside· there are clean mattings and even kneeling-cushions. No windows of course, nor any other opening than the door; for the building is half-buried in the flank of the mountain. We lunch ... The station-keeper tells us that recently a student walked from Gotemba to the top of the mountain and back again – in geta! Geta are heavy wooden sandals, or clogs, held to the foot only by a thong passing between the great and the second toe. The feet of that student must have been made of steel!

Having rested, I go out to look around. Far below white clouds are rolling over the landscape in huge fluffy wreaths. Above the hut, and actually trickling down over it, the sable cone soars to the sky. But the amazing sight is the line of the monstrous slope to the left – a line that now shows no curve whatever, but shoots down below the clouds, and up to the gods only know where (for I cannot see the end of it), straight as a tightened bowstring. The right flank is rocky and broken. But as for the left, I never dreamed it possible that a line so absolutely straight and smooth, and extending for so enormous a distance at such an amazing angle, could exist even in a volcano. That stupendous pitch gives me a sense of dizziness, and a totally unfamiliar feeling of wonder. Such regularity appears unnatural, frightful; seems even artificial – but artificial upon a superhuman and demoniac scale. I imagine that to fall thence from above would be to fall for leagues. Absolutely nothing to take hold of. But the gōriki assure me that there is no danger on that slope: it is all soft sand.

IV

Though drenched with perspiration by the exertion of the first climb, I am already dry, and cold ... Up again ... The ascent is at first through ashes and sand as before; but presently large stones begin to mingle with the sand; and the way is always growing steeper ... I constantly slip. There is nothing firm, nothing resisting to stand upon: loose stones and cinders roll down at every step ... If a big lava-block were to detach itself from above! ... In spite of my helpers and of the staff, I continually slip, and am all in perspiration again. Almost every stone that I tread upon turns under me. How is it that no stone ever turns under the feet of the gōriki? *They* never slip — never make a false step — never seem less at ease than they would be in walking over a matted floor. Their small brown broad feet always poise upon the shingle at exactly the right angle. They are heavier men than I; but they move lightly as birds ... Now I have to stop for rest every half a dozen steps ... The line of broken straw sandals follows the zigzags we take ... At last — at last another door in the face of the mountain. Enter the fourth station, and fling myself down upon the mats. Time, 10.30 a.m. Height, only 7,937 feet — yet it seemed such a distance!

Off again ... Way worse and worse ... Feel a new distress due to the rarefaction of the air. Heart beating as in a high fever ... Slope has become very rough. It is no longer soft ashes and sand mixed with stones, but stones only — fragments of lava, lumps of pumice, scoriae of every sort, all angled as if freshly broken with a hammer. All would likewise seem to have been expressly shaped so as to turn upside-down when trodden upon. Yet I must confess that they never turn under the feet of the gōriki ... The cast-off sandals strew the slope in ever-increasing numbers ... But for the gōriki I should have had ever so many bad tumbles: they cannot prevent me from slipping; but they never allow me to fall. Evidently I am not fitted to climb mountains ... Height, 8,659 feet — but the fifth station is shut up! Must keep zigzagging on to the next. Wonder how I shall ever be able to reach it! ... And there are people still alive who have climbed Fuji three and four times, *for pleasure!* ... Dare not look back. See nothing but the black stones always turning under me, and the bronzed feet of those marvelous gōriki who never slip, never pant, and never perspire ... Staff begins to hurt my hand ... Gōriki push and pull: it is shameful of me, I know, to give them so much trouble ... Ah! sixth station! — may all the myriads of the gods bless my gōriki! Time, 2.07 p.m. Height, 9,317 feet.

Resting, I gaze through the doorway at the abyss below. The land is now dimly visible only through rents in a prodigious wilderness of white clouds; and within these rents everything looks almost black ... The horizon has risen frightfully — has expanded monstrously ... My gōriki warn me that the summit is still miles away. I have been too slow. We must hasten upward.

Certainly the zigzag is steeper than before ... With the stones now mingle angular rocks; and we sometimes have to flank queer black bulks that look like basalt ... On the right rises, out of sight, a jagged black hideous ridge — an ancient lava-stream. The line of the left slope still shoots up, straight as a bow-string ... Wonder if the way will become any steeper; doubt whether it can possibly become any rougher. Rocks dislodged by my feet roll down soundlessly; I am afraid to look after them. Their noiseless vanishing gives me a sensation like the sensation of falling in dreams ...

There is a white gleam overhead — the lowermost verge of an immense stretch of snow ... Now we are skirting a snow-filled gully, the lowermost of those white patches which, at first sight of the summit this morning, seemed scarcely an inch long. It will take an hour to pass it ... A guide runs forward, while I rest upon my staff, and returns with a large ball of snow. What curious snow! Not flaky, soft, white snow, but a mass of transparent globules, exactly like glass beads. I eat some, and find it deliciously refreshing ... The seventh station is closed. How shall I get to the eighth? ... Happily, breathing has become less difficult ... the wind is upon us again, and black dust with it. The gōriki keep close to me, and advance with caution ...

177

I have to stop for rest at every turn on the path – cannot talk for weariness ... I do not feel – I am much too tired to feel ... How I managed it, I do not know; but I have actually got to the eighth station! Not for a thousand millions of dollars will I go one step further today. Time, 4.40 p.m. Height, 10,693 feet.

V

It is much too cold here for rest without winter clothing; and now I learn the worth of the heavy robes provided by the guides. The robes are blue, with big white Chinese characters on the back, and are padded thickly as bed-quilts; but they feel light; for the air is really like the frosty breath of February ... A meal is preparing; I notice that charcoal at this elevation acts in a refractory manner, and that a fire can be maintained only by constant attention ... Cold and fatigue sharpen appetite: we consume a surprising quantity of Zō-sui – rice boiled with eggs and a little meat. By reason of my fatigue and of the hour, it has been decided to remain here for the night.

Tired as I am, I cannot but limp to the doorway to contemplate the amazing prospect. From within a few feet of the threshold, the ghastly slope of rocks and cinders drops down into a prodigious disk of clouds miles beneath us – clouds of countless forms, but mostly wreathings and fluffy pilings; and the whole huddling mass, reaching almost to the horizon, is blinding white under the sun. (By the Japanese, this tremendous cloud-expanse is well named Wata-no-Umi, 'the Sea of Cotton.') The horizon itself – enormously risen, phantasmally expanded – seems halfway up above the world: a wide luminous belt ringing the hollow vision. Hollow, I call it, because extreme distances below the sky-line are sky-colored and vague, so that the impression you receive is not of being on a point under a vault, but of being upon a point rising into a stupendous blue sphere, of which this huge horizon would represent the equatorial zone. To turn away from such a spectacle is not possible. I watch and watch until the dropping sun changes the colors – turning the Sea of Cotton into a Fleece of Gold. Half-round the horizon a yellow glory grows and burns. Here and there beneath it, through cloud-rifts, colored vaguenesses define: I now see golden water, with long purple headlands reaching into it, with ranges of violet peaks thronging behind it — these glimpses curiously resembling portions of a tinted topographical map. Yet most of the landscape is pure delusion. Even my guides, with their long experience and their eagle-sight, can scarcely distinguish the real from the unreal; for the blue and purple and violet clouds moving under the Golden Fleece exactly mock the outlines and the tones of distant peaks and capes: you can detect what is vapor only by its slowly shifting shape ... Brighter and brighter glows the gold. Shadows come from the west — shadows flung by cloud-pile over cloud-pile; and these, like evening shadows upon snow, are violaceous blue ... Then orange tones appear in the horizon; then smouldering crimson. And now the greater part of the Fleece of Gold has changed to cotton again — white cotton mixed with pink ... Stars thrill out. The cloud-waste uniformly whitens — thickening and packing to the horizon. The west glooms. Night rises· and all things darken except that wondrous unbroken world-round of white — the Sea of Cotton.

The station-keeper lights his lamps, kindles a fire of twigs. prepares our beds. Outside it is bitterly cold, and, with the fall of night becoming colder. Still I cannot turn away from that astounding vision ... Countless stars now flicker and shiver in the blue-black sky. Nothing whatever of the material world remains visible. except the black slope of the peak before my feet. The enormous cloud-disk below continues white; but to all appearance it has become a liquidly level white. without forms — a white flood. It is no longer the Sea of Cotton. It is a Sea of Milk, the Cosmic Sea of ancient Indian legend — and always self-luminous, as with ghostly quickenings.

VI

Squatting by the wood fire, I listen to the gōriki and the station-keeper telling of strange happenings on the mountain. One incident discussed I remember reading something about in a Tōkyō paper: I now hear it retold by the lips of a man who figured in it as a hero.

A Japanese meteorologist named Nonaka attempted last year the rash undertaking of passing the winter on the summit of Fuji for purposes of scientific study. It might not be difficult to winter upon the peak in a solid observatory furnished with a good stove, and all necessary comforts; but Nonaka could afford only a small wooden hut, in which he would be obliged to spend the cold season *without fire!* His young wife insisted on sharing his labors and dangers. The couple began their sojourn on the summit toward the close of September. In midwinter news was brought to Gotemba that both were dying.

Relatives and friends tried to organize a rescue-party. But the weather was frightful; the peak was covered with snow and ice; the chances of death were innumerable; and the gōriki would not risk their lives. Hundreds of dollars could not tempt them. At last a desperate appeal was made to them as representatives of Japanese courage and hardihood: they were assured that to suffer a man of science to perish, without making even one plucky effort to save him, would disgrace the country; they were told that the national honor was in their hands. This appeal brought forward two volunteers. One was a man of great strength and daring, nicknamed by his fellow-guides Oni-guma, 'the Demon-Bear,' the other was the elder of my gōriki. Both believed that they were going to certain destruction. They took leave of their friends and kindred, and drank with their families the farewell cup of water — midzu-no-sakazuki — in which those about to be separated by death pledge each other. Then, after having thickly wrapped themselves in cotton-wool, and made all possible preparation for ice climbing, they started — taking with them a brave army surgeon who had offered his services, without fee, for the rescue. After surmounting extraordinary difficulties, the party reached the hut; but the inmates refused to open! Nonaka protested that he would rather die than face the shame of failure in his undertaking; and his wife said that she had resolved to die with her husband. Partly by forcible, and partly by gentle means, the pair were restored to a better state of mind. The surgeon administered medicines and cordials; the patients, carefully wrapped up, were strapped to the backs of the guides; and the descent was begun. My gōriki, who carried the lady, believes that the gods helped him on the ice-slopes. More than once, all thought themselves lost; but they reached the foot of the mountain without one serious mishap. After weeks of careful nursing, the rash young couple were pronounced out of danger. The wife suffered less, and recovered more quickly, than the husband.

*

The gōriki have cautioned me not to venture outside during the night without calling them. They will not tell me why; and their warning is peculiarly uncanny. From previous experiences during Japanese travel, I surmise that the danger implied is supernatural; but I feel that it would be useless to ask questions.

The door is closed and barred. I lie down between the guides, who are asleep in a moment, as I can tell by their heavy breathing. I cannot sleep immediately; perhaps the fatigues and the surprises of the day have made me somewhat nervous. I look up at the rafters of the black roof — at packages of sandals, bundles of wood, bundles of many indistinguishable kinds there stowed away or suspended, and making queer shadows in the lamplight ... It is terribly cold, even under my three quilts; and the sound of the wind outside is wonderfully like the sound of great surf — a constant succession of bursting roars, each followed by a prolonged hiss. The hut, half buried under tons of rock and drift, does not move; but the sand does, and trickles down between the rafters; and small stones also move after each fierce gust, with a rattling just like the clatter of shingle in the pull of a retreating wave.

4 a.m. — Go out alone, despite last evening's warning, but keep close to the door. There is a great and icy blowing. The Sea of Milk is unchanged: it lies far below this wind. Over it the moon is dying ... The guides, perceiving my absence, spring up and join me. I am reproved for not having awakened them. They will not let me stay outside alone: so I turn in with them.

Dawn — a zone of pearl grows round the world. The stars vanish; the sky brightens. A wild sky, with dark wrack drifting at an enormous height. The Sea of Milk has turned again into cotton, and there are wide rents in it. The desolation of the black slope, all the ugliness of slaggy rock and angled stone, again defines ... Now the cotton becomes disturbed; it is breaking up. A yellow glow runs along the east like the glare of a wind-blown fire ... Alas! I shall not be among the fortunate mortals able to boast of viewing from Fuji the first lifting of the sun! Heavy clouds have drifted across the horizon at the point where he should rise ... Now I know that he has risen, because the upper edges of those purple rags of cloud are burning like charcoal. But I have been so disappointed!

More and more luminous the hollow world. League-wide heapings of cottony cloud roll apart. Fearfully far away there is a light of gold upon water: the sun here remains viewless, but the ocean sees him. It is not a flicker, but a burnished glow; at such a distance ripplings are invisible ... Further and further scattering, the clouds unveil a vast gray and blue landscape – hundreds and hundreds of miles throng into vision at once. On the right I distinguish Tōkyō bay, and Kamakura, and the holy island of Enoshima (no bigger than the dot over this letter 'i'); on the left the wilder Suruga coast, and the blue-toothed promontory of Idzu, and the place of the fishing-village where I have been summering – the merest pin-point in that tinted dream of hill and shore. Rivers appear but as sun-gleams on spider-threads; fishing-sails are white dust clinging to the gray-blue glass of the sea. And the picture alternately appears and vanishes while the clouds drift and shift across it, and shape themselves into spectral islands and mountains and valleys of all Elysian colors ...

VII

6.40 a.m. – Start for the top ... Hardest and roughest stage of the journey, through a wilderness of lava-blocks. The path zigzags between ugly masses that project from the slope like black teeth. The trail of cast-away sand. ʒ is wider than ever ... Have to rest every few minutes ... Reach another long patch of the snow that looks like glass-beads, and eat some. The next station – a half-station – is closed; and the ninth has ceased to exist ... A sudden fear comes to me, not of the ascent, but of the prospective descent by a route which is too steep even to permit of comfortably sitting down. But the guides assure me that there will be no difficulty, and that most of the return journey will be by another way – over the interminable level which I wondered at yesterday – nearly all soft sand, with very few stones. It is called the hashiri ('glissade'); and we are to descend at a run! ...

All at once a family of field-mice scatter out from under my feet in panic; and the gōriki behind me catches one, and gives it to me. I hold the tiny shivering life for a moment to examine it, and set it free again. These little creatures have very long pale noses. How do they live in this waterless desolation – and at such an altitude

— especially in the season of snow? For we are now at a height of more than eleven thousand feet! The gōriki say that the mice find roots growing under the stones ...

Wilder and steeper; for me, at least, the climbing is sometimes on all fours. There are barriers which we surmount with the help of ladders. There are fearful places with Buddhist names, such as the Sai-no-Kawara, or Dry Bed of the River of Souls — a black waste strewn with heaps of rock, like those stone-piles which, in Buddhist pictures of the underworld, the ghosts of children build ...

Twelve thousand feet, and something — the top! Time, 8.20 a.m. ... Stone huts; Shintō shrine with tōrii; icy well, called the Spring of Gold; stone tablet bearing a Chinese poem and the design of a tiger; rough walls of lava-blocks round these things, possibly for protection against the wind. Then the huge dead crater — probably between a quarter of a mile and half a mile wide, but shallowed up to within three or four hundred feet of the verge by volcanic detritus — a cavity horrible even in the tones of its yellow crumbling walls, streaked and stained with every hue of scorching. I perceive that the trail of straw sandals ends *in* the crater. Some hideous over-hanging cusps of black lava — like the broken edges of a monstrous cicatrix — project on two sides several hundred feet above the opening; but I certainly shall not take the trouble to climb them. Yet these — seen through the haze of a hundred miles, through the soft illusion of blue spring-weather — appear as the opening snowy petals of the bud of the Sacred Lotus! ... No spot in this world can be more horrible, more atrociously dismal, than the cindered tip of the Lotus as you stand upon it.

But the view — the view for a hundred leagues — and the light of the far faint dreamy world — and the fairy vapors of morning — and the marvelous wreathings of cloud· all this, and only this, consoles me for the labor and the pain ... Other pilgrims, earlier climbers — poised upon the highest crag, with faces turned to the tremendous East — are clapping their hands in Shintō prayer, saluting the mighty Day ... The immense poetry of the moment enters into me with a thrill. I know that the colossal vision before me has already become a memory ineffaceable — a memory of which no luminous detail can fade, and the dust of these eyes be mingled with the dust of the myriad million eyes that also have looked, in ages forgotten before my birth, from the summit supreme of Fuji to the Rising of the Sun.

PART TWO

Reflections

In a Japanese Garden

I

My little two-story house by the Ōhashigawa, although dainty as a bird-cage, proved much too small for comfort at the approach of the hot season — the rooms being scarcely higher than steamship cabins, and so narrow that an ordinary mosquito-net could not be suspended in them. I was sorry to lose the beautiful lake view, but I found it necessary to remove to the northern quarter of the city, into a very quiet street behind the mouldering castle. My new home is a katchiū-yashiki, the ancient residence of some samurai of high rank. It is shut off from the street, or rather roadway, skirting the castle moat by a long, high wall coped with tiles. One ascends to the gateway, which is almost as large as that of a temple court, by a low broad flight of stone steps; and projecting from the wall, to the right of the gate, is a lookout window, heavily barred, like a big wooden cage. Thence, in feudal days, armed retainers kept keen watch on all who passed by — invisible watch, for the bars are set so closely that a face behind them cannot be seen from the roadway. Inside the gate the approach to the dwelling is also walled in on both sides, so that the visitor, unless privileged, could see before him only the house entrance, always closed with white shōji. Like all samurai homes, the residence itself is but one story high, but there are fourteen rooms within, and these are lofty, spacious, and beautiful. There is, alas, no lake view nor any charming prospect. Part of the O-Shiroyama, with the castle on its summit, half concealed by a park of pines, may be seen above the coping of the front wall, but only a part; and scarcely a hundred yards behind the house rise densely wooded heights, cutting off not only the horizon, but a large slice of the sky as well. For this immurement, however, there exists fair compensation in the shape of a very pretty garden, or rather a series of garden spaces, which surround the dwelling on three sides. Broad verandas overlook these, and from a certain veranda angle I can enjoy the sight of two gardens at once. Screens of bamboos and woven rushes, with wide gateless openings in their midst, mark the boundaries of the three divisions of the pleasure-grounds. But these structures are not intended to serve as true fences; they are ornamental, and only indicate where one style of landscape gardening ends and another begins.

II

Now a few words upon Japanese gardens in general.

After having learned — merely by seeing, for the practical knowledge of the art requires years of study and experience, besides a natural, instinctive sense of beauty — something about the Japanese manner of arranging flowers, one can thereafter consider European ideas of floral decoration only as vulgarities. This observation is not the result of any hasty enthusiasm, but a conviction settled by long residence in the interior. I have come to understand the unspeakable loveliness of a solitary spray of blossoms arranged as only a Japanese expert knows how to arrange it — not by simply poking the spray into a vase, but by perhaps one whole hour's labor of trimming and posing and daintiest manipulation — and therefore I cannot think now of what we Occidentals call a 'bouquet' as anything but a vulgar murdering of flowers, an outrage upon the color-sense, a brutality, an abomination. Somewhat in the same way, and for similar reasons, after having learned what an old Japanese garden is, I can remember our costliest gardens at home only as ignorant displays of what wealth can accomplish in the creation of incongruities that violate nature.

Now a Japanese garden is not a flower garden; neither is it made for the purpose of cultivating plants. In nine cases out of ten there is nothing in it resembling a flower-bed. Some gardens may contain scarcely a sprig of green; some have nothing green at all, and consist entirely of rocks and pebbles and sand, although these are exceptional.[1] As a rule, a Japanese garden is a landscape garden, yet its existence does not depend upon any fixed allowance of space. It may cover one acre or many acres. It may also be only ten feet square. It may, in extreme cases, be much less; for a certain kind of Japanese garden can be contrived small enough to put in a tokonoma. Such a garden, in a vessel no larger than a fruit-dish, is called koniwa or tokoniwa, and may occasionally be seen in the tokonoma of humble little dwellings so closely squeezed between other structures as to possess no ground in which to cultivate an outdoor garden. (I say 'an outdoor garden,' because there are indoor gardens, both upstairs and downstairs, in some large Japanese houses.) The tokoniwa is usually made in some curious bowl, or shallow carved box, or quaintly shaped vessel impossible to describe by any English word. Therein are created minuscule hills with minuscule houses upon them, and microscopic ponds and rivulets spanned by tiny humped bridges; and queer wee plants do duty for trees, and curiously formed pebbles stand for rocks, and there are tiny tōrō, perhaps a tiny torii as well – in short, a charming and living model of a Japanese landscape.

Another fact of prime importance to remember is that, in order to comprehend the beauty of a Japanese garden, it is necessary to understand – or at least to learn to understand – the beauty of stones. Not of stones quarried by the hand of man, but of stones shaped by nature only. Until you can feel, and keenly feel, that stones have character, that stones have tones and values, the whole artistic meaning of a Japanese garden cannot be revealed to you. In the foreigner, however aesthetic he may be, this feeling needs to be cultivated by study. It is inborn in the Japanese; the soul of the race comprehends Nature infinitely better than we do, at least in her visible forms. But although, being an Occidental, the true sense of the beauty of stones can be reached by you only through

1. Such as the garden attached to the abbot's palace at Tokuwamonji, cited by Mr Conder, which was made to commemorate the legend of stones which bowed themselves in assent to the doctrine of Buddha. At Togo-ike, in Tottori-ken, I saw a very large garden consisting almost entirely of stones and sand. The impression which the designer had intended to convey was that of approaching the sea over a verge of dunes, and the illusion was beautiful.

long familiarity with the Japanese use and choice of them, the characters of the lessons to be acquired exist everywhere about you, if your life be in the interior. You cannot walk through a street without observing tasks and problems in the aesthetics of stones for you to master. At the approaches to temples, by the side of roads, before holy groves, and in all parks and pleasure-grounds, as well as in all cemeteries, you will notice large, irregular, flat slabs of natural rock — mostly from the river-beds and water-worn — sculptured with ideographs, but unhewn. These have been set up as votive tablets, as commemorative monuments, as tombstones, and are much more costly than the ordinary cut-stone columns and haka chiseled with the figures of divinities in relief. Again, you will see before most of the shrines, nay, even in the grounds of nearly all large homesteads, great irregular blocks of granite or other hard rock, worn by the action of torrents, and converted into water-basins (chodzu-bachi) by cutting a circular hollow in the top. Such are but common examples of the utilization of stones even in the poorest villages; and if you have any natural artistic sentiment, you cannot fail to discover, sooner or later, how much more beautiful are these natural forms than any shapes from the hand of the stone-cutter. It is probable, too, that you will become so habituated at last to the sight of inscriptions cut upon rock surfaces, especially if you travel much through the country, that you will often find yourself involuntarily looking for texts or other chiselings where there are none, and could not possibly be, as if ideographs belonged by natural law to rock formation. And stones will begin, perhaps, to assume for you a certain individual or physiognomical aspect — to suggest moods and sensations, as they do to the Japanese. Indeed, Japan is particularly a land of suggestive shapes in stone, as high volcanic lands are apt to be; and such shapes doubtless addressed themselves to the imagination of the race at a time long prior to the date of that archaic text which tells of demons in Izumo 'who made rocks, and the roots of trees, and leaves, and the foam of the green waters to speak.'

As might be expected in a country where the suggestiveness of natural forms is thus recognized, there are in Japan many curious beliefs and superstitions concerning stones. In almost every province there are famous stones supposed to be sacred or haunted, or to possess miraculous powers, such as the Women's Stone at the temple of Hachiman at Kamakura, and the Sesshō-seki, or Death Stone of Nasu, and the Wealth-giving Stone at Enoshima, to which pilgrims pay reverence. There are even legends of stones having manifested sensibility, like the tradition of the Nodding Stones which bowed down before the monk Daita when he preached unto them the word of Buddha; or the ancient story from the Kojiki, that the Emperor O-Jin, being augustly intoxicated, 'smote with his august staff a great stone in the middle of the Ohosaka road; *whereupon the stone ran away!*'[2]

Now stones are valued for their beauty; and large stones selected for their shape may have an aesthetic worth of hundreds of dollars. And large stones form the skeleton, or framework, in the design of old Japanese gardens. Not only is every stone chosen with a view to its particular expressiveness of form, but every stone in the garden or about the premises has its separate and individual name, indicating its purpose or its decorative duty. But I can tell you only a little, a very little, of the folk-lore of a Japanese garden; and if you want to know more about stones and their names, and about the philosophy of gardens, read the unique essay of Mr Conder on the Art of Landscape Gardening in Japan,[3] and his beautiful book on the Japanese Art of Floral Decoration; and also the brief but charming chapter on Gardens, in Morse's Japanese Homes.[4]

III

No effort to create an impossible or purely ideal landscape is made in the Japanese garden. Its artistic purpose is to copy faithfully the attractions of a veritable landscape, and to convey the real impression

2. The *Kojiki*, translated by Professor B. H. Chamberlain, p. 254.

3. Since this paper was written, Mr Conder has published a beautiful illustrated volume – 'Landscape Gardening in Japan. By Josiah Conder, F.R.I., B.A. Tōkyō: 1893.' A photographic supplement to the work gives views of the most famous gardens in the capital and elsewhere.

4. The observations of Dr Rein on Japanese gardens are not to be recommended, in respect either to accuracy or to comprehension of the subject. Rein spent only two years in Japan, the larger part of which time he devoted to the study of the lacquer industry, the manufacture of silk and paper, and other practical matters. On these subjects his work is justly valued. But his chapters on Japanese manners and customs, art, religion, and literature show extremely little acquaintance with those topics.

that a real landscape communicates. It is therefore at once a picture and a poem; perhaps even more a poem than a picture. For as nature's scenery, in its varying aspects, affects us with sensations of joy or of solemnity, of grimness or of sweetness, of force or of peace, so must the true reflection of it in the labor of the landscape gardener create not merely an impression of beauty, but a mood in the soul. The grand old landscape gardeners, those Buddhist monks who first introduced the art into Japan, and subsequently developed it into an almost occult science, carried their theory yet farther than this. They held it possible to express moral lessons in the design of a garden, and abstract ideas, such as Chastity, Faith, Piety, Content, Calm, and Connubial Bliss. Therefore were gardens contrived according to the character of the owner, whether poet, warrior, philosopher, or priest. In those ancient gardens (the art, alas, is passing away under the withering influence of the utterly commonplace Western taste) there were expressed both a mood of nature and some rare Oriental conception of a mood of man.

I do not know what human sentiment the principal division of my garden was intended to reflect; and there is none to tell me. Those by whom it was made passed away long generations ago, in the eternal transmigration of souls. But as a poem of nature it requires no interpreter. It occupies the front portion of the grounds, facing south; and it also extends west to the verge of the northern division of the garden, from which it is partly separated by a curious screen-fence structure. There are large rocks in it, heavily mossed; and divers fantastic basins of stone for holding water; and stone lamps green with years; and a shachihoko, such as one sees at the peaked angles of castle roofs – a great stone fish, an idealized porpoise, with its nose in the ground and its tail in the air.[5] There are miniature hills, with old trees upon them; and there are long slopes of green, shadowed by flowering shrubs, like river banks; and there are green knolls like islets. All these verdant elevations rise from spaces of pale yellow sand, smooth as a surface of silk and miming the curves and meanderings of a river course. These sanded spaces are not to be trodden upon; they are much too beautiful for that. The least speck of dirt would mar their effect; and it requires

5. This attitude of the shachihoko is somewhat *de rigueur*, whence the common expression 'shachihoko dai,' signifying 'to stand on one's head.'

the trained skill of an experienced native gardener – a delightful old man he is – to keep them in perfect form. But they are traversed in various directions by lines of flat unhewn rock slabs, placed at slightly irregular distances from one another, exactly like stepping-stones across a brook. The whole effect is that of the shores of a still stream in some lovely, lonesome, drowsy place.

There is nothing to break the illusion, so secluded the garden is. High walls and fences shut out streets and contiguous things; and the shrubs and the trees, heightening and thickening toward the boundaries, conceal from view even the roofs of the neighboring katchiū-yashiki. Softly beautiful are the tremulous shadows of leaves on the sunned sand; and the scent of flowers comes thinly sweet with every waft of tepid air; and there is a humming of bees.

IV

By Buddhism all existences are divided into Hijō, things without desire, such as stones and trees; and Ujō, things having desire, such as men and animals. This division does not, so far as I know, find expression in the written philosophy of gardens; but it is a convenient one. The folk-lore of my little domain relates both to the inanimate and the animate. In natural order, the Hijō may be considered first, beginning with a singular shrub near the entrance of the yashiki, and close to the gate of the first garden.

Within the front gateway of almost every old samurai house, and usually near the entrance of the dwelling itself, there is to be seen a small tree with large and peculiar leaves. The name of this tree in Izumo is tegashiwa, and there is one beside my door. What the scientific name of it is I do not know; nor am I quite sure of the etymology of the Japanese name. However, there is a word tegashi, meaning a bond for the hands; and the shape of the leaves of the tegashiwa somewhat resembles the shape of a hand.

Now, in old days, when the samurai retainer was obliged to leave his home in order to accompany his daimyō to Yedo, it was customary, just before his departure, to set before him a baked tai[6] served up

6. The magnificent perch called tai (*Serranus marginulis*), which is very common along the Izumo coast, is not only justly prized as the most delicate of Japanese fish, but is also held to be an emblem of good fortune. It is a ceremonial gift at weddings and on congratulatory occasions. The Japanese call it also 'the king of fishes.'

on a tegashiwa leaf. After this farewell repast, the leaf upon which the tai had been served was hung up above the door as a charm to bring the departed knight safely back again. This pretty superstition about the leaves of the tegashiwa had its origin not only in their shape but in their movement. Stirred by a wind they seemed to beckon — not indeed after our Occidental manner, but in the way that a Japanese signs to his friend to come by gently waving his hand up and down with the palm toward the ground.

Another shrub to be found in most Japanese gardens is the nanten,[7] about which a very curious belief exists. If you have an evil dream, a dream which bodes ill luck, you should whisper it to the nanten early in the morning, and then it will never come true.[8] There are two varieties of this graceful plant: one which bears red berries, and one which bears white. The latter is rare. Both kinds grow in my garden. The common variety is placed close to the veranda (perhaps for the convenience of dreamers); the other occupies a little flower-bed in the middle of the garden, together with a small citron-tree. This most dainty citron-tree is called 'Buddha's fingers,'[9] because of the wonderful shape of its fragrant fruits. Near it stands a kind of laurel, with lanciform leaves glossy as bronze; it is called by the Japanese yuzuri-ha,[10] and is almost as common in the gardens of old samurai homes as the tegashiwa itself. It is held to be a tree

7. *Nandina domestica.*

8. The most lucky of all dreams, they say in Izumo, is a dream of Fuji, the Sacred Mountain. Next in order of good omen is dreaming of a falcon (taka). The third best subject for a dream is the eggplant (nasubi). To dream of the sun or of the moon is very lucky; but it is still more so to dream of stars. For a young wife it is most fortunate to dream of *swallowing a star*: this signifies that she will become the mother of a beautiful child. To dream of a cow is a good omen; to dream of a horse is lucky, but it signifies traveling. To dream of rain or fire is good. Some dreams are held in Japan, as in the West, 'to go by contraries.' Therefore, to dream of having one's house burned up, or of funerals, or of being dead, or of talking to the ghost of a dead person, is good. Some dreams which are good for women mean the reverse when dreamed by men; for example, it is good for a woman to dream that her nose bleeds, but for a man this is very bad. To dream of much money is a sign of loss to come. To dream of the koi, or of any fresh-water fish, is the most unlucky of all. This is curious, for in other parts of Japan the koi is a symbol of good fortune.

9. Tebushukan: *Citrus sarkodactilis.*

10. 'Yuzuru' signifies to resign in favor of another; 'ha' signifies a leaf. The botanical name, as given in Hepburn's dictionary, is *Daphniphillum macropodum.*

of good omen, because no one of its old leaves ever falls off before a new one, growing behind it, has well developed. For thus the yuzuri-ha symbolizes hope that the father will not pass away before his son has become a vigorous man, well able to succeed him as the head of the family. Therefore, on every New Year's Day the leaves of the yuzuri-ha, mingled with fronds of fern, are attached to the shimenawa which is then suspended before every Izumo home.

v

The trees, like the shrubs, have their curious poetry and legends. Like the stones, each tree has its special landscape name according to its position and purpose in the composition. Just as rocks and stones form the skeleton of the ground-plan of a garden, so pines form the framework of its foliage design. They give body to the whole. In this garden there are five pines – not pines tormented into fantasticalities, but pines made wondrously picturesque by long and tireless care and judicious trimming. The object of the gardener has been to develop to the utmost possible degree their natural tendency to rugged line and massings of foliage – that spiny sombre-green foliage which Japanese art is never weary of imitating in metal inlay or golden lacquer. The pine is a symbolic tree in this land of symbolism. Ever green, it is at once the emblem of unflinching purpose and of vigorous old age; and its needle-shaped leaves are credited with the power of driving demons away.

There are two sakuranoki,[11] Japanese cherry-trees – those trees whose blossoms, as Professor Chamberlain so justly observes, are 'beyond comparison more lovely than anything Europe has to show.' Many varieties are cultivated and loved; those in my garden bear blossoms of the most ethereal pink, a flushed white. When, in spring, the trees flower, it is as though fleeciest masses of cloud faintly tinged by sunset had floated down from the highest sky to fold themselves about the branches. This comparison is no poetical exaggeration; neither is it original: it is an ancient Japanese description of the most marvelous floral exhibition which nature is capable of making. The reader who has never seen a cherry-tree blossoming in Japan cannot possibly imagine the delight of the spectacle. There

11. *Cerasus pseudo-cerasus* (Lindley).

are no green leaves; these come later: there is only one glorious burst of blossoms, veiling every twig and bough in their delicate mist; and the soil beneath each tree is covered deep out of sight by fallen petals as by a drift of pink snow.

But these are cultivated cherry-trees. There are others which put forth their leaves before their blossoms, such as the yamazakura, or mountain cherry.[12] This too, however, has its poetry of beauty and of symbolism. Sang the great Shintō writer and poet, Motowori:

> *Shikishima no*
> *Yamato-gokoro wo*
> *Hito-towaba,*
> *Asa-hi ni niou*
> *Yamazakura bana.*[13]

Whether cultivated or uncultivated, the Japanese cherry-trees are emblems. Those planted in old samurai gardens were not cherished for their loveliness alone. Their spotless blossoms were regarded as symbolizing that delicacy of sentiment and blamelessness of life belonging to high courtesy and true knightliness. 'As the cherry flower is first among flowers,' says an old proverb, 'so should the warrior be first among men.'

Shadowing the western end of this garden, and projecting its smooth dark limbs above the awning of the veranda, is a superb umenoki, Japanese plum-tree, very old, and originally planted here, no doubt, as in other gardens, for the sake of the sight of its blossoming. The flowering of the umenoki,[14] in the earliest spring, is scarcely less astonishing than that of the cherry-tree, which does not bloom for a full month later; and the blossoming of both is celebrated by

12. About this mountain cherry there is a humorous saying which illustrates the Japanese love of puns. In order fully to appreciate it, the reader should know that Japanese nouns have no distinction of singular and plural. The word 'ha,' as pronounced, may signify either 'leaves' or 'teeth;' and the word 'hana,' either 'flowers' or 'nose.' The yamazakura puts forth its ha (leaves) before its hana (flowers). Wherefore a man whose ha (teeth) project in advance of his hana (nose) is called a yamazakura. Prognathism is not uncommon in Japan, especially among the lower classes.

13. 'If one should ask you concerning the heart of a true Japanese, point to the wild cherry flower glowing in the sun.'

14. There are three noteworthy varieties: one bearing red, one pink and white, and one pure white flowers.

popular holidays. Nor are these, although the most famed, the only flowers thus loved. The wistaria, the convolvulus, the peony, each in its season, form displays of efflorescence lovely enough to draw whole populations out of the cities into the country to see them. In Izumo, the blossoming of the peony is especially marvelous. The most famous place for this spectacle is the little island of Daikonshima, in the grand Naka-umi lagoon, about an hour's sail from Matsue. In May the whole island flames crimson with peonies; and even the boys and girls of the public schools are given a holiday, in order that they may enjoy the sight.

Though the plum flower is certainly a rival in beauty of the sakura-no-hana, the Japanese compare woman's beauty — physical beauty — to the cherry flower, never to the plum flower. But womanly virtue and sweetness, on the other hand, are compared to the ume-no-hana, never to the cherry blossom. It is a great mistake to affirm, as some writers have done, that the Japanese never think of comparing a woman to trees and flowers. For grace, a maiden is likened to a slender willow;[15] for youthful charm, to the cherry-tree in flower; for sweetness of heart, to the blossoming plum-tree. Nay, the old Japanese poets have compared woman to all beautiful things. They have even sought similes from flowers for her various poses, for her movements, as in the verse:

> *Tateba shakuyaku;*[16]
> *Suwareba botan;*
> *Aruku sugatawa*
> *Himeyuri*[17] *no hana.*[18]

Why, even the names of the humblest country girls are often those of beautiful trees or flowers prefixed by the honorific

15. The expression 'yanagi-goshi,' 'a willow-waist,' is one of several in common use comparing slender beauty to the willow-tree.

16. *Peonia albiflora.* The name signifies the delicacy of beauty. The simile of the botan (the tree peony) can be fully appreciated only by one who is acquainted with the Japanese flower.

17. Some say keshiyuri (poppy) instead of himeyuri. The latter is a graceful species of lily, *Lilium callosum.*

18. 'Standing, she is a shakuyaku; seated, she is a botan; and the charm of her figure in walking is the charm of a himeyuri.'

O:[19] O-Matsu (Pine), O-Také (Bamboo), O-Umé (Plum), O-Hana
(Blossom), O-Iné (Ear-of-Young-Rice), not to speak of the professional
flower-names of dancing-girls and of jorō. It has been argued with
considerable force that the origin of certain tree-names borne by girls
must be sought in the folk-conception of the tree as an emblem of
longevity, or happiness, or good fortune, rather than in any popular
idea of the beauty of the tree in itself. But however this may be,
proverb, poem, song, and popular speech today yield ample proof that
the Japanese comparisons of women to trees and flowers are in no wise
inferior to our own in aesthetic sentiment.

VI

That trees, at least Japanese trees, have souls cannot seem an unnatural
fancy to one who has seen the blossoming of the umenoki and the
sakuranoki. This is a popular belief in Izumo and elsewhere. It is
not in accord with Buddhist philosophy, and yet in a certain sense
it strikes one as being much closer to cosmic truth than the old
Western orthodox notion of trees as 'things created for the use of
man.' Furthermore, there exist several odd superstitions about particular
trees, not unlike certain West Indian beliefs which have had a good
influence in checking the destruction of valuable timber. Japan, like
the tropical world, has its goblin trees. Of these, the enoki (*Celtis
willdenowiana*) and the yanagi (drooping willow) are deemed especially
ghostly, and are rarely now to be found in old Japanese gardens.
Both are believed to have the power of haunting. 'Enoki ga bakeru,'
the Izumo saying is. You will find in a Japanese dictionary the word
'bakeru' translated by such terms as 'to be transformed,' 'to be meta-
morphosed,' 'to be changed,' etc.; but the belief about these trees
is very singular, and cannot be explained by any such rendering
of the verb 'bakeru.' The tree itself does not change form or place,
but a spectre called Ki-no o-baké disengages itself from the tree

19. In the higher classes of Japanese society today, the honorific *O* is not, as
a rule, used before the names of girls, and showy appellations are not given to
daughters. Even among the poor respectable classes, names resembling those of geisha,
etc., are in disfavor. But those above cited are good, honest, everyday names.

and walks about in various guises.[20] Most often the shape assumed by the phantom is that of a beautiful woman. The tree spectre seldom speaks, and seldom ventures to go very far away from its tree. If approached, it immediately shrinks back into the trunk or the foliage. It is said that if either an old yanagi or a young enoki be cut, blood will flow from the gash. When such trees are very young it is not believed that they have supernatural habits, but they become more dangerous the older they grow.

There is a rather pretty legend — recalling the old Greek dream of dryads — about a willow-tree which grew in the garden of a samurai of Kyōto. Owing to its weird reputation, the tenant of the homestead desired to cut it down; but another samurai dissuaded him, saying: 'Rather sell it to me, that I may plant it in my garden. That tree has a soul; it were cruel to destroy its life.' Thus purchased and transplanted, the yanagi flourished well in its new home, and its spirit, out of gratitude, took the form of a beautiful woman, and became the wife of the samurai who had befriended it. A charming boy was the result of this union. A few years later, the daimyō to whom the ground belonged gave orders that the tree should be cut down. Then the wife wept bitterly, and for the first time revealed to her husband the whole story. 'And now,' she added, 'I know that I must die; but our child will live, and you will always love him. This thought is my only solace.' Vainly the astonished and terrified husband sought to retain her. Bidding him farewell forever, she vanished into the tree. Needless to say that the samurai did everything in his power to persuade the daimyō to forego his purpose. The prince wanted the tree for the reparation of a great Buddhist temple, the San-jiu-san-gen-dō.[21] The tree was felled, but, having fallen, it suddenly became so heavy that three hundred men

20. Mr Satow has found in Hirata a belief to which this seems to some extent akin, the curious Shintō doctrine 'according to which a divine being throws off portions of itself by a process of fissure, thus producing what are called waki-mi-tama — parted spirits, with separate functions.' The great god of Izumo, Oho-kuni-nushi-no-Kami, is said by Hirata to have three such 'parted spirits:' his rough spirit (ara-mi-tama) that punishes, his gentle spirit (nigi-mi-tama) that pardons, and his benedictory or beneficent spirit (saka-mi-tama) that blesses. There is a Shintō story that the rough spirit of this god once met the gentle spirit without recognizing it.

21. Perhaps the most impressive of all the Buddhist temples in Kyōto. It is dedicated to Kwannon of the Thousand Hands, and is said to contain 33,333 of her images.

could not move it. Then the child, taking a branch in his little hand, said, 'Come,' and the tree followed him, gliding along the ground to the court of the temple.

Although said to be a bakemono-ki, the enoki sometimes receives highest religious honors; for the spirit of the god Kōjin, to whom old dolls are dedicated, is supposed to dwell within certain very ancient enoki trees, and before these are placed shrines whereat people make prayers.

VII

The second garden, on the north side, is my favorite. It contains no large growths. It is paved with blue pebbles, and its centre is occupied by a pondlet — a miniature lake fringed with rare plants, and containing a tiny island, with tiny mountains and dwarf peach-trees and pines and azaleas, some of which are perhaps more than a century old, though scarcely more than a foot high. Nevertheless, this work, seen as it was intended to be seen, does not appear to the eye in miniature at all. From a certain angle of the guest-room looking out upon it, the appearance is that of a real lake shore with a real island beyond it, a stone's throw away. So cunning the art of the ancient gardener who contrived all this, and who has been sleeping for a hundred years under the cedars of Gesshoji, that the illusion can be detected only from the zashiki by the presence of an ishidōrō, or stone lamp, upon the island. The size of the ishidōrō betrays the false perspective, and I do not think it was placed there when the garden was made.

Here and there at the edge of the pond, and almost level with the water, are placed large flat stones, on which one may either stand or squat, to watch the lacustrine population or to tend the water-plants. There are beautiful water-lilies, whose bright green leaf-disks float oilily upon the surface (*Nuphar japonica*), and many lotus plants of two kinds, those which bear pink and those which bear pure white flowers. There are iris plants growing along the bank, whose blossoms are prismatic violet, and there are various ornamental grasses and ferns and mosses. But the pond is essentially a lotus pond; the lotus plants make its greatest charm. It is a delight to watch every phase of their marvelous growth, from the first unrolling of the leaf to the fall of the last flower. On rainy days. especially the lotus plants are worth observing. Their great cup-shaped leaves, swaying high above the pond, catch the rain and hold it a while; but always after the water in the leaf reaches a certain level the stem bends, and empties the leaf with a loud plash, and then straightens again. Rain-water upon a lotus-leaf is a favorite subject with Japanese metal-workers, and metal-work only can reproduce the effect, for the motion and color of water moving upon the green oleaginous surface are exactly those of quicksilver.

VIII

The third garden, which is very large, extends beyond the inclosure containing the lotus pond to the foot of the wooded hills which form the northern and northeastern boundary of this old samurai quarter. Formerly all this broad level space was occupied by a bamboo grove; but it is now little more than a waste of grasses and wild flowers. In the northeast corner there is a magnificent wall, from which ice-cold water is brought into the house through a most ingenious little aqueduct of bamboo pipes; and in the northwestern end, veiled by tall weeds, there stands a very small stone shrine of Inari, with two proportionately small stone foxes sitting before it. Shrine and images are chipped and broken, and thickly patched with dark green moss. But on the east side of the house one little square of soil belonging to this large division of the garden is still cultivated. It is devoted entirely to chrysanthemum plants, which are shielded from heavy rain and strong sun by slanting frames of light wood fashioned like shōji, with panes of white paper, and supported like awnings upon thin posts of bamboo. I can venture to add nothing to what has already been written about these marvelous products of Japanese floriculture considered in themselves; but there is a little story relating to chrysanthemums which I may presume to tell.

There is one place in Japan where it is thought unlucky to cultivate chrysanthemums, for reasons which shall presently appear· and that place is in the pretty little city of Himeji, in the province of Harima. Himeji contains the ruins of a great castle of thirty turrets; and a daimyō used to dwell therein whose revenue was one hundred and fifty-six thousand koku of rice. Now, in the house of one of that daimyō's chief retainers there was a maidservant, of good family, whose name was O-Kiku; and the name 'Kiku' signifies a chrysanthemum flower. Many precious things were intrusted to her charge, and among others ten costly dishes of gold. One of these was suddenly missed, and could not be found; and the girl, being responsible therefore, and knowing not how otherwise to prove her innocence, drowned herself in a well. But ever thereafter her ghost, returning nightly, could be heard counting the dishes slowly, with sobs:

Ichi-mai,	Yo-mai,	Shichi-mai,
Ni-mai,	Go-mai,	Hachi-mai,
San-mai,	Roku-mai,	Ku-mai —

Then would be heard a despairing cry and a loud burst of weeping; and again the girl's voice counting the dishes plaintively: 'One — two — three — four — five — six — seven — eight — *nine —*'

Her spirit passed into the body of a strange little insect, whose head faintly resembles that of a ghost with long disheveled hair; and it is called O-Kiku-mushi, or 'the fly of O-Kiku;' and it is found, they say, nowhere save in Himeji. A famous play was written about O-Kiku, which is still acted in all the popular theatres, entitled Banshu-O-Kiku-no-Sara-ya-shiki; or, The Manor of the Dish of O-Kiku of Banshu.

Some declare that Banshu is only the corruption of the name of an ancient quarter of Tōkyō (Yedo), where the story should have been laid. But the people of Himeji say that part of their city now called Go-Ken-Yashiki is identical with the site of the ancient manor. What is certainly true is that to cultivate chrysanthemum flowers in the part of Himeji called Go-Ken-Yashiki is deemed unlucky, because the name of O-Kiku signifies 'Chrysanthemum.' Therefore, nobody, I am told, ever cultivates chrysanthemums there.

IX

Now of the ujō, or things having desire, which inhabit these gardens.

There are four species of frogs: three that dwell in the lotus pond, and one that lives in the trees. The tree frog is a very pretty little creature, exquisitely green; it has a shrill cry, almost like the note of a semi; and it is called amagaeru, or 'the rain frog,' because, like its kindred in other countries, its croaking is an omen of rain. The pond frogs are called babagaeru, shinagaeru, and Tono-san-gaeru. Of these, the first named variety is the largest and the ugliest: its color is very disagreeable, and its full name ('babagaeru' being a decent abbreviation) is quite as offensive as its hue. The shinagaeru, or 'striped frog,' is not handsome, except by comparison with the previously mentioned creature. But the Tono-san-gaeru, so called after a famed daimyō who left behind him a memory of great splendor, is beautiful: its color is a fine bronze-red.

Besides these varieties of frogs there lives in the garden a huge uncouth goggle-eyed thing which, although called here hikigaeru, I take to be a toad. 'Hikigaeru' is the term ordinarily used for a bullfrog. This creature enters the house almost daily to be fed, and seems to have no fear even of strangers. My people consider it a luck bringing visitor; and it is credited with the power of drawing all the mosquitoes out of a room into its mouth by simply sucking its breath in. Much as it is cherished by gardeners and others, there is a legend about a goblin toad of old times, which, by thus sucking in its breath, drew into its mouth, not insects, but men.

The pond is inhabited also by many small fish; imori, or newts, with bright red bellies; and multitudes of little water-beetles, called maimaimushi, which pass their whole time in gyrating upon the surface of the water so rapidly that it is almost impossible to distinguish their shape clearly. A man who runs about aimlessly to and fro, under the influence of excitement, is compared to a maimaimushi. And there are some beautiful snails, with yellow stripes on their shells. Japanese children have a charm-song which is supposed to have power to make the snail put out its horns:

> *Daidaimushi,[22] daidaimushi, tsuno chitto dashare!*
> *Ame kaze fuku kara tsuno chitto dashare![23]*

The playground of the children of the better classes has always

22. Daidaimushi in Izumo. The dictionary word is dedemushi. The snail is supposed to be very fond of wet weather; and one who goes out much in the rain is compared to a snail – dedemushi no yona.

23. 'Snail, snail, put out your horns a little: it rains and the wind is blowing, so put out your horns, just for a little while.'

been the family garden, as that of the children of the poor is the temple court. It is in the garden that the little ones first learn something of the wonderful life of plants and the marvels of the insect world; and there, also, they are first taught those pretty legends and songs about birds and flowers which form so charming a part of Japanese folk-lore. As the home training of the child is left mostly to the mother, lessons of kindness to animals are early inculcated; and the results are strongly marked in after life. It is true, Japanese children are not entirely free from that unconscious tendency to cruelty characteristic of children in all countries, as a survival of primitive instincts. But in this regard the great moral difference between the sexes is strongly marked from the earliest years. The tenderness of the woman-soul appears even in the child. Little Japanese girls who play with insects or small animals rarely hurt them, and generally set them free after they have afforded a reasonable amount of amusement. Little boys are not nearly so good, when out of sight of parents or guardians. But if seen doing anything cruel, a child is made to feel ashamed of the act, and hears the Buddhist warning, 'Thy future birth will be unhappy, if thou dost cruel things.'

Somewhere among the rocks in the pond lives a small tortoise – left in the garden, probably, by the previous tenants of the house. It is very pretty, but manages to remain invisible for weeks at a time. In popular mythology, the tortoise is the servant of the divinity Kompira;[24] and if a pious fisherman finds a tortoise, he writes upon his back characters signifying 'Servant of the Deity Kompira,' and then gives it a drink of saké and sets it free. It is supposed to be very fond of saké.

Some say that the land tortoise, or 'stone tortoise,' only, is the servant of Kompira, and the sea tortoise, or turtle, the servant of the Dragon Empire beneath the sea. The turtle is said to have the power to create, with its breath, a cloud, a fog, or a magnificent palace. It figures in the beautiful old folk-tale of Urashima.[25] All tortoises are supposed to live for a thousand years, wherefore one of the most frequent symbols of longevity in Japanese art is a tortoise.

24. A Buddhist divinity, but within recent times identified by Shintō with the god Kotohira.
25. See Professor Chamberlain's version of it in The Japanese Fairy-Tale Series, with charming illustrations by a native artist.

But the tortoise most commonly represented by native painters and metal-workers has a peculiar tail, or rather a multitude of small tails, extending behind it like the fringes of a straw rain-coat, mino, whence it is called minogamé. Now, some of the tortoises kept in the sacred tanks of Buddhist temples attain a prodigious age, and certain water-plants attach themselves to the creatures' shells and stream behind them when they walk. The myth of the minogamé is supposed to have had its origin in old artistic efforts to represent the appearance of such tortoises with confervæ fastened upon their shells.

x

Early in summer the frogs are surprisingly numerous, and, after dark, are noisy beyond description; but week by week their nightly clamor grows feebler, as their numbers diminish under the attacks of many enemies. A large family of snakes, some fully three feet long, make occasional inroads into the colony. The victims often utter piteous cries, which are promptly responded to, whenever possible, by some inmate of the house, and many a frog has been saved by my servant-girl, who, by a gentle tap with a bamboo rod, compels the snake to let its prey go. These snakes are beautiful swimmers. They make themselves quite free about the garden; but they come out only on hot days. None of my people would think of injuring or killing one of them. Indeed, in Izumo it is said that to kill a snake is unlucky. 'If you kill a snake without provocation,' a peasant assured me, 'you will afterwards find its head in the komebitsu [the box in which cooked rice is kept] when you take off the lid.'

But the snakes devour comparatively few frogs. Impudent kites and crows are their most implacable destroyers; and there is a very pretty weasel which lives under the kura (godown), and which does not hesitate to take either fish or frogs out of the pond, even when the lord of the manor is watching. There is also a cat which poaches in my preserves, a gaunt outlaw, a master thief, which I have made sundry vain attempts to reclaim from vagabondage. Partly because of the immorality of this cat, and partly because it happens to have a long tail, it has the evil reputation of being a nekomata, or goblin cat.

It is true that in Izumo some kittens are born with long tails;

but it is very seldom that they are suffered to grow up with long tails. For the natural tendency of cats is to become goblins; and this tendency to metamorphosis can be checked only by cutting off their tails in kittenhood. Cats are magicians, tails or no tails, and have the power of making corpses dance. Cats are ungrateful. 'Feed a dog for three days,' says a Japanese proverb, 'and he will remember your kindness for three years; feed a cat for three years and she will forget your kindness in three days.' Cats are mischievous: they tear the mattings, and make holes in the shōji, and sharpen their claws upon the pillars of tokonoma. Cats are under a curse: only the cat and the venomous serpent wept not at the death of Buddha; and these shall never enter into the bliss of the Gokuraku. For all these reasons, and others too numerous to relate, cats are not much loved in Izumo, and are compelled to pass the greater part of their lives out of doors.

XI

Not less than eleven varieties of butterflies have visited the neighborhood of the lotus pond within the past few days. The most common variety is snowy white. It is supposed to be especially attracted by the na, or rapeseed plant; and when little girls see it, they sing:

> *Chō-chō, chō-chō, na no ha ni tomare;*
> *Na no ha ga iyenara, te ni tomare.*[26]

But the most interesting insects are certainly the semi (cicadae). These Japanese tree crickets are much more extraordinary singers than even the wonderful cicadae of the tropics; and they are much less tiresome, for there is a different species of semi, with a totally different song, for almost every month during the whole warm season. There are, I believe, seven kinds; but I have become familiar with only four. The first to be heard in my trees is the natsuzemi, or summer semi: it makes a sound like the Japanese monosyllable *ji*, beginning wheezily, slowly swelling into a crescendo shrill as the blowing of steam, and dying away in another wheeze. This *j-i-i-iiiiiiiiii* is so deafening that when two or three natsuzemi come close to

26. 'Butterfly, little butterfly, light upon the *na* leaf. But if thou dost not like the na leaf, light, I pray thee, upon my hand.'

the window I am obliged to make them go away. Happily the natsuzemi is soon succeeded by the minminzemi, a much finer musician, whose name is derived from its wonderful note. It is said 'to chant like a Buddhist priest reciting the kyō:' and certainly, upon hearing it the first time, one can scarcely believe that one is listening to a mere cicada. The minminzemi is followed, early in autumn, by a beautiful green semi, the higurashi, which makes a singularly clear sound, like the rapid ringing of a small bell — *kana-kana-kana-kana-kana*. But the most astonishing visitor of all comes still later, the tsuku-tsuku-bōshi.[27] I fancy this creature can have no rival in the whole world of cicadae: its music is exactly like the song of a bird. Its name, like that of the minminzemi, is onomatopoetic; but in Izumo the sounds of its chant are given thus:

Tsuku-tsuku uisu,[28]
Tsuku-tsuku uisu,

Tsuku-tsuku uisu;
　　Ui-ōsu,
　　Ui-ōsu,
　　Ui-ōsu,
　　Ui-ōs-s-s-s-s-s-s-su.

However, the semi are not the only musicians of the garden. Two remarkable creatures aid their orchestra. The first is a beautiful bright green grasshopper, known to the Japanese by the curious name of hotoke-no-uma, or 'the horse of the dead.' This insect's head really bears some resemblance in shape to the head of a horse — hence the fancy. It is a queerly familiar creature, allowing itself to be taken in the hand without struggling, and generally making itself quite at home in the house, which it often enters. It makes a very thin sound, which the Japanese write as a repetition of the syllables *jun-ta;* and the name junta is sometimes given to the grasshopper itself. The other insect is also a green grasshopper, somewhat larger, and much shyer: it is called gisu,[29] on account of its chant:

27. 'Bōshi' means 'a hat;' 'tsukeru,' 'to put on.' But this etymology is more than doubtful.

28. Some say 'Chokko-chokko-uisu.' 'Uisu' would be pronounced in English very much like 'weece,' the final *u* being silent. 'Uiōsu' would be something like 'we-oce.'

29. Pronounced almost as 'geece.'

> Chon,
> > Gisu;
> Chon,
> > Gisu;
> Chon,
> > Gisu;
> Chon ... (ad libitum).

Several lovely species of dragon-flies (tombō) hover about the pondlet on hot bright days. One variety – the most beautiful creature of the kind I ever saw, gleaming with metallic colors indescribable, and spectrally slender – is called Tenshi-tombō, 'the Emperor's dragon-fly.' There is another, the largest of Japanese dragon-flies, but somewhat rare, which is much sought after by children as a plaything. Of this species it is said that there are many more males than females; and what I can vouch for as true is that, if you catch a female, the male can be almost immediately attracted by exposing the captive. Boys, accordingly, try to secure a female, and when one is captured they tie it with a thread to some branch, and sing a curious little song, of which these are the original words:

> Konna[30] danshō Korai ō
> Adzuma no metō ni makete
> Nigeru wa haji dewa naikai?

Which signifies, 'Thou, the male, King of Korea, dost thou not feel shame to flee away from the Queen of the East?' (This taunt is an allusion to the story of the conquest of Korea by the Empress Jin-gō.) And the male comes invariably, and is also caught. In Izumo the first seven words of the original song have been corrupted into 'konna unjo Korai abura no mito;' and the name of the male dragon-fly, unjo, and that of the female, mito, are derived from two words of the corrupted version.

XII

On warm nights all sorts of unbidden guests invade the house in multitudes. Two varieties of mosquitoes do their utmost to make life unpleasant, and these have learned the wisdom of not approaching

---

30. Contraction of 'kore naru.'

a lamp too closely; but hosts of curious and harmless things cannot be prevented from seeking their death in the flame. The most numerous victims of all, which come thick as a shower of rain, are called Sanemori. At least they are so called in Izumo, where they do much damage to growing rice.

Now the name Sanemori is an illustrious one, that of a famous warrior of old times belonging to the Genji clan. There is a legend that while he was fighting with an enemy on horseback his own steed slipped and fell in a rice-field, and he was consequently overpowered and slain by his antagonist. He became a rice-devouring insect, which is still respectfully called, by the peasantry of Izumo, Sanemori-San. They light fires, on certain summer nights, in the rice-fields to attract the insect, and beat gongs and sound bamboo flutes, chanting the while, 'O Sanemori, augustly deign to come hither!' A kannushi performs a religious rite, and a straw figure representing a horse and rider is then either burned or thrown into a neighboring river or canal. By this ceremony it is believed that the fields are cleared of the insect.

This tiny creature is almost exactly the size and color of a rice-husk. The legend concerning it may have arisen from the fact that its body, together with the wings, bears some resemblance to the helmet of a Japanese warrior.[31]

Next in number among the victims of fire are the moths, some of which are very strange and beautiful. The most remarkable is an enormous creature popularly called okori-chōchō, or the 'ague

---

31. A kindred legend attaches to the shiwan, a little yellow insect which preys upon cucumbers. The shiwan is said to have been once a physician, who, being detected in an amorous intrigue, had to fly for his life; but as he went his foot caught in a cucumber vine, so that he fell and was overtaken and killed, and his ghost became an insect, the destroyer of cucumber vines.

In the zoological mythology and plant mythology of Japan there exist many legends offering a curious resemblance to the old Greek tales of metamorphoses. Some of the most remarkable bits of such folk-lore have originated, however, in comparatively modern time. The legend of the crab called heikegani, found at Nagato, is an example. The souls of the Taira warriors who perished in the great naval battle of Dan-no-ura (now Seto-Nakai), 1185, are supposed to have been transformed into heikegani. The shell of the heikegani is certainly surprising. It is wrinkled into the likeness of a grim face, or rather into exact semblance of one of those black iron visors or masks, which feudal warriors wore in battle, and which were shaped like frowning visages.

moth,' because there is a superstitious belief that it brings intermittent fever into any house it enters. It has a body quite as heavy and almost as powerful as that of the largest humming-bird, and its struggles, when caught in the hand, surprise by their force. It makes a very loud whirring sound while flying. The wings of one which I examined measured, outspread, five inches from tip to tip, yet seemed small in proportion to the heavy body. They were richly mottled with dusky browns and silver grays of various tones.

Many flying night-comers, however, avoid the lamp. Most fantastic of all visitors is the tōrō or kamakiri, called in Izumo kamakaké, a bright green praying mantis, extremely feared by children for its capacity to bite. It is very large. I have seen specimens over six inches long. The eyes of the kamakaké are a brilliant black at night, but by day they appear grass-colored, like the rest of the body. The mantis is very intelligent and surprisingly aggressive. I saw one attacked by a vigorous frog easily put its enemy to flight. It fell a prey subsequently to other inhabitants of the pond, but it required the combined efforts of several frogs to vanquish the monstrous insect, and even then the battle was decided only when the kamakaké had been dragged into the water.

Other visitors are beetles of divers colors, and a sort of small roach called goki-kaburi, signifying 'one whose head is covered with a bowl.' It is alleged that the goki-kaburi likes to eat human eyes, and is therefore the abhorred enemy of Ichibata-Sama — Yakushi-Nyorai of Ichibata — by whom diseases of the eye are healed. To kill the goki-kiburi is consequently thought to be a meritorious act in the sight of this Buddha. Always welcome are the beautiful fireflies (hotaru), which enter quite noiselessly, and at once seek the darkest place in the house, slow-glimmering, like sparks moved by a gentle wind. They are supposed to be very fond of water; wherefore children sing to them this little song:

> *Hotaru kōe midzu nomashō;*
> *Achi no midzu wa nigaizo;*
> *Kochi no midzu wa amaizo.*[32]

A pretty gray lizard, quite different from some which usually haunt

32. 'Come, firefly, I will give you water to drink. The water of that place is bitter; the water here is sweet.'

the garden, also makes its appearance at night, and pursues its prey along the ceiling. Sometimes an extraordinarily large centipede attempts the same thing, but with less success, and has to be seized with a pair of fire-tongs and thrown into the exterior darkness. Very rarely, an enormous spider appears. This creature seems inoffensive. If captured, it will feign death until certain that it is not watched, when it will run away with surprising swiftness if it gets a chance. It is hairless, and very different from the tarantula, or fukurogumo. It is called miyamagumo, or mountain spider. There are four other kinds of spiders common in this neighborhood: tenagakumo, or 'long-armed spider;' hiratakumo, or 'flat spider;' jikumo, or 'earth spider;' and totatekumo, or 'door-shutting spider.' Most spiders are considered evil beings. A spider seen anywhere at night, the people say, should be killed; for all spiders that show themselves after dark are goblins. While people are awake and watchful, such creatures make themselves small; but when everybody is fast asleep, then they assume their true goblin shape, and become monstrous.

XIII

The high wood of the hill behind the garden is full of bird life. There dwell wild uguisu, owls, wild doves, too many crows, and a queer bird that makes weird noises at night — long deep sounds of *hoo, hoo.* It is called awamakidori or the 'millet-sowing bird,' because when the farmers hear its cry, they know that it is time to plant the millet. It is quite small and brown, extremely shy, and, so far as I can learn, altogether nocturnal in its habits.

But rarely, very rarely, a far stranger cry is heard in those trees at night, a voice as of one crying in pain the syllables '*ho-to-to-gi-su.*' The cry and the name of that which utters it are one and the same, hototogisu.

It is a bird of which weird things are told; for they say it is not really a creature of this living world, but a night wanderer from the Land of Darkness. In the Meido its dwelling is among those sunless mountains of Shide over which all souls must pass to reach the place of judgment. Once in each year it comes; the time of its coming is the end of the fifth month, by the antique counting of moons; and the peasants, hearing its voice, say one to the other, 'Now must we

sow the rice; for the Shide-no-taosa is with us.' The word taosa signifies the head man of a mura, or village, as villages were governed
in the old days; but why the hototogisu is called the taosa of Shide
I do not know. Perhaps it is deemed to be a soul from some shadowy
hamlet of the Shide hills, whereat the ghosts are wont to rest on
their weary way to the realm of Emma, the King of Death.

Its cry has been interpreted in various ways. Some declare that
the hototogisu does not really repeat its own name, but asks, 'Honzon
kaketaka?' ('Has the honzon[33] been suspended?') Others, resting their
interpretation upon the wisdom of the Chinese, aver that the bird's
speech signifies, 'Surely it is better to return home.' This, at least,
is true: that all who journey far from their native place, and hear the
voice of the hototogisu in other distant provinces, are seized with
the sickness of longing for home.

Only at night, the people say, is its voice heard, and most often
upon the nights of great moons; and it chants while hovering high
out of sight, wherefore a poet has sung of it thus:

> Hito koe wa.
> Tsuki ga naitaka
> Hototogisu![34]

And another has written:

> Hototogisu
> Nakitsuru kuta wo

> Nagamureba,
> Tada ariake no
> Tsuki zo nokoreru.[35]

The dweller in cities may pass a lifetime without hearing the hototogisu. Caged, the little creature will remain silent and die. Poets often

33 By honzon is here meant the sacred kakemono, or picture, exposed to public
view in the temples only upon the birthday of the Buddha, which is the eighth day
of the old fourth month. Honzon also signifies the principal image in a Buddhist temple.

34. 'A solitary voice!
Did the Moon cry?
'Twas but the hototogisu.'

35. 'When I gaze towards the place where I heard the hototogisu cry, lo! there
is naught save the wan morning moon.'

wait vainly in the dew, from sunset till dawn, to hear the strange
cry which has inspired so many exquisite verses. But those who have
heard found it so mournful that they have likened it to the cry of
one wounded suddenly to death.

> *Hototogisu*
> *Chi ni naku koe wa*
> *Ariake no*
> *Tsuki yori hokani*
> *Kiku hito mo nashi.*[36]

Concerning Izumo owls, I shall content myself with citing a
composition by one of my Japanese students:

'The Owl is a hateful bird that sees in the dark. Little children who
cry are frightened by the threat that the Owl will come to take them
away; for the Owl cries, "Ho! ho! sorōtto kōka! sorōtto kōka!" which
means, "Thou! must I enter slowly?" It also cries, "Noritsuke hose! ho!
ho!" which means, "Do thou make the starch to use in washing
tomorrow!" And when the women hear that cry, they know that tomorrow will be a fine day. It also cries, "Tototo," "The man dies," and
"Kōtokokko," "The boy dies." So people hate it. And crows hate it
so much that it is used to catch crows. The Farmer puts an Owl in
the rice-field; and all the crows come to kill it, and they get caught
fast in the snares. This should teach us not to give way to our dislikes
for other people.'

The kites which hover over the city all day do not live in the
neighborhood. Their nests are far away upon the blue peaks; but they
pass much of their time in catching fish, and in stealing from back
yards. They pay the wood and the garden swift and sudden piratical
visits; and their sinister cry – *pi-yorōyorō, pi-yorōyorō* – sounds at intervals over the town from dawn till sundown. Most insolent of all
feathered creatures they certainly are – more insolent than even their
fellow-robbers, the crows. A kite will drop five miles to filch a tai
out of a fish-seller's bucket, or a fried cake out of a child's hand, and
shoot back to the clouds before the victim of the theft has time to

36. 'Save only the morning moon, none heard the heart's-blood cry of the hototogisu.'

stoop for a stone. Hence the saying, 'to look as surprised as if one's aburagé[37] had been snatched from one's hand by a kite.' There is, moreover, no telling what a kite may think proper to steal. For example, my neighbor's servant-girl went to the river the other day, wearing in her hair a string of small scarlet beads made of rice-grains prepared and dyed in a certain ingenious way. A kite lighted upon her head, and tore away and swallowed the string of beads. But it is great fun to feed these birds with dead rats or mice which have been caught in traps overnight and subsequently drowned. The instant a dead rat is exposed to view a kite pounces from the sky to bear it away. Sometimes a crow may get the start of the kite, but the crow must be able to get to the woods very swiftly indeed in order to keep his prize. The children sing this song:

> *Tobi, tobi, maute mise!*
> *Ashita no ba ni*
> *Karasu ni kakushite*
> *Nezumi yaru.*[38]

The mention of dancing refers to the beautiful balancing motion of the kites wings in flight. By suggestion this motion is poetically compared to the graceful swaying of a maiko, or dancing-girl, extending her arms and waving the long wide sleeves of her silken robe.

Although there is a numerous sub-colony of crows in the wood behind my house, the headquarters of the corvine army are in the pine grove of the ancient castle grounds, visible from my front rooms. To see the crows all flying home at the same hour every evening is an interesting spectacle, and popular imagination has found an amusing comparison for it in the hurry-skurry of people running to a fire. This explains the meaning of a song which children sing to the crows returning to their nests:

> *Ato no karasu saki ine,*
> *Ware ga iye ga yakeru ken,*
> *Hayō inde midzu kake,*

37. A sort of doughnut made of bean flour, or tofu.
38. 'Kite, kite, let me see you dance, and tomorrow evening, when the crows do not know, I will give you a rat.'

Midzu ga nakya yarozo,
Amattara ko ni yure,
Ko ga nakya modose.[39]

Confucianism seems to have discovered virtue in the crow. There is a Japanese proverb, 'Karasu ni hampo no ko ari,' meaning that the crow performs the filial duty of hampo, or, more literally, 'the filial duty of hampo exists in the crow.' 'Hampo' means, literally, 'to return a feeding.' The young crow is said to requite its parents' care by feeding them when it becomes strong. Another example of filial piety has been furnished by the dove. 'Hato ni sanshi no rei ari' – the dove sits three branches below its parent, or, more literally, 'has the three-branch etiquette to perform.'

The cry of the wild dove (yamabato), which I hear almost daily from the wood, is the most sweetly plaintive sound that ever reached my ears. The Izumo peasantry say that the bird utters these words, which it certainly seems to do if one listens to it after having learned the alleged syllables:

> *Tété*
> > *poppō,*
> *Kaka*
> > *poppō,*
> *Tété*
> > *poppō,*
> *Kaka*
> > *poppō,*
> *Tété . . . (sudden pause).*

'Tété' is the baby word for 'father,' and 'kaka' for 'mother;' and 'poppō' signifies, in infantile speech, 'the bosom.'[40]

Wild uguisu also frequently sweeten my summer with their song, and sometimes come very near the house, being attracted, apparently, by the chant of my caged pet. The uguisu is very common in this province. It haunts all the woods and the sacred groves in the neigh-

39. 'O tardy crow, hasten forward! Your house is all on fire. Hurry to throw water upon it. If there be no water, I will give you. If you have too much, give it to your child. If you have no child, then give it back to me.'

40. The words 'papa' and 'mamma' exist in Japanese baby language, but their meaning is not at all what might be supposed. Mamma, or, with the usual honorific, O-mamma, means 'boiled rice.' Papa means 'tobacco.'

borhood of the city, and I never made a journey in Izumo during the warm season without hearing its note from some shadowy place. But there are uguisu and uguisu. There are uguisu to be had for one or two yen, but the finely trained, cage-bred singer may command not less than a hundred.

It was at a little village temple that I first heard one curious belief about this delicate creature. In Japan, the coffin in which a corpse is borne to burial is totally unlike an Occidental coffin. It is a surprisingly small square box, wherein the dead is placed in a sitting posture. How any adult corpse can be put into so small a space may well be an enigma to foreigners. In cases of pronounced *rigor mortis* the work of getting the body into the coffin is difficult even for the professional dōshin-bozu. But the devout followers of Nichiren claim that after death their bodies will remain perfectly flexible; and the dead body of an uguisu, they affirm, likewise never stiffens, for this little bird is of their faith, and passes its life in singing praises unto the Sutra of the Lotus of the Good Law.

XIV

I have already become a little too fond of my dwelling-place. Each day, after returning from my college duties, and exchanging my teacher's uniform for the infinitely more comfortable Japanese robe, I find more than compensation for the weariness of five class-hours in the simple pleasure of squatting on the shaded veranda overlooking the gardens. Those antique garden walls, high-mossed below their ruined coping of tiles, seem to shut out even the murmur of the city's life. There are no sounds but the voices of birds, the shrilling of semi, or, at long, lazy intervals, the solitary plash of a diving frog. Nay, those walls seclude me from much more than city streets. Outside them hums the changed Japan of telegraphs and newspapers and steamships; within dwell the all-reposing peace of nature and the dreams of the sixteenth century. There is a charm of quaintness in the very air, a faint sense of something viewless and sweet all about one; perhaps the gentle haunting of dead ladies who looked like the ladies of the old picture-books, and who lived here when all this was new. Even in the summer light – touching the gray strange shapes of stone, thrilling through the foliage of the long-loved trees – there is the tenderness of a phantom caress. These are the gardens of the past. The future will know them only as dreams, creations of a forgotten art, whose charm no genius may reproduce.

Of the human tenants here no creature seems to be afraid. The little frogs resting upon the lotus-leaves scarcely shrink from my touch; the lizards sun themselves within easy reach of my hand; the water-snakes glide across my shadow without fear; bands of semi establish their deafening orchestra on a plum branch just above my head, and a praying mantis insolently poses on my knee. Swallows and sparrows not only build their nests on my roof, but even enter my rooms without concern – one swallow has actually built its nest in the ceiling of the bath-room – and the weasel purloins fish under my very eyes without any scruples of conscience. A wild uguisu perches on a cedar by the window, and in a burst of savage sweetness challenges my caged pet to a contest in song; and always through the golden air, from the green twilight of the mountain pines, there purls to me the plaintive, caressing, delicious call of the yamabato:

> *Tété*
>   *poppō,*
> *Kaka*
>   *poppō,*
> *Tété*
>   *poppō,*
> *Kaka*
>   *poppō,*
> *Tété. . .*

No European dove has such a cry. He who can hear, for the first time, the voice of the yamabato without feeling a new sensation at his heart little deserves to dwell in this happy world.

Yet all this – the old katchiū-yashiki and its gardens – will doubtless have vanished forever before many years. Already a multitude of gardens, more spacious and more beautiful than mine, have been converted into rice-fields or bamboo groves; and the quaint Izumo city, touched at last by some long-projected railway line – perhaps even within the present decade – will swell, and change, and grow common-place, and demand these grounds for the building of factories and mills. Not from here alone, but from all the land the ancient peace and the ancient charm seem doomed to pass away. For impermanency is the nature of things, more particularly in Japan; and the changes and the changers shall also be changed until there is found no place for them — and regret is vanity. The dead art that made the beauty of this place was the art, also, of that faith to which belongs the all-consoling text, *'Verily, even plants and trees, rocks and stones, all shall enter into Nirvana.'*

Survivals

In the gardens of certain Buddhist temples there are trees which have been famous for centuries — trees trained and clipped into extraordinary shapes. Some have the form of dragons; others have the form of pagodas, ships, umbrellas. Supposing that one of these trees were abandoned to its own natural tendencies, it would eventually lose the queer shape so long imposed upon it; but the outline would not be altered for a considerable time, as the new leafage would at first unfold only in the direction of least resistance: that is to say, within limits originally established by the shears and the pruning-knife. By sword and law the old Japanese society had been pruned and clipped, bent and bound, just like such a tree; and after the reconstructions of the Meiji period — after the abolition of the daimiates, and the suppression of the military class — it still maintained its former shape, just as the tree would continue to do when first abandoned by the gardener. Though delivered from the bonds of feudal law, released from the shears of military rule, the great bulk of the social structure preserved its ancient aspect; and the rare spectacle bewildered and delighted and deluded the Western observer. Here indeed was Elf-land — the strange, the beautiful, the grotesque, the very mysterious — totally unlike aught of strange and attractive ever beheld elsewhere. It was not a world of the nineteenth century after Christ, but a world of many centuries before Christ: yet this fact — the wonder of wonders — remained unrecognized; and it remains unrecognized by most people even to this day.

Fortunate indeed were those privileged to enter this astonishing fairy-land thirty odd years ago, before the period of superficial change, and to observe the unfamiliar aspects of its life: the universal urbanity, the smiling silence of crowds, the patient deliberation of toil, the absence of misery and struggle. Even yet, in those remoter districts where alien influence has wrought but little change, the charm of the old existence lingers and amazes; and the ordinary traveler can little understand what it means. That all are polite, that nobody quarrels, that everybody smiles, that pain and sorrow remain invisible, that the new police have nothing to do, would seem to prove a morally superior humanity. But for the trained sociologist it would prove something different, and suggest something very terrible. It would prove to him that this society had been moulded under immense coercion, and that the coercion must have been exerted uninterruptedly for thousands of years. He would immediately perceive that ethics and custom had not yet become dissociated, and that the conduct of each person was regulated by the will of the rest. He would know that personality could not develop in such a social medium – that no individual superiority dare assert itself, that no competition would be tolerated. He would understand that the outward charm of this life – its softness, its smiling silence as of dreams – signified the rule of the dead. He would recognize that between those minds and the minds of his own epoch no kinship of thought, no community of sentiment, no sympathy whatever, could exist – that the separating gulf was not to be measured by thousands of leagues, but only by thousands of years – that the psychological interval was hopeless as the distance from planet to planet. Yet this knowledge probably would not – certainly should not – blind him to the intrinsic charm of things. Not to feel the beauty of this archaic life is to prove oneself insensible to all beauty. Even that Greek world, for which our scholars and poets profess such loving admiration, must have been in many ways a world of the same kind, whose daily mental existence no modern mind could share.

Now that the great social tree, so wonderfully clipped and cared for during many centuries, is losing its fantastic shape, let us try to see how much of the original design can still be traced.

Under all the outward aspects of individual activity that modern Japan presents to the visitor's gaze, the ancient conditions really persist to an extent that no observation could reveal. Still the immemorial cult rules all the land. Still the family law, the communal law, and (though in a more irregular manner) the clan law control every action of existence. I do not refer to any written law, but only to the old unwritten religious law, with its host of obligations deriving from ancestor-worship. It is true that many changes − and, in the opinion of the wise, too many changes − have been made in civil legislation; but the ancient proverb 'Government laws are only seven-day laws' still represents popular sentiment in regard to hasty reforms. The old law, the law of the dead, is that by which the millions prefer to act and think. Though ancient social groupings have been officially abolished, regroupings of a corresponding sort have been formed, instinctively, throughout the country districts. In theory the individual is free; in practice he is scarcely more free than were his forefathers. Old penalties for breach of custom have been abrogated; yet communal opinion is able to compel the ancient obedience. Legal enactments can nowhere effect immediate change of sentiment and long-established usage − least of all among a people of such fixity of character as the Japanese. Young persons are no more at liberty now than were their fathers and mothers under the Shōgunate to marry at will, to invest their means and efforts in undertakings not sanctioned by family approval, to consider themselves in any way enfranchised from family authority; and it is probably better for the present that they are not. No man is yet complete master of his activities, his time, or his means.

Though the individual is now registered, and made directly accountable to the law, while the household has been relieved from its ancient responsibility for the acts of its members, still the family practically remains the social unit, retaining its patriarchal organization and its particular cult. Not unwisely, the modern legislators have protected this domestic religion: to weaken its bond at this time were to weaken the foundations of the national moral life − to introduce disintegrations into the most deeply seated structures of the social organism. The new codes forbid the man who becomes by succession the head of a house to abolish that house: he is not permitted to suppress a cult. No legal presumptive heir to the headship of a family can enter into another family as adopted son or husband; nor can he abandon the paternal house to establish an independent family of his own.[1] Provision has been made to meet extraordinary cases;

1. That is to say, he cannot separate himself from the family in law; but he is free to live in a separate house. The tendency to further disintegration of the family is shown by a custom which has been growing of late years, especially in Tōkyō: the

but no individual is allowed, without good and sufficient reason, to free himself from those traditional obligations which the family-cult imposes. As regards adoption, the new law maintains the spirit of the old, with fresh provision for the conservation of the family religion, permitting any person of legal age to adopt a son, on the simple condition that the person adopted shall be younger than the adopter. The new divorce laws do not permit the dismissal of a wife for sterility alone (and divorce for such cause had long been condemned by Japanese sentiment); but, in view of the facilities given for adoption, this reform does not endanger the continuance of the cult. An interesting example of the manner in which the law still protects ancestor-worship is furnished by the fact that an aged and childless widow, last representative of her family, is not permitted to remain without an heir. She must adopt a son if she can: if she cannot, because of poverty, or for other reasons, the local authorities will provide a son for her — that is to say, a male heir to maintain the family-worship. Such official interference would seem to us tyrannical: it is simply paternal, and represents the continuance of an ancient regulation intended to protect the bereaved against what Eastern faith still deems the supreme misfortune — the extinction of the home-cult ... In other respects the later codes allow of individual liberty unknown in previous generations. But the ordinary person would not dream of attempting to claim a legal right opposed to common opinion. Family and public sentiment are still more potent than law. The Japanese newspapers frequently record tragedies resulting from the prevention or dissolution of unions; and these tragedies afford strong proof that most young people would prefer even suicide to the probable consequence of a successful appeal to law against family decision.

*

custom of demanding, as a condition of marriage, that the bride shall not be obliged to live in the same house with the parents of the bridegroom. This custom is yet confined to certain classes, and has been adversely criticized. Many young men, on marrying, leave the parental home to begin independent housekeeping, though remaining legally attached to their parents' families, of course ... It will perhaps be asked, What becomes of the cult in such cases? The cult remains in the parental home. When the parents die, then the ancestral tablets are transferred to the home of the married son.

The communal form of coercion is less apparent in the large cities; but everywhere it endures to some extent, and in the agricultural districts it remains supreme. Between the new conditions and the old there is this difference, that the man who finds the yoke of his district hard to bear can now flee from it: he could not do so fifty years ago. But he can flee from it only to enter into another state of subordination of nearly the same kind. Full advantage, nevertheless, has been taken of this modern liberty of movement: thousands yearly throng to the cities; other thousands travel over the country, from province to province, working for a year or a season in one place, then going to another, with little more to hope for than experience of change. Emigration also has been taking place upon an extensive scale; but for the common class of emigrants, at least, the advantage of emigration is chiefly represented by the chance of earning larger wages. A Japanese emigrant community abroad organizes itself upon the home-plan;[2] and the individual emigrant probably finds himself as much under communal coercion in Canada, Hawaii, or the Philippine Islands as he could ever have been in his native province. Needless to say that in foreign countries such coercion is more than compensated by the aid and protection which the communal organization insures. But with the constantly increasing number of restless spirits at home, and the ever-widening experience of Japanese emigrants abroad, it would seem likely that the power of the commune for compulsory cooperation must become considerably weakened in the near future.

As for the tribal or clan law, it survives to the degree of remaining almost omnipotent in administrative circles, and in all politics. Voters, officials, legislators, do not follow principles in our sense of the word:

2. Except as regards the communal cult, perhaps. The domestic cult is transplanted; emigrants who go abroad, accompanied by their families, take the ancestral tablets with them. To what extent the communal cult may have been established in emigrant communities, I have not yet been able to learn. It would appear, however, that the absence of Ujigami in certain emigrant settlements is to be accounted for solely by the pecuniary difficulty of constructing such temples and maintaining competent officials. In Formosa, for example, though the domestic ancestor-cult is maintained in the homes of the Japanese settlers, Ujigami have not yet been established. The government, however, has erected several important Shintō temples; and I am told that some of these will probably be converted into Ujigami when the Japanese population has increased enough to justify the measure.

they follow men, and obey commands. In these spheres of action the penalties of disobedience of orders are endless as well as serious: by a single such offence one may array against oneself powers that will continue their hostile operation for years and years, unreasoningly, implacably, blindly, with the weight and persistence of natural forces

of winds or tides. Any comprehension of the history of Japanese politics during the last fifteen years is not possible without some knowledge of clan history. A political leader, fully acquainted with the history of clan parties, and their offshoots, can accomplish marvelous things; and even foreign residents, with long experience of Japanese life, have been able, by pressing upon clan interests, to exercise a very real power in government circles. But to the ordinary foreigner, Japanese contemporary politics must appear a chaos, a disintegration, a hopeless flux. The truth is that most things remain, under varying outward forms, 'as all were ordered, ages since,' though the shiftings have become more rapid, and the results less obvious, in the haste of an era of steam and electricity.

The greatest of living Japanese statesmen, the Marquis Ito, long ago perceived that the tendency of political life to agglomerations, to clan groupings, presented the most serious obstacle to the successful working of constitutional government. He understood that this tendency could be opposed only by considerations weightier than clan interests, considerations worthy of supreme sacrifice. He therefore formed a party of which every member was pledged to pass over clan interests, clique interests, personal and every other kind of interests, for the sake of national interests. Brought into collision with a hostile Cabinet in 1903, this party achieved the feat of controlling its animosities even to the extent of maintaining its foes in power; but large fragments broke off in the process. So profoundly is the grouping tendency, the clan sentiment, identified with national character, that the ultimate success of Marquis Ito's policy must still be considered doubtful. Only a national danger – the danger of war – has yet been able to weld all parties together, to make all wills work as one.

Not only politics, but nearly all phases of modern life, yield evidence that the disintegration of the old society has been superficial rather than fundamental. Structures dissolved have recrystallized, taking forms dissimilar in aspect to the original forms, but inwardly built upon the same plan. For the dissolutions really effected represented only a separation of masses, not a breaking up of substance into independent units; and these masses, again cohering, continue to act only as masses. Independence of personal action, in the Western sense, is still almost inconceivable. The individual of every class above the lowest must continue to be at once coercer and coerced. Like an atom within a solid body, he can vibrate; but the orbit of his vibration is fixed. He must act and be acted upon in ways differing little from those of ancient time.

As for being acted upon, the average man is under three kinds of pressure: pressure from above, exemplified in the will of his superiors; pressure about him, represented by the common will of his fellows and equals; pressure from below, represented by the general sentiment of his inferiors. And this last sort of coercion is not the least formidable.

Individual resistance to the first kind of pressure — that represented by authority — is not even to be thought of, because the superior represents a clan, a class, an exceedingly multiple power of some description; and no solitary individual, in the present order of things, can strive against a combination. To resist injustice he must find ample support, in which case his resistance does not represent individual action.

Resistance to the second kind of pressure — communal coercion — signifies ruin, loss of the right to form a part of the social body.

Resistance to the third sort of pressure, embodied in the common sentiment of inferiors, may result in almost anything — from momentary annoyance to sudden death — according to circumstances.

In all forms of society these three kinds of pressure are exerted to some degree; but in Japanese society, owing to inherited tendency, and traditional sentiment, their power is tremendous.

Thus, in every direction, the individual finds himself confronted by the despotism of collective opinion: it is impossible for him to act with safety except as one unit of a combination. The first kind of pressure deprives him of moral freedom, exacting unlimited obedience to orders; the second kind of pressure denies him the right to use his best faculties in the best way for his own advantage (that is to say, denies him the right of free competition); the third kind of pressure compels him, in directing the actions of others, to follow tradition, to forbear innovations, to avoid making any changes, however beneficial, which do not find willing acceptance on the part of his inferiors.

These are the social conditions which, under normal circumstances, make for stability, for conservation; and they represent the will of the dead. They are inevitable to a militant state; they make the strength of that state; they render facile the creation and maintenance of formidable armies. But they are not conditions favourable to success in the future international competition – in the industrial struggle for existence against societies incomparably more plastic, and of higher mental energy.

Insect-Musicians

Mushi yo mushi,
Naïté ingwa ga
Tsukuru nara?

   'O insect, insect! — think you that Karma can be exhausted by song?' —
Japanese poem

I

If you ever visit Japan, be sure to go to at least one temple-
festival — en-nichi. The festival ought to be seen at night, when everything shows to the best advantage in the glow of countless lamps
and lanterns. Until you have had this experience, you cannot know
what Japan is, you cannot imagine the real charm of queerness and
prettiness, the wonderful blending of grotesquery and beauty, to be
found in the life of the common people.

   In such a night you will probably let yourself drift awhile with
the stream of sightseers through dazzling lanes of booths full of toys
indescribable — dainty puerilities, fragile astonishments, laughter-
making oddities; you will observe representations of demons, gods,
and goblins; you will be startled by mandō — immense lantern-
transparencies, with monstrous faces painted upon them; you will have
glimpses of jugglers, acrobats, sword-dancers, fortune-tellers; you will
hear everywhere, above the tumult of voices, a ceaseless blowing of
flutes and booming of drums. All this may not be worth stopping for.
But presently, I am almost sure, you will pause in your promenade to
look at a booth illuminated like a magic-lantern, and stocked with tiny
wooden cages out of which an incomparable shrilling proceeds. The
booth is the booth of a vender of singing-insects; and the storm of noise

227

is made by the insects. The sight is curious; and a foreigner is nearly always attracted by it.

But having satisfied his momentary curiosity, the foreigner usually goes on his way with the idea that he has been inspecting nothing more remarkable than a particular variety of toys for children. He might easily be made to understand that the insect-trade of Tōkyō alone represents a yearly value of thousands of dollars; but he would certainly wonder if assured that the insects themselves are esteemed for the peculiar character of the sounds which they make. It would not be easy to convince him that in the aesthetic life of a most refined and artistic people, these insects hold a place not less important or well deserved than that occupied in Western civilization by our thrushes, linnets, nightingales, and canaries. What stranger could suppose that a literature one thousand years old – a literature full of curious and delicate beauty – exists upon the subject of these short-lived insect-pets?

The object of the present paper is, by elucidating these facts, to show how superficially our travelers might unconsciously judge the most interesting details of Japanese life. But such misjudgments are as natural as they are inevitable. Even with the kindest of intentions it is impossible to estimate correctly at sight anything of the extra-ordinary in Japanese custom, because the extraordinary nearly always relates to feelings, beliefs, or thoughts about which a stranger cannot know anything.

Before proceeding further, let me observe that the domestic insects of which I am going to speak are mostly night-singers, and must not be confounded with the semi (cicadae), mentioned in former essays of mine. I think that the cicadae – even in a country so exceptionally rich as is Japan in musical insects – are wonderful melodists in their own way. But the Japanese find as much difference between the notes of night-insects and of cicadae as we find between those of larks and sparrows; and they relegate their cicadae to the vulgar place of chatterers. Semi are therefore never caged. The national liking for caged insects does not mean a liking for mere noise; and the note of every insect in public favor must possess either some rhythmic charm, or some mimetic quality celebrated in poetry or legend. The same fact is true of the Japanese liking for the chant of frogs. It would be a mistake to suppose that all kind of frogs are considered musical; but there are particular species of very small frogs having sweet notes; and these are caged and petted.

Of course, in the proper meaning of the word, insects do not *sing*; but in the following pages I may occasionally employ the terms 'singer' and 'singing-insect,' partly because of their convenience, and partly because of their correspondence with the language used by Japanese insect-dealers and poets describing the 'voices' of such creatures.

II

There are many curious references in the old Japanese classic literature to the custom of keeping musical insects. For example, in the chapter entitled 'Nowaki'[1] of the famous novel *Genji Monogatari*, written in the latter part of the tenth century by the Lady Murasaki-Shikibu, it is stated: ' The maids were ordered to descend to the garden, and give some water to the insects.' But the first definite mention of cages for singing-insects would appear to be the following passage from a work entitled *Chomon-Shu*: 'On the twelfth day of the eighth month of the second year of Kaho [1095 A.D.], the Emperor ordered his pages and chamberlains to go to Sagano and find some insects. The Emperor gave them a cage of network of bright purple thread. All, even the head chaplain and his attendants, taking horses from the Right and the Left Imperial Mews, then went on horseback to hunt for insects. Tokinori Ben, at that time holding the office of Kurando,[2] proposed to the party as they rode toward Sagano a subject for poetical composition. The subject was, *Looking for insects in the fields*. On reaching Sagano, the party dismounted, and walked in various directions for a distance of something more than ten chō,[3]

1. Nowaki is the name given to certain destructive storms usually occurring toward the end of autumn. All the chapters of the *Genji Monogatari* have remarkably poetical and effective titles. There is an English translation, by Mr Kenchō Suyematsu, of the first seventeen chapters.

2. The Kurando, or Kurōdo, was an official intrusted with the care of the imperial records.

3. A chō is about one-fifteenth of a mile.

and sent their attendants to catch the insects. In the evening they returned to the palace. They put into the cage some hagi[4] and omina-meshi [for the insects]. The cage was respectfully presented to the Empress. There was saké-drinking in the palace that evening; and many poems were composed. The Empress and her court-ladies joined in the making of the poems.'

This would appear to be the oldest Japanese record of an insect-hunt, though the amusement may have been invented earlier than the period of Kaho. By the seventeenth century it seems to have become a popular diversion; and night-hunts were in vogue as much as day-hunts. In the *Teikoku Bunshū*, or collected works of the poet Teikoku, who died during the second year of Shōwō (1653), there has been preserved one of the poet's letters which contains a very interesting passage on the subject. 'Let us go insect-hunting this evening,' writes the poet to his friend. 'It is true that the night will be very dark, since there is no moon; and it may seem dangerous to go out. But there are many people now going to the graveyards every night, because the Bon festival is approaching;[5] therefore the way to the fields will not be lonesome for us. I have prepared many lanterns; so the hata-ori, matsumushi, and other insects will probably come to the lanterns in great number.'

It would also seem that the trade of insect-seller (mushiya) existed in the seventeenth century; for in a diary of that time, known as the Diary of Kikaku, the writer speaks of his disappointment at not finding any insect-dealers in Yedo — tolerably good evidence that he had met such persons elsewhere. 'On the thirteenth day of the sixth month of the fourth year of Teikyo [1687], I went out,' he writes, 'to look for kirigirisu-sellers. I searched for them in Yotsuya, in Kōjimachi, in Hongō, in Yushimasa, and in both divisions of Kanda-Sudamachō;[6] but I found none.'

4. Hagi is the name commonly given to the bush-clover. Ominameshi is the common term for the *Valeriana officinalis*.

5. That is to say, there are now many people who go every night to the grave-yards, to decorate and prepare the graves before the great Festival of the Dead.

6. Most of these names survive in the appellations of well-known districts of the present Tōkyō.

As we shall presently see, the kirigirisu was not sold in Tōkyō until about one hundred and twenty years later.

But long before it became the fashion to keep singing insects, their music had been celebrated by poets as one of the aesthetic pleasures of the autumn. There are charming references to singing-insects in poetical collections made during the tenth century, and doubtless containing many compositions of a yet earlier period. And just as places famous for cherry, plum, or other blossoming trees are still regularly visited every year by thousands and tens of thousands, merely for the delight of seeing the flowers in their seasons, so in ancient times city-dwellers made autumn excursions to country districts simply for the pleasure of hearing the chirruping choruses of crickets and of locusts — the night-singers especially. Centuries ago places were noted as pleasure resorts solely because of this melodious attraction; such were Musashino (now Tōkyō), Yatano in the province of Echizen, and Mano in the province of Ōmi. Somewhat later, probably, people discovered that each of the principal species of singing-insects haunted by preference some particular locality, where its peculiar chanting could be heard to the best advantage; and eventually no less than eleven places became famous throughout Japan for different kinds of insect-music.

The best places to hear the matsumushi were:

(1) Arashiyama, near Kyōto, in the province of Yamashiro;

(2) Sumiyoshi, in the province of Settsu;

(3) Miyagino, in the province of Mutsu.

The best places to hear the suzumushi were:

(1) Kagura-ga-Oka, in Yamashiro;

(2) Ogura-yama, in Yamashiro;

(3) Suzuka-yama, in Isé;

(4) Narumi, in Owari.

The best places to hear the kirigirisu were:

(1) Sagano, in Yamashiro;

(2) Takeda-no-Sato, in Yamashiro;

(3) Tatsuta-yama, in Yamato;

(4) Ono-no-Shinowara, in Ōmi.

Afterwards, when the breeding and sale of singing-insects became a lucrative industry, the custom of going into the country to hear

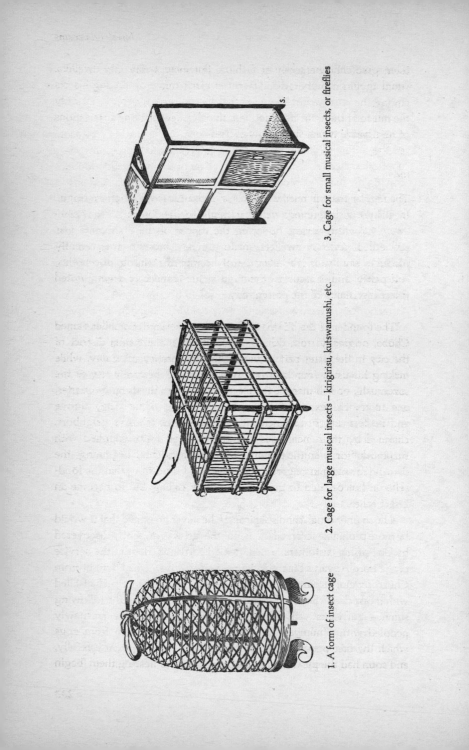

3. Cage for small musical insects, or fireflies

2. Cage for large musical insects – kirigirisu, kutswamushi, etc.

1. A form of insect cage

them gradually went out of fashion. But even today city-dwellers, when giving a party, will sometimes place cages of singing-insects among the garden shrubbery, so that the guests may enjoy not only the music of the little creatures, but also those memories or sensations of rural peace which such music evokes.

III

The regular trade in musical insects is of comparatively modern origin. In Tōkyō its beginnings date back only to the Kwansei era (1789–1800), at which period, however, the capital of the Shōgunate was still called Yedo. A complete history of the business was recently placed in my hands – a history partly compiled from old documents, and partly from traditions preserved in the families of several noted insect-merchants of the present day.

The founder of the Tōkyō trade was an itinerant food-seller named Chūzō, originally from Echigo, who settled in the Kanda district of the city in the latter part of the eighteenth century. One day, while making his usual rounds, it occurred to him to capture a few of the suzumushi, or bell-insects, then very plentiful in the Negishi quarter, and to try the experiment of feeding them at home. They throve and made music in confinement; and several of Chūzō's neighbors, charmed by their melodious chirruping, asked to be supplied with suzumushi for a consideration. From this accidental beginning, the demand for suzumushi grew rapidly to such proportions that the food-seller at last decided to give up his former calling and to become an insect-seller.

Chūzō only caught and sold insects: he never imagined that it would be more profitable to breed them. But the fact was presently discovered by one of his customers, a man named Kiriyama, then in the service of the Lord Aoyama Shimodzuké-no-Kami. Kiriyama had bought from Chūzō several suzumushi, which were kept and fed in a jar half-filled with moist clay. They died in the cold season; but during the following summer Kiriyama was agreeably surprised to find the jar newly peopled with a number of young ones, evidently born from eggs which the first prisoners had left in the clay. He fed them carefully, and soon had the pleasure, my chronicler says, of hearing them 'begin to sing in small voices.' Then he resolved to make some experiments; and, aided by Chūzō, who furnished the males and females, he succeeded in breeding not only suzumushi, but three other kinds of singing-insects also — kantan, matsumushi, and kutsuwamushi. He discovered, at the same time, that, by keeping his jars in a warm room, the insects could be hatched considerably in advance of the natural season. Chūzō sold for Kiriyama these home-bred singers; and both men found the new undertaking profitable beyond expectation.

The example set by Kiriyama was imitated by a tabiya, or stocking-maker, named Yasubei (commonly known as Tabiya Yasubei by reason of his calling), who lived in Kanda-ku. Yasubei likewise made careful study of the habits of singing insects, with a view to their breeding and nourishment; and he soon found himself able to carry on a small trade in them. Up to that time the insects sold in Yedo would seem to have been kept in jars or boxes: Yasubei conceived the idea of having special cages manufactured for them. A man named Kondō, vassal to the Lord Kamei of Honjō-ku, interested himself in the matter, and made a number of pretty little cages which delighted Yasubei, and secured a large order from him. The new invention found public favor at once: and Kondō soon afterwards established the first manufactory of insect-cages.

The demand for singing-insects increased from this time so rapidly that Chūzō soon found it impossible to supply all his would-be customers directly. He therefore decided to change his business to wholesale trade, and to sell to retail dealers only. To meet orders, he purchased largely from peasants in the suburbs and elsewhere. Many persons were employed by him; and Yasubei and others paid him a fixed annual sum for sundry rights and privileges.

Some time after this Yasubei became the first itinerant vender of singing-insects. He walked through the streets crying his wares; but hired a number of servants to carry the cages. Tradition says that while going his rounds he used to wear a katabira[7] made of a much-esteemed silk stuff called sukiya, together with a fine Hakata-girdle;

7. Katabira is a name given to many kinds of light textures used for summer-robes. The material is usually hemp, but sometimes, as in the case referred to here, of fine silk. Some of these robes are transparent, and very beautiful. Hakata, in Kyūshū, is still famous for the silk girdles made there. The fabric is very heavy and strong.

and that this elegant way of dressing proved of much service to him in his business.

Two men, whose names have been preserved, soon entered into competition with Yasubei. The first was Yasakura Yasuzō, of Honjō-ku, by previous occupation a sahainin, or property-agent. He prospered, and became widely known as Mushi-Yasu — 'Yasu-the-Insect-Man.' His success encouraged a former fellow-sahainin, Genbei of Uyeno, to go into the same trade. Genbei likewise found insect-selling a lucrative occupation, and earned for himself the sobriquet of Mushi-Gen, by which he is yet remembered. His descendants in Tōkyō today are amé-manufacturers;[8] but they still carry on the hereditary insect-business during the summer and autumn months; and one of the firm was kind enough to furnish me with many of the facts recorded in this little essay.

Chūzō, the father and founder of all this curious commerce, died without children; and sometime in the period of Bunsei (1818–29) his business was taken over by a distant relative named Yamasaki Seïchirō. To Chūzō's business, Yamasaki joined his own — that of a toy-merchant. About the same time a law was passed limiting the number of insect-dealers in the municipality to thirty-six. The thirty-six then formed themselves into a guild, called the Ōyama-Kō ('Ōyama Society'), having for patron the divinity Sekison-Sama of the mountain Ōyama in Sagami Province.[9] But in business the association was known as the Yedō-Mushi-Kō, or Yedo Insect-Company.

It is not until after this consolidation of the trade that we hear of the kirigirisu — the same musical insect which the poet Kikaku had vainly tried to buy in the city in 1687 — being sold in Yedo. One of the guild known as Mushiya Kojirō ('Kojirō the Insect-Merchant'), who did business in Honjō-Ku, returning to the city after a short visit to his native place in Kadzusa, brought back with him a number of kirigirisu, which he sold at a good profit. Although long famous elsewhere, these insects had never before been sold in Yedo.

---

8. *Amé* is a nutritive gelatinous extract obtained from wheat and other substances. It is sold in many forms — as candy, as a syrupy liquid resembling molasses, as a sweet hot drink, as a solid jelly. Children are very fond of it. Its principal element is starch-sugar.

9. Ōyama mountain in Sagami is a great resort of pilgrims. There is a celebrated temple there, dedicated to Iwanaga-Himé ('Long-Rock Princess'), sister of the beautiful Goddess of Fuji. Sekison-San is a popular name both for the divinity and for the mountain itself.

'When Midzu Echizen-no-Kami,' says the chronicle, 'became machi-bugyō (or chief magistrate) of Yedo, the law limiting the number of insect-dealers to thirty-six, was abolished.' Whether the guild was subsequently dissolved the chronicle fails to mention.

Kiriyama, the first to breed singing-insects artificially, had, like Chūzō, built up a prosperous trade. He left a son, Kaméjirō, who was adopted into the family of one Yumoto, living in Waséda, Ushigomé-ku. Kaméjirō brought with him to the Yumoto family the valuable secrets of his father's occupation; and the Yumoto family is still celebrated in the business of insect-breeding.

Today the greatest insect-merchant in Tōkyō is said to be Kawasumi Kanésaburō, of Samonchō in Yotsuya-ku. A majority of the lesser dealers obtain their autumn stock from him. But the insects bred artificially, and sold in summer, are mostly furnished by the Yumoto house. Other noted dealers are Mushi-Sei, of Shitaya-ku, and Mushi-Toku, of Asakusa. These buy insects caught in the country, and brought to the city by the peasants. The wholesale dealers supply both insects and cages to multitudes of itinerant venders who do business in the neighborhood of the parish-temples during the en-nichi, or religious festivals – especially after dark. Almost every night of the year there are en-nichi in some quarter of the capital; and the insect-sellers are rarely idle during the summer and autumn months.

Perhaps the following list of current Tōkyō prices[10] for singing-insects may interest the reader:

Suzumushi	3 sen 5 rin, to	4 sen
Matsumushi	4 „	„ 5 „
Kantan	10 „	„ 12 „
Kin-hibari	10 „	„ 12 „
Kusa-hibari	10 „	„ 12 „
Kuro-hibari	8 „	„ 12 „
Kutsuwamushi	10 „	„ 15 „
Yamato-suzu	8 „	„ 12 „
Kirigirisu	12 „	„ 15 „
Emma-kōrogi	5 „	
Kanétataki	12 „	
Umaoi	10 „	

10. Prices for the year 1897.

These prices, however, rule only during the busy period of the insect trade. In May and the latter part of June the prices are high — for only artificially bred insects are then in the market. In July kirigirisu brought from the country will sell as low as one sen. The kantan, kusa-hibari, and Yamato-suzu sell sometimes as low as two sen. In August the Emma-kōrogi can be bought even at the rate of ten for one sen; and in September the kuro-hibari, kanétataki, and umaoi sell for one or one and a half sen each. But there is little variation at any season in the prices of suzumushi and of matsumushi. These are never very dear, but never sell at less than three sen; and there is always a demand for them. The suzumushi is the most popular of all; and the greater part of the profits annually made in the insect-trade is said to be gained on the sale of this insect.

IV

As will be seen from the foregoing price-list, twelve varieties of musical insects are sold in Tōkyō. Nine can be artificially bred — namely the suzumushi, matsumushi, kirigirisu, kantan, kutsuwamushi, Emma-kōrogi, kin-hibari, kusa-hibari (also called Asa-suzu), and the Yamato-suzu, or Yoshino-suzu. Three varieties, I am told, are not bred for sale, but captured for the market: these are the kanétataki, umaoi or hataori, and kuro-hibari. But a considerable number of all the insects annually offered for sale are caught in their native haunts.

The night-singers are, with few exceptions, easily taken. They are captured with the help of lanterns. Being quickly attracted by light,

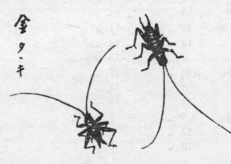

Kanétataki 'The Bell-Ringer' (*natural size*)

they approach the lanterns; and when near enough to be observed, they can readily be covered with nets or little baskets. Males and females are usually secured at the same time, for the creatures move about in couples. Only the males sing; but a certain number of females are always taken for breeding purposes. Males and females are kept in the same vessel only for breeding: they are never left together in a cage, because the male ceases to sing when thus mated, and will die in a short time after pairing.

The breeding pairs are kept in jars or other earthen vessels half-filled with moistened clay, and are supplied every day with fresh food. They do not live long: the male dies first, and the female survives only until her eggs have been laid. The young insects hatched from them shed their skin in about forty days from birth, after which they grow more rapidly, and soon attain their full development. In their natural state these creatures are hatched a little before the Doyō, or Period of Greatest Heat by the old calendar — that is to say, about the middle of July — and they begin to sing in October. But when bred in a warm room, they are hatched early in April; and, with careful feeding, they can be offered for sale before the end of May. When very young, their food is triturated and spread for them upon a smooth piece of wood; but the adults are usually furnished with unprepared food, consisting of parings of eggplant, melon rind, cucumber rind, or the soft interior parts of the white onion. Some insects, however, are specially nourished — the abura-kirigirisu, for example, being fed with sugar-water and slices of musk-melon.

v

All the insects mentioned in the Tōkyō price-lists are not of equal interest; and several of the names appear to refer only to different varieties of one species, though on this point I am not positive. Some of the insects do not seem to have yet been scientifically classed; and I am no entomologist. But I can offer some general notes on the more important among the little melodists, and free translations of a few out of the countless poems about them, beginning with the matsumushi, which was celebrated in Japanese verse a thousand years ago:

Matsumushi[11]

As ideographically written, the name of this creature signifies 'pine-insect;' but, as pronounced, it might mean also 'waiting-insect,' since the verb 'matsu,' 'to wait,' and the noun 'matsu,' 'pine,' have the same

Matsumushi (*slightly enlarged*)

sound. It is chiefly upon this double meaning of the word as uttered that a host of Japanese poems about the matsumushi are based. Some of these are very old, dating back to the tenth century at least.

Although by no means a rare insect, the matsumushi is much esteemed for the peculiar clearness and sweetness of its notes — onomatopoetically rendered in Japanese by the syllables chin-chirorīn, chin-chirorīn — little silvery shrillings which I can best describe as resembling the sound of an electric bell heard from a distance. The matsumushi haunts pine-woods and cryptomeria-groves, and makes its music at night. It is a very small insect, with a dark-brown back, and a yellowish belly.

Perhaps the oldest extant verses upon the matsumushi are those contained in the *Kokinshū* — a famous anthology compiled in the year 905 by the court-poet Tsurayuki and several of his noble friends. Here we first find that play on the name of the insect as pronounced, which was to be repeated in a thousand different keys by a multitude of poets through the literature of more than nine hundred years:

> Aki no no ni
> Michi mo madoinu;

11. *Calyptotryphus marmoratus* (?).

> Matsumushi no
> Koe suru kata ni
> Yadoya karamashi.

'In the autumn-fields I lose my way; perhaps I might ask for lodging in the direction of the cry of the waiting insect' – that is to say, 'might sleep tonight in the grass where the insects are waiting for me.' There is in the same work a much prettier poem on the matsumushi by Tsurayuki.

> With dusk begins to cry the male of the Waiting-insect;
>   I, too, await my beloved, and, hearing, my longing grows.

The following poems on the same insect are less ancient but not less interesting:

> Forever past and gone, the hour of the promised advent! –
> Truly the Waiter's voice is a voice of sadness now!

> Parting is sorrowful always – even the parting with autumn!
> O plaintive matsumushi, add not thou to my pain!

> Always more clear and shrill, as the hush of the night grows deeper,
> The Waiting-insect's voice; and I that wait in the garden
> Feel enter into my heart the voice and the moon together.

Suzumushi[12]

The name signifies 'bell-insect;' but the bell of which the sound is thus referred to is a very small bell, or a bunch of little bells such as a Shintō priestess uses in the sacred dances. The suzumushi is a great favorite with insect-fanciers, and is bred in great numbers for the market. In the wild state it is found in many parts of Japan; and at night the noise made by multitudes of suzumushi in certain lonesome places might easily be mistaken – as it has been by myself more than once – for the sound of rapids. The Japanese description of the insect as resembling 'a watermelon seed' – the black kind – is excellent. It is very small, with a black back, and a white or yellowish belly. Its tintinnabulation – *ri-i-i-i-in*, as the Japanese render the sound – might easily be mistaken for the tinkling of a suzu. Both the matsumushi

---

12. *Homeogryllus japonicus.*

and the suzumushi are mentioned in Japanese poems of the period of Engi (901—922).

Suzumushi (*slightly enlarged*)

Some of the following poems on the suzumushi are very old; others are of comparatively recent date:

> Yes, my dwelling is old: weeds on the roof are growing;
> But the voice of the suzumushi — that will never be old!
> Today united in love, we who can meet so rarely!
> Hear how the insects ring! — their bells to our hearts keep time.
>
> The tinkle of tiny bells — the voices of suzumushi,
> I hear in the autumn-dusk — and think of the fields at home.
>
> Even the moonshine sleeps on the dews of the garden-grasses;
> Nothing moves in the night but the suzumushi's voice.
>
> Heard in these alien fields, the voice of the suzumushi —
> Sweet in the evening-dusk — sounds like the sound of home.
>
> Vainly the suzumushi exhausts its powers of pleasing,
> Always, the long night through, my tears continue to flow!
>
> Hark to those tinkling tones, the chant of the suzumushi!
> If a jewel of dew could sing, it would tinkle with such a voice!
>
> Foolish-fond I have grown — I feel for the suzumushi! —
> In the time of the heavy rains, what will the creature do?

Hataori-mushi

The hataori is a beautiful bright-green grasshopper, of very graceful shape. Two reasons are given for its curious name, which signifies 'the Weaver.' One is that, when held in a particular way. the struggling

241

gestures of the creature resemble the movements of a girl weaving. The other reason is that its music seems to imitate the sound of the reed and shuttle of a hand-loom in operation — *Ji-i-i-i* — *chon-chon!* — *ji-i-i-i* — *chon-chon!*

There is a pretty folk-story about the origin of the hataori and the kirigirisu, which used to be told to Japanese children in former times. Long, long ago, says the tale, there were two very dutiful daughters who supported their old blind father by the labor of their hands. The elder girl used to weave, and the younger to sew. When the old blind father died at last, these good girls grieved so much that they soon died also. One beautiful morning, some creatures of a kind never seen before were found making music above the graves of the sisters. On the tomb of the elder was a pretty green insect, producing sounds like those made by a girl weaving — *ji-i-i-i, chon-chon! ji-i-i-i, chon-chon!* This was the first hataori-mushi. On the tomb of the younger sister was an insect which kept crying out, 'Tsuzuré — sasé, sasé! — tsuzuré, tsuzuré — sasé, sasé, sasé!' ('Torn clothes — patch, patch them up! — torn clothes, torn clothes — patch up, patch up, patch up!') This was the first kirigirisu. Then everybody knew that the spirits of the good sisters had taken those shapes. Still every autumn they cry to wives and daughters to work well at the loom, and warn them to repair the winter garments of the household before the coming of the cold.

Such poems as I have been able to obtain about the hataori consist of nothing more than pretty fancies. Two, of which I offer free renderings, are ancient — the first by Tsurayuki; the second by a poetess classically known as 'Akinaka's Daughter':

> Weaving-insects I hear; and the fields, in their autumn-colors,
> Seem of Chinese-brocade — was this the weavers' work?

> Gossamer-threads are spread over the shrubs and grasses:
> Weaving-insects I hear — do they weave with spider-silk?

Umaoi

The umaoi is sometimes confounded with the hataori, which it much resembles. But the true umaoi — (called junta in Izumo) — is a shorter and thicker insect than the hataori, and has at its tail a hook-shaped protuberance, which the weaver-insect has not. Moreover, there is some difference in the sounds made by the two creatures. The music

Umaoi (*natural size*)

of the umaoi is not *'ji-i-i-i, – chon-chon,'* but *'zu-ï-in-tzō! – zu-ï-in-tzō!'* – say the Japanese.

Kirigirisu[13]

There are different varieties of this much-prized insect. The abura-kirigirisu, a day-singer, is a delicate creature, and must be carefully nourished in confinement. The tachi-kirigirisu, a night-singer, is more

Kirigirisu (*natural size*)

commonly found in the market. Captured kirigirisu sold in Tōkyō are mostly from the neighbourhood of Itabashi, Niiso, and Todogawa; and these, which fetch high prices, are considered the best. They are large vigorous insects, uttering very clear notes. From Kujiukuri in Kadzusa other and much cheaper kirigirisu are brought to the capital;

13. *Locusta japonica* (?).

but these have a disagreeable odor, suffer from the attacks of a peculiar parasite, and are feeble musicians.

As stated elsewhere, the sounds made by the kirigirisu are said to resemble those of the Japanese words 'Tsuzuré – sasé! sasé!' ('Torn clothes – patch up! patch up!'); and a large proportion of the many poems written about the insect depend for interest upon ingenious but untranslatable allusions to those words. I offer renderings therefore of only two poems on the kirigirisu – the first by an unknown poet in the *Kokinshū*; the second by Tadafusa:

> O Kirigirisu! when the clover changes color,
> Are the nights then sad for you as for me that cannot sleep?

> O Kirigirisu! cry not, I pray, so loudly!
> Hearing, my sorrow grows – and the autumn-night is long!

Kusa-hibari

The kusa-hibari, or 'Grass-Lark' – also called Asa-suzu, or 'Morning-Bell;' Yabu-suzu, or 'the Little Bell of the Bamboo-groove;' Aki-kazé, or 'Autumn-Wind;' and Ko-suzu-mushi, or 'the Child of the Bell Insect' – is a day-singer. It is very small – perhaps the smallest of the insect-choir, except the Yamato-suzu.

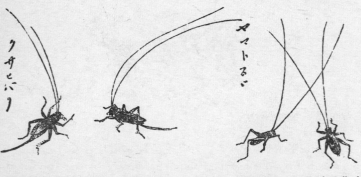

Kusa-hibari (*natural size*)

Yamato-suzu ('Little-Bell of Yamato') (*natural size*)

Kin-hibari

The kin-hibari, or 'Golden Lark,' used to be found in great numbers about the neighborhood of the well-known Shino-bazu-no-iké — the great lotus-pond of Uyeno in Tōkyō; but of late years it has become scarce there. The kin-hibari now sold in the capital are brought from Todogawa and Shimura.

Kin-hibari (*natural size*)

Kuro-hibari

The kuro-hibari, or 'Black Lark,' is rather uncommon, and comparatively dear. It is caught in the country about Tōkyō, but is never bred.

Kuro-hibari (*natural size*)

Kōrogi

There are many varieties of this night-cricket — called kōrogi from its music: '*kiri-kiri-kiri-kiri! — kōro-kōro-kōro-kōro! — ghi-ï-ï-ï-ï-ï!*' One variety, the ebi-kōrogi, or 'shrimp-kōrogi,' does not make any sound. But the uma-kōrogi, or 'horse-kōrogi,' the Oni-kōrogi, or 'Demon-kōrogi,' and the Emma-kōrogi, or 'Cricket-of-Emma[14] (King of the Dead),' are all good musicians. The color is blackish-brown, or black; the singing varieties have curious wavy markings on the wings.

An interesting fact regarding the kōrogi is that mention of it is made in the very oldest collection of Japanese poems known, the

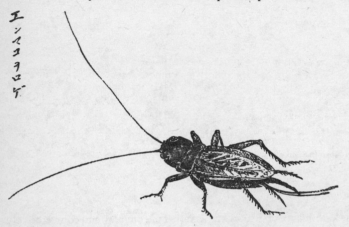

Emma-dōrogi (*natural size*)

Emma-kōrogi

14. In Sanskrit *Yama*. Probably this name was given to the insect on account of its large staring eyes. Images of King Emma are always made with very big and awful eyes.

Manyōshu, probably compiled about the middle of the eighth century. The following lines, by an unknown poet, which contain this mention are therefore considerably more than eleven hundred years old:

> Nīwa-kusa ni
> Murasamé furité
> Kōrogi no
> Naku oto kikeba
> Aki tsukinikeri.

'Showers have sprinkled the garden-grass. Hearing the sound of the crying of the kōrogi, I know that the autumn has come.'

Kutsuwamushi

There are several varieties of this extraordinary creature – also called onomatopoetically gatcha-gatcha – which is most provokingly

Kutsuwamushi (*natural size*)

described in dictionaries as 'a kind of noisy cricket'! The variety commonly sold in Tōkyō has a green back, and a yellowish-white abdomen; but there are also brown and reddish varieties. The kut-suwamushi is difficult to capture, but easy to breed. As the tsuku-tsuku-bōshi is the most wonderful musician among the sun-loving cicadae, or semi, so the kutsuwamushi is the most wonderful of night-crickets. It owes its name, which means 'The Bridle-bit-Insect,' to its noise, which resembles the jingling and ringing of the old-fashioned Japanese bridle-bit (kutsuwa). But the sound is really much louder and much more complicated than ever was the jingling of a single kutsuwa; and the accuracy of the comparison is not easily discerned while the creature is storming beside you. Without the evidence of one's own eyes, it were hard to believe that so small a life could make so prodigious a noise. Certainly the vibratory apparatus in this insect must be very complicated. The sound begins with a thin sharp whizzing, as of leaking steam, and slowly strengthens; then to the whizzing is suddenly added a quick dry clatter, as of castanets; and then, as the whole machinery rushes into operation, you hear, high above the whizzing and the clatter, a torrent of rapid ringing tones like the tapping of a gong. These, the last to begin, are also the first to cease; then the castanets stop; and finally the whizzing dies; but the full orchestra may remain in operation for several hours at a time, without a pause. Heard from far away at night the sound is pleasant, and is really so much like the ring-ing of a bridle-bit that when you first listen to it you cannot but feel how much real poetry belongs to the name of this insect, celebrated from of old as 'playing at ghostly escort in ways where no man can pass.'

The most ancient poem on the kutsuwamushi is perhaps the follow-ing, by the Lady Idzumi-Shikibu:

> Waga seko wa
> Koma ni makasété
> Kinikeri to,
> Kiku ni kikasuru
> Kutsuwamushi kana!

— which might be thus freely rendered:

> Listen! — his bridle rings; that is surely my husband
> Homeward hurrying now — fast as the horse can bear him! ...
> Ah! my ear was deceived! — only the Kutsuwamushi!

Kantan

This insect — also called kantan-gisu, and kantan-no-kirigirisu — is a dark-brown night-cricket. Its note — *'zi-i-i-i-in'* — is peculiar. I can only compare it to the prolonged twang of a bow-string. But this comparison is not satisfactory, because there is a penetrant metallic quality in the twang, impossible to describe.

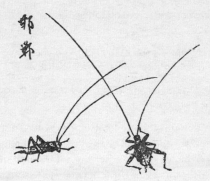

Kantan (*natural size*)

VI

Besides poems about the chanting of particular insects, there are countless Japanese poems, ancient and modern, upon the voices of night-insects in general, chiefly in relation to the autumn season. Out of a multitude I have selected and translated a few of the more famous only, as typical of the sentiment or fancy of hundreds. Although some of my renderings are far from literal as to language, I believe that they express with tolerable faithfulness the thought and feeling of the originals:

Not for my sake alone, I know, is the autumn's coming;
Yet, hearing the insects sing, at once my heart grows sad.

KOKINSHŪ

Faint in the moonshine sounds the chorus of insect-voices:
Tonight the sadness of autumn speaks in their plaintive tone.

I never can find repose in the chilly nights of autumn,
Because of the pain I hear in the insects' plaintive song.

How must it be in the fields where the dews are falling thickly!
In the insect-voices that reach me I hear the tingling of cold.

Never I dare to take my way through the grass in autumn:
Should I tread upon insect-voices,[15] what would my feelings be!

The song is ever the same, but the tones of the insects differ,
Maybe their sorrows vary, according to their hearts.

IDZUMI-SHIKIBU

Changed is my childhood's home – all but those insect-voices:
I think they are trying to speak of happier days that were.

These trembling dews on the grass – are they tears for the death of autumn? –
Tears of the insect-singers that now so sadly cry?

It might be thought that several of the poems above given were intended to express either a real or an affected sympathy with imagined insect-pain. But this would be a wrong interpretation. In most compositions of this class, the artistic purpose is to suggest, by indirect means, various phases of the emotion of love – especially that melancholy which lends its own passional tone to the aspects and the voices of nature. The baroque fancy that dew might be insect-tears is by its very exaggeration intended to indicate the extravagance of grief, as well as to suggest that human tears have been freshly shed. The verses in which a woman declares that her heart has become too affectionate, since she cannot but feel for the bell-insect during a heavy shower, really bespeak the fond anxiety felt for some absent beloved, traveling in the time of the great rains. Again, in the lines about 'treading on insect-voices,' the dainty scruple is uttered only as a hint of that intensification of feminine tenderness which love creates. And a still more remarkable example of this indirect double-suggestiveness is offered by the little poem prefacing this article:

'O insect, insect! – think you that Karma can be exhausted by song?'

15. Mushi no koe fumu.

The Western reader would probably suppose that the insect-condition, or insect-state-of-being, is here referred to; but the real thought of the speaker, presumably a woman, is that her own sorrow is the result of faults committed in former lives, and is therefore impossible to alleviate.

It will have been observed that a majority of the verses cited refer to autumn and to the sensations of autumn. Certainly Japanese poets have not been insensible to the real melancholy inspired by autumn — that vague strange annual revival of ancestral pain: dim inherited sorrow of millions of memories associated through millions of years with the death of summer — but in nearly every utterance of this melancholy, the veritable allusion is to grief of parting. With its color-changes, its leaf-whirlings, and the ghostly plaint of its insect-voices, autumn Buddhistically symbolizes impermanency, the certainty of bereavement, the pain that clings to all desire, and the sadness of isolation.

But even if these poems on insects were primarily intended to shadow amorous emotion, do they not reflect also for us the subtlest influences of nature — wild pure nature — upon imagination and memory? Does not the place accorded to insect-melody, in the home-life as well as in the literature of Japan, prove an aesthetic sensibility developed in directions that yet remain for us almost unexplored? Does not the shrilling booth of the insect-seller at a night-festival proclaim even a popular and universal comprehension of things divined in the West only by our rarest poets: the pleasure-pain of autumn's beauty, the weird sweetness of the voices of the night, the magical quickening of remembrance by echoes of forest and field? Surely we have something to learn from the people in whose mind the simple chant of a cricket can awaken whole fairy-swarms of tender and delicate fancies. We may boast of being their masters in the mechanical, their teachers of the artificial in all its varieties of ugliness; but in the knowledge of the natural, in the feeling of the joy and beauty of earth, they exceed us like the Greeks of old. Yet perhaps it will be only when our blind aggressive industrialism has wasted and sterilized their paradise — substituting everywhere for beauty the utilitarian, the conventional, the vulgar, the utterly hideous —

that we shall begin with remorseful amazement to comprehend the charm of that which we destroyed.

Kusa-Hibari

I

His cage is exactly two Japanese inches high and one inch and a half wide: its tiny wooden door, turning upon a pivot, will scarcely admit the tip of my little finger. But he has plenty of room in that cage — room to walk, and jump, and fly; for he is so small that you must look very carefully through the brown-gauze sides of it in order to catch a glimpse of him. I have always to turn the cage round and round, several times, in a good light, before I can discover his whereabouts; and then I usually find him resting in one of the upper corners, clinging, upside down, to his ceiling of gauze.

Imagine a cricket about the size of an ordinary mosquito, with a pair of antennae much longer than his own body, and so fine that you can distinguish them only against the light. Kusa-Hibari, or 'Grass-Lark,' is the Japanese name of him; and he is worth in the market exactly twelve cents: that is to say, very much more than his weight in gold. Twelve cents for such a gnat-like thing!

By day he sleeps or meditates, except while occupied with the slice of fresh eggplant or cucumber which must be poked into his cage every morning ... To keep him clean and well fed is somewhat troublesome: could you see him, you would think it absurd to take any pains for the sake of a creature so ridiculously small.

But always at sunset the infinitesimal soul of him awakens; then the room begins to fill with a delicate and ghostly music of indescribable sweetness — a thin, thin silvery rippling and trilling as of tiniest electric bells. As the darkness deepens, the sound becomes sweeter, sometimes swelling till the whole house seems to vibrate with the elfish resonance, sometimes thinning down into the faintest imaginable thread of a voice. But loud or low, it keeps a penetrating quality that is weird .. All night the atomy thus sings: he ceases only when the temple bell proclaims the hour of dawn.

Now this tiny song is a song of love, vague love of the unseen and unknown. It is quite impossible that he should ever have seen or known, in this present existence of his, not even his ancestors, for many generations back, could have known anything of the night-life of the fields, or the amorous value of song. They were born of eggs hatched in a jar of clay, in the shop of some insect-merchant; and they dwelt thereafter only in cages. But he sings the song of his race as it was sung a myriad years ago, and as faultlessly as if he understood the exact significance of every note. Of course he did not learn the song. It is a song of organic memory — deep, dim memory of other quintillions of lives, when the ghost of him shrilled at night from the dewy grasses of the hills. Then that song brought him love — and death. He has forgotten all about death; but he remembers the love. And therefore he sings now — for the bride that will never come.

So that his longing is unconsciously retrospective: he cries to the dust of the past — he calls to the silence and the gods for the return of time ... Human lovers do very much the same thing without knowing it. They call their illusion an Ideal; and their Ideal is, after all, a mere shadowing of race-experience, a phantom of organic memory. The living present has very little to do with it ... Perhaps this atomy also has an ideal, or at least the rudiment of an ideal; but, in any event, the tiny desire must utter its plaint in vain.

The fault is not altogether mine. I had been warned that if the creature were mated, he would cease to sing and would speedily die. But, night after night, the plaintive, sweet, unanswered trilling touched me like a reproach, became at last an obsession, an affliction, a torment of conscience; and I tried to buy a female. It was too late in the season; there were no more kusa-hibari for sale, either males or females. The insect-merchant laughed and said, 'He ought to have died about the twentieth day of the ninth month.' (It was already the second day of the tenth month.) But the insect-merchant did not know that I have a good stove in my study, and keep the temperature at above 75° F. Wherefore my grass-lark still sings at the close of the eleventh month, and I hope to keep him alive until the Period of Greatest Cold. However, the rest of his generation are probably dead: neither for love nor money could I now find him a mate. And were I to set him free in order that he might make the search for himself, he could not possibly live through a single night, even if fortunate enough to escape by day the multitude of his natural enemies in the garden — ants, centipedes, and ghastly earth-spiders.

II

Last evening — the twenty-ninth of the eleventh month — an odd feeling came to me as I sat at my desk: a sense of emptiness in the room. Then I became aware that my grass-lark was silent, contrary to his wont. I went to the silent cage, and found him lying dead beside a dried-up lump of eggplant as gray and hard as a stone. Evidently he had not been fed for three or four days; but only the night before his death he had been singing wonderfully, so that I foolishly imagined him to be more than usually contented. My student, Aki, who loves insects, used to feed him; but Aki had gone into the country for a week's holiday, and the duty of caring for the grass-lark had devolved upon Hana, the housemaid. She is not sympathetic, Hana the housemaid. She says that she did not forget the mite — but there was no more eggplant. And she had never thought of substituting a slice of onion or of cucumber! ... I spoke words of reproof to Hana the housemaid, and she dutifully expressed contrition. But the fairy-music has stopped; and the stillness reproaches, and the room is cold, in spite of the stove.

Absurd! ... I have made a good girl unhappy because of an insect half the size of a barley-grain! The quenching of that infinitesimal life troubles me more than I could have believed possible ... Of course, the mere habit of thinking about a creature's wants — even the wants of a cricket — may create, by insensible degrees, an imaginative interest, an attachment of which one becomes conscious only when the relation is broken. Besides, I had felt so much, in the hush of the night, the charm of the delicate voice, telling of one minute existence dependent upon my will and selfish pleasure, as upon the favour of a god, telling me also that the atom of ghost in the tiny cage, and the atom of ghost within myself, were forever but one and the same in the deeps of the Vast of being ... And then to think of the little creature hungering and thirsting, night after night, and day after day, while the thoughts of his guardian deity were turned to the weaving of dreams! ... How bravely, nevertheless, he sang on to the very end – an atrocious end, for he had eaten his own legs! ... May the gods forgive us all – especially Hana the housemaid!

Yet, after all, to devour one's own legs for hunger is not the worst that can happen to a being cursed with the gift of song. There are human crickets who must eat their own hearts in order to sing.

A Glimpse of Tendencies

I

The foreign concession of an open port one striking contrast to its Far Eastern environment. In the well-ordered ugliness of its streets one finds suggestions of places not on this side of the world, just as though fragments of the Occident had been magically brought oversea: bits of Liverpool, of Marseilles, of New York, of New Orleans, and bits also of tropical towns in colonies twelve or fifteen thousand miles away. The mercantile buildings — immense by comparison with the low light Japanese shops — seem to utter the menace of financial power. The dwellings, of every conceivable design — from that of an Indian bungalow to that of an English or French country-manor, with turrets and bow-windows — are surrounded by commonplace gardens of clipped shrubbery; the white roadways are solid and level as tables, and bordered with boxed-up trees. Nearly all things conventional in England or America have been domiciled in these districts. You see church steeples and factory chimneys and telegraph poles and street lamps. You see warehouses of imported brick with iron shutters, and shop-fronts with plate-glass windows, and sidewalks, and cast-iron railings. There are morning and evening and weekly newspapers; clubs and reading-rooms and bowling alleys; billiard halls and bar-rooms; schools and bethels. There are electric-light and telephone companies; hospitals, courts, jails, and a foreign police. There are foreign lawyers, doctors, and druggists; foreign grocers, confectioners, bakers, dairymen; foreign dressmakers and tailors; foreign school-teachers and music-teachers. There is a town-hall, for municipal business and public meetings of all kinds — likewise for amateur theatricals or lectures and concerts; and very rarely some dramatic company, on a tour of the world, halts there awhile to make men laugh and women cry like they used to do at home. There are cricket grounds, racecourses, public parks – or, as we should call them in England, 'squares' – yachting associations, athletic societies, and swimming baths. Among the familiar noises are the endless tinkling of piano practice, the crashing of a town band, and an occasional wheezing of accordions: in fact, one misses only the organ-grinder. The population is English, French, German, American, Danish, Swedish, Swiss, Russian, with a thin sprinkling of Italians and Levantines. I had almost forgotten the Chinese. They are present in multitude, and have a little corner of the district to themselves. But the dominant element is English and American – the English being in the majority. All the faults and some of the finer qualities of the masterful races can be studied here to better advantage than beyond seas, because everybody knows all about everybody else in communities so small – mere oases of Occidental life in the vast unknown of the Far East. Ugly stories may be heard which are not worth writing about; also stories of nobility and generosity – about good brave things done by men who pretend to be selfish, and wear conventional masks to hide what is best in them from public knowledge.

But the domains of the foreigner do not stretch beyond the distance of an easy walk, and may shrink back again into nothing before many years – for reasons I shall presently dwell upon. His settlements developed precociously – almost like 'mushroom cities' in the great American West – and reached the apparent limit of their development soon after solidifying.

About and beyond the concession, the 'native town' – the real Japanese city – stretches away into regions imperfectly known. To the average settler this native town remains a world of mysteries; he may not think it worth his while to enter it for ten years at a time. It has no interest for him, as he is not a student of native customs, but simply a man of business; and he has no time to think how queer it all is. Merely to cross the concession line is almost the same thing as to cross the Pacific Ocean – which is much less wide than the difference between the races. Enter alone into the interminable narrow maze of Japanese streets, and the dogs will bark at you, and the children stare at you as if you were the only foreigner they ever saw. Perhaps they will even call after you 'Ijin,' 'Tōjin,' or 'Ke-tōjin' – the last of which signifies 'hairy foreigner,' and is not intended as a compliment.

For a long time the merchants of the concessions had their own way in everything, and forced upon the native firms methods of business to which no Occidental merchant would think of submitting — methods which plainly expressed the foreign conviction that all Japanese were tricksters. No foreigner would then purchase anything until it had been long enough in his hands to be examined and re-examined and 'exhaustively' examined, or accept any order for imports unless the order were accompanied by 'a substantial payment of bargain money.'[1] Japanese buyers and sellers protested in vain; they found themselves obliged to submit. But they bided their time — yielding only with the determination to conquer. The rapid growth of the foreign town, and the immense capital successfully invested therein, proved to them how much they would have to learn before being able to help themselves. They wondered without admiring, and traded with the foreigners or worked for them, while secretly detesting them. In old Japan the merchant ranked below the common peasant; but these foreign invaders assumed the tone of princes and the insolence of conquerors. As employers they were usually harsh, and sometimes brutal. Nevertheless they were wonderfully wise in the matter of making money; they lived like kings and paid high salaries. It was desirable that young men should suffer in their service for the sake of learning things which would have to be learned to save the country from passing under foreign rule. Some day Japan would have a mercantile marine of her own, and foreign banking agencies, and foreign credit, and be well able to rid herself of these haughty strangers: in the meanwhile they should be endured as teachers.

So the import and export trade remained entirely in foreign hands, and it grew from nothing to a value of hundreds of millions; and Japan was well exploited. But she knew that she was only paying to learn; and her patience was of that kind which endures so long as to be mistaken for oblivion of injuries. Her opportunities came in the natural order of things. The growing influx of aliens seeking fortune gave her the first advantage. The intercompetition for Japanese trade broke down old methods; and new firms being glad to take

1. See *Japan Mail,* 21 July 1895.

orders and risks without 'bargain-money,' large advance-payments could no longer be exacted. The relations between foreigners and Japanese simultaneously improved, as the latter showed a dangerous capacity for sudden combination against ill-treatment, could not be cowed by revolvers, would not suffer abuse of any sort, and knew how to dispose of the most dangerous rowdy in the space of a few minutes. Already the rougher Japanese of the ports, the dregs of the populace, were ready to assume the aggressive on the least provocation.

Within two decades from the founding of the settlements, those foreigners who once imagined it a mere question of time when the whole country would belong to them, began to understand how greatly they had underestimated the race. The Japanese had been learning wonderfully well – 'nearly as well as the Chinese.' They were supplanting the small foreign shopkeepers; and various establishments had been compelled to close because of Japanese competition. Even for large firms the era of easy fortune-making was over; the period of hard work was commencing. In early days all the personal wants of foreigners had necessarily been supplied by foreigners, so that a large retail trade had grown up under the patronage of the wholesale trade. The retail trade of the settlements was evidently doomed. Some of its branches had disappeared; the rest were visibly diminishing.

Today the economic foreign clerk or assistant in a business house cannot well afford to live at the local hotels. He can hire a Japanese cook at a very small sum per month, or can have his meals sent him from a Japanese restaurant at five to seven sen per plate. He lives in a house constructed in 'semi-foreign style,' and owned by a Japanese. The carpets or mattings on his floor are of Japanese manufacture. His furniture is supplied by a Japanese cabinet-maker. His suits, shirts, shoes, walking-cane, umbrella, are 'Japanese make': even the soap on his washstand is stamped with Japanese ideographs. If a smoker, he buys his Manilla cigars from a Japanese tobacconist half a dollar cheaper per box than any foreign house would charge him for the same quality. If he wants books, he can buy them at much lower prices from a Japanese than from a foreign book-dealer, and select his purchases from a much larger and better-selected stock. If he wants a photograph taken, he goes to a Japanese gallery; no foreign photographer could make a living in Japan. If he wants curios, he visits a Japanese house; the foreign dealer would charge him a hundred per cent dearer.

On the other hand, if he be a man of family, his daily marketing is supplied by Japanese butchers, fishmongers, dairymen, fruit-sellers, vegetable-dealers. He may continue for a time to buy English or American hams, bacon, canned goods, etc. from some foreign provision-dealer; but he has discovered that Japanese stores now offer the same class of goods at lower prices. If he drinks good beer, it probably comes from a Japanese brewery; and if he wants a good quality of ordinary wine or liquor, Japanese storekeepers can supply it at rates below those of the foreign importer. Indeed, the only things he cannot buy from the Japanese houses are just those things which he cannot afford — high-priced goods such as only rich men are likely to purchase. And finally, if any of his family become sick, he can consult a Japanese physician who will charge him a fee perhaps one tenth less than he would have had to pay a foreign physician in former times. Foreign doctors now find it very hard to live — unless they have something more than their practice to rely upon. Even when the foreign doctor brings down his fee to a dollar a visit, the high-class Japanese doctor can charge two, and still crush competition; for he furnishes the medicine himself at prices which would ruin a foreign apothecary. There are doctors and doctors, of course, as in all countries; but the German-speaking Japanese physician capable of directing a public or military hospital is not easily surpassed in his profession; and the average foreign physician cannot possibly compete with him. He furnishes no prescriptions to be taken to a drugstore: his drugstore is either at home or in a room of the hospital he directs.

These facts, taken at random out of a multitude, imply that foreign shops, or, as we call them in America, 'stores,' will soon cease to be. The existence of some has been prolonged only by needless and foolish trickery on the part of some petty Japanese dealers — attempts to sell abominable decoctions in foreign bottles under foreign labels, to adulterate imported goods, or to imitate trademarks. But the common sense of the Japanese dealers, as a mass, is strongly opposed to such immorality, and the evil will soon correct itself.

The native storekeepers can honestly undersell the foreign ones, because they are able not only to underlive them, but to make fortunes during the competition.

This has been for some time well recognized in the concessions. But the delusion prevailed that the great exporting and importing firms were impregnable; that they could still control the whole volume of commerce with the West; and that no Japanese companies could find means to oppose the weight of foreign capital, or to acquire the business methods according to which it was employed. Certainly the retail trade would go. But that signified little. The great firms would remain and multiply, and would increase their capacities.

III

During all this time of outward changes the real feeling between the races — the mutual dislike of Oriental and Occidental — had continued to grow. Of the nine or ten English papers published in the open ports, the majority expressed, day after day, one side of this dislike, in the language of ridicule or contempt; and a powerful native press retorted in kind, with dangerous effectiveness. If the 'anti-Japanese' newspapers did not actually represent — as I believe they did — an absolute majority in sentiment, they represented at least the weight of foreign capital, and the preponderant influences of the settlements. The English 'pro-Japanese' newspapers, though conducted by shrewd men, and distinguished by journalistic abilities of no common order, could not appease the powerful resentment provoked by the language of their contemporaries. The charges of barbarism or immorality printed in English were promptly answered by the publication in Japanese dailies of the scandals of the open ports, for all the millions of the empire to know. The race question was carried into Japanese politics by a strong anti-foreign league; the foreign concessions were openly denounced as hotbeds of vice; and the national anger became so formidable that only the most determined action on the part of the government could have prevented disastrous happenings. Nevertheless oil was still poured on the smothered fire by foreign editors, who at the outbreak of the war with China openly took the part of China. This policy was pursued throughout the campaign. Reports of imaginary reverses were printed recklessly; undeniable victories were unjustly belittled; and after the war had been decided, the cry was raised that the Japanese 'had been allowed to become dangerous.' Later on, the interference of Russia was applauded, and the sympathy of England condemned by men of English blood. The effect of such utterances at such a time was that of insult never to be forgiven upon a people who never forgive. Utterances of hate they were, but also utterances of alarm – alarm excited by the signing of those new treaties, bringing all aliens under Japanese jurisdiction – and fear, not ill-founded, of another anti-foreign agitation with the formidable new sense of national power behind it. Premonitory symptoms of such agitation were really apparent in a general tendency to insult or jeer at foreigners, and in some rare but exemplary acts of violence. The government again found it necessary to issue proclamations and warnings against such demonstrations of national anger; and they ceased almost as quickly as they began. But there is no doubt that their cessation was due largely to recognition of the friendly attitude of England as a naval power, and the worth of her policy to Japan in a moment of danger to the world's peace. England too, had first rendered treaty-revision possible, in spite of the passionate outcries of her own subjects in the Far East; and the leaders of the people were grateful. Otherwise the hatred between settlers and Japanese might have resulted quite as badly as had been feared.

In the beginning, of course, this mutual antagonism was racial, and therefore natural; and the irrational violence of prejudice and malignity developed at a later day was inevitable with the ever-increasing conflict of interests. No foreigner really capable of estimating the conditions could have seriously entertained any hope of a *rapprochement.* The barriers of racial feeling, of emotional differentiation, of language, of manners and beliefs, are likely to remain insurmountable for centuries. Though instances of warm friendship, due to the mutual attraction of exceptional natures able to divine each other intuitively, might be cited, the foreigner, as a general rule, understands the Japanese quite as little as the Japanese understands him. What is worse for the alien than miscomprehension is the simple fact that he is in the position of an invader. Under no ordinary circumstances need he expect to be treated like a Japanese; and this not merely because he has more money at his command, but because of his race. One price for the foreigner, another for the Japanese, is the common regulation — except in those Japanese stores which depend almost exclusively upon foreign trade. If you wish to enter a Japanese theatre, a figure-show, any place of amusement, or even an inn, you must pay a virtual tax upon your nationality. Japanese artisans, laborers, clerks, will not work for you at Japanese rates — unless they have some other object in view than wages. Japanese hotel-keepers — except in those hotels built and furnished especially for European or American travelers — will not make out your bill at regular prices. Large hotel-companies have been formed which maintain this rule — companies controlling scores of establishments throughout the country, and able to dictate terms to local storekeepers and to the smaller hostelries. It has been generously confessed that foreigners ought to pay higher than Japanese for accommodation, since they give more trouble; and this is true. But under even these facts race-feeling is manifest. Those innkeepers who build for Japanese custom only, in the great centres, care nothing for foreign custom, and often lose by it — partly because well-paying native guests do not like hotels patronized by foreigners, and partly because the Western guest wants all to himself the room which can be rented more profitably to a Japanese party of five or eight. Another fact not generally understood in connection with this is that in Old Japan the question of recompense for service was left to honor. The Japanese innkeeper always supplied (and in the country often still supplies) food at scarcely more than cost; and his real profit depended upon the conscience of the customer. Hence the importance of the chadai, or present of tea-money, to the hotel. From the poor a very small sum, from the rich a larger sum, was expected, according to services rendered. In like manner the hired servant expected to be remunerated according to his master's ability to pay, even more than according to the value of the work done; the artist preferred, when working for a good patron, never to name a price: only the merchant tried to get the better of his customers by bargaining — the immoral privilege of his class. It may be readily imagined that the habit of trusting to honor for payment produced no good results in dealing with Occidentals. All matters of buying and selling we think of as 'business;' and business in the West is not conducted under purely abstract ideas of morality, but at best under relative and partial ideas of morality. A generous man extremely dislikes to have the price of an article which he wants to buy left to his conscience; for, unless he knows exactly the value of the material and the worth of the labor, he feels obliged to make such over-payment as will assure him that he has done more than right; while the selfish man takes advantage of the situation to give as nearly next to nothing as he can. Special rates have to be made, therefore, by the Japanese in all dealings with foreigners. But the dealing itself is made more or less aggressive, according to circumstance, because of race antagonism. The foreigner has not only to pay higher rates for every kind of skilled labor, but must sign costlier leases, and submit to higher rents. Only the lowest class of Japanese servants can be hired even at high wages by a foreign household; and their stay is usually brief, as they dislike the service required of them. Even the apparent eagerness of educated Japanese to enter foreign employ is generally misunderstood; their veritable purpose being simply, in most cases, to fit themselves for the same sort of work in Japanese business houses, stores, and hotels. The average Japanese would prefer to work fifteen hours a day for one of his own countrymen than eight hours a day for a foreigner paying higher wages. I have seen graduates of the university working as servants; but they were working only to learn special things.

IV

Really the dullest foreigner could not have believed that a people of forty millions, uniting all their energies to achieve absolute national independence, would remain content to leave the management of their country's import and export trade to aliens, especially in view of the feeling in the open ports. The existence of foreign settlements in Japan, under consular jurisdiction, was in itself a constant exasperation to national pride, an indication of national weakness. It had so been proclaimed in print, in speeches by members of the anti-foreign league, in speeches made in parliament. But knowledge of the national desire to control the whole of Japanese commerce, and the periodical manifestations of hostility to foreigners as settlers, excited only temporary uneasiness. It was confidently asserted that the Japanese could only injure themselves by any attempt to get rid of foreign negotiators. Though alarmed at the prospect of being brought under Japanese law, the merchants of the concessions never imagined a successful attack upon large interests possible, except by violation of that law itself. It signified little that the Nippon Yusen Kwaisha had become, during the war, one of the largest steamship companies in the world; that Japan was trading directly with India and China; that Japanese banking agencies were being established in the great manufacturing centres abroad; that Japanese merchants were sending their sons to Europe and America for a sound commercial education. Because Japanese lawyers were gaining a large foreign *clientèle*; because Japanese shipbuilders, architects, engineers, had replaced foreigners in government service, it did not at all follow that the foreign agents controlling the import and export trade with Europe and America could be dispensed with. The machinery of commerce would be useless in Japanese hands; and capacity for other professions by no means augured latent capacity for business. The foreign capital invested in Japan could not be successfully threatened by any combinations formed against it. Some Japanese houses might carry on a small import business; but the export trade required a thorough knowledge of business conditions on the other side of the world, and such connections and credits as the Japanese could not obtain. Nevertheless the self-confidence of the foreign importers and exporters was rudely broken in July 1895, when a British house, having brought suit against a Japanese company in a Japanese court for refusal to accept delivery of goods ordered, and having won a judgment for nearly thirty thousand dollars, suddenly found itself confronted and menaced by a guild whose power had never been suspected. The Japanese firm did not appeal against the decision of the court: it expressed itself ready to pay the whole sum at once — if required. But the guild to which it belonged informed the triumphant plaintiffs that a compromise would be to their advantage. Then the English house discovered itself threatened with a boycott which could utterly ruin it — a boycott operating in all the industrial centres of the Empire. The compromise was promptly effected at considerable loss to the foreign firm; and the settlements were dismayed. There was much denunciation of the immorality of the proceeding.[1] But it was

1. A Kobé merchant of great experience, writing to the *Kobé Chronicle* of 7 August 1895, observed: 'I am not attempting to defend boycotts; but I firmly believe from what has come to my knowledge that in each and every case there has been provocation irritating the Japanese. rousing their feelings and their sense of justice, and driving them to combination as a defense.'

a proceeding against which the law could do nothing; for boycotting cannot be satisfactorily dealt with under law; and it afforded proof positive that the Japanese were able to force foreign firms to submit to their dictation – by foul means if not by fair. Enormous guilds had been organized by the great industries – combinations whose moves, perfectly regulated by telegraph, could ruin opposition, and could set at defiance even the judgment of tribunals. The Japanese had attempted boycotting in previous years with so little success that they were deemed incapable of combination. But the new situation showed how well they had learned through defeat, and that with further improvement of organization they could reasonably expect to get the foreign trade under control – if not into their own hands. It would be the next great step toward the realization of the national desire – *Japan only for the Japanese*. Even though the country should be opened to foreign settlement, foreign investments would always be at the mercy of Japanese combinations.

v

The foregoing brief account of existing conditions may suffice to prove the evolution in Japan of a social phenomenon of great significance. Of course the prospective opening of the country under new treaties, the rapid development of its industries, and the vast annual increase in the volume of trade with America and Europe will probably bring about some increase of foreign settlers; and this temporary result might deceive many as to the inevitable drift of things. But old merchants of experience even now declare that the probable further expansion of the ports will really mean the growth of a native competitive commerce that must eventually dislodge foreign merchants. The foreign settlements, as communities, will disappear: there will remain only some few great agencies, such as exist in all the chief ports of the civilized world; and the abandoned streets of the concessions, and the costly foreign houses on the heights will be peopled and tenanted by Japanese. Large foreign investments will not be made in the interior. And even Christian mission-work must be left to native missionaries; for just as Buddhism never took definite form in Japan until the teaching of its doctrines was left entirely to Japanese priests, so Christianity will never take any fixed shape till it has been so remodeled as to harmonize with the emotional and social life of the race. Even thus remodeled it can scarcely hope to exist except in the form of a few small sects.

The social phenomenon exhibited can be best explained by a simile. In many ways a human society may be compared biologically with an individual organism. Foreign elements introduced forcibly into the system of either, and impossible to assimilate, set up irritations and partial disintegration, until eliminated naturally or removed artificially. Japan is strengthening herself through elimination of disturbing elements; and this natural process is symbolized in the resolve to regain possession of all the concessions, to bring about the abolishment of consular jurisdiction, to leave nothing under foreign control within the Empire. It is also manifested in the dismissal of foreign employees, in the resistance offered by Japanese congregations to the authority of foreign missionaries, and in the resolute boycotting of foreign merchants. And behind all this race-movement there is more than race-feeling: there is also the definite conviction that foreign help is proof of national feebleness, and that the Empire remains disgraced before the eyes of the commercial world, so long as its import and export trade are managed by aliens. Several large Japanese firms have quite emancipated themselves from the domination of foreign middlemen; large trade with India and China is being carried on by Japanese steamship companies; and communication with the Southern States of America is soon to be established by the Nippon Yusen Kwaisha, for the direct importation of cotton. But the foreign settlements remain constant sources of irritation; and their commercial conquest by untiring national effort will alone satisfy the country, and will prove, even better than the war with China, Japan's real place among nations. That conquest, I think, will certainly be achieved.

VI

What of the future of Japan? No one can venture any positive prediction on the assumption that existing tendencies will continue far into that future. Not to dwell upon the grim probabilities of war, or the possibility of such internal disorder as might compel indefinite suspension of the constitution, and lead to a military dictatorship

– a resurrected Shogunate in modern uniform – great changes there will assuredly be, both for better and for worse. Supposing these changes normal, however, one may venture some qualified predictions, based upon the reasonable supposition that the race will continue, through rapidly alternating periods of action and reaction, to assimilate its new-found knowledge with the best relative consequences.

Physically, I think, the Japanese will become before the close of the next century much superior to what they now are. For such belief there are three good reasons. The first is that the systematic military and gymnastic training of the able-bodied youth of the Empire ought in a few generations to produce results as marked as those of the military system in Germany – increase in stature, in average girth of chest, in muscular development. Another reason is that the Japanese of the cities are taking to a richer diet, a flesh diet; and that a more nutritive food must have physiological results favoring growth. Immense numbers of little restaurants are everywhere springing up, in which 'Western Cooking' is furnished almost as cheaply as Japanese food. Thirdly, the delay of marriage necessitated by education and by military service must result in the production of finer and finer generations of children. As immature marriages become the exception rather than the rule, children of feeble constitution will correspondingly diminish in number. At present the extraordinary differences of stature noticeable in any Japanese crowd seem to prove that the race is capable of great physical development under a severer social discipline.

Moral improvement is hardly to be expected – rather the reverse. The old moral ideals of Japan were at least quite as noble as our own; and men could really live up to them in the quiet benevolent times of patriarchal government. Untruthfulness, dishonesty, and brutal crime were rarer than now, as official statistics show, the percentage of crime having been for some years steadily on the increase – which proves of course, among other things, that the struggle for existence has been intensified. The old standard of chastity, as represented in public opinion, was that of a less developed society than our own; yet I do not believe it can be truthfully asserted that the moral conditions were worse than with us. In one respect they were certainly better; for the virtue of Japanese wives was generally in all ages

269

above suspicion.[2] If the morals of men were much more open to reproach, it is not necessary to cite Lecky for evidence as to whether a much better state of things prevails in the Occident. Early marriages were encouraged to guard young men from temptations to irregular life; and it is only fair to suppose that in a majority of cases this result was obtained. Concubinage, the privilege of the rich, had its evil side; but it had also the effect of relieving the wife from the physical strain of rearing many children in rapid succession. The social conditions were so different from those which Western religion assumes to be the best possible that an impartial judgment of them cannot be ecclesiastical. One fact is indisputable, that they were unfavorable to professional vice; and in many of the larger fortified towns — the seats of princes — no houses of prostitution were suffered to exist. When all things are fairly considered, it will be found that Old Japan might claim, in spite of her patriarchal system, to have been less open to reproach even in the matter of sexual morality than many a Western country. The people were better than their laws asked them to be. And now that the relations of the sexes are to be regulated by new codes — at a time when new codes are really needed — the changes which it is desirable to bring about cannot result in immediate good. Sudden reforms are not made by legislation. Laws cannot directly create sentiment; and real social progress can be made only through change of ethical feeling developed by long discipline and training. Meanwhile increasing pressure of

2. The statement has been made that there is no word for chastity in the Japanese language. This is true in the same sense only that we might say there is no word for chastity in the English language, because such words as honor, virtue, purity, chastity, have been adopted into English from other languages. Open any good Japanese-English dictionary and you will find many words for chastity. Just as it would be ridiculous to deny that the word 'chastity' is modern English, because it came to us through the French from the Latin, so it is ridiculous to deny that Chinese moral terms, adopted into the Japanese tongue more than a thousand years ago, are Japanese today. The statement, like a majority of missionary statements on these subjects, is otherwise misleading; for the reader is left to infer the absence of an adjective as well as a noun — and the purely Japanese adjectives signifying chaste are numerous. The word most commonly used applies to both sexes, and has the old Japanese sense of firm, strict, resisting, honorable. The deficiency of abstract terms in a language by no means implies the deficiency of concrete moral ideas — a fact which has been vainly pointed out to missionaries more than once.

population and increasing competition must tend, while quickening intelligence, to harden character and develop selfishness.

Intellectually there will doubtless be great progress, but not a progress so rapid as those who think that Japan has really transformed herself in thirty years would have us believe. However widely diffused among the people, scientific education cannot immediately raise the average of practical intelligence to the Western level. The common capacity must remain lower for generations. There will be plenty of remarkable exceptions, indeed; and a new aristocracy of intellect is coming into existence. But the real future of the nation depends rather upon the general capacity of the many than upon the exceptional capacity of the few. Perhaps it depends especially upon the development of the mathematical faculty, which is being everywhere assiduously cultivated. At present this is the weak point, hosts of students being yearly debarred from the more important classes of higher study through inability to pass in mathematics. At the Imperial naval and military colleges, however, such results have been obtained as suffice to show that this weakness will eventually be remedied. The most difficult branches of scientific study will become less formidable to the children of those who have been able to distinguish themselves in such branches.

In other respects, some temporary retrogression is to be looked for. Just so certainly as Japan has attempted that which is above the normal limit of her powers, so certainly must she fall back to that limit — or, rather, below it. Such retrogression will be natural as well as necessary: it will mean nothing more than a recuperative preparation for stronger and loftier efforts. Signs of it are even now visible in the working of certain state-departments, notably in that of education. The idea of forcing upon Oriental students a course of study above the average capacity of Western students, the idea of making English the language, or at least one of the languages of the country, and the idea of changing ancestral modes of feeling and thinking for the better by such training were wild extravagances. Japan must develop her own soul: she cannot borrow another. A dear friend whose life has been devoted to philology once said to me while commenting upon the deterioration of manners among the students of Japan: 'Why, the English language itself has been a demoralizing influence!' There was much depth in that observation. Setting the whole Japanese nation to study English (the language of a people who are being forever preached to about their 'rights,' and never about their 'duties') was almost an imprudence. The policy was too wholesale as well as too sudden. It involved great waste of money and time, and it helped to sap ethical sentiment. In the future Japan will learn English, just as England learns German. But if this study has been wasted in some directions, it has not been wasted in others. The influence of English has effected modifications in the native tongue, making it richer, more flexible, and more capable of expressing the new forms of thought created by the discoveries of modern science. This influence must long continue. There will be a considerable absorption of English — perhaps also of French and German words — into Japanese: indeed, this absorption is already marked in the changing speech of the educated classes, not less than in the colloquial of the ports which is mixed with curious modifications of foreign commercial words. Furthermore, the grammatical structure of Japanese is being influenced; and though I cannot agree with a clergyman who lately declared that the use of the passive voice by Tōkyō street-urchins announcing the fall of Port Arthur — 'Ryojunko ga senryo serareta!' — represented the working of 'divine providence,' I do think it afforded some proof that the Japanese language, assimilative like the genius of the race, is showing capacity to meet all demands made upon it by the new conditions.

Perhaps Japan will remember her foreign teachers more kindly in the twentieth century. But she will never feel toward the Occident, as she felt toward China before the Meiji era, the reverential respect due by ancient custom to a beloved instructor; for the wisdom of China was voluntarily sought, while that of the West was thrust upon her by violence. She will have some Christian sects of her own; but she will not remember our American and English missionaries as she remembers even now those great Chinese priests who once educated her youth. And she will not preserve relics of our sojourn, carefully wrapped in septuple coverings of silk, and packed away in dainty whitewood boxes, because we had no new lesson of beauty to teach her, nothing by which to appeal to her emotions.

The Japanese Family

The great general idea, the fundamental idea, underlying every persistent ancestor-worship is that the welfare of the living depends upon the welfare of the dead. Under the influence of this idea, and of the cult based upon it, were developed the early organization of the family, the laws regarding property and succession, the whole structure, in short, of ancient society, whether in the Western or the Eastern world.

But before considering how the social structure in Old Japan was shaped by the ancestral cult, let me again remind the reader that there were at first no other gods than the dead. Even when Japanese ancestor-worship evolved a mythology, its gods were only transfigured ghosts – and this is the history of all mythology. The ideas of heaven and hell did not exist among the primitive Japanese, nor any notion of metempsychosis. The Buddhist doctrine of rebirth – a late borrowing – was totally inconsistent with the archaic Japanese beliefs, and required an elaborate metaphysical system to support it. But we may suppose the early ideas of the Japanese about the dead to have been much like those of the Greeks of the pre-Homeric era. There was an underground world to which spirits descended; but they were supposed to haunt by preference their own graves, or their 'ghost-houses.' Only by slow degrees did the notion of their power of ubiquity become evolved. But even then they were thought to be particularly attached to their tombs, shrines, and homesteads. Hirata wrote, in the early part of the nineteenth century: 'The spirits of the dead continue to exist in the unseen world which is everywhere about us; and they all become gods of varying character and degrees of influence. Some reside in temples built in their honour; others hover near their tombs; and they continue to render service to their prince, parents, wives, and children, as when in the body.'

Evidently 'the unseen world' was thought to be in some sort a duplicate of the visible world, and dependent upon the help of the living for its prosperity. The dead and the living were mutually dependent. The all-important necessity for the ghost was sacrificial worship; the all-important necessity for the man was to provide for the future cult of his own spirit; and to die without assurance of a cult was the supreme calamity ... Remembering these facts we can understand better the organization of the patriarchal family, shaped to maintain and to provide for the cult of its dead, any neglect of which cult was believed to involve misfortune.

The reader is doubtless aware that in the old Aryan family the bond of union was not the bond of affection, but a bond of religion, to which natural affection was altogether subordinate. This condition characterizes the patriarchal family wherever ancestor-worship exists. Now the Japanese family, like the ancient Greek or Roman family, was a religious society in the strictest sense of the term; and a religious society it yet remains. Its organization was primarily shaped in accordance with the requirements of ancestor-worship; its later imported doctrines of filial piety had been already developed in China to meet the needs of an older and similar religion. We might expect to find in the structure, the laws, and the customs of the Japanese family many points of likeness to the structure and the traditional laws of the old Aryan household, because the law of sociological evolution admits of only minor exceptions. And many such points of likeness are obvious. The materials for a serious comparative study have not yet been collected: very much remains to be learned regarding the past history of the Japanese family. But, along certain general lines, the resemblances between domestic institutions in ancient Europe and domestic institutions in the Far East can be clearly established.

Alike in the early European and in the old Japanese civilization it was believed that the prosperity of the family depended upon the exact fulfilment of the duties of the ancestral cult; and, to a considerable degree, this belief rules the life of the Japanese family today. It is still thought that the good fortune of the household depends on the observance of its cult, and that the greatest possible calamity is to die without leaving a male heir to perform the rites and to make the offerings. The paramount duty of filial piety among the early Greeks and Romans was to provide for the perpetuation of the family cult; and celibacy was therefore generally forbidden, the obligation to marry being enforced by opinion where not enforced by legislation. Among the classes of Old Japan, marriage was also, as a general rule, obligatory in the case of a male heir; otherwise, where celibacy was not condemned by law, it was condemned by custom. To die without offspring was in the case of a younger son, chiefly a personal misfortune; to die without leaving a male heir, in the case of an elder son and successor, was a crime against the ancestors, the cult being thereby threatened with extinction. No excuse existed for remaining childless: the family law in Japan, precisely as in ancient Europe, having amply provided against such a contingency. In case that a wife proved barren, she might be divorced. In case that there were reasons for not divorcing her, a concubine might be taken for the purpose of obtaining an heir. Furthermore, every family representative was privileged to adopt an heir. An unworthy son, again, might be disinherited, and another young man adopted in his place. Finally, in case that a man had daughters but no son, the succession and the continuance of the cult could be assured by adopting a husband for the eldest daughter.

But, as in the antique European family, daughters could not inherit: descent being in the male line, it was necessary to have a male heir. In old Japanese belief, as in old Greek and Roman belief, the father, not the mother, was the life-giver; the creative principle was masculine; the duty of maintaining the cult rested with the man, not with the woman.[1]

The woman shared the cult; but she could not maintain it. Besides, the daughters of the family, being destined, as a general rule, to marry into other households, could bear only a temporary relation to the home-cult. It was necessary that the religion of the wife should be the religion of the husband; and the Japanese, like the Greek

1. Wherever, among ancestor-worshipping races, descent is in the male line, the cult follows the male line. But the reader is doubtless aware that a still more primitive form of society than the patriarchal – the matriarchal – is supposed to have had its ancestor-worship. Mr Spencer observes: 'What has happened when descent in the female line obtains is not clear. I have met with no statement showing that, in societies characterized by this usage, the duty of administering to the double of the dead man devolved on one of his children rather than on others' – *Principles of Sociology*, Vol. III, para. 601.

woman, on marrying into another household, necessarily became attached to the cult of her husband's family. For this reason especially, the females in the patriarchal family are not equal to the males; the sister cannot rank with the brother. It is true that the Japanese daughter, like the Greek daughter, could remain attached to her own family even after marriage, providing that a husband were adopted for her − that is to say, taken into the family as a son. But even in this case, she could only share in the cult, which it then became the duty of the adopted husband to maintain.

The constitution of the patriarchal family everywhere derives from its ancestral cult; and before considering the subjects of marriage and adoption in Japan, it will be necessary to say something about the ancient family-organization. The ancient family was called uji − a word said to have originally signified the same thing as the modern term uchi, 'interior,' or 'household,' but certainly used from very early times in the sense of 'name' − clan-name especially. There were two kinds of uji: the ō-uji, or great families, and the ko-uji, or lesser families − either term signifying a large body of persons united by kinship and by the cult of a common ancestor. The ō-uji corresponded in some degree to the Greek γένος or the Roman *gens*: the ko-uji were its branches, and subordinate to it. The unit of society was the uji. Each ō-uji, with its dependent ko-uji, represented something like a *phratry* or *curia*; and all the larger groups making up the primitive Japanese society were but multiplications of the uji − whether we call them clans, tribes, or hordes. With the advent of a settled civilization, the greater groups necessarily divided and subdivided; but the smallest subdivision still retained its primal organization. Even the modern Japanese family partly retains that organization. It does not mean only a household: it means rather what the Greek or Roman family became after the dissolution of the *gens*. With ourselves the family has been disintegrated: when we talk of a man's family, we mean his wife and children. But the Japanese family is still a large group. As marriages take place early, it may consist, even as a household, of great-grandparents, grand-parents, parents, and children − sons and daughters of several genera-tions; but it commonly extends much beyond the limits of one household. In early times it might constitute the entire population of a village or town; and there are still in Japan large communities of persons all bearing the same family name. In some districts it was formerly the custom to keep all the children, as far as possible, within the original family group – husbands being adopted for all the daughters. The group might thus consist of sixty or more persons, dwelling under the same roof; and the houses were of course constructed, by successive extension, so as to meet the requirement. (I am mentioning these curious facts only by way of illustration.) But the greater uji, after the race had settled down, rapidly multiplied; and although there are said to be house-communities still in some remote districts of the country, the primal patriarchal groups must have been broken up almost everywhere at some very early period. Thereafter the main cult of the uji did not cease to be the cult also of its subdivisions: all members of the original *gens* continued to worship the common ancestor, or uji-no-kami, 'the god of the uji.' By degrees the ghost-house of the uji-no-kami became transformed into the modern Shintō parish-temple; and the ancestral spirit became the local tutelar god, whose modern appellation, ujigami, is but a shortened form of his ancient title, uji-no-kami. Meanwhile, after the general establishment of the domestic cult, each separate household maintained the special cult of its own dead, in addition to the communal cult. This religious condition still continues. The family may include several households; but each household maintains the cult of its dead. And the family-group, whether large or small, preserves its ancient constitution and character; it is still a religious society, exacting obedience, on the part of all its members, to traditional custom.

So much having been explained, the customs regarding marriage and adoption, in their relation to the family hierarchy, can be clearly understood. But a word first regarding this hierarchy, as it exists today. Theoretically the power of the head of the family is still supreme in the household. All must obey the head. Furthermore, the females must obey the males – the wives, the husbands; and the younger members of the family are subject to the elder members. The children must not only obey the parents and grandparents, but must observe among themselves the domestic law of seniority: thus the younger brother should obey the elder brother, and the younger sister the elder sister. The rule of precedence is enforced gently, and is cheerfully obeyed even in small matters: for example, at meal-time, the elder boy is served first, the second son next, and so on – an exception being made in the case of a very young child, who is not obliged to wait. This custom accounts for an amusing popular term often applied in jest to a second son, 'Master Cold-Rice' (Hiaméshi-San); as the second son, having to wait until both infants and elders have been served, is not likely to find his portion desirably hot when it reaches him ... Legally, the family can have but one responsible head. It may be the grandfather, the father, or the eldest son; and it is generally the eldest son, because according to a custom of Chinese origin, the old folks usually resign their active authority as soon as the eldest son is able to take charge of affairs.

The subordination of young to old, and of females to males – in fact, the whole existing constitution of the family – suggests a great deal in regard to the probably stricter organization of the patri-archal family, whose chief was at once ruler and priest, with almost unlimited powers. The organization was primarily, and still remains, religious: the marital bond did not constitute the family; and the relation of the parent to the household depended upon his or her relation to the family as a religious body. Today also, the girl adopted into a household as wife ranks only as an adopted child: marriage signifies adoption. She is called 'flower-daughter' (hana-yomé). In like manner, and for the same reasons, the young man received into a household as a husband of one of the daughters, ranks merely as an adopted son. The adopted bride or bridegroom is necessarily subject to the elders, and may be dismissed by their decision. As for the adopted husband, his position is both delicate and difficult – as an old Japanese proverb bears witness: 'Konuka san-go aréba, mukoyoshi to naruna' ('While you have even three gō[2] of rice-bran left, do not become a son-in-law'). Jacob does not have to wait for Rachel: he is given to Rachel on demand; and his service then begins. And after twice seven years of service, Jacob may be sent away. In that event his children do not any more belong to him, but to the family. His adoption may have had nothing to do with affection; and his dismissal may have nothing to do with misconduct. Such matters, however they may be settled in law, are really decided by

2. A gō is something more than a pint.

family interests – interests relating to the maintenance of the house and of its cult.[3]

It should not be forgotten that, although a daughter-in-law or a son-in-law could in former times be dismissed almost at will, the question of marriage in the old Japanese family was a matter of religious importance – marriage being one of the chief duties of filial piety. This was also the case in the early Greek and Roman family; and the marriage ceremony was performed, as it is now performed in Japan, not at a temple, but in the home. It was a rite of the family religion – the rite by which the bride was adopted into the cult in the supposed presence of the ancestral spirits. Among the primitive Japanese there was probably no corresponding ceremony; but after the establishment of the domestic cult, the marriage ceremony became a religious rite, and this it still remains. Ordinary marriages are not, however, performed before the household shrine or in front of the ancestral tablets, except under certain circumstances. The rule, as regards such ordinary marriages, seems to be that if the parents of the bridegroom are yet alive, this is not done; but if they are dead, then the bridegroom leads his bride before their mortuary tablets, where she makes obeisance. Among the nobility, in former times at least, the marriage ceremony appears to have been more distinctly religious – judging from the following curious relation in the book *Shōrei-Hikki*, or 'Record of Ceremonies'[4]: 'At the weddings of the great, the bridal-chamber is composed of three rooms thrown into one [by removal of the sliding-screens ordinarily separating them], and newly decorated ... The shrine for the image of the family-god is placed upon a shelf adjoining the sleeping-place.' It is noteworthy also that Imperial marriages are always officially announced to the ancestors; and that the marriage of the heir-apparent, or other male offspring of the Imperial house, is performed before the Kashiko-dokoro, or imperial temple of the ancestors, which stands within the palace-grounds.[5] As a general rule it would appear that the evolu-

3. Recent legislation has been in favor of the mukoyoshi; but, as a rule, the law is seldom resorted to except by men dismissed from the family for misconduct, and anxious to make profit by the dismissal.

4. The translation is Mr Mitford's. There are no 'images' of the family-god, and I suppose that the family's Shintō shrine is meant, with its ancestral tablets.

5. This was the case at the marriage of the present Crown-Prince.

tion of the marriage-ceremony in Japan chiefly followed Chinese precedent; and in the Chinese patriarchal family the ceremony is in its own way quite as much of a religious rite as the early Greek or Roman marriage. And though the relation of the Japanese rite to the family cult is less marked, it becomes sufficiently clear upon investigation. The alternate drinking of rice-wine, by bridegroom and bride, from the same vessels, corresponds in a sort to the Roman *confarreatio*. By the wedding-rite the bride is adopted into the family religion. She is adopted not only by the living but by the dead; she must thereafter revere the ancestors of her husband as her own ancestors; and should there be no elders in the household, it will become her duty to make the offerings, as representative of her husband. With the cult of her own family she has nothing more to do; and the funeral ceremonies performed upon her departure from the parental roof – the solemn sweeping-out of the house-rooms, the lighting of the death-fire before the gate – are significant of this religious separation.

Speaking of the Greek and Roman marriage, M. de Coulanges observes: 'Une telle religion ne pouvait pas admettre la polygamie.' As relating to the highly developed domestic cult of those communities considered by the author of *La Cité antique*, his statement will scarcely be called in question. But as regards ancestor-worship in general, it would be incorrect, since polygamy or polygyny, and polyandry may coexist with ruder forms of ancestor-worship. The Western Aryan societies, in the epoch studied by M. de Coulanges, were practically monogamic. The ancient Japanese society was polygynous; and polygyny persisted, after the establishment of the domestic cult. In early times, the marital relation itself would seem to have been indefinite. No distinction was made between the wife and the concubines: 'they were classed together as "women."'[6] Probably under Chinese influence the distinction was afterwards sharply drawn; and with the progress of civilization, the general tendency was towards monogamy, although the ruling classes remained polygynous. In the fifty-fourth article of Iyeyasu's legacy, this phase of the social condition is clearly expressed – a condition which prevailed down to the present era: 'The position a wife holds towards a concubine is the same as that of a lord to his vassal. The Emperor has

6. Satow: *The Revival of Pure Shintau.*

twelve imperial concubines. The princes may have eight concubines. Officers of the highest class may have five mistresses. A Samurai may have two handmaids. All below this are ordinary married men.'

This would suggest that concubinage had long been (with some possible exceptions) an exclusive privilege; and that it should have persisted down to the period of the abolition of the daimiates and of the military class, is sufficiently explained by the militant character of the ancient society.[7] Though it is untrue that domestic ancestor-worship cannot coexist with polygamy or polygyny (Mr Spencer's term is the most inclusive), it is at least true that such worship is favored by the monogamic relation, and tends therefore to establish it, since monogamy insures to the family succession a stability that no other relation can offer. We may say that, although the old Japanese society was not monogamic, the natural tendency was toward monogamy, as the condition best according with the religion of the family, and with the moral feeling of the masses.

Once that the domestic ancestor-cult had become universally established, the question of marriage, as a duty of filial piety, could not be judiciously left to the will of the young people themselves. It was a matter to be decided by the family, not by the children; for mutual inclination could not be suffered to interfere with the requirements of the household religion. It was not a question of affection, but of religious duty; and to think otherwise was impious. Affection might and ought to spring up from the relation. But any affection powerful enough to endanger the cohesion of the family would be condemned. A wife might therefore be divorced because her husband had become too much attached to her; an adopted husband might be divorced because of his power to exercise, through affection, too great an influence upon the daughter of the house. Other causes would probably be found for the divorce in either case – but they would not be difficult to find.

For the same reason that connubial affection could be tolerated only within limits, the natural rights of parenthood (as we understand them) were necessarily restricted in the old Japanese household. Marriage being for the purpose of obtaining heirs to perpetuate the

7. See especially Herbert Spencer's chapter, 'The Family,' in Vol. I, *Principles of Sociology*, para. 315.

cult, the children were regarded as belonging to the family rather than to the father and mother. Hence, in case of divorcing the son's wife, or the adopted son-in-law — or of disinheriting the married son — the children would be retained by the family. For the natural right of the young parents was considered subordinate to the religious rights of the house. In opposition to those rights, no other rights could be tolerated. Practically, of course, according to more or less fortunate circumstances, the individual might enjoy freedom under the paternal roof; but theoretically and legally there was no freedom in the old Japanese family for any member of it — not excepting even its acknowledged chief, whose responsibilities were great. Every person, from the youngest child up to the grandfather, was subject to somebody else; and every act of domestic life was regulated by traditional custom.

Like the Greek or Roman father, the patriarch of the Japanese family appears to have had in early times powers of life and death over all the members of the household. In the ruder ages the father might either kill or sell his children; and afterwards, among the ruling classes his powers remained almost unlimited until modern times. Allowing for certain local exceptions, explicable by tradition, or class exceptions, explicable by conditions of servitude, it may be said that originally the Japanese paterfamilias was at once ruler, priest, and magistrate within the family. He could compel his children to marry or forbid them to marry; he could disinherit or repudiate them; he could ordain the profession or calling which they were to follow; and his power extended to all members of the family, and to the household dependents. At different epochs limits were placed to the exercise of this power in the case of the ordinary people; but in the military class, the *patria potestas* was almost unrestricted. In its extreme form, the paternal power controlled everything — the right to life and liberty, the right to marry, or to keep the wife or husband already espoused, the right to one's own children, the right to hold property, the right to hold office, the right to choose or follow an occupation. The family was a despotism.

It should not be forgotten, however, that the absolutism prevailing in the patriarchal family has its justification in a religious belief, in the conviction that everything should be sacrificed for the sake of the cult, and every member of the family should be ready to give up even life, if necessary, to assure the perpetuity of the succession. Remembering this, it becomes easy to understand why, even in communities otherwise advanced in civilization, it should have seemed right that a father could kill or sell his children. The crime of a son might result in the extinction of a cult through the ruin of the family — especially in a militant society like that of Japan, where the entire family was held responsible for the acts of each of its members, so that a capital offence would involve the penalty of death on the whole of the household, including the children. Again, the sale of a daughter, in time of extreme need, might save a house from ruin; and filial piety exacted submission to such sacrifice for the sake of the cult.

As in the Aryan family,[8] property descended by right of primogeniture from father to son, the eldest-born, even in cases where the other property was to be divided among the children, always inheriting the homestead. The homestead property was, however, family property; and it passed to the eldest son as representative, not as individual. Generally speaking, sons could not hold property, without the father's consent, during such time as he retained his headship. As a rule — to which there were various exceptions — a daughter could not inherit; and in the case of an only daughter, for whom a husband had been adopted, the homestead property would pass to the adopted husband, because (until within recent times) a woman could not become the head of a family. This was the case also in the Western Aryan household, in ancestor-worshipping times.

To modern thinking, the position of woman in the old Japanese family appears to have been the reverse of happy. As a child she was subject, not only to the elders, but to all the male adults of the household. Adopted into another household as wife, she merely passed into a similar state of subjection, unalleviated by the affection which parental and fraternal ties assured her in the ancestral home. Her retention in the family of her husband did not depend upon his affection, but upon the will of the majority, and especially of

8. The laws of succession in Old Japan differed considerably according to class, place, and era; the entire subject has not yet been fully treated; and only a few safe general statements can be ventured at the present time.

the elders. Divorced, she could not claim her children: they belonged to the family of the husband. In any event her duties as wife were more trying than those of a hired servant. Only in old age could she hope to exercise some authority; but even in old age she was under tutelage – throughout her entire life she was in tutelage. 'A woman can have no house of her own in the Three Universes,' declared an old Japanese proverb. Neither could she have a cult of her own: there was no special cult for the women of a family – no ancestral rite distinct from that of the husband. And the higher the rank of the family into which she entered by marriage, the more difficult would be her position. For a woman of the aristocratic class no freedom existed: she could not even pass beyond her own gate except in a palanquin (kago) or under escort; and her existence as a wife was likely to be embittered by the presence of concubines in the house.

Such was the patriarchal family in old times; yet it is probable that conditions were really better than the laws and the customs would suggest. The race is a joyous and kindly one; and it discovered, long centuries ago, many ways of smoothing the difficulties of life, and of modifying the harsher exactions of law and custom. The great powers of the family-head were probably but seldom exercised in cruel directions. He might have legal rights of the most formidable character; but these were required by reason of his responsibilities, and were not likely to be used against communal judgment. It must be remembered that the individual was not legally considered in former times: the family only was recognized; and the head of it legally existed only as representative. If he erred, the whole family was liable to suffer the penalty of his error. Furthermore, every extreme exercise of his authority involved proportionate responsibilities. He could divorce his wife, or compel his son to divorce the adopted daughter-in-law; but in either case he would have to account for this action to the family of the divorced; and the divorce-right, especially in the samurai class, was greatly restrained by the fear of family resentment, the unjust dismissal of a wife being counted as an insult to her kindred. He might disinherit an only son; but in that event he would be obliged to adopt a kinsman. He might kill or sell either son or daughter; but unless he belonged to some abject class, he would have to justify his action to the community.[9] He might be reckless in his management of the family property; but in that case an appeal to communal authority was possible, and the appeal might result in his deposition. So far as we are able to judge from the remains of old Japanese law which have been studied, it would seem to have been the general rule that the family-head could not sell or alienate the estate. Though the family-rule was despotic, it was the rule of a body rather than of a chief; the family-head really exercising authority in the name of the rest ... In this sense, the family still remains a despotism; but the powers of its legal head are now checked, from within as well as from without, by later custom. The acts of adoption, disinheritance, marriage, or divorce are decided usually by general consent; and the decision of the household and kindred is required in the taking of any important step to the disadvantage of the individual.

Of course the old family-organization had certain advantages which largely compensated the individual for his state of subjection. It was a society of mutual help; and it was not less powerful to give aid than to enforce obedience. Every member could do something to assist another member in case of need: each had a right to the protection of all. This remains true of the family today. In a well-conducted household, where every act is performed according to the old forms of courtesy and kindness, where no harsh word is ever spoken, where the young look up to the aged with affectionate respect, where those whom years have incapacitated for more active duty, take upon themselves the care of the children, and render priceless service in teaching and training, an ideal condition has been realized. The daily life of such a home – in which the endeavour of each is to make existence as pleasant as possible for all, in which the bond of union is really love and gratitude – represents religion in the best and purest sense; and the place is holy ...

It remains to speak of the dependants in the ancient family. Though the fact has not yet been fully established, it is probable that the

9. Samurai fathers might kill a daughter convicted of unchastity, or kill a son guilty of any action calculated to disgrace the family name. But they would not sell a child. The sale of daughters was practised only by the abject classes, or by families of other castes reduced to desperate extremities. A girl might, however, sell herself for the sake of her family.

first domestics were slaves or serfs; and the condition of servants in later times — especially of those in families of the ruling classes — was much like that of slaves in the early Greek and Roman families. Though necessarily treated as inferiors, they were regarded as members of the household: they were trusted familiars, permitted to share in the pleasures of the family, and to be present at most of its reunions. They could legally be dealt with harshly; but there is little doubt that, as a rule, they were treated kindly, absolute loyalty being expected from them. The best indication of their status in past times is furnished by yet surviving customs. Though the power of the family over the servant no longer exists in law or in fact, the pleasant features of the old relation continue; and they are of no little interest. The family takes a sincere interest in the welfare of its domestics, almost such interest as would be shown in the case of poorer kindred. Formerly, the family furnishing servants to a household of higher rank stood to the latter in the relation of vassal to liege-lord; and between the two there existed a real bond of loyalty and kindliness. The occupation of servant was then hereditary; children were trained for the duty from an early age. After the manservant or maidservant had arrived at a certain age, permission to marry was accorded; and the relation of service then ceased, but not the bond of loyalty. The children of the married servants would be sent, when old enough, to work in the house of the master, and would leave it only when the time also came for them to marry. Relations of this kind still exist between certain aristocratic families and former vassal-families, and conserve some charming traditions and customs of hereditary service, unchanged for hundreds of years.

In feudal times, of course, the bond between master and servant was of the most serious kind; the latter being expected, in case of need, to sacrifice life and all else for the sake of the master or of the master's household. This also was the loyalty demanded of the Greek and Roman domestic, before there had yet come into existence that inhuman form of servitude which reduced the toiler to the condition of a beast of burden; and the relation was partly a religious one. There does not seem to have been in ancient Japan any custom corresponding to that, described by M. de Coulanges, of adopting the Greek or Roman servant into the household cult. But as the Japanese vassal-families furnishing domestics were, as vassals, necessarily attached to the clan-cult of their lord, the relation of the servant to the family was to some extent a religious bond.

The reader will be able to understand, from the facts of this chapter, to what extent the individual was sacrificed to the family, as a religious body. From servant to master — up through all degrees of the household hierarchy — the law of duty was the same: obedience absolute to custom and tradition. The ancestral cult permitted no individual freedom: nobody could live according to his or her pleasure; everyone had to live according to rule. The individual did not even have a legal existence; the family was the unit of society. Even its patriarch existed in law as representative only, responsible both to the living and the dead. His public responsibility, however, was not determined merely by civil law. It was determined by another religious bond, that of the ancestral cult of the clan or tribe; and this public form of ancestor-worship was even more exacting than the religion of the home.

PART THREE

Relations

作品と人

A Conservative

作
品
と
人

Amazakaru
Hi no iru kuni ni
Kite wa aredo,
Yamato-nishiki no
Iro wa kawaraji.

I

He was born in a city of the interior, the seat of a daimyō of three hundred thousand koku, where no foreigner had ever been. The yashiki of his father, a samurai of high rank, stood within the outer fortifications surrounding the prince's castle. It was a spacious yashiki; and behind it and around it were landscape gardens, one of which contained a small shrine of the god of armies. Forty years ago there were many such homes. To artist eyes the few still remaining seem like fairy palaces, and their gardens like dreams of the Buddhist paradise.

But sons of samurai were severely disciplined in those days; and the one of whom I write had little time for dreaming. The period of caresses was made painfully brief for him. Even before he was invested with his first hakama, or trousers – a great ceremony in that epoch – he was weaned as far as possible from tender influence, and taught to check the natural impulses of childish affection. Little comrades would ask him mockingly, 'Do you still need milk?' if they saw him walking out with his mother, although he might love her in the house as demonstratively as he pleased, during the hours he could pass by her side. These were not many. All inactive pleasures were severely restricted by his discipline; and even comforts, except during illness, were not allowed him. Almost from the time he could speak he was enjoined to consider duty the guiding motive of life, self-control the first requisite of conduct, pain and death matters of no consequence in the selfish sense.

There was a grimmer side to this Spartan discipline, designed to cultivate a cold sternness never to be relaxed during youth, except in the screened intimacy of the home. The boys were inured to sights of blood. They were taken to witness executions; they were expected to display no emotions and they were obliged, on their return home, to quell any secret feeling of horror by eating plentifully of rice tinted blood-color by an admixture of salted plum juice. Even more difficult things might be demanded of a very young boy – to go alone at midnight to the execution-ground, for example, and bring back a head in proof of courage. For the fear of the dead was held not less contemptible in a samurai than the fear of man. The samurai child was pledged to fear nothing. In all such tests, the demeanor exacted was perfect impassiveness; any swaggering would have been judged quite as harshly as any sign of cowardice.

As a boy grew up, he was obliged to find his pleasures chiefly in those bodily exercises which were the samurai's early and constant preparations for war – archery and riding, wrestling and fencing. Playmates were found for him; but these were older youths, sons of retainers, chosen for ability to assist him in the practice of martial exercises. It was their duty also to teach him how to swim, to handle a boat, to develop his young muscles. Between such physical training and the study of the Chinese classics the greater part of each day was divided for him. His diet, though ample, was never dainty; his clothing, except in time of great ceremony, was light and coarse; and he was not allowed the use of fire merely to warm himself. While studying of winter mornings, if his hands became too cold to use the writing brush, he would be ordered to plunge them into icy water to restore the circulation; and if his feet were numbed by frost, he would be told to run about in the snow to make them warm. Still more rigid was his training in the special etiquette of the military class; and he was early made to know that the little sword in his girdle was neither an ornament nor a plaything. He was shown how to use it, how to take his own life at a moment's notice, without shrinking, whenever the code of his class might so order.[1]

1. 'Is that really the head of your father?' a prince once asked of a samurai boy only seven years old. The child at once realized the situation. The freshly severed

Also in the matter of religion, the training of a samurai boy was peculiar. He was educated to revere the ancient gods and the spirits of his ancestors; he was well schooled in the Chinese ethics; and he was taught something of Buddhist philosophy and faith. But he was likewise taught that hope of heaven and fear of hell were for the ignorant only; and that the superior man should be influenced in his conduct by nothing more selfish than the love of right for its own sake, and the recognition of duty as a universal law.

Gradually, as the period of boyhood ripened into youth, his conduct was less subjected to supervision. He was left more and more free to act upon his own judgment, but with full knowledge that a mistake would not be forgotten; that a serious offense would never be fully condoned; and that a well-merited reprimand was more to be dreaded than death. On the other hand, there were few moral dangers against which to guard him. Professional vice was then strictly banished from many of the provincial castle-towns; and even so much of the non-moral side of life as might have been reflected in popular romance and drama, a young samurai could know little about. He was taught to despise that common literature appealing either to the softer emotions or the passions, as essentially unmanly reading; and the public theater was forbidden to his class.[2] Thus, in that innocent provincial life of Old Japan, a young samurai might grow up exceptionally pure-minded and simple-hearted.

So grew up the young samurai concerning whom these things are written — fearless, courteous, self-denying, despising pleasure, and ready at an instant's notice to give his life for love, loyalty, or honor.

---

head set before him was not his father's: the daimyō had been deceived, but further deception was necessary. So the lad, after having saluted the head with every sign of reverential grief, suddenly cut out his own bowels. All the prince's doubts vanished before that bloody proof of filial piety; the outlawed father was able to make good his escape; and the memory of the child is still honored in Japanese drama and poetry.

2. Samurai women, in some provinces at least, could go to the public theater. The men could not, without committing a breach of good manners. But in samurai homes, or within the grounds of the yashiki, some private performances of a particular character were given. Strolling players were the performers. I know several charming old shizoku who have never been to a public theater in their lives, and refuse all invitations to witness a performance. They still obey the rules of their samurai education.

But though already a warrior in frame and spirit, he was in years scarcely more than a boy when the country was first startled by the coming of the Black Ships.

II

The policy of Iyemitsu, forbidding any Japanese to leave the country under pain of death, had left the nation for two hundred years ignorant of the outer world. About the colossal forces gathering beyond seas nothing was known. The long existence of the Dutch settlement at Nagasaki had in no wise enlightened Japan as to her true position – an Oriental feudalism of the sixteenth century menaced by a Western world three centuries older. Accounts of the real wonders of that world would have sounded to Japanese ears like stories invented to please children, or have been classed with ancient tales of the fabled palaces of Hōrai. The advent of the American fleet, 'the Black Ships,' as they were then called, first awakened the government to some knowledge of its own weakness, and of danger from afar.

National excitement at the news of the second coming of the Black Ships was followed by consternation at the discovery that the Shogunate confessed its inability to cope with the foreign powers. This could mean only a peril greater than that of the Tartar invasion in the days of Hōjo Tokimuné, when the people had prayed to the gods for help, and the Emperor himself, at Isé, had besought the spirits of his fathers. Those prayers had been answered by sudden darkness, a sea of thunder, and the coming of that mighty wind still called Kami-kazé, 'the Wind of the Gods,' by which the fleets of Kublai Khan were given to the abyss. Why should not prayers now also be made? They were, in countless homes and at thousands of shrines. But the Superior Ones gave this time no answer; the Kami-kazé did not come. And the samurai boy, praying vainly before the little shrine of Hachiman in his father's garden, wondered if the gods had lost their power, or if the people of the Black Ships were under the protection of stronger gods.

III

It soon became evident that the foreign 'barbarians' were not to be driven away. Hundreds had come, from the East as well as from the West; and all possible measures for their protection had been taken; and they had built queer cities of their own upon Japanese soil. The government had even commanded that Western knowledge was to be taught in all schools; that the study of English was to be made an important branch of public education; and that public education itself was to be remodeled upon Occidental lines. The government had also declared that the future of the country would depend upon the study and mastery of the languages and the science of the foreigners. During the interval, then, between such study and its successful results, Japan would practically remain under alien domination. The fact was not, indeed, publicly stated in so many words; but the signification of the policy was unmistakable. After the first violent emotions provoked by knowledge of the situation, after the great dismay of the people, and the suppressed fury of the samurai, there arose an intense curiosity regarding the appearance and character of those insolent strangers who had been able to obtain what they wanted by mere display of superior force. This general curiosity was partly satisfied by an immense production and distribution of cheap colored prints, picturing the manner and customs of the barbarians, and the extraordinary streets of their settlements. Caricatures only those flaring wood-prints could have seemed to foreign eyes. But caricature was not the conscious object of the artist. He tried to portray foreigners as he really saw them; and he saw them as green-eyed monsters, with red hair like Shōjo,[3] and with noses like Tengu,[4] wearing clothes of absurd forms and colors; and dwelling in structures like storehouses or prisons. Sold by hundreds of thousands throughout the interior, these prints must have created many uncanny ideas. Yet as attempts to depict the unfamiliar they were only innocent. One should be able to study those old drawings in order to comprehend

3. Apish mythological beings with red hair, delighting in drunkenness.

4. Mythological beings of several kinds, supposed to live in the mountains. Some have long noses.

just how we appeared to the Japanese of that era; how ugly, how grotesque, how ridiculous.

The young samurai of the town soon had the experience of seeing a real Western foreigner, a teacher hired for them by the prince. He was an Englishman. He came under the protection of an armed escort; and orders were given to treat him as a person of distinction. He did not seem quite so ugly as the foreigners in the Japanese prints: his hair was red, indeed, and his eyes of a strange color; but his face was not disagreeable. He at once became, and long remained, the subject of tireless observation. How closely his every act was watched could never be guessed by any one ignorant of the queer superstitions of the pre-Meiji era concerning ourselves. Although recognized as intelligent and formidable creatures, Occidentals were not generally regarded as quite human; they were thought of as more closely allied to animals than to mankind. They had hairy bodies of queer shape; their teeth were different from those of men; their internal organs were also peculiar; and their moral ideas those of goblins. The timidity which foreigners then inspired, not, indeed, to the samurai, but to the common people, was not a physical, but a superstitious fear. Even the Japanese peasant has never been a coward. But to know his feelings in that time toward foreigners, one must also know something of the ancient beliefs, common to both Japan and China, about animals gifted with supernatural powers, and capable of assuming human form; about the existence of races half human and half superhuman; and about the mythical beings of the old picture-books — goblins long-legged and long-armed and bearded (ashinaga and tenaga), whether depicted by the illustrators of weird stories or comically treated by the brush of Hokusai. Really the aspect of the new strangers seemed to afford confirmation of the fables related by a certain Chinese Herodotus; and the clothing they wore might seem to have been devised for the purpose of hiding what would prove them not human. So the new English teacher, blissfully ignorant of the fact, was studied surreptitiously, just as one might study a curious animal! Nevertheless, from his students he experienced only courtesy: they treated him by that Chinese code which ordains that 'even the shadow of a teacher must not be trodden on.' In any event it would have mattered little to samurai students whether their teacher were perfectly human or not, so long as he could teach. The hero Yoshitsuné had been taught the art of the sword by a Tengu. Beings not human had proved themselves scholars and poets.[5] But behind the never-lifted mask of delicate courtesy, the stranger's habits were minutely noted; and the ultimate judgment, based upon the comparison of such observation, was not altogether flattering. The teacher himself could never have imagined the comments made upon him by his two-sworded pupils; nor would it have increased his peace of mind, while overlooking compositions in the class-room, to have understood their conversation:

'See the color of his flesh, how soft it is! To take off his head with a single blow would be very easy.'

Once he was induced to try their mode of wrestling, just for fun, he supposed. But they really wanted to take his physical measure. He was not very highly estimated as an athlete.

'Strong arms he certainly has,' one said. 'But he does not know how to use his body while using his arms; and his loins are very weak. To break his back would not be difficult.'

'I think,' said another, 'that it would be easy to fight with foreigners.'

'With swords it would be very easy,' responded a third; 'but they are more skillful than we in the use of guns and cannon.'

'We can learn all that,' said the first speaker. 'When we have learned Western military matters, we need not care for Western soldiers.'

'Foreigners,' observed another, 'are not hardy like we are. They soon tire, and they fear cold. All winter our teacher must have a great fire in his room. To stay there five minutes gives me the headache.'

*

5. There is a legend that when Toryōko, a great poet, who was the teacher of Sugiwara-no-Michizané (now deified as Tenjin), was once passing the Gate called Ra-jō-mon, of the Emperor's palace at Kyōto, he recited aloud this single verse which he had just composed:

Clear is the weather and fair; and the wind waves the
hair of young willows.

Immediately a deep mocking voice from the gateway continued the poem, thus:

Melted and vanished the ice; the waves comb the locks of old mosses.

Toryōko looked, but there was no one to be seen. Reaching home, he told his pupil about the matter, and repeated the two compositions. Sugiwara-no-Michizané praised the second one, saying: 'Truly the words of the first are the words of a poet; but the words of the second are the words of a Demon!'

But for all that, the lads were kind to their teacher, and made him love them.

IV

Changes came as great earthquakes come, without warning: the transformation of daimiates into prefectures, the suppression of the military class, the reconstruction of the whole social system. These events filled the youth with sadness, although he felt no difficulty in transferring his allegiance from prince to emperor, and although the wealth of his family remained unimpaired by the shock. All this reconstruction told him of the greatness of the national danger, and announced the certain disappearance of the old high ideals, and of nearly all things loved. But he knew regret was vain. By self-transformation alone could the nation hope to save its independence; and the obvious duty of the patriot was to recognize necessity, and fitly prepare himself to play the man in the drama of the future.

In the samurai school he had learned much English, and he knew himself able to converse with Englishmen. He cut his long hair, put away his swords, and went to Yokohama that he might continue his study of the language under more favorable conditions. At Yokohama everything at first seemed to him both unfamiliar and repellent. Even the Japanese of the port had been changed by foreign contact: they were rude and rough; they acted and spoke as common people would not have dared to do in his native town. The foreigners themselves impressed him still more disagreeably: it was the period when new settlers could assume the tone of conquerors to the conquered, and when the life of the 'open ports' was much less decorous than now. The new buildings of brick or stuccoed timber revived for him unpleasant memories of the Japanese colored pictures of foreign manners and customs; and he could not quickly banish the fancies of his boyhood concerning Occidentals. Reason, based on larger knowledge and experience, fully assured him what they really were; but to his emotional life the intimate sense of their kindred humanity still failed to come. Race-feeling is older than intellectual development; and the superstitions attaching to race-feeling are not easy to get rid of. His soldier-spirit, too, was stirred at times by ugly things heard or seen — incidents that filled him with the hot impulse of his fathers to avenge a cowardice or to redress a wrong. But he learned to conquer his repulsions as obstacles to knowledge: it was the patriot's duty to study calmly the nature of his country's foes. He trained himself at last to observe the new life about him without prejudice – its merits not less than its defects; its strength not less than its weakness. He found kindness; he found devotion to ideals – ideals not his own, but which he knew how to respect because they exacted, like the religion of his ancestors, abnegation of many things.

Through such appreciation he learned to like and to trust an aged missionary entirely absorbed in the work of educating and proselytizing. The old man was especially anxious to convert this young samurai, in whom aptitudes of no common order were discernible; and he spared no pains to win the boy's confidence. He aided him in many ways, taught him something of French and German, of Greek and Latin, and placed entirely at his disposal a private library of considerable extent. The use of a foreign library, including works of history, philosophy, travel, and fiction, was not a privilege then easy for Japanese students to obtain. It was gratefully appreciated; and the owner of the library found no difficulty at a later day in persuading his favored and favorite pupil to read a part of the New Testament. The youth expressed surprise at finding among the doctrines of the 'Evil Sect' ethical precepts like those of Confucius. To the old missionary he said: 'This teaching is not new to us; but it is certainly very good. I shall study the book and think about it.'

V

The study and the thinking were to lead the young man much further than he had thought possible. After the recognition of Christianity as a great religion came recognitions of another order, and various imaginings about the civilization of the races professing Christianity. It then seemed to many reflective Japanese, possibly even to the keen minds directing the national policy, that Japan was doomed to pass altogether under alien rule. There was hope, indeed; and while even the ghost of hope remained, the duty for all was plain. But the power that could be used against the Empire was irresistible. And studying the enormity of that power, the young Oriental could not but ask himself, with a wonder approaching awe, whence and how it had been gained. Could it, as his aged teacher averred, have some occult relation to a higher religion? Certainly the ancient Chinese philosophy, which declared the prosperity of peoples proportionate to their observance of celestial law and their obedience to the teaching of sages, countenanced such a theory. And if the superior force of Western civilization really indicated the superior character of Western ethics, was it not the plain duty of every patriot to follow that higher faith, and to strive for the conversion of the whole nation? A youth of that era, educated in Chinese wisdom, and necessarily ignorant of the history of social evolution in the West, could never have imagined that the very highest forms of material progress were developed chiefly though a merciless competition out of all harmony with Christian idealism, and at variance with every great system of ethics. Even today in the West unthinkable millions imagine some divine connection between military power and Christian belief; and utterances are made in our pulpits implying divine justification for political robberies, and heavenly inspiration for the invention of high explosives. There still survives among us the superstition that races professing Christianity are divinely destined to rob or exterminate races holding other beliefs. Some men occasionally express their conviction that we still worship Thor and Odin – the only difference being that Odin has become a mathematician, and that the Hammer Mjölnir is now worked by steam. But such persons are declared by the missionaries to be atheists and men of shameless lives.

Be this as it may, a time came when the young samurai resolved to proclaim himself a Christian, despite the opposition of his kindred. It was a bold step; but his early training had given him firmness; and he was not to be moved from his decision even by the sorrow of his parents. His rejection of the ancestral faith would signify more than temporary pain for him: it would mean disinheritance, the contempt of old comrades, loss of rank, and all the consequences of bitter poverty. But his samurai training had taught him to despise self. He saw what he believed to be his duty as a patriot and as a truth-seeker; and he followed it without fear or regret.

VII

Those who hope to substitute their own Western creed in the room of one which they wreck by the aid of knowledge borrowed from modern science do not imagine that the arguments used against the ancient faith can be used with equal force against the new. Unable himself to reach the higher levels of modern thought, the average missionary cannot foresee the result of his small teaching of science upon an Oriental mind naturally more powerful than his own. He is therefore astonished and shocked to discover that the more intelligent his pupil, the briefer the term of that pupil's Christianity. To destroy personal faith in a fine mind previously satisfied with Buddhist cosmogony, because innocent of science, is not extremely difficult. But to substitute, in the same mind, Western religious emotions for Oriental, Presbyterian or Baptist dogmatisms for Chinese and Buddhist ethics, is not possible. The psychological difficulties in the way are never recognized by our modern evangelists. In former ages, when the faith of the Jesuits and the friars was not less superstitious than the faith they strove to supplant, the same deep-lying obstacles existed; and the Spanish priest, even while accomplishing marvels by his immense sincerity and fiery zeal, must have felt that to fully realize his dream he would need the sword of the Spanish soldier. Today the conditions are far less favorable for any work of conversion than they ever were in the sixteenth century. Education has been secularized and remodeled upon a scientific basis; our religions are being changed into mere social recognitions of ethical necessities; the functions of our clergy are being gradually transformed into those of a moral police; and the multitude of our church-spires proves no increase of our faith, but only the larger growth of our respect for conventions. Never can the conventions of the Occident become those of the Far East; and never will foreign missionaries be suffered in Japan to take the role of a police of morals. Already the most liberal of our churches, those of broadest culture, begin to recognize the vanity of missions. But it is not necessary to drop old dogmatisms in order to perceive the truth: thorough education should be enough to reveal it; and the most educated of nations, Germany, sends no missionaries to work in the interior of Japan. A result of missionary efforts, much more significant than the indispensable yearly report of new conversions, has been the reorganization of the native religions, and a recent government mandate insisting upon the higher education of the native priesthoods. Indeed, long before this mandate the wealthier sects had established Buddhist schools on the Western plan; and the Shinshū could already boast of its scholars, educated in Paris or at Oxford — men whose names are known to Sanskritists the world over. Certainly Japan will need higher forms of faith than her medieval ones; but these must be themselves evolved from the ancient forms — from within, never from without. A Buddhism strongly fortified by Western science will meet the future needs of the race.

The young convert at Yokohama proved a noteworthy example of missionary failures. Within a few years after having sacrificed a fortune in order to become a Christian — or, rather. the member of a foreign religious sect — he publicly renounced the creed accepted at such a cost. He had studied and comprehended the great minds of the age better than his religious teachers, who could no longer respond to the questions he propounded, except by the assurance that books of which they had recommended him to study parts were dangerous to faith as wholes. But as they could not prove the fallacies alleged to exist in such books, their warnings availed nothing. He had been converted to dogmatism by imperfect reasoning; by larger and deeper reasoning he found his way beyond dogmatism. He passed from the church after an open declaration that its tenets were not based upon true reason or fact; and that he felt himself obliged to accept the opinions of men whom his teachers had called the enemies of Christianity. There was great scandal at his 'relapse.'

The real 'relapse' was yet far away. Unlike many with a similar experience, he knew that the religious question had only receded for him, and that all he had learned was scarcely more than the alphabet of what remained to learn. He had not lost belief in the relative value of creeds, in the worth of religion as a conserving and restraining force. A distorted perception of one truth — the truth of a relation subsisting between civilizations and their religions — had first deluded him into the path that led to his conversion. Chinese philosophy had taught him that which modern sociology recognizes in the law that societies without priesthoods have never developed; and Buddhism had taught him that even delusions — the parables, forms, and symbols presented as actualities to humble minds – have their value and their justification in aiding the development of human goodness. From such a point of view, Christianity had lost none of its interest for him; and though doubting what his teacher had told him about the superior morality of Christian nations, not at all illustrated in the life of the open ports, he desired to see for himself the influence of religion upon morals in the Occident; to visit European countries and to study the causes of their development and the reason of their power.

This he set out to do sooner than he had purposed. That intellectual quickening which had made him a doubter in religious matters had made him also a free-thinker in politics. He brought down upon himself the wrath of the government by public expressions of opinion antagonistic to the policy of the hour; and, like others equally imprudent under the stimulus of new ideas, he was obliged to leave the country. Thus began for him a series of wanderings destined to carry him round the world. Korea first afforded him a refuge; then China, where he lived as a teacher; and at last he found himself on board a steamer bound for Marseilles. He had little money; but he did not ask himself how he was going to live in Europe. Young, tall, athletic, frugal and inured to hardship, he felt sure of himself; and he had letters to men abroad who could smooth his way.

But long years were to pass before he could see his native land again.

VIII

During those years he saw Western civilization as few Japanese ever saw it; for he wandered through Europe and America, living in many cities, and toiling in many capacities – sometimes with his brain, oftener with his hands – and so was able to study the highest and the lowest, the best and the worst of the life about him. But he saw with the eyes of the Far East; and the ways of his judgments were not as our ways. For even as the Occident regards the Far East, so does the Far East regard the Occident, only with this difference: that what each most esteems in itself is least likely to be esteemed by the other. And both are partly right and partly wrong; and there never has been, and never can be, perfect mutual comprehension.

303

Larger than all anticipation the West appeared to him, a world of giants; and that which depresses even the boldest Occidental who finds himself, without means or friends, alone in a great city must often have depressed the Oriental exile: that vague uneasiness aroused by the sense of being invisible to hurrying millions; by the ceaseless roar of traffic drowning voices; by monstrosities of architecture without a soul; by the dynamic display of wealth forcing mind and hand, as mere cheap machinery, to the uttermost limits of the possible. Perhaps he saw such cities as Doré saw London: sullen majesty of arched glooms, and granite deeps opening into granite deeps beyond range of vision, and mountains of masonry with seas of labor in turmoil at their base, and monumental spaces displaying the grimness of ordered power slow-gathering through centuries. Of beauty there was nothing to make appeal to him between those endless cliffs of stone which walled out the sunrise and the sunset, the sky and the wind. All that which draws us to great cities repelled or oppressed him; even luminous Paris soon filled him with weariness. It was the first foreign city in which he made a long sojourn. French art, as reflecting the aesthetic thought of the most gifted of European races, surprised him much, but charmed him not at all. What surprised him especially were its studies of the nude, in which he recognized only an open confession of the one human weakness which, next to disloyalty or cowardice, his stoical training had taught him to most despise. Modern French literature gave him other reasons for astonishment. He could little comprehend the amazing art of the story-teller; the worth of the workmanship in itself was not visible to him; and if he could have been made to understand it as a European understands, he would have remained none the less convinced that such application of genius to production signified social depravity. And gradually, in the luxurious life of the capital itself, he found proof for the belief suggested to him by the art and the literature of the period. He visited the pleasure resorts, the theaters, the opera; he saw with the eyes of an ascetic and a soldier, and wondered why the Western conception of the worth of life differed so little from the Far-Eastern conception of folly and of effeminacy. He saw fashionable balls, and exposures *de rigueur* intolerable to the Far-Eastern sense of modesty, artistically calculated to suggest what would cause a Japanese woman to die of shame; and he wondered at criticisms he had heard about the natural, modest, healthy half-nudity of Japanese toiling under a summer sun. He saw cathedrals and churches in vast number, and near to them the palaces of vice, and establishments enriched by the stealthy sale of artistic obscenities. He listened to sermons by great preachers; and he heard blasphemies against all faith and love by priest-haters. He saw the circles of wealth, and the circles of poverty, and the abysses underlying both. The 'restraining influence' of religion he did not see. That world had no faith. It was a world of mockery and masquerade and pleasure-seeking selfishness, ruled not by religion, but by police; a world into which it were not good that a man should be born.

England, more sombre, more imposing, more formidable, furnished him with other problems to consider. He studied her wealth, forever growing, and the nightmares of squalor forever multiplying in the shadow of it. He saw the vast ports gorged with the riches of a hundred lands, mostly plunder; and knew the English still like their forefathers, a race of prey; and thought of the fate of her millions if she should find herself for even a single month unable to compel other races to feed them. He saw the harlotry and drunkenness that make night hideous in the world's greatest city; and he marveled at the conventional hypocrisy that pretends not to see, and. at the religion that utters thanks for existing conditions, and at the ignorance that sends missionaries where they are not needed, and at the enormous charities that help disease and vice to propagate their kind. He saw also the declaration of a great Englishman[6] who had traveled in many countries that one tenth of the population of England were professional criminals or paupers. And this in spite of the myriads of churches, and the incomparable multiplication of

6. 'Although we have progressed vastly beyond the savage state in intellectual achievements, we have not advanced equally in morals ... It is not too much to say that the mass of our populations have not at all advanced beyond the savage code of morals, and have in many cases sunk below it. A deficient morality is the great blot of modern civilization ... Our whole social and moral civilization remains in a state of barbarism ... We are the richest country in the world; and yet nearly one twentieth of our population are parish paupers, and one thirtieth known criminals. Add to these the criminals who escape detection, and the poor who live mainly or partly on private charity (which, according to Dr Hawkesley, expends seven millions sterling annually in London alone), and we may be sure that more than ONE-TENTH of our population are actually Paupers and Criminals' – ALFRED RUSSEL WALLACE.

laws! Certainly English civilization showed less than any other the pretended power of that religion which he had been taught to believe the inspiration of progress. English streets told him another story: there were no such sights to be seen in the streets of Buddhist cities. No: this civilization signified a perpetual wicked struggle between the simple and the cunning, the feeble and the strong, force and craft combining to thrust weakness into a yawning and visible hell. Never in Japan had there been even the sick dream of such conditions. Yet the merely material and intellectual results of those conditions he could not but confess to be astonishing; and though he saw evil beyond all he could have imagined possible, he also saw much good, among both poor and rich. The stupendous riddle of it all, the countless contradictions, were above his powers of interpretation.

He liked the English people better than the people of other countries he had visited; and the manners of the English gentry impressed him as not unlike those of the Japanese samurai. Behind their formal coldness he could discern immense capacities of friendship and enduring kindness, kindness he experienced more than once; the depth of emotional power rarely wasted; and the high courage that had won the dominion of half a world. But ere he left England for America, to study a still vaster field of human achievement, mere differences of nationality had ceased to interest him: they were blurred out of visibility in his growing perception of Occidental civilization as one amazing whole, everywhere displaying — whether through imperial, monarchial, or democratic forms — the working of the like merciless necessities with the like astounding results, and everywhere based on ideas totally the reverse of Far-Eastern ideas. Such civilization he could estimate only as one having no single emotion in harmony with it — as one finding nothing to love while dwelling in its midst, and nothing to regret in the hour of leaving it forever. It was as far away from his soul as the life of another planet under another sun. But he could understand its cost in terms of human pain, feel the menace of its weight, and divine the prodigious range of its intellectual power. And he hated it, hated its tremendous and perfectly calculated mechanism; hated its utilitarian stability; hated its conventions, its greed, its blind cruelty, its huge hypocrisy, the foulness of its want and the insolence of its wealth. Morally, it was monstrous; conventionally, it was brutal. Depths of degradation unfathomable it had shown him, but no ideals equal to the ideals of his youth. It was all one great wolfish struggle; and that so much real goodness as he had found in it could exist seemed to him scarcely less than miraculous. The real sublimities of the Occident were intellectual only, far, steep, cold heights of pure knowledge, below whose perpetual snow-line emotional ideals die. Surely the old Japanese civilization of benevolence and duty was incomparably better in its comprehension of happiness, in its moral ambitions, its larger faith, its joyous courage, its simplicity and unselfishness, its sobriety and contentment. Western superiority was *not* ethical. It lay in forces of intellect developed through suffering incalculable, and used for the destruction of the weak by the strong.

And, nevertheless, that Western science whose logic he knew to be irrefutable assured him of the larger and larger expansion of the power of that civilization, as of an irresistible, inevitable, measureless inundation of world-pain. Japan would have to learn the new forms of action, to master the new forms of thought, or to perish utterly. There was no other alternative. And then the doubt of all doubts came to him, the question which all the sages have had to face: *Is the universe moral?* To that question Buddhism had given the deepest answer.

But whether moral or immoral the cosmic process, as measured by infinitesimal human emotion, one conviction remained with him that no logic could impair: the certainty that man should pursue the highest moral ideal with all his power to the unknown end, even though the suns in their courses should fight against him. The necessities of Japan would oblige her to master foreign science, to adopt much from the material civilization of her enemies; but the same necessities could not compel her to cast bodily away her ideas of right and wrong, of duty and of honor. Slowly a purpose shaped itself in his mind — a purpose which was to make him in after years a leader and a teacher: to strive with all his strength for the conservation of all that was best in the ancient life, and to fearlessly oppose further introduction of anything not essential to national self-preservation, or helpful to national self-development. Fail he well might, and without shame; but he could hope at least to save something of worth from the drift of wreckage. The wastefulness of Western life had impressed him more than its greed of pleasure and its capacity for pain: in the clean poverty of his own land he saw strength; in her unselfish thrift, the sole chance of competing with the Occident. Foreign civilization had taught him to understand, as he could never otherwise have understood, the worth and the beauty of his own; and he longed for the hour of permission to return to the country of his birth.

IX

It was through the transparent darkness of a cloudless April morning, a little before sunrise, that he saw again the mountains of his native land — far lofty sharpening sierras, towering violet-black out of the circle of an inky sea. Behind the steamer which was bearing him back from exile the horizon was slowly filling with rosy flame. There were some foreigners already on deck, eager to obtain the first and fairest view of Fuji from the Pacific; for the first sight of Fuji at dawn is not to be forgotten in this life or the next. They watched the long procession of the ranges, and looked over the jagged looming into the deep night, where stars were faintly burning still — and they could not see Fuji. 'Ah!' laughed an officer they questioned, 'you are looking too low! higher up — much higher!' Then they looked up, up, up into the heart of the sky, and saw the mighty summit pinkening like a wondrous phantom lotus-bud in the flush of the coming day: a spectacle that smote them dumb. Swiftly the eternal snow yellowed into gold, then whitened as the sun reached out beams to it over the curve of the world, over the shadowy ranges, over the very stars, it seemed; for the giant base remained viewless. And the night fled utterly; and soft blue light bathed all the hollow heaven; and colors awoke from sleep; and before the gazers there opened the luminous bay of Yokohama, with the sacred peak, its base ever invisible, hanging above all like a snowy ghost in the arch of the infinite day.

Still in the wanderer's ears the words rang, '*Ah! you are looking too low! — higher up — much higher!*' — making vague rhythm with an immense, irresistible emotion swelling at his heart. Then everything dimmed: he saw neither Fuji above, nor the nearing hills below, changing their vapory blue to green; nor the crowding of the ships in the bay; nor anything of the modern Japan; he saw the Old.

The land-wind, delicately scented with odors of spring, rushed to him, touched his blood, and startled from long-closed cells of memory the shades of all that he had once abandoned and striven to forget. He saw the faces of his dead: he knew their voices over the graves of the years. Again he was a very little boy in his father's yashiki, wandering from luminous room to room, playing in sunned spaces where leaf-shadows trembled on the matting, or gazing into the soft green dreamy peace of the landscape garden. Once more he felt the light touch of his mother's hand guiding his little steps to the place of morning worship, before the household shrine, before the tablets of the ancestors; and the lips of the man murmured again, with sudden new-found meaning, the simple prayer of the child.

Kimiko

作品と人

Wasuraruru
Mi naran to omō
Kokoro koso
Wasuré nu yori mo
Omoi nari-keré.[1]

I

The name is on a paper lantern at the entrance of a house in the
Street of the Geisha.

Seen at night the street is one of the queerest in the world. It
is narrow as a gangway; and the dark shining woodwork of the
house-fronts, all tightly closed, each having a tiny sliding door with
paper panes that look just like frosted glass, makes you think of
first-class passenger-cabins. Really the buildings are several stories
high; but you do not observe this at once — especially if there be
no moon — because only the lower stories are illuminated up to
their awnings, above which all is darkness. The illumination is made
by lamps behind the narrow paper-paned doors, and by the paper
lanterns hanging outside, one at every door. You look down the
street between two lines of these lanterns — lines converging far
off into one motionless bar of yellow light. Some of the lanterns
are egg-shaped, some cylindrical; others four-sided or six-sided; and
Japanese characters are beautifully written upon them. The street
is very quiet — silent as a display of cabinet-work in some great
exhibition after closing-time. This is because the inmates are mostly
away, attending banquets and other festivities. Their life is of the
night.

1. 'To wish to be forgotten by the beloved is a soul-task harder far than trying
not to forget' — Poem by Kimiko.

The legend upon the first lantern to the left as you go south is '*Kinoya: uchi O-Kata;*' and that means 'The House of Gold wherein O Kata dwells.' The lantern to the right tells of the House of Nishimura, and of a girl Miyotsuru, which name signifies The Stork Magnificently Existing. Next upon the left comes the House of Kajita; and in that house are Kohana, the Flower-Bud, and Hinako, whose face is pretty as the face of a doll. Opposite is the House of Nagaye, wherein live Kimika and Kimiko ... And this luminous double litany of names is half a mile long.

The inscription on the lantern of the last-named house reveals the relationship between Kimika and Kimiko, and yet something more; for Kimiko is styled Ni-dai-me, an honorary untranslatable title which signifies that she is only Kimiko No. 2. Kimika is the teacher and mistress: she has educated two geisha, both named, or rather renamed by her, Kimiko; and this use of the same name twice is proof positive that the first Kimiko — Ichi-dai-me — must have been celebrated. The professional appellation borne by an unlucky or unsuccessful geisha is never given to her successor.

If you should ever have good and sufficient reason to enter the house, pushing open that lantern-slide of a door which sets a gong-bell ringing to announce visits, you might be able to see Kimika, provided her little troupe be not engaged for the evening. You would find her a very intelligent person, and well worth talking to. She can tell, when she pleases, the most remarkable stories, real flesh-and-blood stories, true stories of human nature. For the Street of the Geisha is full of traditions, tragic, comic, melodramatic; every house has its memories; and Kimika knows them all. Some are very, very terrible; and some would make you laugh; and some would make you think. The story of the first Kimiko belongs to the last class. It is not one of the most extraordinary; but it is one of the least difficult for Western people to understand.

II

There is no more Ichi-dai-me Kimiko: she is only a remembrance. Kimika was quite young when she called that Kimiko her professional sister.

'An exceedingly wonderful girl,' is what Kimika says of Kimiko.

To win any renown in her profession, a geisha must be pretty or very clever; and the famous ones are usually both, having been selected at a very early age by their trainers according to the promise of such qualities. Even the commoner class of singing-girls must have some charm in their best years, if only that *beauté du diable* which inspired the Japanese proverb that even a devil is pretty at eighteen.[2] But Kimiko was much more than pretty. She was according to the Japanese ideal of beauty; and that standard is not reached by one woman in a hundred thousand. Also she was more than clever: she was accomplished. She composed very dainty poems, could arrange flowers exquisitely, perform tea-ceremonies faultlessly, embroider, make silk mosaic: in short, she was genteel. And her first public appearance made a flutter in the fast world of Kyōto. It was evident that she could make almost any conquest she pleased, and that fortune was before her.

But it soon became evident, also, that she had been perfectly trained for her profession. She had been taught how to conduct herself under almost any possible circumstances; for what she could not have known Kimika knew everything about: the power of beauty, and the weakness of passion; the craft of promises and the worth of indifference; and all the folly and evil in the hearts of men. So Kimiko made few mistakes and shed few tears. By and by she proved to be, as Kimika wished, slightly dangerous. So a lamp is to night-fliers: otherwise some of them would put it out. The duty of the lamp is to make pleasant things visible: it has no malice. Kimiko had no malice, and was not too dangerous. Anxious parents discovered that she did not want to enter into respectable families, nor even to lend herself to any serious romances. But she was not particularly merciful to that class of youths who sign documents with their own blood, and ask a dancing-girl to cut off the extreme end of the little finger of her left hand as a pledge of eternal affection. She was mischievous enough with them to cure them of their folly. Some rich folks who offered her lands and houses on condition of owning her, body and soul, found her less merciful. One proved generous enough to purchase her freedom unconditionally, at a price which made Kimika a rich woman; and Kimiko was grateful – but she remained a geisha.

2. 'Oni mo jiuhachi, azami no hana.' There is a similar saying of a dragon: 'ja mo hatachi' ('even a dragon at twenty').

She managed her rebuffs with too much tact to excite hate, and knew how to heal despairs in most cases. There were exceptions, of course. One old man, who thought life not worth living unless he could get Kimiko all to himself, invited her to a banquet one evening, and asked her to drink wine with him. But Kimika, accustomed to read faces, deftly substituted tea (which has precisely the same color) for Kimiko's wine, and so instinctively saved the girl's precious life, for only ten minutes later the soul of the silly host was on its way to the Meido alone, and doubtless greatly disappointed ... After that night Kimika watched over Kimiko as a wild cat guards her kitten.

The kitten became a fashionable mania, a craze, a delirium, one of the great sights and sensations of the period. There is a foreign prince who remembers her name: he sent her a gift of diamonds which she never wore. Other presents in multitude she received from all who could afford the luxury of pleasing her; and to be in her good graces, even for a day, was the ambition of the 'gilded youth.' Nevertheless she allowed no one to imagine himself a special favorite, and refused to make any contracts for perpetual affection. To any protests on the subject she answered that she knew her place. Even respectable women spoke not unkindly of her, because her name never figured in any story of family unhappiness. She really kept her place. Time seemed to make her more charming. Other geisha grew into fame, but no one was even classed with her. Some manufacturers secured the sole right to use her photograph for a label; and that label made a fortune for the firm.

But one day the startling news was abroad that Kimiko had at last shown a very soft heart. She had actually said goodbye to Kimika, and had gone away with somebody able to give her all the pretty dresses she could wish for, somebody eager to give her social position also, and to silence gossip about her naughty past, somebody willing to die for her ten times over, and already half dead for love of her. Kimika said that a fool had tried to kill himself because of Kimiko, and that Kimiko had taken pity on him, and nursed him back to foolishness. Taiko Hideyoshi had said that there were only two things in this world which he feared — a fool and a dark night. Kimika had always been afraid of a fool; and a fool had taken Kimiko away.

And she added, with not unselfish tears, that Kimiko would never come back to her: it was a case of love on both sides for the time of several existences.

Nevertheless, Kimika was only half right. She was very shrewd indeed; but she had never been able to see into certain private chambers in the soul of Kimiko. If she could have seen, she would have screamed for astonishment.

III

Between Kimiko and other geisha there was a difference of gentle blood. Before she took a professional name, her name was Ai, which, written with the proper character, means love. Written with another character the same word-sound signifies grief. The story of Ai was a story of both grief and love.

She had been nicely brought up. As a child she had been sent to a private school kept by an old samurai, where the little girls squatted on cushions before little writing-tables twelve inches high, and where the teachers taught without salary. In these days when teachers get better salaries than civil-service officials, the teaching is not nearly so honest or so pleasant as it used to be. A servant always accompanied the child to and from the school-house, carrying her books, her writing-box, her kneeling cushion, and her little table.

Afterwards she attended an elementary public school. The first 'modern' text-books had just been issued — containing Japanese translations of English, German, and French stories about honor and duty and heroism, excellently chosen, and illustrated with tiny innocent pictures of Western people in costumes never of this world. Those dear pathetic little text-books are now curiosities: they have long been superseded by pretentious compilations much less lovingly and sensibly edited. Ai learned well. Once a year, at examination time, a great official would visit the school, and talk to the children as if they were all his own, and stroke each silky head as he distributed the prizes. He is now a retired statesman, and has doubtless forgotten Ai; and in the schools of today nobody caresses little girls, or gives them prizes.

Then came those reconstructive changes by which families of rank were reduced to obscurity and poverty; and Ai had to leave school.

Many great sorrows followed, till there remained to her only her mother and an infant sister. The mother and Ai could do little but weave; and by weaving alone they could not earn enough to live. House and lands first, then, article by article, all things not necessary to existence – heirlooms, trinkets, costly robes, crested lacquer-ware – passed cheaply to those whom misery makes rich, and whose wealth is called by the people 'Namida no kane,' – 'the Money of Tears.' Help from the living was scanty, for most of the samurai families of kin were in like distress. But when there was nothing left to sell, not even Ai's little school-books, help was sought from the dead.

For it was remembered that the father of Ai's father had been buried with his sword, the gift of a daimyō; and that the mountings of the weapon were of gold. So the grave was opened, and the grand hilt of curious workmanship exchanged for a common one and the ornaments of the lacquered sheath removed. But the good blade was not taken, because the warrior might need it. Ai saw his face as he sat erect in the great red-clay urn which served in lieu of coffin to the samurai of high rank when buried by the ancient rite. His features were still recognizable after all those years of sepulture; and he seemed to nod a grim assent to what had been done as his sword was given back to him.

At last the mother of Ai became too weak and ill to work at the loom; and the gold of the dead had been spent. Ai said: 'Mother, I know there is but one thing now to do. Let me be sold to the dancing-girls.' The mother wept, and made no reply. Ai did not weep, but went out alone.

She remembered that in other days, when banquets were given in her father's house, and dancers served the wine, a free geisha named Kimika had often caressed her. She went straight to the house of Kimika. 'I want you to buy me,' said Ai; 'and I want a great deal of money.' Kimika laughed, and petted her, and made her eat, and heard her story, which was bravely told, without one tear. 'My child,' said Kimika, 'I cannot give you a great deal of money; for I have very little. But this I can do: I can promise to support your mother. That will be better than to give her much money for you, because your mother, my child, has been a great lady, and therefore cannot know how to use money cunningly. Ask your honored mother to sign the bond, promising that you will stay with me till you are twenty-four years old, or until such time as you can pay me back. And what money I can now spare, take home with you as a free gift.'

Thus Ai became a geisha; and Kimika renamed her Kimiko, and kept the pledge to maintain the mother and the child-sister. The mother died before Kimiko became famous; the little sister was put to school. Afterwards those things already told came to pass.

The young man who had wanted to die for love of a dancing-girl was worthy of better things. He was an only son; and his parents, wealthy and titled people, were willing to make any sacrifice for him, even that of accepting a geisha for daughter-in-law. Moreover, they were not altogether displeased with Kimiko, because of her sympathy for their boy.

Before going away, Kimiko attended the wedding of her young sister, Umé, who had just finished school. She was good and pretty. Kimiko had made the match, and used her wicked knowledge of men in making it. She chose a very plain, honest, old-fashioned mer-chant — a man who could not have been bad, even if he tried. Umé did not question the wisdom of her sister's choice, which time proved fortunate.

IV

It was in the period of the fourth moon that Kimiko was carried away to the home prepared for her, a place in which to forget all the unpleasant realities of life, a sort of fairy-palace lost in the charmed repose of great shadowy silent high-walled gardens. Therein she might have felt as one reborn, by reason of good deeds, into the realm of Hōrai. But the spring passed, and the summer came — and Kimiko remained simply Kimiko. Three times she had contrived, for reasons unspoken, to put off the wedding-day.

In the period of the eighth moon, Kimiko ceased to be playful, and told her reasons very gently but very firmly: 'It is time that I should say what I have long delayed saying. For the sake of the mother who gave me life, and for the sake of my little sister, I have lived in hell. All that is past; but the scorch of the fire is upon me, and there is no power that can take it away. It is not for such as I to enter into an honored family, nor to bear you a son, nor to build up your house ... Suffer me to speak; for in the knowing of wrong I am very, very much wiser than you ... Never shall I be your wife to become your shame. I am your companion only, your play-fellow, your guest of an hour – and this not for any gifts. When I shall be no longer with you – nay! certainly that day must come! – you will have clearer sight. I shall still be dear to you, but not in the same way as now – which is foolishness. You will remember these words out of my heart. Some true sweet lady will be chosen for you, to become the mother of your children. I shall see them; but the place of a wife I shall never take, and the joy of a mother I must never know. I am only your folly, my beloved – an illusion, a dream, a shadow flitting across your life. Somewhat more in later time I may become, but a wife to you never – neither in this existence nor in the next. Ask me again – and I go.'

In the period of the tenth moon, and without any reason imaginable, Kimiko disappeared, vanished, utterly ceased to exist.

v

Nobody knew when or how or whither she had gone. Even in the neighborhood of the home she had left, none had seen her pass. At first it seemed that she must soon return. Of all her beautiful and precious things – her robes, her ornaments, her presents: a fortune in themselves – she had taken nothing. But weeks passed without word or sign; and it was feared that something terrible had befallen her. Rivers were dragged, and wells were searched. Inquiries were made by telegraph and by letter. Trusted servants were sent to look for her. Rewards were offered for any news – especially a reward to Kimika, who was really attached to the girl, and would have been only too happy to find her without any reward at all. But the mystery remained a mystery. Application to the authorities would have been useless: the fugitive had done no wrong, broken no law; and the vast machinery of the imperial police-system was not to be set in motion by the passionate whim of a boy. Months grew into years;

but neither Kimika, nor the little sister in Kyōto, nor any one of the thousands who had known and admired the beautiful dancer, ever saw Kimiko again.

But what she had foretold came true; for time dries all tears and quiets all longing; and even in Japan one does not really try to die twice for the same despair. The lover of Kimiko became wiser; and there was found for him a very sweet person for wife, who gave him a son. And other years passed; and there was happiness in the fairy-home where Kimiko had once been.

There came to that home one morning, as if seeking alms, a traveling nun; and the child, hearing her Buddhist cry of '*Ha−i! ha−i!*' ran to the gate. And presently a house-servant, bringing out the customary gift of rice, wondered to see the nun caressing the child, and whispering to him. Then the little one cried to the servant 'Let me give!' − and the nun pleaded from under the veiling shadow of her great straw hat: 'Honorably allow the child to give me.' So the boy put the rice into the mendicant's bowl. Then she thanked him, and asked: 'Now will you say again for me the little word which I prayed you to tell your honored father?' And the child lisped: '*Father, one whom you will never see again in this world says that her heart is glad because she has seen your son.*'

The nun laughed softly, and caressed him again, and passed away swiftly; and the servant wondered more than ever, while the child ran to tell his father the words of the mendicant.

But the father's eyes dimmed as he heard the words, and he wept over his boy. For he, and only he, knew who had been at the gate, and the sacrificial meaning of all that had been hidden.

Now he thinks much, but tells his thought to no one.

He knows that the space between sun and sun is less than the space between himself and the woman who loved him.

He knows it were vain to ask in what remote city, in what fantastic riddle of narrow nameless streets, in what obscure little temple known only to the poorest poor, she waits for the darkness before the Dawn of the immeasurable Light, when the Face of the Teacher will smile upon her, in tones of sweetness deeper than ever came from human lover's lips: '*O my daughter in the Law, thou hast practised the perfect way; thou hast believed and understood the highest truth; therefore come I now to meet and to welcome thee!*'

The Story of Mimi-Nashi-Hōïchi

More than seven hundred years ago, at Dan-no-ura, in the Straits of Shimonoséki, was fought the last battle of the long contest between the Heiké, or Taira clan, and the Genji, or Minamoto clan. There the Heiké perished utterly. with their women and children, and their infant emperor likewise — now remembered as Antoku Tennō. And that sea and shore have been haunted for seven hundred years ... Elsewhere I told you about the strange crabs found there, called Heiké crabs, which have human faces on their backs, and are said to be the spirits of Heiké warriors.[1] But there are many strange things to be seen and heard along that coast. On dark nights thousands of ghostly fires hover about the beach, or flit above the waves — pale lights which the fishermen call Oni-bi, or demon-fires; and, whenever the winds are up, a sound of great shouting comes from that sea, like a clamor of battle.

In former years the Heiké were much more restless than they now are. They would rise about ships passing in the night, and try to sink them; and at all times they would watch for swimmers, to pull them down. It was in order to appease those dead that the Buddhist temple, Amidaji, was built at Akamagaséki.[2] A cemetery also was made close by, near the beach; and within it were set up monuments inscribed with the names of the drowned emperor and of his great vassals; and Buddhist services were regularly performed there, on behalf of the spirits of them. After the temple had been built, and the tombs erected, the Heiké gave less trouble than before; but they continued to do queer things at intervals — proving that they had not found the perfect peace.

*

1. See my *Kottō* for a description of these curious crabs.
2. Or Shimonoséki. The town is also known by the name of Bakkan.

Some centuries ago there lived at Akamagaséki a blind man named Hōïchi, who was famed for his skill in recitation and in playing upon the biwa.[3] From childhood he had been trained to recite and to play; and while yet a lad he had surpassed his teachers. As a professional biwa-hōshi he became famous chiefly by his recitations of the history of the Heiké and the Genji; and it is said that when he sang the song of the battle of Dan-no-ura 'even the goblins [kijin] could not refrain from tears.'

At the outset of his career, Hōïchi was very poor; but he found a good friend to help him. The priest of the Amidaji was fond of poetry and music; and he often invited Hōïchi to the temple to play and recite. Afterwards, being much impressed by the wonderful skill of the lad, the priest proposed that Hōïchi should make the temple his home; and this offer was gratefully accepted. Hōïchi was given a room in the temple-building; and, in return for food and lodging, he was required only to gratify the priest with a musical performance on certain evenings, when otherwise disengaged.

One summer night the priest was called away to perform a Buddhist service at the house of a dead parishioner; and he went there with his acolyte, leaving Hōïchi alone in the temple. It was a hot night; and the blind man sought to cool himself on the veranda before his sleeping-room. The veranda overlooked a small garden in the rear of the Amidaji. There Hōïchi waited for the priest's return, and tried to relieve his solitude by practicing upon his biwa. Midnight passed; and the priest did not appear. But the atmosphere was still too warm for comfort within doors; and Hōïchi remained outside. At last he heard steps approaching from the back gate. Somebody crossed the garden, advanced to the veranda, and halted directly in front of him — but it was not the priest. A deep voice called

3. The biwa, a kind of four-stringed lute, is chiefly used in musical recitative. Formerly the professional minstrels who recited the *Heiké-Monogatari*, and other tragical histories, were called biwa-hōshi, or 'lute-priests.' The origin of this appellation is not clear; but it is possible that it may have been suggested by the fact that 'lute-priests,' as well as blind shampooers, had their heads shaven, like Buddhist priests. The biwa is played with a kind of plectrum, called bachi, usually made of horn.

the blind man's name – abruptly and unceremoniously, in the manner of a samurai summoning an inferior:

'Hoïchi!'

Hōïchi was too much startled, for the moment, to respond; and the voice called again, in a tone of harsh command:

'Hōïchi!'

'*Hai!*' answered the blind man, frightened by the menace in the voice, 'I am blind! – I cannot know who calls!'

'There is nothing to fear,' the stranger exclaimed, speaking more gently. 'I am stopping near this temple, and have been sent to you with a message. My present lord, a person of exceedingly high rank, is now staying in Akamagaséki, with many noble attendants. He wished to view the scene of the battle of Dan-no-ura; and today he visited that place. Having heard of your skill in reciting the story of the battle, he now desires to hear your performance: so you will take your biwa and come with me at once to the house where the august assembly is waiting.'

In those times, the order of a samurai was not to be lightly disobeyed. Hōïchi donned his sandals, took his biwa, and went away with the stranger, who guided him deftly, but obliged him to walk very fast. The hand that guided was iron; and the clank of the warrior's stride proved him fully armed – probably some palace-guard on duty. Hōïchi's first alarm was over: he began to imagine himself in good luck; for, remembering the retainer's assurance about a 'person of exceedingly high rank,' he thought that the lord who wished to hear the recitation could not be less than a daimyō of the first class. Presently the samurai halted; and Hōïchi became aware that they had arrived at a large gateway; and he wondered, for he could not remember any large gate in that part of the town, except the main gate of the Amidaji. 'Kaimon!'[4] the samurai called, and there was a sound of unbarring; and the twain passed on. They traversed a space of garden, and halted again before some entrance; and the retainer cried in a loud voice, 'Within there! I have brought Hōïchi.' Then came sounds of feet hurrying, and screens sliding, and rain-doors opening, and voices of women in converse. By the language

4. A respectful term, signifying the opening of a gate. It was used by samurai when calling to the guards on duty at a lord's gate for admission.

of the women Hōïchi knew them to be domestics in some noble household; but he could not imagine to what place he had been conducted. Little time was allowed him for conjecture. After he had been helped to mount several stone steps, upon the last of which he was told to leave his sandals, a woman's hand guided him along interminable reaches of polished planking, and round pillared angles too many to remember, and over widths amazing of matted floor, into the middle of some vast apartment. There he thought that many great people were assembled: the sound of the rustling of silk was like the sound of leaves in a forest. He heard also a great humming of voices, talking in undertones; and the speech was the speech of courts.

Hōïchi was told to put himself at ease, and he found a kneeling-cushion ready for him. After having taken his place upon it, and tuned his instrument, the voice of a woman — whom he divined to be the Rōjo, or matron in charge of the female service, addressed him, saying:

'It is now required that the history of the Heiké be recited, to the accompaniment of the biwa.'

Now the entire recital would have required a time of many nights: therefore Hōïchi ventured a question:

'As the whole of the story is not soon told, what portion is it augustly desired that I now recite?'

The woman's voice made answer:

'Recite the story of the battle at Dan-no-ura, for the pity of it is the most deep.'[5]

Then Hōïchi lifted up his voice, and chanted the chant of the fight on the bitter sea — wonderfully making his biwa to sound like the straining of oars and the rushing of ships, the whirr and the hissing of arrows, the shouting and trampling of men, the crashing of steel upon helmets, the plunging of slain in the flood. And to left and right of him, in the pauses of his playing, he could hear voices murmuring praise: 'How marvelous an artist!' — 'Never in our own province was playing heard like this!' — 'Not in all the empire is there another singer like Hōïchi!' Then fresh courage came to him, and he played and sang yet better than before; and a hush of wonder

5. Or the phrase might be rendered, 'for the pity of that part is the deepest.' The Japanese word for pity in the original text is 'awaré.'

deepened about him. But when at last he came to tell the fate of the fair and helpless – the piteous perishing of the women and children, and the death-leap of Nii-no Ama, with the imperial infant in her arms – then all the listeners uttered together one long, long shuddering cry of anguish; and thereafter they wept and wailed so loudly and so wildly that the blind man was frightened by the violence of the grief that he had made. For much time the sobbing and the wailing continued. But gradually the sounds of lamentation died away; and again, in the great stillness that followed, Hōïchi heard the voice of the woman whom he supposed to be the Rōjo.

She said:

'Although we had been assured that you were a very skillful player upon the biwa, and without an equal in recitative, we did not know that anyone could be so skillful as you have proved yourself tonight. Our lord has been pleased to say that he intends to bestow upon you a fitting reward. But he desires that you shall perform before him once every night for the next six nights – after which time he will probably make his august return-journey. Tomorrow night, therefore, you are to come here at the same hour. The retainer who tonight conducted you will be sent for you ... There is another matter about which I have been ordered to inform you. It is required that you shall speak to no one of your visits here, during the time of our lord's august sojourn at Akamagaséki. As he is traveling incognito,[6] he commands that no mention of these things be made ... You are now free to go back to your temple.'

After Hōïchi had duly expressed his thanks, a woman's hand conducted him to the entrance of the house, where the same retainer who had before guided him, was waiting to take him home. The retainer led him to the veranda at the rear of the temple and there bade him farewell.

It was almost dawn when Hōïchi returned; but his absence from the temple had not been observed, as the priest, coming back at a very late hour, had supposed him asleep. During the day Hōïchi

6. 'Traveling incognito' is at least the meaning of the original phrase – making a disguised august-journey' (shinobi no go-ryokō).

was able to take some rest; and he said nothing about his strange adventure. In the middle of the following night the samurai again came for him, and led him to the august assembly, where he gave another recitation with the same success that had attended his previous performance. But during this second visit his absence from the temple was accidentally discovered; and after his return in the morning he was summoned to the presence of the priest. who said to him, in a tone of kindly reproach:

'We have been very anxious about you, friend Hōïchi. To go out, blind and alone, at so late an hour, is dangerous. Why did you go without telling us? I could have ordered a servant to accompany you. And where have you been?'

Hōïchi answered, evasively:

'Pardon me, kind friend! I had to attend to some private business; and I could not arrange the matter at any other hour.'

The priest was surprised, rather than pained, by Hōïchi's reticence: he felt it to be unnatural, and suspected something wrong. He feared that the blind lad had been bewitched or deluded by some evil spirits. He did not ask any more questions; but he privately instructed the men-servants of the temple to keep watch upon Hōïchi's movements, and to follow him in case that he should again leave the temple after dark.

On the very next night, Hōïchi was seen to leave the temple; and the servants immediately lighted their lanterns, and followed after him. But it was a rainy night, and very dark; and before the temple-folks could get to the roadway, Hōïchi had disappeared. Evidently he had walked very fast, a strange thing, considering his blindness; for the road was in a bad condition. The men hurried through the streets, making inquiries at every house which Hōïchi was accustomed to visit; nobody could give them any news of him. At last, as they were returning to the temple by way of the shore, they were startled by the sound of a biwa, furiously played, in the cemetery of the Amidaji. Except for some ghostly fires — such as usually flitted there on dark nights — all was blackness in that direction. But the men at once hastened to the cemetery; and there, by the help of their lanterns, they discovered Hōïchi, sitting alone in the rain before the memorial tomb of Antoku Tennō, making his biwa resound, and loudly chanting the chant of the battle of Dan-no-rua.

And behind him, and about him, and everywhere above the tombs, the fires of the dead were burning, like candles. Never before had so great a host of Oni-bi appeared in the sight of mortal man ...

'Hōïchi San! – Hōïchi San!' the servants cried, 'you are bewitched! ... Hōïchi San!'

But the blind man did not seem to hear. Strenuously he made his biwa to rattle and ring and clang; more and more wildly he chanted the chant of the battle of Dan-no-rua. They caught hold of him; they shouted into his ear:

'Hōïchi San! – Hōïchi San! – come home with us at once!'

Reprovingly he spoke to them:

'To interrupt me in such a manner, before this august assembly, will not be tolerated.'

Whereat, in spite of the weirdness of the thing, the servants could not help laughing. Sure that he had been bewitched, they now seized him, and pulled him up on his feet, and by main force hurried him back to the temple, where he was immediately relieved of his wet clothes, by order of the priest, and reclad, and made to eat and drink. Then the priest insisted upon a full explanation of his friend's astonishing behavior.

Hōïchi long hesitated to speak. But at last, finding that his conduct had really alarmed and angered the good priest, he decided to abandon his reserve; and he related everything that had happened from the time of the first visit of the samurai.

The priest said:

'Hōïchi, my poor friend, you are now in great danger! How unfortunate that you did not tell me all this before! Your wonderful skill in music has indeed brought you into strange trouble. By this time you must be aware that you have not been visiting any house whatever, but have been passing your nights in the cemetery, among the tombs of the Heiké; and it was before the memorial-tomb of Antoku Tennō that our people tonight found you, sitting in the rain. All that you have been imagining was illusion – except the calling of the dead. By once obeying them, you have put yourself in their power. If you obey them again, after what has already occurred, they will tear you in pieces. But they would have destroyed you, sooner or later, in any event ... Now I shall not be able to remain with you tonight: I am called away to perform another service. But, before I go, it will be necessary to protect your body by writing holy texts upon it.'

Before sundown the priest and his acolyte stripped Hōïchi: then, with their writing-brushes, they traced upon his breast and back, head and face and neck, limbs and hands and feet — even upon the soles of his feet, and upon all parts of his body — the text of the holy sutra called *Hannya-Shin-Kyō*.[7] When this had been done, the priest instructed Hōïchi, saying:

'Tonight, as soon as I go away, you must seat yourself on the veranda, and wait. You will be called. But, whatever may happen, do not answer, and do not move. Say nothing, and sit still — as if meditating. If you stir, or make any noise, you will be torn asunder. Do not get frightened; and do not think of calling for help — because no help could save you. If you do exactly as I tell you, the danger will pass, and you will have nothing more to fear.'

After dark the priest and the acolyte went away; and Hōïchi seated himself on the veranda, according to the instructions given him. He laid his biwa on the planking beside him, and, assuming the attitude of meditation, remained quite still, taking care not to cough, or to breathe audibly. For hours he stayed thus.

Then, from the roadway, he heard the steps coming. They passed the gate, crossed the garden, approached the veranda, stopped — directly in front of him.

---

7. The Smaller Pragña-Pâramitâ-Hridaya-Sutra is thus called in Japanese. Both the smaller and larger sutras called Pragña-Pâramitâ ('Transcendent Wisdom') have been translated by the late Professor Max Müller, and can be found in volume xlix of the *Sacred Books of the East* ('Buddhist Mahâyâna Sutras'). Apropos of the magical use of the text, as described in this story, it is worth remarking that the subject of the sutra is the Doctrine of the Emptiness of Forms — that is to say, of the unreal character of all phenomena or noumena ... 'Form is emptiness; and emptiness is form. Emptiness is not different from form; form is not different from emptiness. What is form — that is emptiness. What is emptiness — that is form ... Perception, name, concept, and knowledge, are also emptiness ... There is no eye, ear, nose, tongue, body, and mind ... But when the envelopment of consciousness has been annihilated, then he [the seeker] becomes free from all fear, and beyond the reach of change, enjoying final Nirvâna.'

'Hōïchi!' the deep voice called. But the blind man held his breath, and sat motionless.

'Hōïchi!' grimly called the voice a second time. Then a third time — savagely:

'Hōïchi!'

Hōïchi remained as still as a stone, and the voice grumbled:

'No answer! — that won't do! ... Must see where the fellow is.'

There was a noise of heavy feet mounting upon the veranda. The feet approached deliberately, halted beside him. Then, for long minutes, during which Hōïchi felt his whole body shake to the beating of his heart, there was dead silence.

At last the gruff voice muttered close to him:

'Here is the biwa; but of the biwa-player I see — only two ears! ... So that explains why he did not answer: he had no mouth to answer with — there is nothing left of him but his ears ... Now to my lord those ears I will take — in proof that the august commands have been obeyed, so far as was possible ...'

At that instant Hōïchi felt his ears gripped by fingers of iron, and torn off! Great as the pain was, he gave no cry. The heavy footfalls receded along the veranda, descended into the garden, passed out to the roadway, ceased. From either side of his head, the blind man felt a thick warm trickling; but he dared not lift his hands ...

Before sunrise the priest came back. He hastened at once to the veranda in the rear, stepped and slipped upon something clammy, and uttered a cry of horror; for he saw, by the light of his lantern, that the clamminess was blood. But he perceived Hōïchi sitting there, in the attitude of meditation — with the blood still oozing from his wounds.

'My poor Hōïchi!' cried the startled priest, 'what is this? ... You have been hurt?'

At the sound of his friend's voice, the blind man felt safe. He burst out sobbing, and tearfully told his adventure of the night.

'Poor, poor Hōïchi!' the priest exclaimed, 'all my fault! — my very grievous fault! ... Everywhere upon your body the holy texts had been written — except upon your ears! I trusted my acolyte to do that part of the work; and it was very, very wrong of me not to have made sure that he had done it! ... Well, the matter cannot now be helped; we can only try to heal your hurts as soon as possible ... Cheer up, friend! – the danger is now well over. You will never again be troubled by those visitors.'

With the aid of a good doctor, Hōïchi soon recovered from his injuries. The story of his strange adventure spread far and wide, and soon made him famous. Many noble persons went to Akamagaséki to hear him recite; and large presents of money were given to him, so that he became a wealthy man ... But from the time of his adventure, he was known only by the appellation of Mimi-nashi-Hōïchi: 'Hōïchi-the-Earless.'

Ubazakura

Three hundred years ago, in the village called Asamimura, in the district called Onsengōri, in the province of Iyō, there lived a good man named Tokubei. This Tokubei was the richest person in the district, and the muraosa, or headman, of the village. In most matters he was fortunate; but he reached the age of forty without knowing the happiness of becoming a father. Therefore he and his wife, in the affliction of their childlessness, addressed many prayers to the divinity Fudō Myō Ō, who had a famous temple called Saihōji, in Asamimura.

At last their prayers were heard: the wife of Tokubei gave birth to a daughter. The child was very pretty; and she received the name of Tsuyu. As the mother's milk was deficient, a milk-nurse, called O-Sodé was hired for the little one.

O-Tsuyu grew up to be a very beautiful girl; but at the age of fifteen she fell sick, and the doctors thought that she was going to die. In that time the nurse O-Sodé, who loved O-Tsuyu with a real mother's love, went to the temple Saihōji, and fervently prayed to Fudō-Sama on behalf of the girl. Every day, for twenty-one days, she went to the temple and prayed; and at the end of that time, O-Tsuyu suddenly and completely recovered.

Then there was great rejoicing in the house of Tokubei; and he gave a feast to all his friends in celebration of the happy event. But on the night of the feast the nurse O-Sodé was suddenly taken ill; and on the following morning, the doctor, who had been summoned to attend her, announced that she was dying.

Then the family, in great sorrow, gathered about her bed, to bid her farewell. But she said to them:

'It is time that I should tell you something which you do not know. My prayer has been heard. I besought Fudō-Sama that I might be permitted to die in the place of O-Tsuyu; and this great favor has been granted me. Therefore you must not grieve about my death ... But I have one request to make. I promised Fudō-Sama that I would have a cherry-tree planted in the garden of Saihōji, for a thank-offering and a commemoration. Now I shall not be able myself to plant the tree there: so I must beg that you will fulfill that vow for me ... Goodbye, dear friends; and remember that I was happy to die for O-Tsuyu's sake.'

After the funeral of O-Sodé, a young cherry-tree – the finest that could be found – was planted in the garden of Saihōji by the parents of O-Tsuyu. The tree grew and flourished; and on the sixteenth day of the second month of the following year – the anniversary of O-Sodé's death – it blossomed in a wonderful way. So it continued to blossom for two hundred and fifty-four years, always upon the sixteenth day of the second month; and its flowers, pink and white, were like the nipples of a woman's breasts, bedewed with milk. And the people called it Ubazakura, the Cherry-tree of the Milk-Nurse.

Yuki-Onna

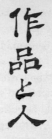

In a village of Musashi Province, there lived two woodcutters: Mosaku and Minokichi. At the time of which I am speaking, Mosaku was an old man; and Minokichi, his apprentice, was a lad of eighteen years. Every day they went together to a forest situated about five miles from their village. On the way to that forest there is a wide river to cross; and there is a ferry-boat. Several times a bridge was built where the ferry is; but the bridge was each time carried away by a flood. No common bridge can resist the current there when the river rises.

Mosaku and Minokichi were on their way home, one very cold evening, when a great snowstorm overtook them. They reached the ferry; and they found that the boatman had gone away, leaving his boat on the other side of the river. It was no day for swimming; and the woodcutters took shelter in the ferryman's hut, thinking themselves lucky to find any shelter at all. There was no brazier in the hut, nor any place in which to make a fire: it was only a two-mat[1] hut, with a single door, but no window. Mosaku and Minokichi fastened the door, and lay down to rest, with their straw raincoats over them. At first they did not feel very cold; and they thought that the storm would soon be over.

The old man almost immediately fell asleep; but the boy, Minokichi, lay awake a long time, listening to the awful wind, and the continual slashing of the snow against the door. The river was roaring; and the hut swayed and creaked like a junk at sea. It was a terrible storm; and the air was every moment becoming colder; and Minokichi shivered under his raincoat. But at last, in spite of the cold, he too fell asleep.

1. That is to say, with a floor-surface of about six feet square.

He was awakened by a showering of snow in his face. The door of the hut had been forced open; and, by the snow-light (yuki-akari), he saw a woman in the room — a woman all in white. She was bending above Mosaku, and blowing her breath upon him; and her breath was like a bright white smoke. Almost in the same moment she turned to Minokichi, and stooped over him. He tried to cry out, but found that he could not utter any sound. The white woman bent down over him, lower and lower, until her face almost touched him; and he saw that she was very beautiful — though her eyes made him afraid. For a little time she continued to look at him; then she smiled, and she whispered: 'I intended to treat you like the other man. But I cannot help feeling some pity for you, because you are so young ... You are a pretty boy, Minokichi; and I will not hurt you now. But, if you ever tell anybody — even your own mother — about what you have seen this night, I shall know it; and then I will kill you ... Remember what I say!'

With these words, she turned from him, and passed through the doorway. Then he found himself able to move; and he sprang up, and looked out. But the woman was nowhere to be seen; and the snow was driving furiously into the hut. Minokichi closed the door, and secured it by fixing several billets of wood against it. He wondered if the wind had blown it open; he thought that he might have been only dreaming, and might have mistaken the gleam of the snowlight in the doorway for the figure of a white woman; but he could not be sure. He called to Mosaku, and was frightened because the old man did not answer. He put out his hand in the dark, and touched Mosaku's face, and found that it was ice! Mosaku was stark and dead ...

By dawn the storm was over; and when the ferryman returned to his station, a little after sunrise, he found Minokichi lying senseless beside the frozen body of Mosaku. Minokichi was promptly cared for, and soon came to himself; but he remained a long time ill from the effects of the cold of that terrible night. He had been greatly frightened also by the old man's death; but he said nothing about the vision of the woman in white. As soon as he got well again, he returned to his calling, going alone every morning to the forest, and coming back at nightfall with his bundles of wood, which his mother helped to sell.

*

One evening, in the winter of the following year, as he was on his way home, he overtook a girl who happened to be traveling by the same road. She was a tall, slim girl, very good-looking; and she answered Minokichi's greeting in a voice as pleasant to the ear as the voice of a song-bird. Then he walked beside her; and they began to talk. The girl said that her name was O-Yuki;[2] that she had lately lost both of her parents; and that she was going to Yedo, where she happened to have some poor relations, who might help her to find a situation as servant. Minokichi soon felt charmed by this strange girl; and the more that he looked at her, the handsomer she appeared to be. He asked her whether she was yet betrothed; and she answered, laughingly, that she was free. Then, in her turn, she asked Minokichi whether he was married, or pledged to marry; and he told her that, although he had only a widowed mother to support, the question of an 'honorable daughter-in-law' had not yet been considered, as he was very young ... After these confidences, they walked on for a long while without speaking; but, as the proverb declares, 'Ki ga aréba, mé mo kuchi hodo ni mono wo iu' ('When the wish is there, the eyes can say as much as the mouth'). By the time they reached the village, they had become very much pleased with each other; and then Minokichi asked O-Yuki to rest awhile at his house. After some shy hesitation, she went there with him; and his mother made her welcome, and prepared a warm meal for her. O-Yuki behaved so nicely that Minokichi's mother took a sudden fancy to her, and persuaded her to delay her journey to Yedo. And the natural end of the matter was that Yuki never went to Yedo at all. She remained in the house, as an 'honorable daughter-in-law.'

O-Yuki proved a very good daughter-in-law. When Minokichi's mother came to die, some five years later, her last words were words of affection and praise for the wife of her son. And O-Yuki bore Minokichi ten children, boys and girls, handsome children all of them, and very fair of skin.

The country-folk thought O-Yuki a wonderful person, by nature different from themselves. Most of the peasant-women age early; but O-Yuki, even after having become the mother of ten children,

---

2. This name, signifying 'Snow,' is not uncommon. On the subject of Japanese female names, see my paper in the volume entitled *Shadowings*.

looked as young and fresh as on the day when she had first come to the village.

One night, after the children had gone to sleep, O-Yuki was sewing by the light of a paper lamp; and Minokichi, watching her, said:

'To see you sewing there, with the light on your face, makes me think of a strange thing that happened when I was a lad of eighteen. I then saw somebody as beautiful and white as you are now – indeed, she was very like you.'

Without lifting her eyes from her work, O-Yuki responded:

'Tell me about her ... Where did you see her?'

Then Minokichi told her about the terrible night in the ferryman's hut, and about the White Woman that had stooped above him, smiling and whispering, and about the silent death of old Mosaku. And he said:

'Asleep or awake, that was the only time that I saw a being as beautiful as you. Of course, she was not a human being; and I was afraid of her – very much afraid – but she was so white! ... Indeed, I have never been sure whether it was a dream that I saw, or the Woman of the Snow.'

O-Yuki flung down her sewing, and arose, and bowed above Minokichi where he sat, and shrieked into his face:

'It was I – I – I! Yuki it was! And I told you then that I would kill you if you ever said one word about it! ... But for those children asleep there, I would kill you this moment! And now you had better take very, very good care of them; for if ever they have reason to complain of you, I will treat you as you deserve!'

Even as she screamed, her voice became thin, like a crying of wind; then she melted into a bright white mist that spired to the roof-beams, and shuddered away through the smoke-hole ... Never again was she seen.

Jikininki

Once, when Musō Kokushi, a priest of the Zen sect, was journeying alone through the province of Mino, he lost his way in a mountain-district where there was nobody to direct him. For a long time he wandered about helplessly; and he was beginning to despair of finding shelter for the night, when he perceived, on the top of a hill lighted by the last rays of the sun, one of those little hermitages, called anjitsu, which are built for solitary priests. It seemed to be in a ruinous condition; but he hastened to it eagerly, and found that it was inhabited by an aged priest, from whom he begged the favor of a night's lodging. This the old man harshly refused; but he directed Musō to a certain hamlet, in the valley adjoining, where lodging and food could be obtained.

Musō found his way to the hamlet, which consisted of less than a dozen farm-cottages; and he was kindly received at the dwelling of the headman. Forty or fifty persons were assembled in the principal apartment, at the moment of Musō's arrival; but he was shown into a small separate room, where he was promptly supplied with food and bedding. Being very tired, he lay down to rest at an early hour; but a little before midnight he was roused from sleep by a sound of loud weeping in the next apartment. Presently the sliding-screens were gently pushed apart; and a young man, carrying a lighted lantern, entered the room, respectfully saluted him, and said:

'Reverend Sir, it is my painful duty to tell you that I am now the responsible head of this house. Yesterday I was only the eldest son. But when you came here, tired as you were, we did not wish that you should feel embarrassed in any way: therefore we did not tell you that father had died only a few hours before. The people whom you saw in the next room are the inhabitants of this village: they all assembled here to pay their last respects to the dead; and now they are going to another village, about three miles off — for, by our custom, no one of us may remain in this village during the night after a death has taken place. We make the proper offerings and prayers; then we go away, leaving the corpse alone. Strange things always happen in the house where a corpse has thus been left: so we think that it will be better for you to come away with us. We can find you good lodging in the other village. But perhaps, as you are a priest, you have no fear of demons or evil spirits; and, if you are not afraid of being left alone with the body, you will be very welcome to the use of this poor house. However, I must tell you that nobody, except a priest, would dare to remain here tonight.'

Musō made answer:

'For your kind intention and your generous hospitality, I am deeply grateful. But I am sorry that you did not tell me of your father's death when I came; for, though I was a little tired, I certainly was not so tired that I should have found any difficulty in doing my duty as a priest. Had you told me, I could have performed the service before your departure. As it is, I shall perform the service after you have gone away; and I shall stay by the body until morning. I do not know what you mean by your words about the danger of staying here alone; but I am not afraid of ghosts or demons: therefore please to feel no anxiety on my account.'

The young man appeared to be rejoiced by these assurances, and expressed his gratitude in fitting words. Then the other members of the family, and the folk assembled in the adjoining room, having been told of the priest's kind promises, came to thank him, after which the master of the house said:

'Now, reverend Sir, much as we regret to leave you alone, we must bid you farewell. By the rule of our village, none of us can stay here after midnight. We beg, kind Sir, that you will take every care of your honorable body, while we are unable to attend upon you. And if you happen to hear or see anything strange during our absence, please tell us of the matter when we return in the morning.'

All then left the house, except the priest, who went to the room where the dead body was lying. The usual offerings had been set before the corpse; and a small Buddhist lamp — tōmyō — was burning.

The priest recited the service, and performed the funeral ceremonies, after which he entered into meditation. So meditating he remained through several silent hours; and there was no sound in the deserted village. But, when the hush of the night was at its deepest, there noiselessly entered a Shape, vague and vast; and in the same moment Musō found himself without power to move or speak. He saw that Shape lift the corpse, as with hands, and devour it, more quickly than a cat devours a rat, beginning at the head, and eating everything: the hair and the bones and even the shroud. And the monstrous Thing, having thus consumed the body, turned to the offerings, and ate them also. Then it went away, as mysteriously as it had come.

When the villagers returned next morning, they found the priest awaiting them at the door of the headman's dwelling. All in turn saluted him; and when they had entered, and looked about the room, no one expressed any surprise at the disappearance of the dead body and the offerings. But the master of the house said to Musō:

'Reverend Sir, you have probably seen unpleasant things during the night: all of us were anxious about you. But now we are very happy to find you alive and unharmed. Gladly we would have stayed with you, if it had been possible. But the law of our village, as I told you last evening, obliges us to quit our houses after a death has taken place, and to leave the corpse alone. Whenever this law has been broken, heretofore, some great misfortune has followed. Whenever it is obeyed, we find that the corpse and the offerings disappear during our absence. Perhaps you have seen the cause.'

Then Musō told of the dim and awful Shape that had entered the death-chamber to devour the body and the offerings. No person seemed to be surprised by his narration; and the master of the house observed:

'What you have told us, reverend Sir, agrees with what has been said about this matter from ancient time.'

Musō then inquired:

'Does not the priest on the hill sometimes perform the funeral-service for your dead?'

'What priest?' the young man asked.

'The priest who yesterday evening directed me to this village,' answered Musō. 'I called at his anjitsu on the hill yonder. He refused me lodging, but told me the way here.'

The listeners looked at each other, as in astonishment; and, after a moment of silence, the master of the house said:

'Reverend Sir, there is no priest and there is no anjitsu on the hill. For the time of many generations there has not been any resident-priest in this neighborhood.'

Musō said nothing more on the subject; for it was evident that his kind hosts supposed him to have been deluded by some goblin. But after having bidden them farewell, and obtained all necessary information as to his road, he determined to look again for the hermitage on the hill, and so to ascertain whether he had really been deceived. He found the anjitsu without any difficulty; and, this time, its aged occupant invited him to enter. When he had done so, the hermit humbly bowed down before him, exclaiming: 'Ah! I am ashamed! – I am very much ashamed! – I am exceedingly ashamed!'

'You need not be ashamed for having refused me shelter,' said Musō. 'You directed me to the village yonder, where I was very kindly treated; and I thank you for that favor.'

'I can give no man shelter,' the recluse made answer; 'and it is not for the refusal that I am ashamed. I am ashamed only that you should have seen me in my real shape – for it was I who devoured the corpse and the offerings last night before your eyes ... Know, reverend Sir, that I am a jikininki[1] – an eater of human flesh. Have pity upon me, and suffer me to confess the secret fault by which I became reduced to this condition.

'A long, long time ago, I was a priest in this desolate region. There was no other priest for many leagues around. So, in that time, the bodies of the mountain-folk who died used to be brought here – sometimes from great distances – in order that I might repeat over them the holy service. But I repeated the service and performed the rites only as a matter of business; I thought only of the food and the clothes that my sacred profession enabled me to gain. And because of this selfish impiety I was reborn, immediately after my death, into the state of a jikininki. Since then I have been obliged

1. Literally, a man-eating goblin. The Japanese narrator gives also the Sanskrit term, *Râkshasa*; but this word is quite as vague as jikininki, since there are many kinds of *Râkshasas*. Apparently the word jikininki signifies here one of the Baramon-Rasetsu-Gaki – forming the twenty-sixth class of pretas enumerated in the old Buddhist books.

to feed upon the corpses of the people who die in this district: every one of them I must devour in the way that you saw last night ... Now, reverend Sir, let me beseech you to perform a ségaki-service[2] for me: help me by your prayers, I entreat you, so that I may be soon able to escape from this horrible state of existence.'

No sooner had the hermit uttered this petition than he disappeared; and the hermitage also disappeared at the same instant. And Musō Kokushi found himself kneeling alone in the high grass, beside an ancient and moss-grown tomb, of the form called go-rinishi,[3] which seemed to be the tomb of a priest.

2. A ségaki-service is a special Buddhist service performed on behalf of beings supposed to have entered into the condition of gaki (pretas), or hungry spirits. For a brief account of such a service, see my *Japanese Miscellany*.

3. Literally, 'five-circle (or 'five-zone') stone.' A funeral monument consisting of five parts superimposed – each of a different form – symbolizing the five mystic elements: Ether, Air, Fire, Water, Earth.

Ningyō-no-Haka

Manyemon had coaxed the child indoors, and made her eat. She appeared to be about eleven years old, intelligent, and pathetically docile. Her name was Iné, which means 'springing rice;' and her frail slimness made the name seem appropriate.

When she began, under Manyemon's gentle persuasion, to tell her story, I anticipated something queer from the accompanying change in her voice. She spoke in a high, thin, sweet tone, perfectly even – a tone changeless and unemotional as the chanting of the little kettle over its charcoal bed. Not unfrequently in Japan one may hear a girl or a woman utter something touching or cruel or terrible in just such a steady, level, penetrating tone, but never anything indifferent. It always means that feeling is being kept under control.

'There were six of us at home,' said Iné, 'mother and father and father's mother, who was very old, and my brother and myself, and a little sister. Father was a hyōguya, a paper-hanger: he papered sliding-screens and also mounted kakemono. Mother was a hairdresser. My brother was apprenticed to a seal-cutter.

'Father and mother did well: mother made even more money than father. We had good clothes and good food; and we never had any real sorrow until father fell sick.

'It was the middle of the hot season. Father had always been healthy: we did not think that his sickness was dangerous, and he did not think so himself. But the very next day he died. We were very much surprised. Mother tried to hide her heart, and to wait upon her customers as before. But she was not very strong, and the pain of father's death came too quickly. Eight days after father's funeral mother also died. It was so sudden that everybody wondered. Then the neighbors told us that we must make a ningyō-no-haka at once, or else there would be another death in our house. My brother said they were right; but he put off doing what they told him. Perhaps he did not have money enough, I do not know; but the haka was not made.'

'What is a ningyō-no-haka?' I interrupted.

'I think,' Manyemon made answer, 'that you have seen many ningyō-no-haka without knowing what they were; they look just like graves of children. It is believed that when two of a family die in the same year, a third also must soon die. There is a saying, "Always three graves". So when two out of one family have been buried in the same year, a third grave is made next to the graves of those two, and in it is put a coffin containing only a little figure of straw, wara-ningyō; and over that grave a small tombstone is set up, bearing a kaimyō.[1] The priests of the temple to which the graveyard belongs write the kaimyō for these little gravestones. By making a ningyō-no-haka it is thought that a death may be prevented .. We listen for the rest, Iné.'

The child resumed:

'There were still four of us — grandmother, brother, myself, and my little sister. My brother was nineteen years old. He had finished his apprenticeship just before father died: we thought that was like the pity of the gods for us. He had become the head of the house. He was very skillful in his business, and had many friends: therefore he could maintain us. He made thirteen yen the first month; that is very good for a seal-cutter. One evening he came home sick: he said that his head hurt him. Mother had then been dead forty-seven days. That evening he could not eat. Next morning he was not able to get up; he had a very hot fever: we nursed him as well as we could, and sat up at night to watch by him; but he did not get better. On the morning of the third day of his sickness we became frightened — because he began to talk to mother. It was the forty-ninth day after mother's death — the day the Soul leaves the house — and brother spoke as if mother was calling him: "Yes, mother, yes! — in a little while I shall come!" Then he told us that mother was pulling him by the sleeve. He would point with his hand and call to us: "There she is! — there! — do you not see her?"

---

1. The posthumous Buddhist name of the person buried is chiseled upon the tomb or haka.

We would tell him that we could not see anything. Then he would say, "Ah! you did not look quick enough: she is hiding now; she has gone down under the floor-mats." All the morning he talked like that. At last grandmother stood up, and stamped her foot on the floor, and reproached mother, speaking very loud. "Taka!" she said, "Taka, what you do is very wrong. When you were alive we all loved you. None of us ever spoke unkind words to you. Why do you now want to take the boy? You know that he is the only pillar of our house. You know that if you take him there will not be anyone to care for the ancestors. You know that if you take him, you will destroy the family name! O Taka, it is cruel! it is shameful! it is wicked!" Grandmother was so angry that all her body trembled. Then she sat down and cried; and I and my little sister cried. But our brother said that mother was still pulling him by the sleeve. When the sun went down, he died.

'Grandmother wept, and stroked us, and sang a little song that she made herself. I can remember it still:

> *Oya no nai ko to*
> *Hamabé no chidori:*
> *Higuré-higuré ni*
> *Sodé shiboru.*[2]

'So the third grave was made, but it was not a ningyō-no-haka; and that was the end of our house. We lived with kindred until winter, when grandmother died. She died in the night – when, nobody knew: in the morning she seemed to be sleeping, but she was dead. Then I and my little sister were separated. My sister was adopted by a tatamiya, a mat-maker, one of father's friends. She is kindly treated: she even goes to school!'

'Aa fushigi na koto da! – aa komatta ne?' murmured Manyemon. Then there was a moment or two of sympathetic silence. Iné prostrated herself in thanks, and rose to depart. As she slipped her feet under

2. 'Children without parents, like the seagulls of the coast. Evening after evening the sleeves are wrung.' The word 'chidori' – indiscriminately applied to many kinds of birds – is here used for seagull. The cries of the seagull are thought to express melancholy and desolation: hence the comparison. The long sleeve of the Japanese robe is used to wipe the eyes as well as to hide the face in moments of grief. To 'wring the sleeve' – that is, to wring the moisture from a tear-drenched sleeve – is a frequent expression in Japanese poetry.

the thongs of her sandals, I moved toward the spot where she had been sitting, to ask the old man a question. She perceived my intention, and immediately made an indescribable sign to Manyemon, who responded by checking me just as I was going to sit down beside him.

'She wishes, he said, 'that the master will honorably strike the matting first.'

'But why?' I asked in surprise, noticing only that under my unshod feet the spot where the child had been kneeling felt comfortably warm.

Manyemon answered:

'She believes that to sit down upon the place made warm by the body of another is to take into one's own life all the sorrow of that other person, unless the place be stricken first.'

Whereat I sat down without performing the rite; and we both laughed.

'Iné,' said Manyemon, 'the master takes your sorrows upon him. He wants' – I cannot venture to render Manyemon's honorifics – 'to understand the pain of other people. You need not fear for him, Iné.'

The Reconciliation

There was a young samurai of Kyōto who had been reduced to poverty by the ruin of his lord, and found himself obliged to leave his home, and to take service with the Governor of a distant province. Before quitting the capital, this samurai divorced his wife, a good and beautiful woman, under the belief that he could better obtain promotion by another alliance. He then married the daughter of a family of some distinction, and took her with him to the district whither he had been called.

But it was in the time of the thoughtlessness of youth, and the sharp experience of want, that the samurai could not understand the worth of the affection so lightly cast away. His second marriage did not prove a happy one; the character of his new wife was hard and selfish; and he soon found every cause to think with regret of Kyōto days. Then he discovered that he still loved his first wife – loved her more than he could ever love the second; and he began to feel how unjust and how thankless he had been. Gradually his repentance deepened into a remorse that left him no peace of mind. Memories of the woman he had wronged – her gentle speech, her smiles, her dainty, pretty ways, her faultless patience – continually haunted him. Sometimes in dreams he saw her at her loom, weaving as when she toiled night and day to help him during the years of their distress: more often he saw her kneeling alone in the desolate little room where he had left her, veiling her tears with her poor worn sleeve. Even in the hours of official duty, his thoughts would wander back to her: then he would ask himself how she was living, what she was doing. Something in his heart assured him that she could not accept another husband, and that she never would refuse to pardon him. And he secretly resolved to seek her out as soon as he could return to Kyōto, then to beg her forgiveness, to take her back, to do everything that a man could do to make atonement. But the years went by.

At last the Governor's official term expired, and the samurai was free. 'Now I will go back to my dear one,' he vowed to himself. 'Ah, what a cruelty, what a folly to have divorced her!' He sent his second wife to her own people (she had given him no children); and hurrying to Kyōto, he went at once to seek his former companion, not allowing himself even the time to change his travelling-garb.

When he reached the street where she used to live, it was late in the night, the night of the tenth day of the ninth month; and the city was silent as a cemetery. But a bright moon made everything visible; and he found the house without difficulty. It had a deserted look: tall weeds were growing on the roof. He knocked at the sliding-doors, and no one answered. Then, finding that the doors had not been fastened from within, he pushed them open, and entered. The front room was matless and empty: a chilly wind was blowing through crevices in the planking; and the moon shone through a ragged break in the wall of the alcove. Other rooms presented a like forlorn condition. The house, to all seeming, was unoccupied. Nevertheless, the samurai determined to visit one other apartment at the further end of the dwelling, a very small room that had been his wife's favorite resting-place. Approaching the sliding-screen that closed it, he was startled to perceive a glow within. He pushed the screen aside, and uttered a cry of joy; for he saw her there, sewing by the light of a paper lamp. Her eyes at the same instant met his own; and with a happy smile she greeted him, asking only: 'When did you come back to Kyōto? How did you find your way here to me, through all those black rooms?' The years had not changed her. Still she seemed as fair and young as in his fondest memory of her; but sweeter than any memory there came to him the music of her voice, with its trembling of pleased wonder.

Then joyfully he took his place beside her, and told her all: how deeply he repented his selfishness, how wretched he had been without her, how constantly he had regretted her, how long he had hoped and planned to make amends; caressing her the while, and asking her forgiveness over and over again. She answered him, with loving gentleness according to his heart's desire, entreating him to cease all self-reproach. It was wrong, she said, that he should have allowed himself to suffer on her account: she had always felt that she was not worthy to be his wife. She knew that he had separated from her, notwithstanding, only because of poverty; and while he lived with her, he had always been kind; and she had never ceased to pray for his happiness. But even if there had been a reason for speaking of amends, this honorable visit would be ample amends — what greater happiness than thus to see him again, though it were only for a moment? 'Only for a moment!' he answered, with a glad laugh, 'say, rather, for the time of seven existences! My loved one, unless you forbid, I am coming back to live with you always — always — always! Nothing shall ever separate us again. Now I have means and friends: we need not fear poverty. Tomorrow my goods will be brought here; and my servants will come to wait upon you; and we shall make this house beautiful ... Tonight,' he added, apologetically, 'I came thus late — without even changing my dress — only because of the longing I had to see you, and to tell you this.' She seemed greatly pleased by these words; and in her turn she told him about all that had happened in Kyōto since the time of his departure — excepting her own sorrows, of which she sweetly refused to speak. They chatted far into the night: then she conducted him to a warmer room, facing south — a room that had been their bridal chamber in former time. 'Have you no one in the house to help you?' he asked, as she began to prepare the couch for him. 'No,' she answered, laughing cheerfully, 'I could not afford a servant; so I have been living all alone.' 'You will have plenty of servants tomorrow,' he said, 'good servants, and everything else that you need.' They lay down to rest, not to sleep: they had too much to tell each other; and they talked of the past and the present and the future, until the dawn was gray. Then, involuntarily, the samurai closed his eyes, and slept.

When he awoke, the daylight was streaming through the chinks of the sliding-shutters; and he found himself, to his utter amazement, lying upon the naked boards of a mouldering floor ... Had he only dreamed a dream? No: she was there; she slept ... He bent above her — and looked — and shrieked; for the sleeper had no face! Before him, wrapped in its grave-sheet only, lay the corpse of a woman —

a corpse so wasted that little remained save the bones, and the long black tangled hair.

Slowly, as he stood shuddering and sickening in the sun, the icy horror yielded to a despair so intolerable, a pain so atrocious, that he clutched at the mocking shadow of a doubt. Feigning ignorance of the neighborhood, he ventured to ask his way to the house in which his wife had lived.

'There is no one in that house,' said the person questioned. 'It used to belong to the wife of a samurai who left the city several years ago. He divorced her in order to marry another woman before he went away; and she fretted a great deal, and so became sick. She had no relatives in Kyōto, and nobody to care for her; and she died in the autumn of the same year – on the tenth day of the ninth month.'

The Case of O-Dai

1

O-Dai pushed aside the lamplet and the incense-cup and the water vessel on the Buddha-shelf, and opened the little shrine before which they had been placed. Within were the ihai, the mortuary tablets of her people — five in all; and a gilded figure of the Bodhisattva Kwannon stood smiling behind them. The ihai of the grandparents occupied the left side; those of the parents the right; and between them was a smaller tablet, bearing the kaimyo of a child-brother with whom she used to play and quarrel, to laugh and cry, in other and happier years. Also the shrine contained a makémono, or scroll, inscribed with the spirit-names of many ancestors. Before that shrine, from her infancy, O-Dai had been wont to pray.

The tablets and the scroll signified more to her faith in former time — very much more — than remembrance of a father's affection and a mother's caress; more than any remembrance of the ever-loving, ever-patient, ever-smiling elders who had fostered her babyhood, carried ner pickaback to every temple-festival, invented her pleasures, consoled her small sorrows, and soothed her fretfulness with song; more than the memory of the laughter and the tears, the cooing and the calling and the running of the dear and mischievous little brother; more than all the traditions of the ancestors.

For those objects signified the actual viewless presence of the lost, the haunting of invisible sympathy and tenderness, the gladness and the grief of the dead in the joy and the sorrow of the living. When, in other time, at evening dusk, she was wont to kindle the lamplet before them, how often had she seen the tiny flame astir with a motion not its own!

*

Yet the ihai is even more than a token to pious fancy. Strange possibilities of transmutation, transubstantiation, belong to it. It serves as temporary body for the spirit between death and birth: each fibre of its incense-penetrated wood lives with a viewless life-potential. The will of the ghost may quicken it. Sometimes, through power of love, it changes to flesh and blood. By help of the ihai the buried mother returns to suckle her babe in the dark. By help of the ihai, the maid consumed upon the funeral pyre may return to wed her betrothed – even to bless him with a son. By power of the ihai, the dead servant may come back from the dust of his rest to save his lord from ruin. Then, after love or loyalty has wrought its will, the personality vanishes; the body again becomes, to outward seeming, only a tablet.

All this O-Dai ought to have known and remembered. Maybe she did; for she wept as she took the tablets and the scroll out of the shrine, and dropped them from a window into the river below. She did not dare to look after them, as the current whirled them away.

II

O-Dai had done this by order of two English missionary-women who, by various acts of seeming kindness, had persuaded her to become a Christian. (Converts are always commanded to bury or to cast away their ancestral tablets.) These missionary-women – the first ever seen in the province – had promised O-Dai, their only convert, an allowance of three yen a month, as assistant, because she could read and write. By the toil of her hands she had never been able to earn more than two yen a month; and out of that sum she had to pay a rent of twenty-five sen for the use of the upper floor of a little house, belonging to a dealer in second-hand goods. Thither, after the death of her parents, she had taken her loom, and the ancestral tablets. She had been obliged to work very hard indeed in order to live. But with three yen a month she could live very well; and the missionary-women had a room for her. She did not think that the people would mind her change of religion.

As a matter of fact they did not much care. They did not know anything about Christianity, and did not want to know; they only laughed at the girl for being so foolish as to follow the ways of the foreign women. They regarded her as a dupe, and mocked her without malice. And they continued to laugh at her, good-humoredly enough, until the day when she was seen to throw the tablets into the river. Then they stopped laughing. They judged the act in itself, without discussing its motives. Their judgment was instantaneous, unanimous. and voiceless. They said no word of reproach to O-Dai. They merely ignored her existence.

The moral resentment of a Japanese community is not always a hot resentment — not the kind that quickly burns itself out. It may be cold. In the case of O-Dai it was cold and silent and heavy like a thickening of ice. No one uttered it. It was altogether spontaneous, instinctive. But the universal feeling might have been thus translated into speech:

'Human society, in this most eastern East, has been held together from immemorial time by virtue of that cult which exacts the gratitude of the present to the past, the reverence of the living for the dead, the affection of the descendant for the ancestor. Far beyond the visible world extends the duty of the child to the parent, of the servant to the master, of the subject to the sovereign. Therefore do the dead preside in the family council, in the communal assembly, in the high seats of judgment, in the governing of cities, in the ruling of the land.

'Against the virtue Supreme of Filial Piety, against the religion of the Ancestors, against all faith and gratitude and reverence and duty, against the total moral experience of her race, O-Dai has sinned the sin that cannot be forgiven. Therefore shall the people account her a creature impure, less deserving of fellowship than the Éta, less worthy of kindness than the dog in the street or the cat upon the roof; since even these, according to their feebler light, observe the common law of duty and affection.

'O-Dai has refused to her dead the word of thankfulness, the whisper of love, the reverence of a daughter. Therefore, now and forever, the living shall refuse to her the word of greeting, the common salutation, the kindly answer.

'O-Dai has mocked the memory of the father who begot her, the memory of the mother whose breasts she sucked, the memory of the elders who cherished her childhood, the memory of the little one who called her Sister. She has mocked at love: therefore all love shall be denied her, all offices of affection.

'To the spirit of the father who begot her, to the spirit of the mother who bore her, O-Dai has refused the shadow of a roof, and the vapor of food, and the offering of water. Even so to her shall be denied the shelter of a roof, and the gift of food, and the cup of refreshment.

'And even as she cast out the dead, the living shall cast her out. As a carcass shall she be in the way, as the small carrion that none will turn to look upon, that none will bury, that none will pity, that none will speak for in prayer to the Gods and the buddhas. As a Gaki[1] she shall be — as a Shōjiki-Gaki — seeking sustenance in refuse-heaps. Alive into hell shall she enter; yet shall her hell remain the single hell, the solitary hell, the hell Kodoku, that spheres the spirit accurst in solitude of fire ...'

III

Unexpectedly the missionary-women informed O-Dai that she would have to take care of herself. Perhaps she had done her best; but she certainly had not been to them of any use whatever, and they required a capable assistant. Moreover, they were going away for some time, and could not take her with them. Surely she could not have been so foolish as to think that they were going to give her three yen per month merely for being a Christian!

O-Dai cried; and they advised her to be brave, and to walk in the paths of virtue. She said that she could not find employment: they told her that no industrious and honest person need ever want for work in this busy world. Then, in desperate terror, she told them truths which they could not understand, and energetically refused to believe. She spoke of a danger imminent; and they answered her with all the harshness of which they were capable, believing that she had confessed herself utterly depraved. In this they were wrong. There was no atom of vice in the girl: an amiable weakness and a childish trustfulness were the worst of her faults. Really she needed help, needed it quickly, needed it terribly. But they could understand only that she wanted money; and that she had threatened to commit sin

1. Preta.

if she did not get it. They owed her nothing, as she had always been paid in advance; and they imagined excellent reasons for denying her further aid of any sort.

So they put her into the street. Already she had sold her loom. She had nothing more to sell except the single robe upon her back, and a few pair of useless tabi, or cleft stockings, which the missionary-women had obliged her to buy, because they thought that it was immodest for a young girl to be seen with naked feet. (They had also obliged her to twist her hair into a hideous back-knot, because the Japanese style of wearing the hair seemed to them ungodly.)

What becomes of the Japanese girl publicly convicted of offending against filial piety? What becomes of the English girl publicly convicted of unchastity?

Of course, had she been strong, O-Dai might have filled her sleeves with stones, and thrown herself into the river, which would have been an excellent thing to do under the circumstances. Or she might have cut her throat, which is more respectable, as the act requires both nerve and skill. But, like most converts of her class, O-Dai was weak: the courage of the race had failed in her. She wanted still to see the sun; and she was not of the sturdy type able to wrestle with the earth for that privilege. Even after fully abjuring her errors, there was left but one road for her to travel.

Said the person who bought the body of O-Dai at a third of the price prayed for:

'My business is an exceedingly shameful business. But even into this business no woman can be received who is known to have done the thing that you have done. If I were to take you into my house, no visitors would come; and the people would probably make trouble. Therefore to Ōsaka, where you are not known, you shall be sent; and the house in Ōsaka will pay the money ...'

So vanished forever O-Dai — flung into the furnace of a city's lust ... Perhaps she existed only to furnish one example of facts that every foreign missionary ought to try to understand.

The Story of Kwashin Koji[1]

During the period of Tenshō[2] there lived, in one of the northern districts of Kyōto, an old man whom the people called Kwashin Koji. He wore a long white beard, and was always dressed like a Shintō priest; but he made his living by exhibiting Buddhist pictures and by preaching Buddhist doctrine. Every fine day he used to go to the grounds of the temple Gion, and there suspend to some tree a large kakemono on which were depicted the punishments of the various hells. This kakemono was so wonderfully painted that all things represented in it seemed to be real; and the old man would discourse to the people crowding to see it, and explain to them the Law of Cause and Effect, pointing out with a buddhist staff (nyoi), which he always carried, each detail of the different torments, and exhorting everybody to follow the teachings of the Buddha. Multitudes assembled to look at the picture and to hear the old man preach about it; and sometimes the mat which he spread before him, to receive contributions, was covered out of sight by the heaping of coins thrown upon it.

Oda Nobunaga was at that time ruler of Kyōto and of the surrounding provinces. One of his retainers, named Arakawa, during a visit to the temple of Gion, happened to see the picture being displayed there; and he afterwards talked about it at the palace. Nobunaga was interested by Arakawa's description, and sent orders to Kwashin Koji to come at once to the palace, and to bring the picture with him.

When Nobunaga saw the kakemono he was not able to conceal his surprise at the vividness of the work: the demons and the tortured spirits actually appeared to move before his eyes; and he heard voices

1. Related in the curious old book *Yasō-Kidan*.
2. The period of Tenshō lasted from A.D. 1573 to 1591. The death of the great captain, Oda Nobunaga, who figures in this story, occurred in 1582.

crying out of the picture; and the blood there represented seemed to be really flowing, so that he could not help putting out his finger to feel if the painting was wet. But the finger was not stained, for the paper proved to be perfectly dry. More and more astonished, Nobunaga asked who had made the wonderful picture. Kwashin Koji answered that it had been painted by the famous Oguri Sōtan,[3] after he had performed the rite of self-purification every day for a hundred days, and practised great austerities, and made earnest prayer for inspiration to the divine Kwannon of Kiyomidzu Temple.

Observing Nobunaga's evident desire to possess the kakemono, Arakawa then asked Kwashin Koji whether he would 'offer it up' as a gift to the great lord. But the old man boldly answered: 'This painting is the only object of value that I possess; and I am able to make a little money by showing it to the people. Were I now to present this picture to the lord, I should deprive myself of the only means which I have to make my living. However, if the lord be greatly desirous to possess it, let him pay me for it the sum of one hundred ryō of gold. With that amount of money I should be able to engage in some profitable business. Otherwise, I must refuse to give up the picture.'

Nobunaga did not seem to be pleased at this reply; and he remained silent. Arakawa presently whispered something in the ear of the lord, who nodded assent; and Kwashin Koji was then dismissed, with a small present of money.

But when the old man left the palace, Arakawa secretly followed him, hoping for a chance to get the picture by foul means. The chance came; for Kwashin Koji happened to take a road leading directly to the heights beyond the town. When he reached a certain lonesome spot at the foot of the hills, where the road made a sudden turn, he was seized by Arakawa, who said to him: 'Why were you so greedy as to ask a hundred ryō of gold? Instead of a hundred ryō of gold, I am now going to give you one piece of iron three feet long.' Then Arakawa drew his sword, and killed the old man, and took the picture.

*

3. Oguri Sōtan was a great religious artist who flourished in the early part of the fifteenth century. He became a Buddhist priest in the later years of his life.

The next day Arakawa presented the kakemono – still wrapped up as Kwashin Koji had wrapped it before leaving the palace – to Oda Nobunaga, who ordered it to be hung up forthwith. But, when it was unrolled, both Nobunaga and his retainer were astounded to find that there was no picture at all – nothing but a blank surface. Arakawa could not explain how the original painting had disappeared; and as he had been guilty – whether willingly or unwillingly – of deceiving his master, it was decided that he should be punished. Accordingly he was sentenced to remain in confinement for a considerable time.

Scarcely had Arakawa completed his term of imprisonment when news was brought to him that Kwashin Koji was exhibiting the famous picture in the grounds of Kitano Temple. Arakawa could hardly believe his ears; but the information inspired him with a vague hope that he might be able, in some way or other, to secure the kakemono, and thereby redeem his recent fault. So he quickly assembled some of his followers, and hurried to the temple; but when he reached it he was told that Kwashin Koji had gone away.

Several days later, word was brought to Arakawa that Kwashin Koji was exhibiting the picture at Kiyomidzu Temple, and preaching about it to an immense crowd. Arakawa made all haste to Kiyomidzu; but he arrived there only in time to see the crowd disperse, for Kwashin Koji had again disappeared.

At last one day Arakawa unexpectedly caught sight of Kwashin Koji in a wine-shop, and there captured him. The old man only laughed good-humoredly on finding himself seized, and said: 'I will go with you; but please wait until I drink a little wine.' To this request Arakawa made no objection; and Kwashin Koji thereupon drank, to the amazement of the bystanders, twelve bowls of wine. After drinking the twelfth he declared himself satisfied; and Arakawa ordered him to be bound with a rope, and taken to Nobunaga's residence.

In the court of the palace Kwashin Koji was examined at once by the Chief Officer, and sternly reprimanded. Finally the Chief Officer said to him: 'It is evident that you have been deluding people by magical practices; and for this offence alone you deserve to be heavily punished. However, if you will now respectfully offer up that picture to the Lord Nobunaga, we shall this time overlook your fault.

Otherwise we shall certainly inflict upon you a very severe punishment.'

At this menace Kwashin Koji laughed in a bewildered way, and exclaimed: 'It is not I who have been guilty of deluding people.' Then, turning to Arakawa, he cried out: 'You are the deceiver! You wanted to flatter the lord by giving him that picture; and you tried to kill me in order to steal it. Surely, if there be any such thing as crime, that was a crime! As luck would have it, you did not succeed in killing me; but if you had succeeded, as you wished, what would you have been able to plead in excuse for such an act? You stole the picture, at all events. The picture that I now have is only a copy. And after you stole the picture, you changed your mind about giving it to Lord Nobunaga; and you devised a plan to keep it for yourself. So you gave a blank kakemono to Lord Nobunaga; and, in order to conceal your secret act and purpose, you pretended that I had deceived you by substituting a blank kakemono for the real one. Where the real picture now is, I do not know. You probably do.'

At these words Arakawa became so angry that he rushed towards the prisoner, and would have struck him but for the interference of the guards. And this sudden outburst of anger caused the Chief Officer to suspect that Arakawa was not altogether innocent. He ordered Kwashin Koji to be taken to prison for the time being; and he then proceeded to question Arakawa closely. Now Arakawa was naturally slow of speech; and on this occasion, being greatly excited, he could scarcely speak at all; and he stammered, and contradicted himself, and betrayed every sign of guilt. Then the Chief Officer ordered that Arakawa should be beaten with a stick until he told the truth. But it was not possible for him even to seem to tell the truth. So he was beaten with a bamboo until his senses departed from him, and he lay as if dead.

Kwashin Koji was told in the prison about what had happened to Arakawa; and he laughed. But after a little while he said to the jailer: 'Listen! That fellow Arakawa really behaved like a rascal; and I purposely brought this punishment upon him, in order to correct his evil inclinations. But now please say to the Chief Officer that Arakawa must have been ignorant of the truth, and that I shall explain the whole matter satisfactorily.'

Then Kwashin Koji was again taken before the Chief Officer, to whom he made the following declaration: 'In any picture of real excellence there must be a ghost; and such a picture, having a will of its own, may refuse to be separated from the person who gave it life, or even from its rightful owner. There are many stories to prove that really great pictures have souls. It is well known that some sparrows, painted upon a sliding-screen [fusuma] by Hōgen Yenshin, once flew away, leaving blank the spaces which they had occupied upon the surface. Also it is well known that a horse, painted upon a certain kakemono, used to go out at night to eat grass. Now, in this present case, I believe the truth to be that, inasmuch as the Lord Nobunaga never became the rightful owner of my kakemono, the picture voluntarily vanished from the paper when it was unrolled in his presence But if you will give me the price that I first asked – one hundred ryō of gold – I think that the painting will then reappear, of its own accord, upon the now blank paper. At all events, let us try! There is nothing to risk, since, if the picture does not reappear, I shall at once return the money.'

On hearing of these strange assertions, Nobunaga ordered the hundred ryō to be paid, and came in person to observe the result, the kakemono was unrolled before him; and, to the amazement of all present, the painting reappeared, with all its details. But the colors seemed to have faded a little; and the figures of the souls and the demons did not look really alive, as before. Perceiving this difference, the lord asked Kwashin Koji to explain the reason of it; and Kwashin Koji replied: 'The value of the painting, as you first saw it, was the value of a painting beyond all price. But the value of the painting, as you now see it, represents exactly what you paid for it, one hundred ryō of gold ... How could it be otherwise?' On hearing this answer. all present felt that it would be worse than useless to oppose the old man any further. He was immediately set at liberty; and Arakawa was also liberated, as he had more than expiated his fault by the punishment which he had undergone.

Now Arakawa had a younger brother named Buichi, also a retainer in the service of Nobunaga. Buichi was furiously angry because Arakawa had been beaten and imprisoned; and he resolved to kill Kwashin Koji. Kwashin Koji no sooner found himself again at liberty than he went straight to a wine-shop, and called for wine. Buichi rushed after him into the shop, struck him down, and cut off his head. Then, taking the hundred ryō that had been paid to the old man, Buichi wrapped up the head and the gold together in a cloth, and hurried home to show them to Arakawa. But when he unfastened the cloth he found, instead of the head, only an empty wine-gourd, and only a lump of filth instead of the gold ... And the bewilderment of the brothers was presently increased by the information that the headless body had disappeared from the wine-shop – none could say how or when.

Nothing more was heard of Kwashin Koji until about a month later, when a drunken man was found one evening asleep in the gateway of Lord Nobunaga's palace, and snoring so loud that every snore sounded like the rumbling of distant thunder. A retainer discovered that the drunkard was Kwashin Koji. For this insolent offence, the old fellow was at once seized and thrown into the prison. But he did not awake; and in the prison he continued to sleep without interruption for ten days and ten nights, all the while snoring so that the sound could be heard to a great distance.

About this time, the Lord Nobunaga came to his death through the treachery of one of his captains, Akéchi Mitsuhidé, who thereupon usurped rule. But Mitsuhidé's power endured only for a period of twelve days.

Now when Mitsuhidé became master of Kyōto, he was told of the case of Kwashin Koji; and he ordered that the prisoner should be brought before him. Accordingly Kwashin Koji was summoned into the presence of the new lord; but Mitsuhidé spoke to him kindly, treated him as a guest, and commanded that a good dinner should be served to him. When the old man had eaten, Mitsuhidé said to him: 'I have heard that you are very fond of wine; how much wine can you drink at a single sitting?' Kwashin Koji answered: 'I do not really know how much; I stop drinking only when I feel intoxication coming on.' Then the lord set a great wine-cup[4] before Kwashin Koji,

4. The term 'bowl' would better indicate the kind of vessel to which the story teller refers. Some of the so-called cups, used on festival occasions, were very large – shallow lacquered basins capable of holding considerably more than a quart. To empty one of the largest size, at a draught, was considered to be no small feat.

and told a servant to fill the cup as often as the old man wished. And Kwashin Koji emptied the great cup ten times in succession, and asked for more; but the servant made answer that the wine-vessel was exhausted. All present were astounded by this drinking-feat; and the lord asked Kwashin Koji: 'Are you not yet satisfied, Sir?' 'Well, yes,' replied Kwashin Koji, 'I am somewhat satisfied; and now, in return for your august kindness, I shall display a little of my art. Be therefore so good as to observe that screen.' He pointed to a large eight-folding screen upon which were painted the Eight Beautiful Views of the Lake of Ōmi (Ōmi-Hakkei); and everybody looked at the screen. In one of the views the artist had represented, far away on the lake, a man rowing a boat – the boat occupying, upon the surface of the screen, a space of less than an inch in length. Kwashin Koji then waved his hand in the direction of the boat; and all saw the boat suddenly turn, and begin to move toward the foreground of the picture. It grew rapidly larger and larger as it approached; and presently the features of the boatmen became clearly distinguishable. Still the boat drew nearer, always becoming larger, until it appeared to be only a short distance away. And, all of a sudden, the water of the lake seemed to overflow, out of the picture into the room; and the room was flooded; and the spectators girded up their robes in haste, as the water rose above their knees. In the same moment the boat appeared to glide out of the screen, a real fishing-boat; and the creaking of the single oar could be heard. Still the flood in the room continued to rise, until the spectators were standing up to their girdles in water. Then the boat came close up to Kwashin Koji; and Kwashin Koji climbed into it; and the boatman turned about, and began to row away very swiftly. And, as the boat receded, the water in the room began to lower rapidly, seeming to ebb back into the screen. No sooner had the boat passed the apparent foreground of the picture than the room was dry again! But still the painted vessel appeared to glide over the painted water, retreating further into the distance, and ever growing smaller, till at last it dwindled to a dot in the offing. And then it disappeared altogether; and Kwashin Koji disappeared with it. He was never again seen in Japan.

Of a Promise Broken[1]

1

'I am not afraid to die,' said the dying wife; 'there is only one thing that troubles me now. I wish that I could know who will take my place in this house.'

'My dear one,' answered the sorrowing husband, 'nobody shall ever take your place in my home. I will never, never marry again.'

At the time that he said this he was speaking out of his heart; for he loved the woman whom he was about to lose.

'On the faith of a samurai?' she questioned, with a feeble smile.

'On the faith of a samurai,' he responded, stroking the pale thin face.

'Then, my dear one,' she said, 'you will let me be buried in the garden – will you not? – near those plum-trees that we planted at the further end? I wanted long ago to ask this; but I thought that if you were to marry again, you would not like to have my grave so near you. Now you have promised that no other woman shall take my place, so I need not hesitate to speak of my wish ... I want so much to be buried in the garden! I think that in the garden I should sometimes hear your voice, and that I should still be able to see the flowers in the spring.'

'It shall be as you wish,' he answered. 'But do not now speak of burial: you are not so ill that we have lost all hope.'

'I have,' she returned; 'I shall die this morning ... But you will bury me in the garden?'

'Yes,' he said, 'under the shade of the plum-trees that we planted; and you shall have a beautiful tomb there.'

'And will you give me a little bell?'

1. Izumo legend.

'Bell —?'

'Yes: I want you to put a little bell in the coffin — such a little bell as the Buddhist pilgrims carry. Shall I have it?'

'You shall have the little bell, and anything else that you wish.'

'I do not wish for anything else,' she said ... 'My dear one, you have been very good to me always. Now I can die happy.'

Then she closed her eyes and died — as easily as a tired child falls asleep. She looked beautiful when she was dead; and there was a smile upon her face.

She was buried in the garden, under the shade of the trees that she loved; and a small bell was buried with her. Above the grave was erected a handsome monument, decorated with the family crest, and bearing the kaimyō *'Greater Elder Sister, Luminous-Shadow-of-the-Plum-Flower-Chamber, dwelling in the Mansion of the Great Sea of Compassion.'*

But, within a twelve-month after the death of his wife, the relatives and friends of the samurai began to insist that he should marry again. 'You are still a young man,' they said, 'and an only son; and you have no children. It is the duty of a samurai to marry. If you die childless, who will there be to make the offerings and to remember the ancestors?'

By many such representations he was at last persuaded to marry again. The bride was only seventeen years old; and he found that he could love her dearly, notwithstanding the dumb reproach of the tomb in the garden.

II

Nothing took place to disturb the happiness of the young wife until the seventh day after the wedding, when her husband was ordered to undertake certain duties requiring his presence at the castle by night. On the first evening that he was obliged to leave her alone, she felt uneasy in a way that she could not explain — vaguely afraid without knowing why. When she went to bed she could not sleep. There was a strange oppression in the air, an indefinable heaviness like that which sometimes precedes the coming of a storm.

About the Hour of the Ox she heard, outside in the night, the clanging of a bell, a Buddhist pilgrim's bell; and she wondered what pilgrim could be passing through the samurai quarter at such a time. Presently, after a pause, the bell sounded much nearer. Evidently the pilgrim was approaching the house; but why approaching from the rear, where no road was? ... Suddenly the dogs began to whine and howl in an unusual and horrible way; and a fear came upon her like the fear of dreams ... That ringing was certainly in the garden ... She tried to get up to waken a servant. But she found that she could not rise, could not move, could not call ... And nearer, and still more near, came the clang of the bell; and oh! how the dogs howled! ... Then, lightly as a shadow steals, there glided into the room a Woman – though every door stood fast, and every screen unmoved – a Woman robed in a grave-robe, and carrying a pilgrim's bell. Eyeless she came, because she had long been dead; and her loosened hair streamed down about her face; and she looked without eyes through the tangle of it, and spoke without a tongue:

'Not in this house – not in this house shall you stay! Here I am mistress still. You shall go; and you shall tell to none the reason of your going. If you tell HIM, I will tear you into pieces!'

So speaking, the haunter vanished. The bride became senseless with fear. Until the dawn she so remained.

Nevertheless, in the cheery light of day, she doubted the reality of what she had seen and heard. The memory of the warning still weighed upon her so heavily that she did not dare to speak of the vision, either to her husband or to anyone else; but she was almost able to persuade herself that she had only dreamed an ugly dream, which had made her ill.

On the following night, however, she could not doubt. Again, at the Hour of the Ox, the dogs began to howl and whine; again the bell resounded, approaching slowly from the garden; again the listener vainly strove to rise and call; again the dead came into the room, and hissed:

'You shall go; and you shall tell to no one why you must go! If you even whisper it to HIM, I will tear you in pieces!'

This time the haunter came close to the couch, and bent and muttered and mowed above it ...

Next morning, when the samurai returned from the castle, his young wife prostrated herself before him in supplication:

'I beseech you,' she said, 'to pardon my ingratitude and my great rudeness in thus addressing you: but I want to go home; I want to go away at once.'

'Are you not happy here?' he asked, in sincere surprise. 'Has any one dared to be unkind to you during my absence?'

'It is not that –' she answered, sobbing. 'Everybody here has been only too good to me ... But I cannot continue to be your wife – I must go away ...'

'My dear,' he exclaimed, in great astonishment, 'it is very painful to know that you have had any cause for unhappiness in this house. But I cannot even imagine why you should want to go away – unless somebody has been very unkind to you ... Surely you do not mean that you wish for a divorce?'

She responded, trembling and weeping.

'If you do not give me a divorce, I shall die!'

He remained for a little while silent, vainly trying to think of some cause for this amazing declaration. Then, without betraying any emotion, he made answer:

'To send you back now to your people, without any fault on your part, would seem a shameful act. If you will tell me a good reason for your wish – any reason that will enable me to explain matters honorably – I can write you a divorce. But unless you give me a reason, a good reason, I will not divorce you, for the honor of our house must be kept above reproach.'

And then she felt obliged to speak; and she told him everything – adding, in an agony of terror:

'Now that I have let you know, she will kill me! – she will kill me! ...'

Although a brave man, and little inclined to believe in phantoms, the samurai was more than startled for the moment. But a simple and natural explanation of the matter soon presented itself to his mind.

'My dear,' he said, 'you are now very nervous; and I fear that someone has been telling you foolish stories. I cannot give you a divorce merely because you have had a bad dream in this house. But I am very sorry indeed that you should have been suffering in such a way during my absence. Tonight, also, I must be at the castle; but you shall not be alone. I will order two of the retainers to keep watch in your room; and you will be able to sleep in peace. They are good men; and they will take all possible care of you.'

Then he spoke to her so considerately and so affectionately that she became almost ashamed of her terrors, and resolved to remain in the house.

III

The two retainers left in charge of the young wife were big, brave, simple-hearted men, experienced guardians of women and children. They told the bride pleasant stories to keep her cheerful. She talked with them a long time, laughed at their good-humored fun, and almost forgot her fears. When at last she lay down to sleep, the men-at-arms took their places in a corner of the room, behind a screen, and began a game of go,[2] speaking only in whispers, that she might not be disturbed. She slept like an infant.

But again at the Hour of the Ox she awoke with a moan of terror — for she heard the bell! ... It was already near, and was coming nearer. She started up; she screamed; but in the room there was no stir, only a silence as of death, a silence growing, a silence thickening. She rushed to the men-at-arms: they sat before their checker-table, motionless, each staring at the other with fixed eyes. She shrieked to them; she shook them; they remained as if frozen ...

Afterwards they said that they had heard the bell, heard also the cry of the bride, even felt her try to shake them into wakefulness; and that, nevertheless, they had not been able to move or speak. From the same moment they had ceased to hear or to see: a black sleep had seized upon them.

Entering his bridal-chamber at dawn, the samurai beheld, by the light of a dying lamp, the headless body of his young wife, lying in a pool of blood. Still squatting before their unfinished game, the two retainers slept. At their master's cry they sprang up, and stupidly they stared at the horror on the floor ...

The head was nowhere to be seen; and the hideous wound showed that it had not been cut off, but *torn off*. A trail of blood led from

2. A game resembling draughts, but much more complicated.

the chamber to an angle of the outer gallery, where the storm-doors appeared to have been riven apart. The three men followed that trail into the garden, over reaches of grass, over spaces of sand, along the bank of an iris-bordered pond, under heavy shadowings of cedar and bamboo. And suddenly, at a turn, they found themselves face to face with a nightmare-thing that chippered like a bat: the figure of the long buried woman, erect before her tomb, in one hand clutching a bell, in the other the dripping head ... For a moment the three stood numbed. Then one of the men-at-arms, uttering a Buddhist invocation, drew, and struck at the shape. Instantly it crumbled down upon the soil, an empty scattering of grave-rags, bones, and hair; and the bell rolled clanking out of the ruin. But the fleshless right hand, though parted from the wrist, still writhed; and its fingers still gripped at the bleeding head, and tore, and mangled, as the claws of the yellow crab cling fast to a fallen fruit ...

['That is a wicked story,' I said to the friend who had related it. 'The vengeance of the dead – if taken at all – should have been taken upon the man.'

'Men think so,' he made answer. 'But that is not the way that a woman feels ...'

He was right.]

MORE ABOUT PENGUINS, PELICANS
AND PUFFINS

For further information about books available from Penguins please write to Dept
EP, Penguin Books Ltd, Harmondsworth, Middlesex UB7 0DA.

In the U.S.A.: For a complete list of books available from Penguins in the United
States write to Dept DG, Penguin Books, 299 Murray Hill Parkway, East Ruther-
ford, New Jersey 07073.

In Canada: For a complete list of books available from Penguins in Canada
write to Penguin Books Canada Ltd, 2801 John Street, Markham, Ontario
L3R 1B4.

In Australia: For a complete list of books available from Penguins in Australia write
to the Marketing Department, Penguin Books Australia Ltd, P.O. Box 257, Ringwood, Victoria 3134.

In New Zealand: For a complete list of books available from Penguins in New
Zealand write to the Marketing Department, Penguin Books (N.Z.) Ltd, Private
Bag, Takapuna, Auckland 9.

In India: For a complete list of books available from Penguins in India write to
Penguin Overseas Ltd, 706 Eros Apartments, 56 Nehru Place, New Delhi 110019.